Byzantine Greece: Microcosm of Empire?

This volume offers a structured presentation of the progress of research into the internal history of a part of the Byzantine world – Greece – in the centuries before the multiple changes induced or accelerated by the Fourth Crusade. Greece is a large area (several Early and Middle Byzantine provinces), with records, archival, literary, archaeological, architectural, and art-historical, most of which are unequalled in terms of their density and range. This creates opportunities for useful synthesis, and for dialogue with those now engaged in the rewriting, or writing, of the inner history of Byzantium, from Italy to the Caucasus, who have been stimulated by, or involved in, the editing of archives and inscriptions (including sigillographic), and in the publication of monuments, excavations, and surveys (for all of which the 'Greek space', the elladikê khôra, is a particular, and fertile, focus of activity, as the conference showed).

Much of the material presented here can usually only be found in specialised publication, and indeed much in Greek alone. But, properly contextualised, this material about the 'Greek space' deserves to be brought into the dialogues or debates at the heart of Byzantine Studies, for instance about the Late Antique 'boom', urban life, the 'Dark Age', economic change, the nature of the 'Byzantine revival', and of social, socio-economic, and ethnic groups. The studies here synthesise such research, enabling the 'Greek space' as a case study in the evolution of a significant region to the west of Constantinople, to take its place more fully as a point of reference in such dialogues or debates. Equally, it provides frameworks for archaeologists dealing with Greece from Late Antiquity onwards – and there are now many – with which to engage, and it makes available a rich source of comparative material for those studying the other regions of the Byzantine world, whether historically or archaeologically, in Southeastern Europe, Italy, or Turkey.

Archibald Dunn is Teaching Fellow in Byzantine Archaeology in the Centre for Byzantine, Ottoman and Modern Greek Studies at the University of Birmingham, UK.

Brian McLaughlin is a freelance editor, writer, and independent scholar of Byzantine history.

Society for the Promotion of Byzantine Studies

Publications 20

This series publishes a selection of papers delivered at the annual British Spring Symposium of Byzantine Studies, now held under the auspices of the Society for the Promotion of Byzantine Studies. These meetings began fifty years ago in the University of Birmingham and have built an international reputation. Themes cover all aspects of Byzantine history and culture, with papers presented by chosen experts. Selected papers from the symposia have been published regularly since 1992 in a series of titles which have themselves become established as major contributions to the study of the Byzantine world.

Also published in this series:

Inscribing Texts in Byzantium
Continuities and Transformations
Edited by Marc D. Lauxtermann and Ida Toth

Global Byzantium
Papers from the Fiftieth Spring Symposium of Byzantine Studies
Edited by Leslie Brubaker, Rebecca Darley, and Daniel Reynolds

Byzantine Greece: Microcosm of Empire?
Papers from the Forty-sixth Spring Symposium of Byzantine Studies
Edited by Archibald Dunn
With the assistance of Brian McLaughlin

Byzantine Greece: Microcosm of Empire?
Papers from the Forty-Sixth Spring Symposium of Byzantine Studies

**Edited by Archibald Dunn
With the assistance of
Brian McLaughlin**

LONDON AND NEW YORK

First published 2024
by Routledge
4 Park Square, Milton Park, Abingdon, Oxon OX14 4RN

and by Routledge
605 Third Avenue, New York, NY 10158

Routledge is an imprint of the Taylor & Francis Group, an informa business

© 2024 selection and editorial matter, Archibald Dunn; individual chapters, the contributors

The right of Archibald Dunn to be identified as the author of the editorial material, and of the authors for their individual chapters, has been asserted in accordance with sections 77 and 78 of the Copyright, Designs and Patents Act 1988.

All rights reserved. No part of this book may be reprinted or reproduced or utilised in any form or by any electronic, mechanical, or other means, now known or hereafter invented, including photocopying and recording, or in any information storage or retrieval system, without permission in writing from the publishers.

Trademark notice: Product or corporate names may be trademarks or registered trademarks, and are used only for identification and explanation without intent to infringe.

British Library Cataloguing-in-Publication Data
A catalogue record for this book is available from the British Library

Library of Congress Cataloging-in-Publication Data
Names: Spring Symposium of Byzantine Studies (46th : 2013 : University of Birmingham) | Dunn, Archibald, 1953- editor. | McLaughlin, Brian (Historian, Royal Holloway, University of London), editor.
Title: Byzantine Greece: microcosm of empire? : papers from the forty-sixth Spring Symposium of Byzantine Studies / edited by Archibald Dunn, with the assistance of Brian McLaughlin.
Description: New York : Routledge, 2023. | Series: Publications / Society for the Promotion of Byzantine Studies ; 24 | Includes bibliographical references and index. |
Identifiers: LCCN 2023010834 (print) | LCCN 2023010835 (ebook) | ISBN 9781032551968 (hardback) | ISBN 9781032551975 (paperback) | ISBN 9781003429470 (ebook)
Subjects: LCSH: Greece--History--323-1453--Congresses. | Byzantine Empire--History--Congresses.
Classification: LCC DF552 .S68 2013 (print) | LCC DF552 (ebook) | DDC 949.5/02--dc23/eng/20230323
LC record available at https://lccn.loc.gov/2023010834
LC ebook record available at https://lccn.loc.gov/2023010835

ISBN: 978-1-032-55196-8 (hbk)
ISBN: 978-1-032-55197-5 (pbk)
ISBN: 978-1-003-42947-0 (ebk)

DOI: 10.4324/9781003429470

Typeset in Times New Roman
by MPS Limited, Dehradun

Contents

List of Figures	*viii*
Acknowledgments	*xiv*

1 Introduction   1
ARCHIBALD DUNN

PART 1
Late Antique Greece   9

2 The Institutional Church in Early Christian Greece   11
EIRINI ZISIMOU-TRYFONIDI

3 The Early Byzantine Fortress of Velika on the Coast of Kissavos, Thessaly   22
STAVROULA SDROLIA AND SOPHIA DIDIOUMI

4 Urban and Rural Settlement in Early Byzantine Attica (4th–7th Centuries)   38
ELLI TZAVELLA

PART 2
Greece in the Transitional Period   51

5 The 'Byzantine District' of Gortyn (Crete) and the End of a/the Ancient Mediterranean City   53
ENRICO ZANINI

6 Maritime Routes in the Aegean (7th–9th Centuries): The Archaeological Evidence   79
NATALIA POULOU-PAPADIMITRIOU

vi *Contents*

7 The 7th-Century Restoration of the Acheiropoietos
   Basilica and Its Significance for the Urban Continuity of
   Thessalonike during the 'Dark Age' 108
   KONSTANTINOS T. RAPTIS

8 Some Remarks on the 'Dark Age' Architecture of Hagia
   Sophia, Thessalonike 121
   SABINE FEIST

PART 3
Urban and Rural Revival 135

9 Bridging the *Grande Brèche*: Rethinking Coins,
   Ceramics, Corinth, and Commerce in the Centuries
   Following AD 500 137
   G. D. R. SANDERS

10 Byzantine Butrint vis-à-vis 'Dark-Age' Athens: A
    Ceramic Perspective 166
    JOANITA VROOM

11 The Defences of Middle Byzantium in Greece (7th–12th
    Centuries): The Flight to Safety in Town, Countryside,
    and Islands 182
    NIKOS D. KONTOGIANNIS AND MICHAEL HESLOP

12 The Demographic and Economic History of Byzantine
    Greece in the *Long Durée*: The Contribution of the
    Pollen Data 207
    ADAM IZDEBSKI

13 Middle Byzantine Hierissos: Archaeological Research at
    the Entrance to Mount Athos 215
    AIKATERINI TSANANA

PART 4
Patronage and Sacred Space 225

14 Patronage of Religious Foundations in Middle
    Byzantine Greece (867–1204): The Evidence of
    Inscriptions and Donor Portraits 227
    SOPHIA KALOPISSI-VERTI

Contents vii

15 Church-Building in the Peloponnese: Reflections of
    Social and Economic Trends in the Countryside in the
    Middle Byzantine Period   253
    MARIA PAPADAKI

16 Hermits, Monks, and Nuns on Chalke, a Small Island
    of the Dodecanese from Early Christian to Middle
    Byzantine Times   265
    MARIA Z. SIGALA

PART 5
The Bureaucrat, the Bishop, the Farmer, and the Merchant 279

17 Loving the Poor: Charity and Justice in Middle
    Byzantine Greece   281
    TERESA SHAWCROSS

18 Economic Strategies of Landowners and Peasant
    Farmers during the 11th and 12th Centuries in Greece   302
    ALAN HARVEY

19 The Merchant in Middle Byzantine Greece   314
    MARIA GEROLYMATOU

    Index   *330*

Figures

2.1	Louloudies Pierias. The Episcopal Complex [after Marki 2008, Fig. 5. (Ed. by E. Zisimou-Tryfonidi)]	12
2.2	Chalkidiki. The Early Christian basilica at 'Bhiadoudi' [after Pazaras 2009, Fig. 73 (Ed. by E. Zisimou-Tryfonidi)]	13
2.3	Arethousa. Plan of the excavations of the Early Christian basilica [after Karivieri 2009, Fig. 2]	14
2.4	Lavreotic Olympus. The Early Christian basilica and the annex with the oil-press [after Kotzias 1952, Fig. 2]	15
3.1	Map of Kissavos. Velika fortress indicated	23
3.2	The defensive wall of Velika fortress	24
3.3	The walls of the fortress. Detail of the masonry	25
3.4	Guard-chambers	26
3.5	Belt buckle of the Sucidava type	26
3.6	Asia Minor lamp	27
3.7	African Red Slip Ware plate with stamped decoration	27
3.8	Dish belonging to the Central Greek Painted Ware	28
3.9	Lid for *pithoi* with incised decoration	28
3.10	Lid with impressed decoration	29
3.11	LRA 1 amphora	30
3.12	LRA 2 amphora	31
4.1	Location of Attic settlements. Purple: *civitas*. Red: minor urban (*emporia*). Pink: extended rural settlement. Green: rural settlement. Blue: shepherds' pens	39
4.2	Aigosthena: lower town, basilica's ruins	40
4.3	*Civitates* situated on regional routes. Orange: Attic *civitates*. Yellow: selected *civitates* of neighbouring regions	41
4.4	Map of Late Roman Eleusis showing defensive wall, houses, and graves, located during rescue excavations	42
5.1	The field of ruins at Gortyn in the early 18th century AD [after Pitton de Tournefort, J. (1817), *Relation d'un voyage du Levant*. Lyon]	56
5.2	Schematic map of the archaeological site of Gortyn [after Giorgi 2016]	58

Figures   ix

5.3   Schematic map of the archaeological site of Gortyn, showing the remains of the Roman and Early Byzantine urban water system [after Giorgi, 2016]   60
5.4   The Byzantine District of Gortyn and previously excavated monuments   62
5.5   The Byzantine District of Gortyn (GBD) seen from the south   63
5.6   Archaeological plan of the GBD   64
5.7   The large building south of the street, seen from the east   65
5.8   The large building north-west of the street seen from the south   67
5.9   Finds sealed under the collapsed roofs of the large building north-west of the street (*ca.* 8th century)   71
5.10   A 'luxurious' Constantinopolitan tableware and its 'rural' context   72
6.1   Map of Byzantine sites: 1. Constantinople, 2. Corinth, 3. Aigina, 4. Kythera, 5. Melos, 6. Santorini, 7. Herakleion, 8. Gortyn, 9, Itanos, 10. Pseira and Mochlos, 11. Yassi Ada, 12. Cyprus, 13. Cos, 14. Philippi, 15. Chios, 16. Lipsoi, 17. Samos, 18. Islands in Argolid Gulf, 19. Rhodes, 20. Amorgos, 21. Anafi, 22. Kydonia/Chania, 23. Eleutherna (Satellite image courtesy of Visible Earth, NASA; adapted by author)   80
6.2   Glazed White Ware I from Saraçhane (With acknowledgements to Hayes, 1992)   81
6.3   (a) Glazed White Ware I from Yassi Ada (With acknowledgements to Bass, 1982). (b) Glazed White Ware I from Yassi Ada (With acknowledgements to Bass, 1982)   82
6.4   Amphora from Saraçhane, type Hayes 45 (With acknowledgements to Hayes (1992); adapted by author)   84
6.5   Amphora from Bojburun shipwreck. Type Hayes 45/survival of LRA1. (https://nauticalarch.org/projects/bozburun-byzantine-shipwreck-excavation/)   84
6.6   Ovoid amphora from the excavation at Pseira (author created)   85
6.7   (a) Globular amphora from Eupalinos tunnel (With acknowledgements to Hautumm (1981); adapted by author). (b) Globular amphora from Cos (author created with Sophia Didioumi, 2010)   86
6.8   (a) Bronze belt buckle, Messara plain (author created, 2005). (b) Bronze belt buckle, Pseira island (author created, 2005). (c) Bronze belt buckle from Herakleion (author created, 2008). (d) Golden belt buckle from Crete (Ashmolean Museum), from 'Les plaques-boucles byzantines de l'île de Crète (fin VIe-IXe siècle)' by the author (2005)   88

x *Figures*

6.9 (a) The island of Kythera (author created). (b) Agios Georgios sto Vouno and Palaiopolis (Photograph by the author). (c) Agios Georgios sto Vouno and Palaiopolis (Photograph by the author)   92

6.10 (a) Pseira Island (Photograph by the author). (b) Pseira Island (Photograph by the author)   93

6.11 (a) Pseira island: the cistern (Photograph by the author). (b) Mochlos, Loutres: the cistern (Photograph by the author)   95

7.1 Acheiropoietos Basilica: view from the southeast (above); plans (below)   109

7.2 Ionic impost capitals: (a) restored at North Gallery Arcade, (b–o) in situ at South Gallery Arcade, (q–s) in situ at Northeast Tribelon   110

7.3 Cross-section looking east (with, in red, the hypothetical reconstruction of the 7th-century apse and southeast tribelon)   112

7.4 South propylon: (a) the doorframe, (b) the east blind arcade, (c–j) marble pseudo-pilaster capitals   114

7.5 Longitudinal section looking north; hypothetical reconstruction of the 16th century phase with galleries and clerestory   115

8.1 Plan of Hagia Sophia, Thessaloniki (basilica and domed church). S. Feist (based upon Theoharidou 1988: Fig. 2, Pl. I; Hadjitryphonos 1998-1999: Eik. 3b)   122

8.2 Reconstruction of the transverse section of Hagia Sophia (domed church). S. Feist (based upon Theoharidou 1988: pl. V)   123

8.3 Fragments of the basilica's narthex in front of the domed church's west façade. U. Peschlow   124

8.4 Detail of the fragments of the eastern wall of the basilica's narthex in front of the domed church's west façade that testify a former connection between the structures. U. Peschlow   125

8.5 Western Gallery of Hagia Sophia, looking south. S. Feist   126

8.6 Bell tower of Hagia Sophia, view from west. S. Feist   127

8.7 Galleries of Hagia Sophia (photo taken from the Northern Gallery, looking southwest). S. Feist   128

8.8 Northern column of the Western Gallery. S. Feist   129

9.1 Excavation at the Athenian Agora. Removal of the 'Burnt Layers' June 23, 1933. Site Notebook H'-5-43, p. 865, Agora image 2012.34.1153. Note the wooden apparatus in the background. This is the conveyor belt which carried the excavated earth to the dump. Agora Archives   139

Figures xi

9.2 Diameter and weight of *nummi* based on an unscientific sample taken from Burrell 2007, the Athenian Agora and Corinth collections — 143

9.3 Coins of Anastasius I (left) and Zeno (right) charted by diameter (x) and weight (y) — 143

9.4 Phocean Red Slip (PRS) and African Red Slip (AfRS) in 'the deposits of c. 460–75', from Hayes 1972 — 144

9.5 Type XXVIII lamps and one Type XXXI lamp (no. 2490) in 'the deposits of c. 460–75', from Perlzweig 1961. (ASCSA) — 145

9.6 Coins from 'the deposits of c. 460–75' — 146

9.7 A comparison of the coins in 'the deposits of c. 460–75' with two hoards — 146

9.8 Map of Late Roman Corinth from Acrocorinth to Lechaion by James Herbst. Corinth Archives — 148

9.9 An excavated portion of the city wall at Kraneion showing the core, robbed outer face and tombs built against the outer face — 149

9.10 Sebastian Ittar's 1802 plan of the west side of the Isthmus showing the Hexamilion wall and the Roman canal cuttings. Note the seaside fortress and outwork which also appear on the Morosini map of 1670. Corinth Archives — 151

9.11 Section through the city wall (Site Notebook 111, p. 52) showing coin relative to the top of the foundations. Corinth Archives — 152

9.12 Lechaion Harbour. A marks the location of the basilica, B the island monument, and CC the gravel hills. Corinth Archives — 154

9.13 Lechaion Basilica. Corinth Archives — 154

9.14 After Milanovic 2004: 31, table 7. Byzantium c. 1000, income in nomismata — 156

10.1 Map with the four key urban sites of the VIDI research project (J. Vroom) — 167

10.2 Butrint, Western Defences, reconstructed drawing of Tower 1 (W. Euvermans) — 170

10.3 Butrint, Western Defences, reconstructed drawing with finds in the interior of Tower 1 (W. Euvermans) — 171

10.4 Athens, map of the 'Dark Age' wells in the Agora; the line (on the right) marks the Late Roman fortification wall (J. Vroom, E. Tzavella and ASCSA) — 173

10.5 Athens, percentages of local, imported, and unknown ceramic finds from various 'Dark Age' wells in the Agora (J. Vroom, E. Tzavella) — 175

11.1 5th-12th-century fortifications — 183

xii *Figures*

11.2	Boeotia with inset of Antikyra Bay	186
11.3	Walls of Kadmeia, Thebes	187
11.4	Walls of Chalkida	188
11.5	Vroulias	190
11.6	Daskaleio	191
11.7	Kastelli – general view from south	193
11.8	Aghios Konstantinos – cisterns, bastions, and east wall	194
11.9	Galatiani – cistern and views of Kastelli and Aghios Konstantinos	195
11.10	Kalymnos with Byzantine defences and sight lines	196
11.11	The Dodecanese with Byzantine defences and sight lines	197
12.1	Location of pollen sites and analysed regions	209
12.2	Pollen sites from Central Greece and Macedonia with data for the Byzantine period	210
12.3	Key anthropogenic indicators in Central Greece and Macedonia	211
12.4	Key forest taxa in Central Greece	212
12.5	Key forest taxa in Macedonia	213
13.1	Topographic plan of Byzantine and modern Hierissos; excavated sites	216
13.2	(1–3) Ruins of houses dated to the 10th–11th centuries, (4) Middle-Byzantine tombs	217
13.3	(1) Polychrome White Ware sherds, (2) zoomorphic padlock, late 12th century, (3) buckle with a representation of Pegasus, second half of the 11th century	218
13.4	Lead seal of the judge Samonas of Thessaloniki (927 AD)	219
14.1	(a) Episkope, Skyros. Foundation inscription of the bishop of Skyros, Savas (895 AD) (Photo: Michalis Karambinis). (b) Drawing of the inscription after Bouras 1960–1961: pl. 29B	228
14.2	Areia near Nauplion. Monastery of Hagia Monê (Zôodochos Pêgê), west façade. Foundation inscription of the bishop of Argos Leon (1149 AD). (Photograph: Reproduced by kind permission of Dr Anastasia Vassiliou)	236
14.3	Kitta, Mani. Church of Saints Sergios, Bacchos, and Georgios, lintel of west façade. Foundation inscription of a lay donor, Georgios Marasiatis, and his family, third quarter of 12th century. (Photograph: Author created)	239
15.1	State of preservation of the Peloponnesian churches examined (© M. Papadaki)	254
15.2	Chronology of church construction in the Peloponnese (© M. Papadaki)	255
15.3	Distribution of churches based on geographical characteristics (© M. Papadaki)	256

		Figures xiii
15.4	Distribution of churches per region in the Peloponnese (© M. Papadaki)	257
16.1	Map of Chalke	266
16.2	Kellia: the cave and the box-like cell in front of it	267
16.3	Kellia: the Early Christian wall paintings in a cavity of the cave	268
16.4	Kellia: detail of the garland which frames the scene	268
16.5	Kellia: the built cell in front of the cave (photo by Neilos Pitsinos)	269
16.6	Kellia: the head of saint Andrew in the second layer of wall-paintings in the built cell	270
16.7	The mountainous area of Chorio in the interior of Chalke (aerial photograph by P. Matsouka)	272
16.8	Ais Adrias stou Ai Adria to Vouno	273

Acknowledgments

This symposium could not have been realised without the logistical support of the College of Arts and Law of the University of Birmingham; without the daily assistance (with brain and brawn) of the postgraduate students of the Centre for Byzantine, Ottoman and Modern Greek Studies of this university, and of Dr Lisa Montagno; and without the generous financial support of the following: The Society for the Promotion of Byzantine Studies, The Hellenic Foundation, The Seven Pillars of Wisdom Trust, The Michael Marks Charitable Trust, and a kind donor who wished to remain anonymous. I would also like to thank the Institute of Archaeology and Antiquity of this university for the technical support and costs of publicity, including artwork, and to thank the Hellenic Foundation again for their grant towards the costs of publishing illustrations. I would particularly like to thank contributing authors, and the editors, for their patience and understanding, and, last but not least, the NHS and its Greek equivalent during several hospitalisations.

We mourn the untimely loss of contributing author Michael Heslop, Honorary Research Fellow of Royal Holloway College, University of London, who died on 5th April this year. In one of his typical acts of selfless dedication to Byzantine and medieval Greek Studies, he created, donated, and installed, an exhibition of his superb photographs of the Byzantine and Hospitaller fortifications of the Dodecanese at our Symposium.

Archie Dunn
Symposiarch

1 Introduction

Archibald Dunn

This Symposium's exploration of approaches to the history of Early-to-Middle Byzantine Greece feels rather like a contribution to a conference in permanent session or a journal whose presses (or transmissions and alerts) run day and night. So I would argue that we need, at the risk of seeming over-selective among the outpourings of publications (to mention only monographic ones), to highlight a few recent scene-setting – sometimes also game-changing – works in the light of which to think about the various overarching approaches of our contributors: their disciplinary orientations, thematic orientations, and the various spatial scales at which they organise their research (spatial scale being a very important feature of a work of the present type). Contributors conscientiously updated their papers through 2019 (after which we entered a distinctly unpleasant, for some of us, time). But this scene-setting is not a review of publications since 2019. It offers an identification of works which arguably exemplify a range of positive trends or academic benchmarks whose disciplinary significance we have had time to digest. I mention first Florin Curta's *Edinburgh History of the Greeks C.500 to 1050: The Early Middle Ages*, the first modern synthesis dealing with the whole geographical space during our combined periods of interest, and one in which archaeological data plays an important role[1]; John Bintliff's *Complete Archaeology of Greece: From Hunter-Gatherers to the 20th Century A.D.*, which includes a pioneering synthesis of the archaeology of Byzantine Greece as a whole within its *longue-durée* framework[2]; Georgios Deligiannakis's *Dodecanese and the Eastern Aegean Islands in Late Antiquity, AD 300–700*, which takes the synthesis of Early Byzantine historical and archaeological material for a distinct sub-region to a new level[3]; while Myrto Veikou's *Byzantine Epirus: A Topography of Transformation: Settlements of the Seventh-Twelfth Centuries in Southern Epirus and Aetoloakarnania, Greece*, is one of the first works to foreground the Byzantine archaeology of a large area of Greece in its study, and to attempt to integrate the landscape as a dynamic and mutable factor in regional economic history (broadly defined).[4] The late Charalambos Bouras's *Byzantine Athens, 10th–12th Centuries* meanwhile developed a uniquely rich, and therefore methodologically instructive, synthesis of the results of research-led and rescue-led excavations throughout the

DOI: 10.4324/9781003429470-1

2   *Archibald Dunn*

city, with art history and historical enquiry, in an attempt to construct a history of a Middle Byzantine town.[5] But he had also, with Laskarina Boura, in their *Ê elladikê naodomia kata ton 12o aiôna*, created a rich synthesis about the Middle Byzantine monumental architecture of southern Greece which is another kind of benchmark in Byzantine regional studies.[6]

One hesitates to stop there – and there are other, older, pioneering, or otherwise still broadly resonating works – but the point here is to illustrate how effectively the Greek space and its materials, including now its dynamic landscapes in their diachronic configurations (but also paleobotanic residues, as we shall see) can sustain and enrich the multidisciplinary study of the Byzantine world as a whole (if not so demonstrably their much heralded 'interdisciplinary' study).

Our foray into this field consists of several kinds of response to an already rich bibliography, by comparison with the bibliographies for some other territories of the former Byzantine world. That richness is closely connected to the political and cultural history of 'the Greek space' since the fall of the Byzantine Empire, a history which favoured, relatively speaking of course, the preservation of several kinds of archives (many of these located beyond this geographical space in Italy, Malta and Spain), of religious art and architecture, and toponymy, and then subsequently favoured their deliberate *conservation*. We do not engage in these proceedings with that fascinating political and cultural story as such, but it is worthwhile to remind ourselves of some steps in the process whereby the study of Byzantine Greece has come to find itself where it is today.

Firstly, this field of enquiry has, ever since the 19th century, been conducted at several levels of detail and synthesis both within and beyond an expanding political Greece. Some, but by no means all, of this variety was captured by Dionysios Zakythinos in his still-historiographically interesting *Vyzantinê Ellas 392–1204* (first published as an article in 1964).[7] Secondly, the ultimately essential recording of freestanding monuments and excavation of buried monuments played no part in the early histories of Byzantine Greece, although Zakythinos acknowledged the interpretative challenge for historians,[8] nor did the incipient editing of the archives of Mount Athos (which are not rich for the Middle Byzantine period though). Thirdly, archaeologists began concertedly to 'intervene' in this traditional narrative history in the 1930s, using the excavations of the Forum of Corinth[9]; then in the 1950s using the Agora of Athens' excavations.[10] Numismatists soon became involved too.[11] Meanwhile at more 'granular' levels of synthesis, such as those of cities or provinces, the socio-economic history of our periods of interest, the Early to Middle Byzantine, had begun to appear, in the works of O. Tafrali regarding Thessaloniki (in 1913–1919), which even included monumental archaeology, in Paul Lemerle's politico-administrative and ecclesiastical history of eastern Macedonia of 1945[12]; and in a quite new kind of provincial history, Antoine Bon's *Le Péloponnèse byzantin jusqu'en 1204* of 1951.[13] This later made systematic use of chronicles of course, but also of a

Introduction   3

wide range of literary works, archives (in which Lemerle's work is rich), epigraphy, numismatics, and sigillography, to formulate a kind of Byzantine regional history. The die was cast, so to speak.

Gradually from 1945 onwards monographic studies of historico-geographic regions in Greece (but with a northern 'edge' not strictly limited by Modern Greece's northern frontier) in Early and/or Middle Byzantine times, often trying to cover both of these periods, have appeared, in which archaeological data have been deployed increasingly.[14] These and other works offer frameworks for both smaller-scale case studies (particularly archaeological, a development under way since the 1980s which can involve the surviving archives, so with a certain focus upon Macedonia), and, looking ahead, frameworks for cross-regional case studies.[15] Above all, the parallel development of a Byzantine (or Late Roman and Byzantine) historical geography of Greece from the 1970s onwards, by systematising empirical knowledge about a given region's or former province's politico-administrative history, economic geography, historical toponymy, and published archaeology, furnishes a 'platform' for regional and sub-regional studies at any 'setting' of a project's focus. This development too is under way. This phase in the study of Late Roman and Byzantine Greece could be said to begin with Anna Avramea's published thesis on the historical geography of Early and Middle Byzantine Thessaly in 1974.[16] It was immediately followed by the first of the fascicles of the *Tabula Imperii Romani* to deal with Greece (Macedonia, and more recently Thrace and the rest of mainland Greece), and by an ongoing series of volumes of the *Tabula Imperii Byzantini* (which has so far covered Central Greece, Epirus, the Aegean islands, and southern Thrace across Bulgaria, European Turkey, and north-eastern Greece).[17]

Meanwhile the aims of excavators were widening beyond the monumental hearts of Greco-Roman cities, such as Athens or Corinth, and whilst those excavations will continue to contribute to our understanding of Byzantine Greece's evolution (as we learnt in the Symposium: see Chapter 9), it is vital, and is justified by the findings, that resources are found to excavate right across, and indeed beyond, the settlement hierarchy, for instance at rural fortifications (as we see in Chapter 3), and religious complexes and economic installations in the countryside (as we see in Chapters 2, 6, and 16).

The Byzantine archaeology which informs newer regional studies has, as is well known, grown exponentially in quantity. It has been slowly acquiring 'critical mass' since the year 1960 (with the Greek Archaeological Service's methodical reporting of discoveries, and the steady appointment of Byzantine archaeologists and/or art historians throughout its new units.[18] And since 1978–1979 the archaeology of Late Roman and Byzantine Greece has been benefitting substantively from the introduction of the multi-period intensive interdisciplinary survey (now slightly misleadingly and blandly called, obviously for brevity, 'landscape archaeology'), those being the years in which Stanford University's Southern Argolid Survey and Cambridge and Bradford Universities' Boeotian Survey began.[19] As dozens of such surveys have since

4   *Archibald Dunn*

then been launched in every part of Greece (including, at last, Greek Thrace), and as they espouse almost without exception the theoretical merits of sampling the entire visible artefactual record, we are brought, by design or by default, as close as is currently possible to representative samples of Byzantium's archaeological presence without expensive excavations. The pedestrian surveys, sometimes combined with remote sensing, and with the developing sites and monuments records of the archaeological service, and of course texts wherever relevant, are now facilitating new kinds of sub-regional syntheses (a good example of which is presented in outline in Chapter 4).

None of these new developments however supersede or displace historical analysis of social or cultural or economic structures and trends at the regional level. Indeed just such a regional historical study was published by Angeliki Laiou in 1977, based entirely on the archives of Mount Athos.[20] The functioning of the Church in the provinces (Chapter 17), the functioning of provincial markets (Chapter 19), and the functioning of the rural economy throughout Middle Byzantine Greece (Chapter 18), are only captured in their complexity in monastic archives, letters, legislation, or fiscal records (the *Praktika* for instance). The general conclusions of these chapters mesh interestingly with the Middle Byzantine archaeological projects included in these proceedings.

Archaeology challenges many of us, whether engaged in it or with it, to test academically sound ways of combining it with historical enquiry: to design and 'test' such approaches. Correlations between different kinds of fieldwork are common practice now (typically between extensive survey, sites and monuments records, and intensive survey), and correlations between these and the earth sciences and environmental sciences are common in Greece as elsewhere. In practice, the ground of integration will vary, not necessarily stretching far across the range of disciplines that an 'interdisciplinary' survey says that it is bringing together, but nevertheless demonstrating a sound basis for further testing of this great challenge. Such is the case with Chapter 12, a circumspect re-analysis of one of the richest palaeo-environmental sources for the study of Byzantine agriculture and land use more generally, 'preparing' some of the Greek palynological data for testing against (ultimately) historical data. That data will surely concern Late Roman and Byzantine economic *outcomes*.

The challenge meanwhile of a close correlation between *cultural* archaeology and the quintessentially historical topic of relations of production in Byzantine Greece would obviously be a major gain for history, archaeology, and interdisciplinarity itself (which is becoming an end in itself for those who try to 'strategise' research), if it could be demonstrated. And Greece's multiperiod intensive interdisciplinary surveys have been used to try to demonstrate just this possibility, with Cynthia Kosso's bold attempt to 'map' the spectrum of Late Roman-to-Early Byzantine rural sites of all kinds found by these surveys in central and southern Greece since 1978–1979 onto legal and other texts' references to types of rural habitation from the villa 'downwards', and to correlate these sites and their material culture with forms of legal land tenure.[21] The Boeotian Survey (presented at the Symposium), using data more refined than some of the data available to Kosso, has attempted something similar for the *khora* of the polis of Thespiai.[22] But detecting and distinguishing between specific social relations of production in the ceramic landscape is problematic (when we know from texts that a slave could be a farmer, and a tenant could be, depending on the terms of the tenure, in a better situation than a smallholder).

Having said that, sophisticated excavations of Byzantine 'Dark-Age' levels at an urban site (and provincial capital) such as Gortyn in Crete (Chapter 5), or those of Butrint, on the mainland opposite to Corfu (Chapter 10), reveal features and artefacts from which conclusions can be confidently drawn about a continuing elite presence, and long-distance traffic in higher-value goods, which characterise and localise important historical phenomena to which texts of the 7th or 8th centuries offer vanishingly brief allusions that we hardly know how to evaluate. The excavations and remote-sensing surveys of Corinth have meanwhile identified a phase of urban fortification which definitively excluded the old forum in the mid-to-late 6th century, meaning that the forum's abandonment (initially to burials) no longer illustrates 'catastrophic' decline at all (Chapter 9). And the excavations of pottery kilns at Aegean insular sites of the 7th–9th centuries provide detailed case studies of the wide circulation of well-modelled amphorae that seem to reflect the state's introduction of controls upon their volumes (hence on their total values when filled), all of which is a far cry from assumptions about technical decline, localisation of economies, and simplification of networks (Chapter 6). At the level of the individual monument, fresh discoveries (many of them made as a result of careful modern conservation) are revealing the unsuspected extent of restoration and professional reconstruction of great churches from the mid or late 7th century through the 8th century in Thessaloniki and elsewhere (Chapters 8 and 13), while extensive archaeo-logical surveys in the Dodecanese reveal an unsuspected rural monastic movement in the 8th (and later) centuries (Chapter 16). In other words, there is much scope for archaeological case studies of the 7th–8th or 9th centuries to critically inform the modelling of patterns and trends in economic, social, and cultural activities that can be correlated with, and greatly refine, models extrapolated from highly problematic historical sources.

Syntheses of specific types of archaeological data recorded throughout Greece (provenanced inscriptions: Chapter 14) and fortifications in different regions of Greece (Chapter 11), a multidisciplinary correlation between the findings of excavations, intensive surveys, art history, and texts (Chapter 16), rural excavations (Chapter 2), and urban excavations (Chapter 13), demon-strate for the most part a fertile complementarity with historical enquiries in which the contributions of archaeology are quite definitely enhancing our understanding of important phenomena on which written sources shed light but which they will never (for the Middle Byzantine era) fully contextualise,

6   *Archibald Dunn*

reconstruct, or explain. The relatively rich and dateable epigraphy of churches' benefactors of the 9th–12th centuries enables the tracing of the evolution of a rising provincial elite in its institutional relationships (Chapter 14). Case studies of the new fortifications of this period, in their variety, scale, and topography, illuminate the changing security problems of the time, but equally decisions to organise protection of localities of which we know almost nothing historically (Chapter 11). There is much recording and analysis still to be carried out at fortified sites however, and, even where we have documentary materials (see below), the fortifications themselves tend not to be illuminated by these. However, one such archivally recorded *kastron*, Hierissos in the Khalkidike, has become probably one of the best-recorded archaeologically (Chapter 13). The revelations of its artisanal production, consumption, and connections are fascinating to link with its historically documented capacity for collective, and clearly successful, activity in the agricultural (agro-pastoral) sphere. The urbanisation of the Middle Byzantine provincial *kastra* has found a highly instructive case study. The Middle Byzantine countryside as the arena of a rising provincial elite's investments in prestigious pious foundations (of which almost invariably only the church survives) is traced across the Peloponnese in its economic logic by the correlation of the Middle Byzantine material from some of the multiperiod intensive surveys with the chronologies of the contemporary churches in or adjacent to their surveyed zones, and with the agricultural potential of the topographically associated landscapes, in this way making much greater use of the surveys' Middle Byzantine ceramic data than they had done (Chapter 15). But this almost certainly illustrates the variety of ways in which elite endowments could combine forms of monastic retreat with elite residence. In any case, the implantation of new rural fortifications, the rise of new towns at some of them, the rise of a new provincial elite, and its expression of its status and religiosity in variations upon the theme of the private monastery (for which the sources of this period are highly informative), all – thanks to innovative combinations of archaeology, art history, and texts – bring the institutions, social classes, and economic developments of this period into more instructive degrees of focus at the regional and sub-regional level than they would otherwise have done.

Byzantine Greece seems rather familiar because of its ubiquitous monumental presence in modern Greece. But if we try to tie its sites and monuments – those ubiquitous basilicas and small Middle Byzantine cruciform churches, those forts and town walls, and now the traces of the occupation of the remotest countryside revealed by intensive surveys – into accounts of Byzantium, or into local histories of the kinds which are possible across much of the West, we quickly encounter a host of well-known problems. As a consequence, Byzantine Greece is not as familiar as it might seem. But is it inaccessible? Parts of Greece are relatively rich in regional archives (Chapter 13). It is relatively rich in epigraphic (and sigillographic) material (Chapter 14). And the archaeological exploration of Byzantine Greece (research-led and rescue-led) is relatively intense. Specific categories of this material already enrich Byzantine Studies as a whole (studies of its architecture and art, of 'the city', of the rural economy, and of all social classes, for instance). But these categories of data can often be correlated with each other, given their geographical or topographical aspect (archives with extensive and intensive surveys in Central and Eastern Macedonia for instance), so as to illuminate Byzantine Greece itself in its own regional and sub-regional specificities. Without often allowing clear correlations with the narrative history of Byzantium (despite the wishes of previous generations of scholars), this data can instead illuminate the evolution of settlements and installations of all kinds in relation to each other and to the changing political and social institutions of Byzantium. That two-way interchange between syntheses and new case studies via regional studies conducted at varied scales and degrees of intensity is vital for the development of Byzantine Studies.

Notes

1 Curta 2014.
2 Bintliff 2012.
3 Deligiannakis 2016.
4 Veikou 2012; Veikou 2012: 19–41.
5 Bouras 2017.
6 Bouras and Boura 2002.
7 Zakythênos 1965.
8 Zakythênos 1965: 23–35.
9 Setton 1975: ii–iii.
10 Davidson 1937: 227–240; Davidson 1952: 5–6.
11 Bon 1951: 51.
12 Lemerle 1945.
13 Bon 1951.
14 Avramea 1997; Tsougarakis 1988; Bowden 2003; Veikou 2012.
15 Dunn 2009; Atherden and Hall 2009 (both forming one case study).
16 Avramea 1974.
17 *Tabula Imperii Romani* 1: 1931 onwards; *Tabula Imperii Byzantini* 1: 1976 onwards.
18 Karagiannê 2010.
19 Van Andel and Runnels 1987; Bintliff 2007.
20 Laiou-Thomadakis 1977.
21 Kosso 2003.
22 Bintliff *et al.* 2007.

References

Atherden, M., and Hall, J. (2009), 'The Strymon Delta Project: the palynological evidence', in J. Bintliff, and H. Stöger, eds., *Medieval and Post-Medieval Greece. The Corfu Papers*, B.A.R. International Series 2023, Oxford: 33–42.

Avramea, A. (1974), *Ê vyzantinê Thessalia mekhri tou 1204. Symvolê eis tên istorikên geôgraphian.* Athens.

Avraméa, A. (1997), *Le Péloponnèse du IVe au VIIIe siècle.* Paris.

8 Archibald Dunn

Bintliff, J. (2007), 'The contribution of regional survey to the Late Antique debate: Greece in the Mediterranean context', in A. Poulter, ed., *The transition to Late Antiquity: on the Danube and beyond*, Oxford: 649–679.

Bintliff, J. *et al.* (2007), *Testing the hinterland: the work of the Boeotian Survey (1989–1991) in the southern approaches to the city of Thespiai*. Cambridge.

Bintliff, J. (2012), *The complete archaeology of Greece: from hunter-gatherers to the 20th century AD*. Oxford.

Bon, A. (1951), *Le Péloponnèse byzantin jusqu'en 1204*. Paris.

Bouras, Ch. (2017), *Byzantine Athens, 10th–12th centuries*. London.

Bouras, Ch., and Boura, L. (2002), *Ê elladikê naodomia kata ton 12o aiôna*. Athens.

Bowden, W. (2003), *Epirus Vetus. The archaeology of a Late Antique province*. London.

Curta, F. (2014), *The Edinburgh History of the Greeks, C.500 to 1050: The Early Middle Ages*. Edinburgh.

Davidson, G. (1937), 'The Avar invasion of Corinth', *Hesperia* 227–240.

Davidson, G. (1952), *Results of excavations at Corinth conducted by the American School of Classical Studies at Athens. Volume XII. The minor objects*. Princeton.

Deligiannakis, G. (2016), *The Dodecanese and the Eastern Aegean islands in Late Antiquity, AD 300–700*. Oxford.

Dunn, A. (2009), 'Byzantine and Ottoman maritime traffic in the estuary of the Strymon: between environment, state and market', in J. Bintliff, and H. Stöger, eds., *Medieval and Post-Medieval Greece. The Corfu Papers*, B.A.R. International Series 2023, Oxford: 15–32.

Karagiannê, Ph. (2010), *Oi vyzantinoi oikismoi stê Makedonia mesa apo ta arkhaiologika dedomena (4os – 15os aiônas)*. Thessaloniki.

Kosso, C. (2003), *The archaeology of public policy in Late Roman Greece*, B.A.R. International Series 1126, Oxford.

Laiou-Thomadakis, A. (1977), *A peasant society in the Late Byzantine Empire. A social and demographic study*. Princeton.

Lemerle, P. (1945), *Philippes et la Macédoine orientale à l'époque chrétienne et byzantine*. Paris.

Setton, K. (1975), *Athens in the Middle Ages*. London.

Tabula Imperii Byzantini (1976–), Multiple volumes. Österreichische Akademie der Wissenschaften.

Tabula Imperii Romani (1931–) Multiple volumes, multiple publishers.

Tsougarakis, D. (1988), *Byzantine Crete from the 5th century to the Venetian conquest*. Athens.

Van Andel, T., and Runnels, C. (1987), *Beyond the Acropolis: a rural Greek Past*. Stanford.

Veikou, M. (2012), *Byzantine Epirus. A topography of transformation. Settlement of the seventh-twelfth centuries in Southern Epirus and Aetoloakarnania, Greece*. Leiden.

Zakythênos, D. (1965), *Ê vyzantinê Ellas 392–1204*. Athens.

Part 1

Late Antique Greece

2 The Institutional Church in Early Christian Greece

Eirini Zisimou-Tryfonidi

This study aims to enrich our knowledge about the organisation and function of the various institutions of the Church in Early Christian Greece by gathering data from excavation reports and revisiting the relevant epigraphical and literary sources. Several representative examples testify to the regional economic and social role of the Church and put the issues of industrialisation, philanthropy, and pilgrimage at the forefront of discussion.

The motive to explore the establishment and activity of the Early Christian Church's institutions in Greece, based on the study of the economy and material culture of the basilicas' annexes, will be the 38th canon of the Council in Trullo, which states explicitly that the organisation of churches is to follow upon the renovation of the city: Εἴ τις ἐκ βασιλικῆς ἐξουσίας ἐκαινίσθη πόλις, ἢ αὖθις καινισθείη, τοῖς πολιτικοῖς καὶ δημοσίοις τύποις καὶ ἡ τῶν ἐκκλησιαστικῶν πραγμάτων τάξις ἀκολουθείτω ('If by imperial authority any city has been renovated or shall have been renovated, the organisation of ecclesiastical affairs shall follow the pattern of civil and state organisation').[1]

The organisation of ecclesiastical affairs of the 'Christianised' city therefore, had to follow upon the renovation of the 'secular' city. But what do we mean exactly by a 'Christianised city'? In my opinion it could mean partly the architectural development of the Church and its institutions and partly the development of a Christian ideology interconnected with the State and its secular notions. The interaction between the Church and the State, and the concept of co-existence that was formed in the political scene, is well illustrated in Justinian's religious and ecclesiastical policies that went hand-in-hand with the codification and reformation of the civil law. Interestingly, in Justinian's Novel 131 the State accepted the ecclesiastical rules of the ecclesiastical Councils as laws.[2]

However, it is not my purpose here to review and comment in general on the relationship developed between the Church and the State during Early Christian times. Instead, I have chosen to study one particular aspect of this subject, the economy of the institutional Church and to limit myself to a specific region of the Empire, that covered by contemporary Greece. I do not wish to explain particular facts but to place the material culture of the institutional Church in its proper perspective and explore the balance

DOI: 10.4324/9781003429470-3

between certain aspects of imperial law, archaeological and epigraphical evidence, and Church literature.

In order to study all these aspects I have distinguished the function of the institutional Church in three main categories: the institutions of the Church serving the pilgrims, the philanthropic mission of the Church, and the Church's engagement in business. In particular, this chapter will consider the industrial and agricultural activity of the basilicas' annexes in relation to the oil and wine production.[3] The activity of the wine and olive oil workshops has been usually identified through the evidence of presses, crushers, weights and counterweights, basins, and the evidence of large *pithoi* in nearby storage facilities.[4]

The most representative example is the so-called Episcopal Complex at the site of Louloudies in Pieria, Western Macedonia (Figure 2.1). According to the excavators, in Justinian's reign a winery with five rooms was built at the northwest part of the complex and an olive oil press was established respectively and both were related to the upgrading of the episcopal role with administrative activities of a financial character.[5]

Another well-studied example is the site of the sacristy at the Early Christian basilica at Bghiadoudi in Chalkidiki, which was also transformed into a winery while at the same time storerooms were erected to the west of the *exonarthex* (Figure 2.2).[6]

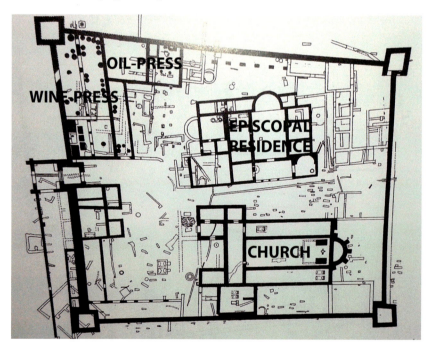

Figure 2.1 Louloudies Pierias. The Episcopal Complex [after Marki 2008, Fig. 5. (Ed. by E. Zisimou-Tryfonidi)].

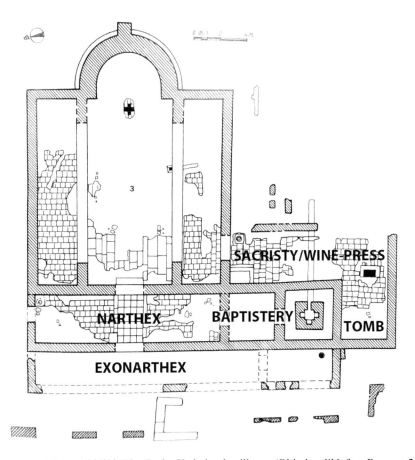

Figure 2.2 Chalkidiki. The Early Christian basilica at 'Bhiadoudi' [after Pazaras 2009, Fig. 73 (Ed. by E. Zisimou-Tryfonidi)].

The northern part of the basilica at Paliambela, at Arethousa, Eastern Macedonia, was also transformed to include an area for wine production and food storage, which has been identified as a multifunctional area for the use of the local community (Figure 2.3).[7] Similarly, part of the transformation at the annexes of the 'Lavreotic Olympos' basilica in Attica, was an olive oil press dated to the early 7th century (Figure 2.4).[8]

On the island of Delos, in the Cyclades, parts of the winepresses or of the rooms where the presses were discovered, at the ruins of the classical city, have been found incised with Christian decorations, graffiti and an invocation to Christ possibly revealing a thriving industrial activity of the local Church.[9]

This material evidence of a specific function of the institutional Church related to the economy of the towns and countryside, as well as to the property of the Church, was established, according to the excavation data, from the middle to the end of the 6th century and continued into the 7th

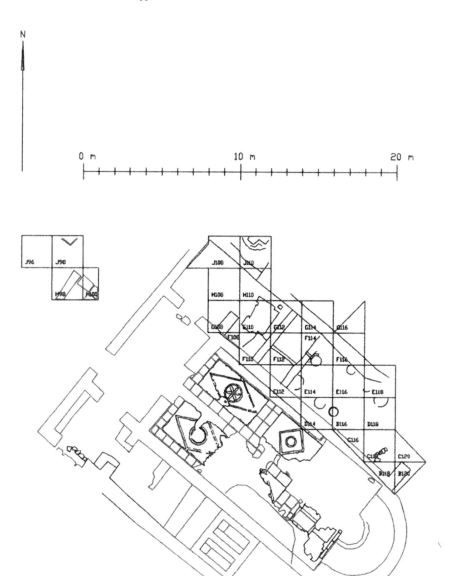

Figure 2.3 Arethousa. Plan of the excavations of the Early Christian basilica [after Karivieri 2009, Fig. 2].

The Institutional Church in Early Christian Greece 15

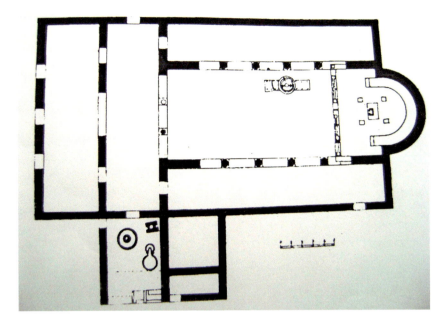

Figure 2.4 Lavreotic Olympus. The Early Christian basilica and the annex with the oil-press [after Kotzias 1952, Fig. 2].

century. Unfortunately it is very difficult to come to conclusions on the specific function of the churches (could they have been used as parish churches?), or to make any assumptions about their urban or rural context.

As part of the transformations observed in the architecture of the 6th century, the organisation of churches was indeed following the State's renovation of the towns. More specifically, Justinian passed a law forbidding lending or divestiture, obviously following the conciliar Canons regarding the economic behaviour of the Church.[10] Later, however, this law changed and churches from all the regions of the Empire (except for Constantinople) were allowed to sell up their movable and immovable property (including property given by the State) in order to pay off their debts including their public debts.[11]

I believe that the annexes of the basilicas discussed above may represent part of the implementation of this law. The establishment of workshops in basilicas' annexes may reflect the opportunity that churches took in response to the requirement of the State to reclaim and invest in their properties. Although more careful investigation needs to be done, it can now be claimed with some certainty that during the 6th and 7th centuries it was not a coincidence that these small-scale industrial establishments were attached to churches. But most importantly the archaeological evidence shows that the Church provided a new model for the organisation of public space in which the Church was the epicentre of the economic and social life of the Greek

16   *Eirini Zisimou-Tryfonidi*

towns by following the existing patterns of civil and state organisation. This was the expression of its secular side, what I would like to call 'secular Christianity'. Although contradictory, the term 'secular Christianity' is a term that may help explain those activities of the Church, which were not directly related to its ritual character but rather to its institutional functions.

The study of representative relevant inscriptions from Early Christian Greece is providing another part of the evidence that may illuminate the institutional organisation of the Church and more specifically its engagement in business.

One of the mosaic inscriptions from the chancel of the Early Christian basilica at Klafsi in Eurytania, names a 'reader and steward': ... ΑΝΑΓΝΩΣΤΟΥ ΚΑΙ ΟΙΚΟ / ΝΟΜΟΥ ΤΗΣ ΕΝΘΑΔΕ / ΑΓΙΩΤΑΤΗΣ ΕΚΚΛΗΣΙΑΣ ... ('Reader and *oikonomos* of this most Holy Church').[12] A steward (*oikonomos*) was nominated by the 26th canon of the Council of Chalcedon, in order to avoid the bishop's involvement in any financial scandal.[13] Another inscription from the Early Christian Church at Olympia mentions a Reader and land lessor (*emphyteutes*), who paved the floors: ΚΥΡΙΑΚΟΣ Ο ΕΥ / ΛΑΒΕΣΤΑΤΟΣ ΑΝΑΓΝΩΣΤΗΣ ΚΑΙ / ΕΜΦΥΤΕΥΤΗΣ / ΤΗΣ ΚΤΗΣΕΟΣ / ΥΠΕΡ ΣΩΤΗΡΙΑΣ / ΕΑΥΤΟΥ ΕΥΞΑΜΕ / ΝΟΣ ΕΚΑΛ(Λ)ΙΕΡΓΗ / ΣΕΝ ΤΗΝ ΣΤΡΩΣΙΝ ('Kyriakos the most pious reader and *emphyteutic* lease-holder decorated the pavement of the building praying for his salvation').[14]

The term 'estate holder' (*emphyteutes*) is most interesting as it suggests further that the church was supported partly by long-term leases. A long-term lease (*emphyteusis*) with a set annual fee was a very common way to let the Church's land during the 6th century.[15] Relevant to the information about long-term leases that this inscription reveals could be the extensive exploitation of vines that is indicated by the archaeological evidence of wineries that have been found around Olympia.[16]

The inscription found in the nave of the Early Christian Church at Molaoi, Laconia, mentions all those who are contributing with good works (*tous kalliergountas*) to the Church: ΜΝΗΣΘΗΤΙ ΚΥΡΙΕ ΚΑΙ ΕΛΕ / ΗΣΟΝ ΠΑΝΤΑΣ ΤΟΥΣ / ΚΑΛΛΙΕΡΓΟΥΝΤΑΣ ΕΝ Τ / Η ΑΓΙΑ ΣΟΥ ΕΚΚΛΗΣΙΑ ('Remember Lord and have mercy on all those doing good works in your Holy Church').[17] Anastasios Orlandos explains the different meanings of the verb *kalliergo* in Church inscriptions, whether as referring to those responsible for the decoration of the church or to those who are taking care of the church.[18] However, I would argue that in many instances the original meaning of this word was figurative and that it actually meant the financial contributions made to the churches.

The same could be argued for the verb *karpophoro* whose derivatives are also found in Church inscriptions. Distinctively, an inscription from Eresos basilica on Lesvos refers to the offerings of the faithful, the so-called '*karpophories*' or '*oblationes*' with which Timagoras the Presbyter and Steward made the mosaic: ΤΙΜΑΓΟΡΑΣ / ΠΡΕΣΒΥΤΕ / ΡΟΣ ΚΑΙ ΟΙΚΟ / ΝΟΜΟΣ ΕΠΟΙ / ΗΣΑ ΑΠΟ ΚΑΡ / ΠΟΦΟΡΙΩΝ ('Timagoras, a presbyter and *oikonomos*, I made (this) from offerings').[19] In this inscription, the phrase 'from offerings' should mean that the mosaic was made from the offerings of the faithful, since Timagoras was a Presbyter, and it implies that the offerings most probably took the form of economic assistance. Another mosaic inscription from the same basilica on Lesvos refers to another mosaic floor that was made using offerings, and which names a certain bishop Ioannis who contributed most probably financially to the erection or decoration of the Eresos basilica: ΕΠΛΗΡΩΘΗ ΤΟ ΕΡΓΟΝ ΕΠΙ ΤΟΥ / ΑΓΙΩΤΑΤΟΥ ΕΠΙΣΚ[ΟΠΟΥ] ΗΜΩΝ / ΙΩΑΝΝΟΥ ΤΟΥ ΚΑΙ Κ[ΑΡΠ]Ο-ΦΟΡΗΣΑΝΤΟΣ ('The work was made with the offering of our most pious bishop Ioannis').[20]

Both inscriptions reveal that both the clergy and laity assisted the church financially. The verb *karpophoro* is mentioned very often in Early Christian inscriptions and it means 'I offer gifts' to the Church or 'I construct something with my own means'. The offerings, or the so-called '*karpophories*' either in kind or in cash, were initially the voluntary offerings from the faithful that were later overshadowed by the income from endowments.[21] In Early Christian inscriptions and in Church literature, usually the language seems to be figurative as they do not seem to have taken the form of regular first fruits, but they were synonymous with offerings of economic value. *Karpophories* were rather directly related to the institutional Church as they constituted the revenues from which the Church supported the clergy, maintained their buildings, engaged in business and distributed charity to the poor.

Finally, I believe that the language used in the previous inscriptions mentioning those that bring offerings and do good works in the church (*tous karpophorountas kai kalliergountas*), was inspired by Church literature and more specifically by John Chrysostom's Divine Liturgy which praises 'those that bring offerings and do good works in the holy and most venerable sanctuary'.

Apart from the material evidence of the industrial activity of the churches' annexes and the evidence of inscriptions regarding the management of their economic activity, there is also evidence that the Church supported and played a crucial role in some specific crafts and trades. More specifically, there is evidence of workshops producing *pithoi*, stamped tiles and bricks, and other vessels for the needs of the Church, revealing that there were industries especially managed for or by the Church.

At the *agora* of Phthiotic Thebes there has been found a pottery workshop producing probably the tiles that were found around the area, inscribed with the words ΕΚΚΛ(ΗΣΙΑ) ΘΗΒ(ΩΝ) ('Church of Thebes').[22] Again in Phthiotic Thebes, at the sacristy of Basilica B was found a *pithos* bearing on its rim the inscription (ΕΚΚΛΗΣΙΑΣ) ΘΗΒ(ΩΝ) ('of the Church of Thebes'),[23] while on the rims of other *pithoi* found at the south annex of the atrium of Basilica A was inscribed the Church that they belonged to, and the amount of their contents: Ε.ΘΒ ('Of the Church of Thebes') and Χ.Μ. ('A thousand *modioi*').[24] Similar inscriptions on bricks and tiles have been found elsewhere

18   *Eirini Zisimou-Tryfonidi*

in Greece, indicating that special orders were made for these basilicas and that very possibly the Church owned its own pottery and terra cotta workshops.[25]

Another factor that contributed decisively to the institutional evolution of the Church is pilgrimage. Although pilgrims were initially part of the religious and festal life of the towns they tended to act as a special category of tourists, and pilgrimage became a way, whether for individuals or for the Church, to make a profit. This resulted in a need for decrees and Canons during the 4th–6th centuries to prohibit severely the exploitation of the veneration of martyrs for economic purposes.

In Greece there are various Early Christian inscriptions that name certain martyrs and holy men who would have been of paramount importance to the local population. To mention a few examples: an inscription on a marble fragment found in Larisa names the martyrs Ioannis, Loukas, Andreas, and Leonides, which has been explained as a *mensa martyrum*: ΜΑΡΤΥΡΩ[Ν] ΙΩΑΝΝΟΥ ΛΟΥΚΑ ΑΝΔΡΕΟΥ ΛΕΩΝΙΔΟΥ ... ./ [ΕΤΕΛΕΙ]ΩΘΗ ΤΟ ΜΑΡΤΥΡΙΟΝ [Τ]Η ΠΡΟ ΙΕ ΚΑΛΕΝΔΩΝ) ΙΑΝ(ΟΥΑΡΙΩΝ / [ΑΝΕΣ]ΤΗΣΕΝ Η ΔΟΥΛΗ ΑΥΤΩΝ ΣΩΤ(ΗΡΙΣ)[26]; an inscription on one of the three burial cavities at the north side of the narthex of the Early Christian basilica at the *agora* of Thasos names the martyr Akakios: ΑΚΑΚΙΟΥ ΜΑΡΤΥΡΟΣ[27]; an inscription on an architectural fragment that has been found at a basilica in Corinth links the complex to the cult of St. Kodratos: [ΑΓΙ]Ε ΚΟΔΡΑΤΕ ΜΝΗΣΘ[ΗΤΙ] ΤΩ ΔΟΥΛΩ ΣΟ[Υ][28]; and an inscribed covering slab from a tomb in Athens informs us of *Hosios* Klematios: Ο ΕΝ ΟΣΙΟΙΣ ΕΠΙΣΚΟΠΟΣ ΚΛΗΜΑΤΙΟΣ.[29]

I would argue however that the most crucial aspect of the process of identifying pilgrimage sites in Greece, is the effective use of the architectural and archaeological evidence of special buildings that were set up to receive the devout supplicants in the places where the memory of a high-profile martyr was venerated.

This is the case of the town of Philippi in northern Greece, which evolved into an important religious centre based on the profound memory of the founding visit of Apostle Paul.[30] Philippi sheds light on the archaeological substance of pilgrimage sites through the architectural and archaeological documentation of the Octagon complex, which is comprised of an octagonal church, annexes including the bathhouse, and the two-storey bishop's residence. The structure identified as the *xenodocheion* formed part of the Octagon's complex and it operated independently.[31] Charalambos Bakirtzis compares the *xenodocheion* at the Octagon's complex, where people could be accommodated, to the spatial arrangement of the *xenodocheion* of St. Menas near Alexandria.[32] The excavation reports of other Early Christian sites in Greece give similar evidence too, such as the identified *xenodocheia* at the Early Christian basilicas of Mytilini,[33] and Samos, to name but a few.[34]

The case of the involvement of the Church in the market economy of the Early Christian towns as the outcome of its institutional activities,

The Institutional Church in Early Christian Greece 19

demonstrates how in order for its institutions to become established, the State supported and promoted it, while the Church in turn followed the existing patterns of civil and state organisation. In fact, the written sources and material evidence show that in time of need the State claimed financial support from the Church, whose annexes' industrial functions, and other institutional activities, enabled her to emerge as an economic powerhouse which also affected decisively the organisation of the public space of the Greek towns.

By focusing on aspects of archaeological and epigraphical documentation, imperial legislation, and Church literature this study has sought to re-examine the forms of economic and social integration of the Church and its institutions. However, as only a fraction of the material concerning this widespread phenomenon has yet been revealed, further scholarship needs to be done in order to shed more light upon the evolving and multifarious roles of the Church's institutions in Early Christian Greece, and indeed the Mediterranean, as well as their consequences in the political, socio-economic, and spatial transformation of towns.

Notes

1 *Syntagma ton Theion kai Hieron Kanonon*, ed. Ralles and Potles 1852: 392.
2 *Corpus Juris Civilis* Nov. 131.1 (545 AD), ed. Schoell and Kroll 1928.
3 For the different functions of the Early Christian basilicas' annexes in Greece, see mailis 2011, especially from 147 for domestic and agricultural function.
4 More specifically, for the identification of olive oil presses in Greece, see Chatzisavvas 2008.
5 Marki 2004; Marki 2008.
6 Pazaras 2009.
7 Karivieri 2002; Karivieri 2004; Karivieri 2009; Karivieri 2017.
8 Kotzias 1952.
9 Bruneau and Fraisse 1984: 713–30; Bruneau 1987: 339–340; Roussel and Launey 1937: no. 2585*bis*.
10 *Corpus Juris Civilis* Nov. 3, 7 (535 AD).
11 *Corpus Juris Civilis* Nov. 3, 46 and 120 (535 AD, 537 AD, 544 AD).
12 Chatzidakis 1958.
13 *Syntagma,* ed. Ralles and Potles 1852: 276–277.
14 Feissel and Philippidis-Braat 1985: 373, no. 155.
15 A long-term lease (*emphyteusis*) with a set annual fee was a very common way to let the Church's land during the 6th century. See Jones 1973: II, 897.
16 Völling 2001.
17 Etzeoglou 1974: 249–250.
18 Orlandos 1933: 83, n. 2.
19 Orlandos 1929: 38–39.
20 Orlandos 1929: 40.
21 For a discussion on the practice of the offerings, see: Jones 1973: II, 894.
22 Lazaridis 1960.
23 Soteriou 1929: 45, 103.
24 Soteriou 1927: 46.
25 Soteriou and Orlandos 1930: 80; Orlandos 1961: 100; Barlas 1966: 100. See also Theocharidou 1985-1986.
26 Soteriou 1932: 7–17; Chalkia 1989: 101–106; Chalkia 2011: 130.

20   *Eirini Zisimou-Tryfonidi*

27 Delvoye 1951: 154–164.
28 Stikas 1962: 54.
29 Travlos 1962: 730.
30 Bakirtzis 1998: 37–48.
31 Bakirtzis 2008: 367–371.
32 Bakirtzis 2008: 371.
33 Evangelidis 1930-1931: 1–40.
34 Schneider 1929: 124–125.

References

Bakirtzis, Ch. (1998), 'Paul and Philippi: the archaeological evidence', in Ch. Bakirtzis and H. Koester, eds., *Philippi at the Time of Paul and after His Death*, Harrisburg, PA: 37–48.

Bakirtzis, Ch. (2008), 'The pilgrims' xenodocheion at Philippi', in E. Chadjitryphonos, ed., *Routes of faith in the Medieval Mediterranean: history, monuments, people, pilgrimage perspectives, International symposium, Thessaloniki 2007*, Thessaloniki: 367–371.

Barla, Ch. (1966), 'Anaskaphe Kephalou Amvrakikou', *PraktArchEt* 121: 95–102.

Bruneau, Ph. (1987), 'Deliaca', *BCH* 111: 313–342.

Bruneau, Ph., and Fraisse, Ph. (1984), 'Pressoirs déliens', *BCH* 108: 713–730.

Chalkia, E. (1989), 'Trapezes Martyron: e semasia tou orou kai e tyche tou sten Ellenike vivliographia', *DChAE* 14: 101–106.

Chatzidakis, E. (1958), 'Anaskaphe Klafsiou Evrytanias', *PraktArchEt* 113: 58–63.

Chatzisavvas, S. (2008), *E elia kai to ladi ston archaio elleniko kosmo*. Athens.

Delvoye, Ch. (1951), 'La basilique paléochrétienne et ses annexes', *BCH* 75: 154–164.

Etzeoglou, R. (1974), 'Palaiochristianike vasilike para tous Molaous Lakonias', *ArchEph*: 244–257.

Evangelidis, D. (1930-31), 'Protovyzantine vasilike Mytilines', *ADelt* 13: 1–40.

Feissel, D., and Philippidis-Braat, A. (1985), 'Inventaires en vue d'un recueil des inscriptions historique de Byzance. III. Inscriptions du Péloponnèse', *TM* 9: 267–395.

Jones, A.H.M. (1973), *The Later Roman Empire 284-602*, 2 vols. [reprint of the 1964 edition]. Oxford.

Karivieri, A. (2002), 'Anaskaphe sten Arethousa to 2002', *To archaiologiko ergo ste Makedonia kai Thrake* 16: 191–195.

Karivieri, A. (2004), 'The pastoral landscape of Paliambela in Arethousa, northern Greece, from antiquity to modern times', in B.S. Frizell, ed., *Man and animal in antiquity, Proceedings of the conference at the Swedish Institute in Rome, September 9-12, 2002*, Rome: 250–251.

Karivieri, A. (2009), 'Along the Via Egnatia: a pastoral economy, religious space and military presence in Arethousa in the Early Byzantine period', in E. Regner von Heijne, C. Kitzler, L. Ahfeldt, and A. Kjellstrom, eds., *From Ephesos to Dalecarlia. Reflections on Body, Space and Time in Medieval and Early Modern Europe*, Stockholm: 31–41.

Karivieri, A., ed. (2017), *The Early Christian basilica of Arethousa in Macedonia I: production, consumption and trade*. Helsinki.

Kotzias, N. (1952), 'Anaskaphai tes vasilikes tou Lavreotikou Olympou', *PraktArchEt* 107: 92–128.

Lazaridis, P. (1960), 'Anaskaphe Neas Anchialou', *PraktArchEt* 115: 60–66.

The Institutional Church in Early Christian Greece 21

Maïlis, A. (2011), *The annexes at the early Christian Basilicas of Greece (4th-6th c.) Architecture and function*, B.A.R., International series 2312. Oxford.

Marki, E. (2004), 'Chorothetese paragogikon kai ergasteriakon drasterioteton sto episkopiko sygkrotema ton Louloudion Pierias', in *Archaiologika tekmeria viotechnikon egkatastaseon kata ten Vyzantine epoche, 5os-15os aionas: Eidiko thema tou 22ou Symposiou Vyzantines kai Metavyzantines Archaiologias kai Technes, Athena, 17-19 Maiou 2002*, Athens: 27–45.

Marki, E. (2008), 'To episkopiko sygkrotema stis Louloudies Kitrous', in G. Aikaterinides, ed., *Archaiologikes trochiodromeseis, Apo ten Thessaloniki ston Platamona*, Athens: 89–115.

Orlandos, A. (1929), 'Ai palaiochristianikai vasilikai tes Lesvou', *ArchDelt*: 1–72.

Orlandos, A. (1933), 'Anaskaphe Sikyonos', *PraktArchEt* 88: 81–90.

Orlandos, A. (1961), 'Anaskaphe Nikopoleos', *PraktArchEt* 116: 98–107.

Pazaras, Th. (2009), *Anaskaphikes ereunes sten perioche tes Epanomes Thessalonikes, to nekrotapheio sto Limori kai e palaiochristianike vasilike sto Mpiadoudi*. Thessaloniki.

Ralles, G., and Potles, M., eds. (1852), *Syntagma ton Theion kai Hieron Kanonon*, 2. Athens.

Roussel, P., and Launey M., eds. (1937), *Inscriptions de Délos*. Paris.

Schneider, A. (1929), 'Samos in frühchristlicher und frühbyzantinischen Zeit', *Athenische Mitteilungen* 54: 97–141.

Schoell, R., and Kroll, W., eds. (1928), *Corpus Juris Civilis*, 3. Berlin.

Soteriou, G. (1927), 'Anaskaphai Neas Anchialou', *PraktArchEt* 82: 44–50.

Soteriou, G. (1929), 'Ai christianikai Thevai tes Thessalias', *ArchEph*: 1–158.

Soteriou, G. (1932), 'Trapeza martyron tou Vyzantinou Mouseiou Athinon', *DChAE*: 7–17.

Soteriou, G., and Orlandos, A. (1930), 'Anaskaphai Nikopoleos', *PraktArchEt* 85: 79–80.

Stikas, E. (1962), 'Anaskaphe koimeteriakes vasilikes Palaias Korinthou', *PraktArchEt* 117: 51–56.

Theocharidou, K. (1985-1986), 'Symvole ste melete tes paragoges oikodomikon keramikon proionton sta Vyzantina kai Metavyzantina chronia', *DChAE* 13: 97–112.

Travlos, I. (1962), 'Christianikai Athinai', *Threskeutike kai Ethike Enkyclopaidia*: 710–758.

Völling, Th. (2001), 'Paragoge krasiou sto hiero tou Olympiou Dios sto proimo Vyzantio', in G.A. Pikoulas, ed., *Oinon historo, Ampelooinike istoria kai archaiologia tes BD Peloponnesou*, Athens: 33–36.

3 The Early Byzantine Fortress of Velika on the Coast of Kissavos, Thessaly

Stavroula Sdrolia and Sophia Didioumi

The fortress of Velika is a fortified settlement of 5.2 acres, situated on a small hill north of the nearby resort, some 500 m from the sea-side (Figure 3.1). Totally covered by vegetation until recently, it has been partly excavated by the archaeological service and restored with funds from the European Community. It was unearthed between 2008 and 2011 by the Seventh Ephorate of Byzantine Antiquities, supported by the Municipality of Melivoia.[1] The site can be identified as the ancient city of Melivoia, the most famous city of Magnesia on the coast of Kissavos.[2] It controlled communication between Macedonia and Demetrias, which was conducted mainly by sea.

The strategic position of the Velika fortress is immediately apparent, surrounded as it is by steep and extensive slopes and river gorges, while enjoying easy access to the sea. The fortification was begun in the Classical period, as is shown from the remains preserved on the southern side, lying below the Byzantine ones, as well as by the ceramic and coin finds, dated to the 4th century BC. The chief part of the city of this period should be sited near the shore: no excavation has been undertaken there so far, with the exception of the uncovering of an ecclesiastic architectural complex of the 6th century AD, including an oil-pressing mill and warehouses.[3]

The fortification wall was traced for a length of 350 m, taking in the eastern and southern sides of the hill (Figure 3.2); the rest of it is still covered by vegetation. It is reinforced by four towers, of rectangular shape, projecting out from the wall up to 3 m. Two of them, identical in shape, house the two entrances of the fortress. The main entrance is in the south-eastern tower, facing the lower town and the fertile plain. It is 2.50 m wide, narrowing to the external part of the wall, with a passage of 1.60 m.[4] A similar entrance existed at the eastern tower. This was blocked at a later phase and replaced by a smaller version, a short distance to the north, near the church. In the area of the southern entrance a series of iron plates was found, coming from the protective covering of the wooden doors. It is unique for this period, but comparable with later examples from the fortress of Torone and monasteries of Mount Athos.[5]

The fortress of Velika is of a strong construction: its walls are of 2 m minimum width (Figure 3.3a), built with a core made of lime-mortar and rubble,

DOI: 10.4324/9781003429470-4

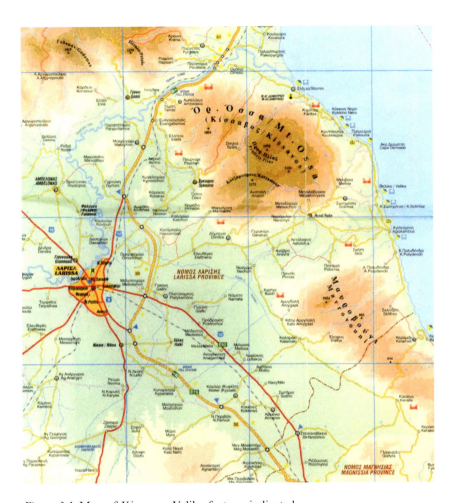

Figure 3.1 Map of Kissavos. Velika fortress indicated.

between faces of rough masonry bonded with mortar (Figure 3.3b). In some parts, stones from the Classical constructions are reused. From the numismatic finds, this work can be placed in the time of Justinian, who is known from Procopius to have renovated the defensive system of Thessaly. Among the fortresses listed by Procopius, Velika can only be associated with Kentavropolis, mentioned as being near Eurymenai in Kokkino Nero.[6] Kentavropolis is usually associated with the fortification of Skiti in the Mavrovouni area,[7] but no Justinianic phase has been attested there and it could possibly be of a later date. The best built parts of the fortress of Velika, in which the mortar partly covers the stone courses, resemble some fortress constructions of nearby areas connected with Justinian, for example the first phase at Platamon,[8] Pydna,[9] and Demetrias.[10] The same feature is observable at the fortification of Kokkino Nero, ancient Eurymenai, also renovated by Justinian.[11]

Figure 3.2 The defensive wall of Velika fortress.

At Velika there are also traces of later repairs, mostly reinforcing structures: such are to be seen in the area of the south-eastern entrance and in the wall east of the church. These were made shortly after the original phase. Stair constructions are visible near the towers, where the width of the fortification wall increases, for which similar examples are known.[12] Traces of bastions have been preserved at the southern side, next to the entrance (Figure 3.3a). From these the total height of the construction can be estimated at 6 m in this area.

The interior of the fortress was densely occupied, as is shown by the excavated zone. The most distinctive building presently revealed is a three-aisled basilica, at the north-eastern corner. Research has been conducted here with the collaboration of the University of Thessaly.[13] The aisles are separated by strong piers, while the apse bears a small *synthronon*, meaning that it was, even circumstantially, an episcopal residence. It is assumed that less-important bishops (*choroepiskopoi*) resided in Kentavropolis and Eurymenai, which were the centres of the region.[14] The apse, protruding through the fortress wall, is connected with a later transformation in this region. The church, built in the 6th century AD, had a second phase, when only the central part was in use.

Little information about the spatial organisation of the settlement is available, because only a small part has been investigated, which includes the zone by the eastern and southern walls. It is apparent that the eastern part is covered by long warehouses, only partly excavated, separated from the wall by a narrow corridor, for which comparisons can be found.[15] A variety of ceramic finds came from this area, including some *pithoi* preserved in situ.

The Early Byzantine Fortress of Velika on the Coast of Kissavos 25

Figure 3.3 The walls of the fortress. Detail of the masonry.

Near the southern gate a series of rectangular buildings can be viewed as guard-chambers,[16] especially the two identical rooms facing the gate (Figure 3.4a, 3.4b). The oblique tripartite building in the level above could be of a slighter later chronology, because it blocked the wall-walk and parapet of the enclosure. Finally, the southern side of the fortress seems to be occupied with large residential buildings. One of them has been partially excavated: a complex of rooms was revealed surrounding a tiled-paved courtyard. It could have housed a state or military official.[17] Belt buckles (Figure 3.5) found in the excavation[18] probably belonged to state officials. One is of the Sucidava type,[19] similar to a belt buckle from the Episcopal Complex at Louloudies near Kitros in Pieria.[20]

The excavation finds include some sculpture from the church, and many sherds of glass vessels, mostly bases, in shapes common in the 6th century AD.

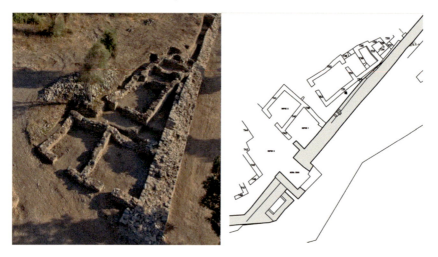

Figure 3.4 Guard-chambers.

Figure 3.5 Belt buckle of the Sucidava type.

Some of the vessels were lamps, as is shown by the copper chains for their suspension.[21] A large variety of metal and ceramic items touches on many aspects of the everyday life of the settlement. The Early Byzantine coins belong to the Justinianic period: the 16-nummion is the most common type, issued in Thessalonike, the seat of the Eparchos of Illyrikon, responsible for the defence of the region and the garrisons of the forts.[22] The only exception is a coin of Justin II of 575, the last numismatic testimony of the settlement. Numismatic finds become scarce after this period, due to general economic decline and the cessation of payments for the army.[23]

A great number of pots, more or less complete, are recorded from the different levels of the excavation. Even now, though the study of the pottery from the Velika excavation is at a preliminary stage, it provides information about chronology, trade routes and the daily life in the fortress of Velika. Imported mould-made clay lamps from Africa (e.g., type Atalante X A, group C1, of the

Figure 3.6 Asia Minor lamp.

Figure 3.7 African Red Slip Ware plate with stamped decoration.

6th century),[24] and Asia Minor (Figure 3.6),[25] have been found in the excavation. African Red Slip Ware dishes are also present in Velika (Figure 3.7) (Hayes Form 104B, stamp type Style E(ii), c. 570–600).[26] Also a few sherds of Late Roman Light Coloured Ware from Asia Minor,[27] and Phocaean Red Slip Ware (Hayes type 3 and 10A) are recorded.[28] But the most common Fine Ware dishes belong to the Central Greek Painted Ware (Figure 3.8).[29] These have a light brown fabric, decorated with herring-bone pattern in a brown paint. Examples of this type of dish have been found in Thessalian Thebes,[30] Demetrias,[31] Delphi,[32] (here of the second half of the 6th century), and in the Agora of Thessalonike.[33] They come from an unknown production centre. Petridis[34] and Karagianni[35] assume that Thessalian Thebes is the production

Figure 3.8 Dish belonging to the Central Greek Painted Ware.

centre, while Hayes' hypothesis[36] that the production centre was at Delphi was not proven by the chemical analysis of the clay.[37] The dishes found in Velika are similar to the material from Thessalian Thebes.

Lids for *pithoi* were also found in situ in the storage rooms, bearing incised decoration of wavy lines, crosses, and birds (Figure 3.9), similar to lids from

Figure 3.9 Lid for *pithoi* with incised decoration.

Figure 3.10 Lid with impressed decoration.

Emporio,[38] and also with a decoration of impressed points, which has a close parallel from Thessalian Thebes.[39]

However the most common related finds at the fortress are clay lids of a smaller size (diameter ca. 15–20 cm), with relief work and with inscriptions (Figure 3.10); they are of local production, probably for small but deep casseroles or storage pots. They bear zones of impressed decoration, crosses with bifid arms, birds, human figures with their hands raised in a prayer and religious inscriptions with invocations, i.e., Κ(ύριε) Β(οήθει) and Θ(εοτόκε) Β (οήθει). Similar lids have been found in the fortresses and cities on the lower Danube, also of local production,[40] of the 4th–6th centuries, an irrefutable witness to the contacts of the two regions. The simultaneous production of this type of lids in Scythia Minor and Velika is maybe connected with a movement of troops or population groups, or maybe only of skilled craftsmen.[41]

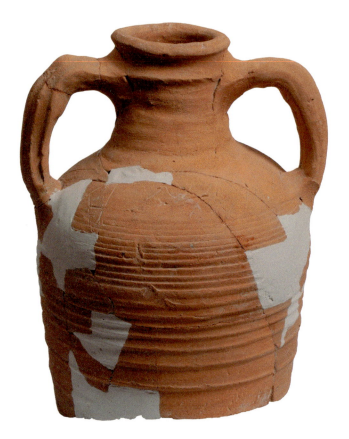

Figure 3.11 LRA 1 amphora.

A large number of commercial amphorae were found in the excavation.[42] Two of the most well-known international types are present: a large quantity of sherds belongs to the LRA 1 type, one of the most common amphora imports on sites throughout the Mediterranean and Black Sea. Most of the Velika examples belong to the LRA 1A transitional and LRA 1B types, according to Pieri's typology, which are dated from the late 5th to early 6th to the middle of the 7th centuries (Figure 3.11).[43] The second type, the LRA 2B (Figure 3.12), dominated the excavation's finds, and are dated mainly to the 6th century.[44] The standard LRA 2A and LRA 2B amphorae have a widespread distribution ranging from Britain to Scythia, from the lower Danube to the Mediterranean Sea.[45] Given the different fabrics of those found in Velika, it is quite possible that they come from various production areas on the Greek mainland and Peloponnese. Two examples of small-sized amphorae imitating the LRA 2, the so called 'LRA 2 *similis*', '*small size*', or '*miniature*' amphorae, found in the fortress, have close parallels in the Argolis area (which we must present elsewhere). The origin of this type is

Figure 3.12 LRA 2 amphora.

attributed to the Saronic Gulf,[46] or Megaris.[47] A small number of amphorae belong to the LRA 3A3 type (Figure 3.12a, 3.12b), dated in the 6th century and produced in the area of Ephesos, the Maeander valley, and Aphrodisias,[48] whose contents were probably wine. A small amount of LRA 4 B1 amphora sherds,[49] and LRA 5[50] represents the vessels produced in the Levant and indicates the trade of Gazan wine to Velika in the 6th century. Only one example belongs to the LRA 8 type.[51] Similar finds, e.g., LRA 1, LRA 2, LRA 3, LRA 4, and LRA 8 amphorae, were found in the major port of Thessaly, Thessalian Thebes, and in the fortresses and cities of the Danube region, for the transportation of wine and olive oil.[52]

Finally, two African amphorae dated to the 7th century were found in the excavation: one emended Spatheion type 3B,[53] and one amphora Spatheion type 3D,[54] of the second half of the 7th century. They belong to the transitional period of the fortification, a testimony of the shipping route from northern Africa to the coast of Thessaly during the 7th century.

Among the major finds, the large quantity of commercial amphorae show the importance to the settlement of the collection and distribution of olive oil and wine, continuing the tradition of ancient Melivoia. Its geographical position gave it an important role in the economy and agrarian exports of Central Greece, led by the large ports of Demetrias and Thessalian Thebes.[55] It also served as an intermediate station between them and Thessalonike.[56] Furthermore, the prevalence of the amphorae connected with the transportation of the *annona militaris* (LRA 1, LRA 2, LRA 3A, LRA 8), places the fortress of Velika in the long list of Aegean centres specialising in the oil and wine trade, a sector so necessary for the troops stationed on the northern *limes* of the Byzantine state.[57] We argue (elsewhere) that these amphorae are cargoes that were brought to the fortified settlement under state control, provisioning the guards of the fortification with agricultural products.

To conclude from the combined examination of the architecture and finds at this present stage of research, one may assume that the fortress of Velika was erected around 540, enclosing a pre-existing settlement on the remains of the ancient acropolis of Melivoia. It underwent repairs and strengthening work during the second half of the century. These repairs may have been necessary after the earthquake of 552 AD or after the Koutrigours' raid of 558 AD.[58] Towards the end of the century and onwards, there seems to be a gradual abandonment of the Velika settlement, with but partial rehabilitation, as one can see from the reduced state of the church. This is a period of massive invasions and a lack of upkeep by the military of the forts, due to state's inefficiency and lack of resources, which dramatically reduces the number of settlements in the Balkans.[59]

As future research progresses, it will permit a hypothesis to be formed about the life of the fortress into the time of transition (late 7th–8th centuries), but it had probably ceased to exist later than that. As with all the nearby sites, the population moved from the coast towards the highlands, seeking protection from invaders by land and sea: a common phenomenon in the coastal sites of Greece.[60] This procedure led to the creation of the Byzantine settlement of Thanatou (present village of Melivoia), on the hilltop at a distance of 7 km from the shore. The name of Velika, which is given to the coastal plain and the main stream, which is similar to *Verliqui,* used in the Byzantine period for the nearby Kissavos Cape,[61] can be connected with the Slavic inhabitants of the transitional period (velik = great). One of the main reasons for the abandonment of the Early Byzantine fortress is the economic decline, as a result of the disruption of the sea traffic of Central Greece during the 7th century,[62] the more so because earlier commerce had mostly been a state initiative.[63] The more characteristic aspects of this phenomenon are the dominance of the Velegezetes Slavs in the area of the Pagasetic Gulf, who besieged Thessalonike in 620 AD and sold wheat in 677 AD, as well as the abandonment of nearby Skiathos in 680 AD.

The Early Byzantine Fortress of Velika on the Coast of Kissavos 33

Apart from the information pertaining to economic and daily-life aspects retrieved, the architectural morphology of the fortress of Velika and its good preservation, without experiencing alterations in the Middle Byzantine period, offer useful information about Early Byzantine fortifications in the Greek countryside.

Notes

1 Sdrolia 2013; Gerousi 2013: 33–34.
2 Helly 2014: 172; Drakoulis 2010: 383.
3 Sdrolia 2009: 587–589; Sdrolia 2016: 128.
4 For similar entrances see Bajenaru 2010: Fig. 126.
5 Papaggelos 2006: 181; Figs. 9–10.
6 Procopius, *De Aedificiis* IV.6.14.
7 Koder and Hild 1976: 186–187; Drakoulis 2010: 383.
8 Fotiadis 2008: 512.
9 Marki 1988: 199, Fig. 12.
10 Karagiorgou 2001a: 203–209.
11 Sdrolia 2015/16: 126.
12 Dinchev 2007: Fig. 32; Bajenaru 2010: 176, Fig. 281.
13 Varalis 2017.
14 Drakoulis 2010: 384.
15 Dinchev 2007: 506; Rizos 2013: 684–688.
16 Dinchev, 2007: 503.
17 Sdrolia, Didioumi, and Koutsoyiannis, forthcoming.
18 Sdrolia 2013: 23 (see fig.).
19 Schultze-Dörrlamm 2002: 146, no. 109, Type D1.
20 Marki 1997: Fig. 5.
21 Pinakoulaki 2017.
22 Nikolaou 2004: 572–574.
23 Dunn 2004: 578–579.
24 Bonifay 2004: 371–372, Fig. 208.
25 Bailey 1988: 391, Pl. 112, nos. Q3192–Q3194.
26 Hayes 1972: 160–166, Figs. 30, 31; Hayes 1972: 268, Fig. 52; Bonifay 2004: 205, Fig. 80.
27 Hayes 1992: 93–95, 100–102, 106.
28 Chatzichristou, forthcoming.
29 Hayes 1972, 412–413.
30 Lazarides 1965: 16, Pl. 10a; Iatridou 1976, Pl. 139 α, β.
31 Eiwanger 1981: 40–42, nos. II.160, II.161, II.162.
32 Hayes 1972: 413, Pl. 23b; Petridis 2010a: 129–130, Figs. 230, 231.
33 Karagianni 2010a: Figs. 1–4, 6, Pls. 1a, b, 3a–e, 4d.
34 Petridis 2010b: 90–91.
35 Karagianni 2010a: 5.
36 Hayes 1972: 140, 413.
37 Petridis 2010a: 129–131.
38 Boardman 1989: 113, no. 278, Fig. 42.
39 Iatridou 1976: Pl. 139 ε, στ.
40 Barnea 1965.
41 Didioumi 2017; Didioumi and Sdrolia, forthcoming, with further bibliography.
42 Didioumi and Sdrolia, forthcoming, with further bibliography.
43 Pieri 2005: 70–76, Fig. 25.

34 *Stavroula Sdrolia and Sophia Didioumi*

44 Pieri 2005: 88, Fig. 45, Pls. 25–6.
45 Pieri 2005: 85–93.
46 Hayes 2003: 529.
47 Korossis 2014: 306, Fig. 7.
48 Pieri 2005: 95–97, Figs. 57–59.
49 Pieri 2005: 105–106, Figs. 66, 69b.
50 Pieri 2005: 109–110.
51 Hayes 1992: 67–68, Fig. 23.1, Type 16/17; Pieri 2005: 133, Pl. 51.2, Pl. 52.2.
52 Didioumi and Sdrolia, forthcoming, with further bibliography.
53 Bonifay 2004: 127–129, Fig. 69.
54 Bonifay 2004: 127–129, Fig. 69.
55 Karagiorgou 2001b, 168–195, 213–214, 222–224.
56 Ginalis 2014, 250–252.
57 Karagiorgou 2001c. Curta, 2017.
58 Karagiorgou 2001b: 22–23.
59 Dunn 1997: 142–145; Karagianni 2010b: 75–82; Ciglenečki 2014.
60 Sodini 2007: 331. Geroussi 2013,2013: 41.
61 Koder and Hild 1976: 134.
62 Karagiorgou 2001b: 26.
63 Curta 2010: 209–212.

References

Primary Sources

Haury, J., and Wirth, G., eds. (1964), *Procopii Caesariensis opera omnia, Vol. 4: De Aedificiis.* Leipzig.

Secondary Sources

Bailey, D.M. (1988), *A Catalogue of the Lamps in the British Museum, 3: Roman Provincial Lamps.* London.
Bajenaru, C. (2010), *Minor Fortifications in the Balkan-Danubian Area from Diocletian to Justinian.* Cluj-Napoca.
Barnea, I. (1965), 'Objets céramiques peu connus. Les couvercles de vases de Scythie Mineure', *Dacia* 9: 407–417.
Boardman, J. (1989), 'The Finds', in M. Ballance, J. Boardman, S. Corbett, and S. Hood, eds., *Excavations in Chios 1952–1955: Byzantine Emporio*. The British School at Athens Supplement 20, Oxford: 86–142.
Bonifay, M. (2004), *Études sur la céramique romaine tardive d'Afrique*, British Archaeological Reports, International Series 1301, Oxford.
Chatzichristou, V. (forthcoming), 'Μαγειρικά σκεύη και επιτραπέζια κεραμική από το Κάστρο της Βελίκας', *Αρχαιολογικό Έργο Θεσσαλίας και Στερεάς Ελλάδας, Βόλος, 1–4 Μαρτίου 2018*, 6. Volos.
Ciglenečki, S. (2014), 'The changing relations between city and countryside in Late Antique Illyricum', *Hortus Artium Medievalium* 20/1: 242–245.
Curta, F. (2010), 'Soldiers as 'makeshift peasants' for the occasion. Sixth-century settlement patterns in the Balkans', in T. Burns, and J. Eadie, eds., *Urban Centers and Rural Contexts in Late Antiquity*, Michigan: 199–217.
Curta, F. (2017), 'Coins, Forts and Commercial Exchanges in the Sixth- and Early Seventh-Century Balkans', *Oxford Journal of Archaeology* 36 (4): 439–454.

The Early Byzantine Fortress of Velika on the Coast of Kissavos 35

Didioumi, S. (2017), 'Το κάστρο της Βελίκας και οι σχέσεις με τα παραδουνάβια κάστρα: η μαρτυρία της κεραμικής', in *37ο Συμπόσιο της Χριστιανικής Αρχαιολογικής Εταιρείας, Αθήνα, 12-14 Μαίου 2017*, Τεύχος περιλήψεων, Athens.

Didioumi, S., and Sdrolia, S. (forthcoming), 'Late Roman Amphorae from the castle of Velika, Thessaly (Greece): a preliminary report', in *LRCW 6, 6th International Congress on Late Roman Coarse Ware, Cooking Ware and Amphorae in the Mediterranean, Agrigento 2017*.

Dinchev, V. (2007), 'The fortresses of Thrace and Dacia in the early Byzantine period', in A. Poulter, ed., *The Transition to the Late Antiquity, on the Danube and Beyond*, Proceedings of the British Academy 141, Oxford: 479–546.

Drakoulis, D. (2010), 'Η περιφερειακή οργάνωση της Βορειοανατολικής Θεσσαλικής ακτής κατά την ύστερη Αρχαιότητα', in S. Gouloulis, and S. Sdrolia, eds., *Άγιος Δημήτριος Στομίου, Ιστορία – Τέχνη- Ιστορική Γεωγραφία του μοναστηριού και της περιοχής των εκβολών του Πηνειού*, Larissa: 375–390.

Dunn, A.W. (1997), 'Stages in the transition from the Late Antique to the Middle Byzantine urban centre, in S. Macedonia and S. Thrace', in *Αφιέρωμα στον N.G.L. Hammond, Makedonika Supplement 7*, Thessaloniki: 137–151.

Dunn, A.W. (2004), 'Continuity and change in the Macedonian countryside from Gallienus to Justinian', in W. Bowden, and L. Lavan, eds., *Late Antique Archaeology 2. Recent Research on the Late Antique Countryside*, Leiden: 533–586.

Eiwanger, J. (1981), *Keramik und Kleinfunde aus der Damokratia – Basilika in Demetrias, Demetrias IV*. Bonn.

Fotiadis, P. (2008), 'Η παλαιοχριστιανική φάση της οχύρωσης του Κάστρου του Πλαταμώνα', in N. Graikos, ed., *Η Πιερία στα βυζαντινά και νεότερα χρόνια, 3ο Επιστημονικό Συνέδριο, πρακτικά*, Katerini: 501–512.

Gerousi, E. (2013), 'Rural Greece in the Byzantine period in light of new archaeological evidence', in J. Albani, and E. Chalkia, eds., *Heaven and Earth. Cities and Countryside in Byzantine Greece*, Athens: 30–43.

Ginalis, A. (2014), *Byzantine Ports, Central Greece as a Link between the Mediterranean and the Black Sea*, Unpublished PhD Thesis, University of Oxford.

Hayes, J.W. (1972), *Late Roman Pottery*. London.

Hayes, J.W. (1992), *Excavations at Saraçhane in Istanbul, 2. The Pottery*. Princeton.

Hayes, J.W. (2003), 'Amphores', in Ch. Bakirtzis (ed.), Actes du VIIe Congrès International sur la céramique médiévale en Méditeranée, Thessaloniki 11–16 Octobre, 1999, Athens: 529–534.

Helly, B. (2014), *Géographie et Histoire des Magnètes de Thessalie, I, De la plaine thessalienne aux cités de la côte égéenne, c. 750–300 av. J.-C.* Vareilles.

Iatridou, E. (1976), 'Νέα Αγχίαλος. Οικόπεδο Π. Μάντση', *Αρχαιολογικόν Δελτίον* 31 (1976), *Χρονικά*, B2: 1, 189-192.

Karagianni, F. (2010a), 'Κεραμική με γραπτό διάκοσμο από την Αρχαία Αγορά της Θεσσαλονίκης', in D. Papanikola-Bakirtzi, and D. Kousoulakou, eds., *Επιστημονική συνάντηση για την κεραμική της ύστερης αρχαιότητας στον ελλαδικό χώρο*, Thessaloniki: 295–308.

Karagianni, F. (2010b), *Οι βυζαντινοί οικισμοί στη Μακεδονία μέσα από τα αρχαιολογικά δεδομένα, 4ος–15οςαι*. Thessaloniki.

Karagiorgou, O. (2001a), 'Demetrias and Thebes: the fortunes and misfortunes of two Thessalian port cities in Late Antiquity', in L. Lavan, ed., *Recent Research in Late-Antique Urbanism, Journal* of *Roman Archaeology Supplement* 42: 182–215.

36   Stavroula Sdrolia and Sophia Didioumi

Karagiorgou, O. (2001b), *Urbanism and Economy in Late Antique Thessaly (3th-7th c. AD): The Archaeological Evidence*, Unpublished PhD thesis, University of Oxford.

Karagiorgou, O. (2001c), 'LR2: a container for the military annona on the Danubian border?', in S. Kingsley, and M. Decker, eds., *Economy and Exchange in the East Mediterranean during Late Antiquity*, Oxford: 130–166.

Koder, J., and Hild, F. (1976), *Hellas und Thessalia, Tabula Imperii Byzantini* 1. Vienna.

Korossis, V. (2014), 'Transport and storage vessels and coarse wares from Megara, Attica (Greece). The testimony of the pottery concerning the city during the early Byzantine period', in N. PoulouPapadimitriou, E. Nodarou, and V. Kilikoglou, eds., *LRCW 4, Late Roman Amphorae and Coarse Ware 4. The Mediterranean: a market without frontiers*. B.A.R., International Series 2616, Oxford: 305–312.

Lazarides, P. (1965), 'Ανασκαφαί Νέας Αγχιάλου', *Πρακτικά Αρχαιολογικής Εταιρείας* 1965: 10–23.

Marki, E. (1988), 'Ανασκαφές βυζαντινής Πύδνας', *Αρχαιολογικό Έργο στη Μακεδονία και Θράκη* 2: 195–206.

Marki, E. (1997), 'Λουλουδιές', *Αρχαιολογικό Έργο στη Μακεδονία και Θράκη* 11: 289–296.

Nikolaou, Y. (2004), 'Νομισματική κυκλοφορία στη βυζαντινή Θεσσαλία', *Οβολός* 7, *Το νόμισμα στο Θεσσαλικό χώρο*: 571–586.

Papaggelos, I. (2006), 'Το τέλος της Τορώνης', in *Δώρον, Τιμητικός τόμος στον καθηγητή Νίκο Νικονάνο*, Thessaloniki: 177–188.

Petridis, P. (2010a), *La céramique protobyzantine de Delphes. Une production et son contexte, Fouilles de Delphes 5, Monuments figurés* 4. Paris/Athens.

Petridis, P. (2010b), 'Ρωμαϊκά και Πρωτοβυζαντινά εργαστήρια κεραμικής στον ελλαδικό χώρο', in D. Papanikola-Bakirtzi, and D. Kousoulakou, eds., *Επιστημονική συνάντηση για την κεραμική της Ύστερης Αρχαιότητας από τον ελλαδικό χώρο (3ος-7ος αι. μ.Χ.)*, Thessaloniki: 81–96.

Piéri, D. (2005), *Le commerce du vin oriental à l'époque byzantine (Ve-VIIe siècles). Le témoignage des amphores en Gaule*. Bibliothèque archéologique et historique 174, Beirut.

Pinakoulaki, E. (2017), 'Κάστρο Βελίκας: Τα γυάλινα ευρήματα', in *37ο Συμπόσιο της Χριστιανικής Αρχαιολογικής Εταιρείας, Αθήνα, 12–14 Μαΐου 2017, Τεύχος περιλήψεων*, Athens: 105–106.

Rizos, E. (2013), 'Centres of the Late Roman Military Supply Network in the Balkans: a Survey of horrea', *Jahrbuch des Römisch-Germanischen Zentralmuseums* 60: 659–696.

Schulze-Dörrlamm, M. (2002), Byzantinische Gürtelschnallen und Gürtelbeschläge im Römisch-Germanischen Zentralmuseum. Mainz/Bonn.

Sdrolia, S. (2009), 'Παλαιοχριστιανικές αρχαιότητες στην περιοχή του Κισσάβου', *Αρχαιολογικό Έργο Θεσσαλίας και Στερεάς Ελλάδας* 3, Volos: 585–592.

Sdrolia, S. (2013), *Το Κάστρο της Μελιβοίας, Βελίκα Αγιάς*. Larissa.

Sdrolia, S. (2015/2016), 'Habitation in the region of Mount Ossa during the Early Byzantine Period', *Archaeological Reports* 62 (2015-2016): 125–132.

Sdrolia, S. (2015), 'Κάστρο Βελίκας, Παρατηρήσεις στην οχυρωματική του 6ου αιώνα', *Αρχαιολογικό Έργο Θεσσαλίας και Στερεάς Ελλάδας* 5. Volos.

The Early Byzantine Fortress of Velika on the Coast of Kissavos 37

Sdrolia, S., Didioumi, S., and Koutsoyiannis, D. (forthcoming), 'An early byzantine house in the castle of Velika Larissa, Greece. A possible official residence', in *Abitare nel Mediterraneo Tardoantiquo, II Convegno Internationale del CISEM, Bologna, 2–5 Marzo 2016.*

Sodini, J.P. (2007), 'The transformation of cities in Late Antiquity within the provinces of Macedonia and Epirus', in A. Poulter, ed., *The Transition to the Late Antiquity, on the Danube and Beyond*, Proceedings of the British Academy 141, Oxford: 311–336.

Varalis, I. (2017), 'Κάστρο Βελίκας: Η οικοδομική ιστορία της εκκλησίας', *37ο Συμπόσιο της Χριστιανικής Αρχαιολογικής Εταιρείας, Αθήνα, 12–14 Μαΐου 2017, Τεύχος περιλήψεων.* Athens.

4 Urban and Rural Settlement in Early Byzantine Attica (4th–7th Centuries)

Elli Tzavella

Early Byzantine Attica has attracted the attention of archaeologists, historians and art historians for numerous decades.[1] Research has focused on the urban arrangement of the Athenian Agora,[2] defence,[3] and Early Christian basilicas.[4] Recently, a large number of intensive rescue excavations and surface archaeological surveys have offered an influx of evidence regarding settlement. In the last 15 years, specialists on Late Antiquity and Byzantium have attempted to locate and identify Attic settlements based on parts of this evidence.[5]

The present chapter is based on a systematic collection of the available archaeological and historical evidence regarding Early Byzantine settlement in Attica.[6] Regional studies have often acknowledged the necessity to focus on all different levels of settlement, versus only the 'city', or the bipolar scheme 'city-village', in order to understand the functional relationships between administration, economy, and the natural environment.[7]

Sites are presented following this scheme:

I Historically known *poleis/civitates*, listed as such in the *Synekdemos* of Hierocles. Many, but not all of them had urban features.[8]
II Settlements which, despite not having the title of a *civitas*, and therefore not listed in the *Synekdemos*, are archaeologically attested to have had some urban features.
III Rural settlements, nucleated or dispersed.
IV A fourth category includes farmsteads, hamlets, and pens (not discussed in this article).

Distinction among the above-mentioned categories is often dangerous and is always prone to change based on new archaeological results. Regarding Attica, however, the high number of excavations allows a preliminary attempt for this kind of distinction.

I. Settlements listed in the *Synekdemos*

Attic *civitates*, according to the *Synekdemos*, were four: Athens, Megara, Aigosthena, and Pagai (location: see Figure 4.1).[9] The validity of the

DOI: 10.4324/9781003429470-5

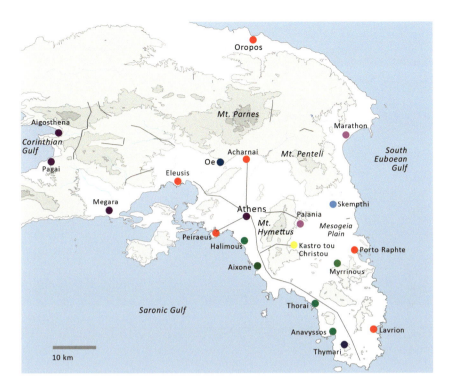

Figure 4.1 Location of Attic settlements. Purple: *civitas*. Red: minor urban (*emporia*). Pink: extended rural settlement. Green: rural settlement. Blue: shepherds' pens.

Source: author.

Synekdemos has been disputed. Regarding the Attic *civitates*, the civic status of Athens and Megara is attested additionally through literary and epigraphic sources, and is therefore not disputed. Aigosthena is attested epigraphically as a *civitas* until the mid-4th century and Pagai until the end of the 3rd century.[10]

The urban features of Athens have been discussed extensively.[11] Megara was protected by a strong ancient city-wall, refurbished in the late 4th and the 5th centuries, according to inscriptions.[12] The city acquired a *stoa* in the Agora in 359/60,[13] three churches,[14] luxurious buildings, and industrial quarters.[15] Its proximity to the important north-south land-route of Greece, as well as to two harbours connecting the Ionian with the Aegean Sea, certainly played a crucial role.

Aigosthena and Pagai were Roman trade colonies. Both sites are harbours. At Aigosthena, a large basilica has been excavated in the lower town (Figure 4.2) and occupation remains in the citadel.[16] The citadel of the strong fortification of the 4th century BC was refurbished in Late Antiquity.[17] The

Figure 4.2 Aigosthena: lower town, basilica's ruins.
Photo: author.

masonry is typical of Late Antique defensive works.[18] Refurbishment of the wall, dedicatory inscriptions, and the continuous function of the harbour suggest that Aigosthena remained a *civitas* until at least the mid-4th century, and that it was reduced to a military and commercial site thereafter, while it lost its urban character by the Early Byzantine period.[19] At Pagai, burials and movable finds suggest some kind of activity and habitation, but nothing can be said about the character of the settlement.[20]

The reasons for the preservation of the civic status of Aigosthena and Pagai, despite their degradation as urban centres, have until now not been discussed. They possibly derived from the fact that both sites played a role in communications both between East and West[21] and between North and South (Figure 4.3). Archaeological research has already shown the protection, in this period, of this north-south route which connects mainland Greece with the Peloponnese, as well as of the Via Egnatia, with forts and fortified *civitates*.[22]

This strategic and economic triangle of Megara, Aigosthena, and Pagai protected the land and sea routes of the broader area. Eleusis, on the contrary, which archaeologically appears as a city with a size comparable with Megara, and also had an important harbour and a fort, was not a *civitas*.

II. Minor urban settlements (*emporia*)

Peiraeus, Eleusis, Oropos, and Steiria (at Porto Raphte) are included in this settlement category, since they all had a dense nexus, a harbour, at least one extensive

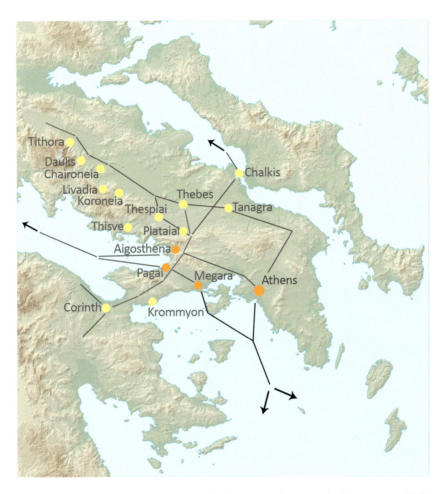

Figure 4.3 Civitates situated on regional routes. Orange: Attic *civitates*. Yellow: selected *civitates* of neighbouring regions.

Source: author.

cemetery indicating a large population, and at least one basilica of considerable size. Lavrion probably belonged to this type of settlement (Figure 4.1).

At Peiraeus, Late Antique houses, including shops and workshops, have been excavated.[23] Amphorae and *terra Sigillata* demonstrate trade contacts with the eastern and western Mediterranean.[24] Burial inscriptions (*IG* II-III² 13505–13509) mention the deceased's occupation (e.g., πλακουντάριος [pastry-cook], μαχεράς [knife-maker], ἰητρός [doctor]), suggesting the existence of a settlement with specialised urban functions.

Eleusis was endowed with at least two known Early Christian churches,[25] while a considerable number of houses has been excavated (Figure 4.4).[26] The

42 *Elli Tzavella*

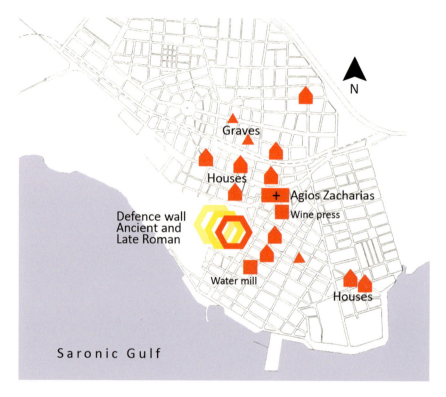

Figure 4.4 Map of Late Roman Eleusis showing defensive wall, houses, and graves, located during rescue excavations.

Source: author.

inhabited area of the settlement expanded during the Early Byzantine period over a previously burial district.[27] Refurbishment of the defence wall is traditionally dated to the reign of Valerian (253–260),[28] while it possibly dates to the Early Byzantine period.[29]

At the coastal site of Oropos (Skala), excavations revealed a three-aisled Early Christian basilica with a baptistery,[30] eight other Early Byzantine buildings (among which one house and three ceramic workshops),[31] and graves.

At Steiria, Porto Raphte, an Early Christian basilica, dated to the 5th century and including two subsequent construction phases, was excavated, along with a very extended cemetery which surrounded it.[32] Burial finds date mainly to the 5th–7th centuries and indicate the existence of a prosperous community. A bath (4th century) and a large apsidal building were excavated nearby, as were sections of the settlement which surrounded these prominent buildings.[33]

A five-aisled basilica has been excavated in the Lavrion harbour.[34] A cemetery excavated in the bay of Panormos/Gaidouromandra revealed 84 graves of the Roman and Early Byzantine periods, some of which contained luxurious objects.[35] These finds attest to habitation and the presence of a wealthy population, while coins continue up until the reign of Heraclius (610–641).

At these sites, continuity of urban character between the ancient and the Late Antique period appears to be due mainly to geographic advantages of these sites—normally a good harbour and, good inland communication. However, not all ancient *demoi* centres with urban features evolved into urban Late Antique settlements. These minor urban centres were inhabited mostly by peasants, but included specialised economic activities. They may be considered as *emporia*, a form of settlement particularly common in this period throughout the Aegean and further east.[36]

III. Rural settlements, nucleated or dispersed

Early Byzantine settlements which show a considerable size but lack attested urban features similar to the ones described above, are Acharnai/Menidi (basin of Athens), Paiania (Mesogeia), Plasi (Marathon), and possibly the settlements at Phoinikia (southeast Attica), Lambrika, and Ennea Pyrgoi (Mesogeia) (Figure 4.1).[37] The aforementioned sites share features such as having more than one basilica (Paiania and Plasi), architectural remains of habitation, or concentration of pottery over an extended area.

Acharnai housed a large bath complex, farmsteads, and cemeteries.[38] Its situation at a regional inland crossroads favoured continuous habitation. Paiania and Plasi were endowed with two Early Christian basilicas each.[39] Moreover, both areas have revealed numerous clusters of settlement. These settlements were extended, but not urban.[40]

The Early Byzantine descendants of Halimous/Alimos, Aixone/Glyphada, Erchia/Spata, Oe (in Aspropyrgos), Thorai/Phoinikia, Anaphlystos/Anavyssos, and Atene were also rural settlements, but possibly less sizeable, or more dispersed, than Acharnai, Paiania, or Plasi.[41] One may suggest that Myrrhinous, which had dispersed habitation in the ancient period, preserved a similar pattern, as suggested by the survival of its cemetery into the Late Roman/Early Byzantine period, the erection of an Early Christian church (Panagia Merenda), and the survival of its name (which suggests that the area was not deserted). Dispersed patterns of settlement existed in Attica already in Antiquity: in the Mesogeia plain, for example, Erchia, Myrrhinouta, Konthyle, and Myrrhinous belonged to this category.[42]

The identification of rural settlements with a dispersed character poses serious methodological problems, especially when excavation is not accompanied with survey. Safer are the results provided by the extensive field survey in Southeast Attica, which localised 87 Early Byzantine sites.[43] Among these, three are churches of very small dimensions (ca. 5 × 8 m), while 20 are shepherd pens, dated through pottery. This settlement pattern, linked to the rocky landscape and the low vegetation, suitable for livestock breeding, differs markedly from the one which predominates in the Attic plains. Early Byzantine pens have been localised also in the eastern part of the Thriasian plain (Oe).[44]

Discussion

The survey in settlement history shows that the bipolar scheme 'town-village' can be broken up in a more nuanced scheme. This involves towns which retained their administrative see as *civitates* until the end of Late Antiquity (Athens, Megara); sites for which the administrative status of a *civitas* is confirmed epigraphically only until the beginning of Late Antiquity, and which were probably reduced to a special role thereafter (military role for Aigosthena; perhaps a commercial role for Pagai). The scheme involves rural sites, both nucleated and dispersed, farmsteads, hamlets, and structures for animal husbandry. This complexity of settlement pattern should be borne in mind when trying to interpret the character of settlements under investigation.

Regarding the sites listed in the *Synekdemos*, it is worth examining their epigraphic and archaeological evidence very closely, since it sometimes bears evidence for a special role. Phases of renovation, which remain unpublished, of the citadel of Aigosthena show, for example, that the site retained a military role, while urban features are not prominent.

The *civitates* listed in the *Synekdemos* (and perhaps certified by other sources) did not have the same role as each other. They were all administered by a *curia*, according to Roman law, and tax collection lay among the most important obligations of this *curia*. However, the role of each *civitas* in a fiscal sense, in a military sense, and (from the 5th century onwards) in an ecclesiastical sense differed. The role of the *civitates* did not evolve the same way during Late Antiquity. Many *civitates* continued to be important as fiscal units during the 4th, 5th, and 6th centuries, and therefore retained their status. Other ones, which stopped fulfilling the fiscal, military and ecclesiastical needs of the *civitates*-network, lost their status as *civitates*.[45] The problem is, that neither the *Synekdemos* nor any other document reflects clearly which *civitates* had lost their civic status by the later part of Late Antiquity, that is, by the 6th and the early 7th centuries.

The upcoming role of *emporia*, highlighted elsewhere in the Empire, becomes clear in Attica as well. They appear to have survived until the first half of the 7th century, as indicated by pottery from Steiria and coins from Lavrion. This is an indication that the 'end' of Late Antiquity at these sites occurred towards the mid-7th century, versus the end of the 6th century. Finds of the 7th century occur in other, rural, sites of Attica.

Most rural settlements presented above are located in the plains, but this is a research-related observation, since modern towns, where rescue archaeology is implemented, are situated on lowland locations. Figure 4.1 depicts only sites which can be securely identified as rural settlements (with green colour); however, many more sites of activity have been located. The plains of Athens and Mesogeia are by far the most intensive districts.

Sites of medium and small size have been revealed in a very large number, thus indicating a relatively high density of population. A major problem remains the chronological precision for activity at a certain site. Reports

Urban and Rural Settlement in Early Byzantine Attica 45

offered by rescue archaeology normally date them to 'Late Antiquity', without giving dates of movable finds. After having established the existence and the location of a great number of rural sites, a next step is specification of the time period in which they were used.

Abbreviations

IG: Inscriptiones Gaecae (Berlin Academy of Sciences).
SEG: Supplementum Epigraphicum Graecum.

Notes

1 This paper forms a preliminary publication of some of my PhD thesis, entitled 'Urban and rural settlement in Early and Middle Byzantine Attica (4th–12th c.)' (Birmingham 2013). I would like to offer sincere thanks to my supervisor, Dr Archibald W. Dunn, for constant support and constructive suggestions throughout my studies. Errors in the present analysis remain mine.
2 Frantz 1988. See also Kerameikos in Bazzechi 2014.
3 On the Post-Herulian wall see Frantz 1988: 5–11 and 125–143 (by J. Travlos); Tsoniotis 2008; Tsoniotis 2016. On the Valerianic wall see Travlos 1960: 161; Theocharaki 2011, esp. 131–137; Theocharaki 2015: 60–68, 232–249. On defence of rural Attica see Fowden 1988.
4 The extensive bibliography on Attic Early Christian churches cannot be inserted here; for a summary see Gini-Tsophopoulou 2001 and Tzavella 2014. A recent contribution to Christian Athens is Baldini 2014.
5 Gini-Tsophopoulou 2001; Mattern 2010; Kontogeorgopoulou 2016.
6 This includes reports of systematic and rescue excavations, studies of monuments, literary sources, numismatics, epigraphy, and sigillography.
7 Dunn 1994; Dunn 2005; Veikou 2009; Veikou 2013.
8 Such as an extended size, dense distribution of buildings, a harbour, often a diversified character of different areas, used for habitation, craftsmanship, religion, and burial.
9 Honigmann (ed.) 1939: 17.
10 *SEG* 23: nos. 266–267 (Aigosthena). *IG* VII: 196 (Pagai): Τὸν κύριον ἡμῶν ἐπι /φανέστατον Καίσαρα Φλ(άβιον) /Οὐαλέρ(ιον) /Κωνστάντιον ἡ πόλις. Constantius Chlorus was nominated Caesar in 292.
11 See above, notes 2–4.
12 *IG* VII: 26; *IG* VII: 93; *IG* VII: 96. For evidence from excavations, see Zorides and Baziotopoulou-Valavani 1983: 33.
13 Zorides 1987: 40; *SEG* 41: no. 412; Avramea 1992-98.
14 Lazarides 1973: 60; Gioles 2002: 89–96.
15 Archaeological reports have been included in several volumes of the *Archaiologikon Deltion*. Reasons of space do not allow their full citation here; see for convenience Tzavella 2013: 353–357, also Korosis 2014a, 2014b.
16 Orlandos 1954. Zoridis 1990: 66–68.
17 Benson 1895: 317f., Plan I: 'Late rubble wall'. No later bibliography. See Tzavella, forthcoming.
18 See for example the masonry of the Hexamilion wall: Gregory 1993.
19 Cf. the situation described in Dunn 2002: 707; fortified *civitates*, some of which did not have urban successors of their Greco-Roman *poleis*.
20 Baziotopoulou-Valavani 2000: 92; Zoridis 1980: 55.

46 *Elli Tzavella*

21 The role of the Corinthian Gulf in east-west communications, prominent in the Early Roman period, resumed in the 6th century and rose further in the 8th: see McCormick 2001: 531–537; Dunn 2006: 44–45.
22 Haldon 1999: Map 3; Poulter 1998 (Louloudies); Rosser 2001 (Thermopylae); Dunn 2002: 708; Aravantinos, Konecny, and Marchese 2003: 300–301 (Plataiai).
23 Grigoropoulos 2016.
24 Grigoropoulos 2010.
25 Agios Zacharias: Soteriou 1929: 183–184. Two further churches are attested epigraphically: Lenormant 1862: 379–381, No. 125, and 381–382 No. 126; Saradi 2011: 284. Furthermore, Travlos (1988: 98), expressed the hypothesis that the *anaktoron* in the *Telesterion* was used as a church in the Early Byzantine period. For more detailed information see Tzavella, forthcoming.
26 Reported in the *Archaeologikon Deltion*; see for convenience Tzavella 2013: 168–169.
27 Papangeli 1997: 62.
28 Ziro 1991: 277–279.
29 Papangeli 2002: 47; Tsouris 2011.
30 Kraniotou 1980: 81.
31 See for convenience Tzavella 2013: 133–134, note 726.
32 Skarmoutsou 1979: 122; Gini-Tsophopoulou 1991: 85–86; Gini-Tsophopoulou and Yangaki 2010. 172 cist graves were found.
33 See for convenience Tzavella 2013: 93–94.
34 Oikonomakou 1981: 55; Gini-Tsophopoulou 1985: 82. Mosaic dated to ca. 425–450: Asimakopoulou-Atzaka 1987: 143.
35 Salliora-Oikonomakou 2001: 160.
36 Veikou 2013: 129–130. Morrisson and Sodini (2002: 179–181) call them 'secondary centres' or 'satellite towns'.
37 Lambrika and Ennea Pyrgoi shared these features in Middle and Late Byzantine times. Their character during the Early Byzantine period is not as clear.
38 See for convenience Tzavella 2013: 34–35.
39 Paiania: Mastrokostas 1956: 27–31; Bouras, Kalogeropoulou, and Andreadi 1969: 234–237; Pallas 1986: 57–59. Plasi (Marathon): Mastrokostas 1970, 18; Mela 1981, 56–57.
40 Paiania: Gini-Tsophopoulou 1994. Marathon: Marinatos 1970, 5. See also Tzavella forthcoming.
41 Halimous: Soteriou 1929: 195; Kaza-Papageorgiou 2006. Aixone: Orlandos 1930; Kaza-Papageorgiou 2000: 112–114. Thorai: Eliot 1962: 67. See for convenience Tzavella 2013, relevant chapters.
42 Steinhauer 1994.
43 Lohmann 1993: Appendix III, Tabelle 16.
44 Platonos-Yota 2005: 23.
45 For a concise description of this process see now Haldon 2016: 11–12.

References

Aravantinos, V., Konecny, A., and Marchese, R. (2003), 'Plataiai in Boeotia: a preliminary report of the 1996–2001 campaigns', *Hesperia* 72: 281–318.
Asimakopoulou-Atzaka, P. (1987), *Σύνταγμα των παλαιοχριστιανικών ψηφιδωτών δαπέδων της Ελλάδος, II. Πελοπόννησος – Στερεά Ελλάδα*. Thessaloniki.
Avramea, A. (1992-98), 'Η επιγραφή του ανθυπάτου Αχαΐας Αμπελίου από τα Μέγαρα', *Horos* 10-12: 327–339.

Baldini, I. (2014), 'Atene: la città christiana', in L. Caliò, E. Lippolis, and V. Parisi, eds., *Gli Ateniesi e il loro modelo di città*, Thiasos Monografie 5, Rome: 309–322.

Baziotopoulou-Valavani, E. (2000), 'Μεγαρίδα', *Archaiologikon Deltion* 55 (B1): 91–93.

Bazzechi, E. (2014), 'Il Ceramico in età tardoantica: sviluppo topographico e mutamenti funzionali', in L. Caliò, E. Lippolis, and V. Parisi, eds., *Gli Ateniesi e il loro modelo di città*, Thiasos Monografie 5, Rome: 337–350.

Benson, E. (1895), 'Aegosthena', *Journal of Hellenic Studies* 15: 314–324.

Bouras, Ch., Kalogeropoulou, A., and Andreadi, E. (1969), *Εκκλησίες της Αττικής*. Athens.

Bouras, Ch., Kaloyeropoulou, A., and Andreade, E. (1970), *Churches of Attica*. Athens.

Dunn, A. (1994), 'The transition from *polis* to *kastron* in the Balkans (III-VII cc.): general and regional perspectives', *Byzantine and Modern Greek Studies* 18: 60–81.

Dunn, A. (2002), 'Was there a militarisation of the southern Balkans during Late Antiquity?', in Ph. Freeman *et al.*, eds., *Limes XVIII. Proceedings of the XVIIIth International Congress of Roman frontier studies*, B.A.R., International Series 1084, Oxford: vol. II, 705–712.

Dunn, A. (2005), 'The problem of Early Byzantine rural settlement in eastern and northern Macedonia', in C. Morrisson, J. Lefort, and J.-P. Sodini, eds., *Les villages dans l' Empire byzantin, IVe – XVe siècle*, Réalités Byzantines 11, Paris: 267–278.

Dunn, A. (2006), 'The rise and fall of towns, loci of maritime traffic, and silk production: the problem of Thisve – Kastorion', in E. Jeffreys, ed., *Byzantine style, religion and civilization. In honour of Sir Steven Runciman*, Cambridge: 39–71.

Eliot, C. (1962), *Coastal demes of Attika. A study of the polity of Kleisthenes*, *Phoenix* Supplement V. Toronto.

Fowden, G. (1988), 'City and mountain in Late Roman Attica', *JHS* 108: 48–59.

Frantz, A. (1988), *The Athenian Agora* XXIV*: Late Antiquity, AD 267-700*. Princeton, NJ.

Gini-Tsophopoulou, E. (1985), 'Ανασκαφικές εργασίες. Λαύριο', *Archaiologikon Deltion* 40 B: 82–83.

Gini-Tsophopoulou, E. (1991), '1η Εφορεία Βυζαντινών Αρχαιοτήτων', *Archaiologikon Deltion* 46 (B1): 75–87.

Gini-Tsophopoulou, E. (1994), 'Νομός Αττικής. Μεσόγεια – Καλύβια, Κάλαμος, Πόρτο Ράφτη, Παιανία', *Archaiologikon Deltion* 49 (B1): 93–95, 104-107.

Gini-Tsophopoulou, E. (2001), 'Τα Μεσόγεια από την επικράτηση του χριστιανισμού έως την οθωμανική κατάκτηση', in Ch. Doumas, ed., *Μεσογαία – Ιστορία και πολιτισμός των Μεσογείων Αττικής, Διεθνής αερολιμένας Αθηνών "Ελευθέριος Βενιζέλος"*, Athens: 148–198.

Gini-Tsophopoulou, E., and Yangaki, A. (2010), 'Παλαιοχριστιανικό νεκροταφείο στη θέση Δρίβλια, Πόρτο Ράφτη: μία πρώτη προσέγγιση της κεραμικής', in D. Papanikola-Bakirtzis, and N. Kousoulakou, eds., *Κεραμική της Ύστερης Αρχαιότητας από τον ελλαδικό χώρο (3ος – 7ος αι. μ.X.)*, Thessaloniki: vol. B, 689–711.

Gioles N. (2002), 'Οι Δέκα Άγιοι Μάρτυρες των Μεγάρων, η εποχή επανεμφάνισής τους και τα κατάλοιπα των παλαιοχριστιανικών μαρτυρίων τους', *DChAE*, series IV 23: 83–98.

Gregory, T. (1993), *Isthmia V. The Hexamilion and the Fortress*, Princeton, NJ.

Grigoropoulos, D. (2010), 'Επιτραπέζια κεραμική και αμφορείς στον Πειραιά κατά την ύστερη ρωμαϊκή περίοδο: γενικές τάσεις στην προμήθεια και κατανάλωση από τον 3ο μέχρι τον 6ο αι. μ.X.', in D. Papanikola-Bakirtzis, and N. Kousoulakou, eds., *Κεραμική της Ύστερης Αρχαιότητας από τον ελλαδικό χώρο (3ος – 7ος αι. μ.X.)*, Thessaloniki: vol. B, 671–688.

48   Elli Tzavella

Grigoropoulos, D. (2016), 'The Piraeus from 86 BC to Late Antiquity: continuity and change in the landscape, function and economy of the port of Roman Athens', *Annual of the British School at Athens* 111: 239–268.

Haldon, J. (1999), *Warfare, State and Society in the Byzantine World, 565–1204*. London.

Haldon, J. (2016) 'Die byzantinische Stadt - Verfall und Wiederaufleben vom 6. bis zum ausgehenden 11. Jahrundert', in: F. Daim & J. Drauschke (eds.), *Hinter den Mauern und auf dem offenen Land. Leben im Byzantinischen Reich*, Verlag des Römisch-Germanischen Zentralmuseums, Mainz: 9–22.

Honigman, E., ed. (1939), *Le Synekdèmos d'Hiéroklès et l'opuscule géographique de Georges de Chypre*. Brussells.

Kaza-Papageorgiou, K. (2000), 'Δάφνη, Άλιμος, Γλυφάδα', *Archaiologikon Deltion* B1(55): 105–114.

Kaza-Papageorgiou, K. (2006), 'Ευώνυμον και Αλιμούς', in *Άλιμος. Όψεις της ιστορίας της πόλης και του δήμου; Alimos: a Greek-English edition of the city's history*, Athens: 11–151.

Kontogeorgopoulou, C. (2016), *Η βυζαντινή Αττική*. Athens.

Korosis, V. (2014a), 'Το πρωτοβυζαντινό παρελθόν των Μεγάρων. Ογδόντα χρόνια σιωπηρής παρουσίας, ιστορία της έρευνας και νέα δεδομένα σχετικά με τη γενέθλια πόλη του Βύζαντα', *34th Symposium of Byzantine and Post-Byzantine Archaeology and Art, Athens 9–11 May 2014*, Abstracts. Athens.

Korosis, V. (2014b), 'Transport and storage vessels and coarse wares from Megara, Attica (Greece). The testimony of pottery in relation to the city during the Early Byzantine period', in N. Poulou-Papadimitriou *et al.*, eds., *LRCW4. Late Roman Coarse Wares, Cooking Wares and Amphorae in the Mediterranean. Archaeology and Archaeometry. The Mediterranean: a market without frontiers*, B.A.R., International Series 2616, Oxford: vol. 1, 305–312.

Kraniotou, L. (1980), 'Σκάλα Ωρωπού. Οδός Αθανασίου Διάκου 5', *Archaiologikon Deltion* 35 (B1): 81–82.

Lazarides, P. (1973), 'Βυζαντινά και Μεσαιωνικά μνημεία νομών Αττικής και Πειραιώς', *Archaiologikon Deltion* 28 (B1): 53–79.

Lenormant, F. (1862), *Recherches archéologiques à Eleusis, exécutées dans le cours de l'année 1860. Recueil des inscriptions*. Paris.

Lohmann, H. (1993), *Atene. Forschungen zu Siedlungs- und Wirtschaftsstruktur des klassischen Attika*. Cologne/Weimar/Vienna.

Marinatos, S. (1970), 'Ανασκαφαί Μαραθώνος', *Praktika Archaiologikes Etaireias*: 5–28.

Mastrokostas, E. (1956), 'Μεσαιωνικά μνημεία Αττικής, Φωκίδος και Μαγνησίας', *Archaiologike Ephemeris*: 27–34.

Mastrokostas, E. (1970), 'Προϊστορική ακρόπολις εν Μαραθώνι', *Archaiologika Analekta ex Athenon* 3: 14–21.

Mattern, T. (2010), 'Eine, skythische Wüste'? Attika in spätantiker und frühbyzantinischer Zeit', in H. Lohmann, and T. Mattern, eds., *Attika. Archäologie einer, zentralen' Kulturlandschaft. Akten der internationalen Tagung vom 18.-20. Mai in Marburg*, Wiesbaden: 201–230.

McCormick, M. (2001), *Origins of the European economy: communications and commerce, AD 300–600*. Cambridge.

Mela, P. (1981), 'Μαραθώνας', *Archaiologikon Deltion* 36 (B1): 56–58.

Urban and Rural Settlement in Early Byzantine Attica   49

Morrisson, C., and Sodini, J.-P. (2002), 'The sixth-century economy', in A. Laiou, ed., *The economic history of Byzantium from the seventh through the fifteenth century*, Washington, DC: 165–213.

Oikonomakou, M. (1981), 'Λαυρεωτική', *Archaiologikon Deltion* 36 (B1): 55–56.

Orlandos, A. (1930), 'La basilique paléochrétienne de Glyphada', *Praktika tes Akademias Athenon* 5: 258–265.

Orlandos, A. (1954), 'Ανασκαφή της βασιλικής των Αιγοσθένων', *Praktika tes Archaiologikes Etaireias*: 129–142.

Pallas, D. (1986), 'Η παλαιοχριστιανική Νοτιοανατολική Αττική', in *Β' Επιστημονική Συνάντηση ΝΑ Αττικής, Καλύβια Αττικής, 25–28/10/1985*, Kalyvia: 43–80.

Papangeli, K. (1997), 'Ελευσίνα', *Archaiologikon Deltion* 52 (B1): 58–65.

Papangeli, K. (2002), *Ελευσίνα: ο αρχαιολογικός χώρος και το μουσείο*. Athens.

Platonos-Yota, M. (2005), 'Κυκλικός περίβολος στη θέση "Σπηλιές" - Καλιστήρι του Δήμου Φυλής', in G. Steinhauer, ed., *Αττικής Οδού περιήγηση/Attiki Odos, an ancient footpath, a modern highway*. Athens: 22–23.

Poulter, A. (1998), 'Field survey at Louloudies: a new Late Roman fortification in Pieria', *BSA* 93, 463–512.

Rosser, J. (2001), 'Evidence for a Justinianic garrison behind Thermopylae at the Dhema Pass', in J. Herrin, M. Mullett, and C. Otten-Froux, eds., *Mosaic. Festschrift for A. H. S. Megaw*, London: 33–42.

Salliora-Oikonomakou, M. (2001), 'Επιγραφές από τη Λαυρεωτική', *Archaiologike Ephemeris*: 159–166.

Saradi, H. (2011), 'Late paganism and Christianisation in Greece', in L. Lavan and M. Mulryan, eds., *The archaeology of late 'paganism'*, Leiden: 263–310.

Skarmoutsou, K. (1979), 'Πόρτο Ράφτη', *Archaiologikon Deltion* 34 B: 122.

Soteriou, G. (1929), 'Αι παλαιοχριστιανικαί βασιλικαί της Ελλάδος', *Archaiologike Ephemeris*: 161–248.

Steinhauer, G. (1994), 'Παρατηρήσεις στην οικιστική μορφή των αττικών δήμων', in W. Coulson *et al.*, eds., *The archaeology of Athens and Attica under the Democracy*, Oxford: 175–189.

Theocharaki, A.-M. (2011), 'The ancient circuit wall of Athens: its changing course and the phases of construction', *Hesperia* 80: 71–156.

Theocharaki, A.-M. (2015), The Ancient Walls of Athens. Athens.

Travlos, I. (1960), *Πολεοδομική εξέλιξις των Αθηνών. Από των προϊστορικών χρόνων μέχρι των αρχών του 19ου αιώνος*. Athens.

Travlos, J. (1988), *Bildlexikon zur Topographie des antiken Attika*. Tübingen.

Tsoniotis, N. (2008), 'Νέα στοιχεία για το ΥΡ τείχος της Αθήνας', in S. Vlizos, ed., *Η Αθήνα κατά τη ρωμαϊκή εποχή. Πρόσφατες ανακαλύψεις, νέες έρευνες*. Athens: 55–74.

Tsoniotis, N. (2016), 'The Benizeli Mansion excavation: latest evidence on the post-Herulian fortification wall in Athens', in R. Frederiksen, S. Muth, P. Schneider, and M. Schnelle, eds., *Focus on Fortifications. New Research on Fortifications in the Ancient Mediterranean and the Near East*, Oxford: 712–724.

Tsouris, K. (2011), 'Μεσοβυζαντινές επεμβάσεις στην οχύρωση της Σπάρτης', International Conference *Defensive architecture in the Peloponnese (5th-15th c.), Loutraki 30/9–1/10/2011*, Abstracts: 69–70.

Tzavella, E. (2013), *Urban and Rural Landscape in Early and Middle Byzantine Attica, 4th-12th c. AD*, Unpublished PhD thesis, University of Birmingham.

50   *Elli Tzavella*

Tzavella, E. (2014), 'Christianisation of Attica. The topography of Early Christian churches', *Pharos* 20.2: 121–158.

Tzavella, E. (forthcoming), *Byzantine Attica. An Archaeology of Settlement and Landscape* (Turnhout).

Veikou, M. (2009), '"Rural towns" and "in-between" or "third" spaces. Settlement patterns in Byzantine Epirus (7th–11th centuries) from an interdisciplinary approach', *Archeologia Medievale* 36: 43–54.

Veikou, M. (2013), 'Settlements in the Greek countryside from the 4th to the 9th centuries: forms and patterns', *Antiquité Tardive* 21: 125–133.

Ziro, D. (1991), *Η κύρια είσοδος του Ιερού της Ελευσίνος*, Library of the Archaeological Society 120, Athens.

Zoridis, P. (1980), 'Μέγαρα, Αλεποχώρι', *Archaiologikon Deltion* 35 (B1): 41–55.

Zoridis, P. (1987), 'Μέγαρα', *Archaiologikon Deltion* 42 B: 34–49.

Zoridis, P. (1990), 'Αιγόσθενα', *Archaiologikon Deltion*, 45 (B1): 66–68.

Zoridis, P., and Baziotopoulou-Valavani, E. (1983), 'Μέγαρα', *Archaiologikon Deltion* 38 B: 30–41.

Part 2

Greece in the Transitional Period

5 The 'Byzantine District' of Gortyn (Crete) and the End of a/the Ancient Mediterranean City[1]

Enrico Zanini

Foreword

This contribution will focus primarily on the possibility of reading into the limited sample of an archaeological excavation the consequence of socio-economic phenomena as complex as those leading to the transformation and the end of an important city in the Early Byzantine Mediterranean.

Secondly, it will concern the possibility of using the same phenomena as indicators of the overall transformation of the idea of the city in the Mediterranean, between the 6th and the 8th–9th centuries AD. But an initial consideration has to be explored in advance, concerning our contemporary notion of the Early Byzantine Mediterranean city.

It is easy to demonstrate that the very idea of the existence of an Early Byzantine model of the city is a product of our time. So, it should be expected that this model will evolve rapidly, not only on the basis of archaeological research (which is a slow producer of new knowledge, by its very nature), but rather on the basis of the very rapid development of historical reflections about the transformation of the Mediterranean world in those centuries.[2] After all, in fact, our concrete knowledge based on that mysterious object we call the Early Byzantine city is extremely limited. Until this moment at least, we can rely on a very limited number of excavations specifically intended to answer this historical question[3]; greater, but not too much, is the number of archaeological sites where Early Byzantine levels or contexts were investigated, more or less hastily, within projects designed to investigate specific aspects of the underlying ancient cities.[4]

There is clearly also a strong statistical bias, because inevitably excavations tend to overestimate a particular aspect of the city, namely the monumental backbone, that has its own pace of transformation, which is not itself necessarily synchronous with the transformation of other aspects of a complex city. From this point of view, it is probable that the image we have today of the Mediterranean city between the 6th and the 8th centuries AD depends to a large extent on the fact that we have essentially investigated the spaces with the highest potential for transformation, namely the public monuments, during a period of deep transformation of the society as a whole. Presumably

DOI: 10.4324/9781003429470-7

54   *Enrico Zanini*

we will discover a quite different image when we investigate the everyday-life spaces, which tend to be much more resilient over a long period.

The second source of evidence we can rely on is obviously the literary sources dating from the 6th to the 8th centuries, that are in some way related with the cities.[5] In this case too, the corpus is continuously growing, mainly thanks to the refinement of critical approaches to texts once classified as marginally interesting for this subject, like, for instance, the lives of saints.

The third source is the continuous changing of our contemporary perception of the idea of ancient city in itself.[6] This can be classified as a source of evidence because it draws our attention to new possible relationships between different types of sources, helping to deepen our analyses in a relevant way.

Once this general framework is established, the next question concerns the evaluation of the relevance of our specific case study. From this point of view, Gortyn can surely be assumed to be a valuable sample, on the basis of a number of considerations. First of all, Gortyn on Crete can be defined as one of the most extensively excavated urban sites all over the Mediterranean. Second, Gortyn qualifies well as an 'average' Mediterranean city: for its physical extent and number of inhabitants; for its politico-administrative and economic role within the Mediterranean framework; for its long lifespan through the Greek, Roman, Late Antique and Early Byzantine ages; and for being the capital city of a large island, then combining the characteristics of insularity and connectivity that marked the Mediterranean framework within a *longue durée* perspective.[7]

From this point of view, Gortyn should theoretically be a 'winner' city, destined to survive the global transformation of the Mediterranean world at the end of Antiquity: located in the very centre of the Roman, Late Antique, and Early Byzantine Mediterranean system, fed by a powerful local economic system, and protected from violent invasions by its insularity. Nonetheless, Gortyn disappeared before the Arab (soft) invasion of Crete, and this makes it an ideal case study to realise an *in vitro* experiment investigating why a city that theoretically should have survived was instead deeply modified and finally 'vanished'.

A point of view

Looking for an answer to our questions deserves firstly a point of view. And my point of view is seeing the city as the intersection point between two different territorial scales.[8] The first scale is that of surrounding microterritory (namely the *chora*); in the case of Gortyn, this micro-territory can be easily recognised in the southern part of Mesarà Plain.

This territory represented, in a *longue durée* perspective, the 'site catchment area' for Gortyn's inhabitants since the beginning of the first structured settlement in the 9th–8th centuries BC; and it preserved this role during the Greek and Roman periods, despite the insertion of the capital city of the newly created Roman province of Crete into the great commercial distributive circuit of the Roman Mediterranean. Furthermore, the *chora* became more and more important in providing food for urban needs in Late Antiquity and Early

Byzantine times, when the range of Mediterranean commerce was reduced progressively. Finally it reached a peak of importance in the last phase of Gortyn's urban life, as the new urban aristocracy found in land ownership the economic base of their social and political power.

The second, and larger, scale is represented by the Mediterranean macro-territory. Gortyn, and Crete, of course, are deeply rooted in the Early Byzantine socio-economic and administrative Mediterranean system. This means that everything we can see occurring in Gortyn and Crete in those centuries is related, in one way or another, to the broad and deep change that marked the contemporary Byzantine world.

The insularity of Crete provides in itself a good image of this: Gortyn is in some way 'melted' into the surrounding countryside (the Roman, Late Antique and Early Byzantine city did not have a circuit wall). So it could be easily seen as a mass of density, or better a mass of intensification,[9] in the settlement pattern of the Cretan island, virtually insulated from the rest of the Early Byzantine Empire. At the same time, Gortyn is part of a complex network connecting to one another all the provincial capitals of the Early Byzantine Mediterranean. And from this point of view, everything of some relevance that happened in Gortyn was related in some way to the complex administrative system that ruled the empire.

In other terms, we could look at this duality as a long-term relationship between a local – then lasting over a long time – micro-ecology and a broader Mediterranean macro-economy, the latter being basically a shorter-term item, historically determined by the political and administrative fortune of the Early Byzantine empire.[10] Once we have adopted this point of view, I believe we could use the relationship between long-term micro-ecology and short-term macro-economy – and indeed the changes over time in this relationship – as one of the major keys to trying to understand the conundrum of the disappearance of Gortyn in the 8th–9th centuries AD, which happened quite independently from the conquest of Crete by a relatively small force of Arabs coming from Spain between 824 and 827/8.[11]

In this perspective, Gortyn can be treated as an interesting example for the study not only of the fate of a single city, but also the transformation of the role of many cities of 'long tradition' in the Early Byzantine Empire, and ultimately the end of the classical city in the Mediterranean Basin.

The site

Gortyn of Crete – and, within it, the so-called 'Early Byzantine District' near the Pythion shrine, hereafter GBD[12] – qualifies as a very interesting site owing to some of its characteristics.

First of all, it is a matter of archaeological visibility and preservation of archaeological potential. The wide area of ancient Gortyn was never re-occupied after its abandonment in the 8th–9th centuries AD, the sole later human settlement being three small villages born in different times among the ruins of the

Figure 5.1 The field of ruins at Gortyn in the early 18th century AD [after Pitton de Tournefort, J. (1817), *Relation d'un voyage du Levant*. Lyon].

northern, western, and eastern peripheries of the ancient site, around respectively the church of St. Titus, the ruins of the ancient episcopal basilica at Mitropolis and the ruins of the Roman amphitheatre. The northern village did not survive until modern times, while the western and eastern villages were at the basis of the modern settlements of 'Agioi Deka' (from a church dedicated to the Ten Saints of Gortyn, persecuted by Decius in 250) and 'Mitropolis' (which name seems clearly related with the ancient basilica).[13] In the space between these hamlets, the ancient site was never reoccupied and it is described by the first modern travellers as an immense field of ruins, crossed by the remains of colonnaded streets and the lines of aqueducts that once served the whole urban surface. This landscape remained visible and relatively untouched until the beginning of the 18th century and was then concealed under the extensive olive groves that left the archaeological stratigraphy quite undisturbed (Figure 5.1).

Secondly, it is matter of the dimension of the investigated area. The site of Gortyn has been under investigation by Italian archaeological teams since the last decades of the 19th century, and more recently some other archaeological work was done by the local Greek Superintendence.[14] In this framework the GBD was partially excavated by Federico Halbherr at the very beginning of the 20th century and was also the focus of some more extensive archaeological field seasons by Antonino Di Vita, the former director of the Italian Archaeological School at Athens (the SAIA), between the 1980s and 1990s. Moreover, within the framework of the general restart of archaeological investigation in Gortyn coordinated since 2000 by the new directors of SAIA, Emanuele Greco and, subsequently, Emanuele Papi, certain Italian teams are now investigating two different parts of the district and some of the surrounding areas.[15] On the whole, we now have available a lot of knowledge about one of the more extensively excavated quarters of an Early Byzantine city, and we are well informed about the insertion of the district itself into the topography and history of the urban fabric of Gortyn between Late Antiquity and Early Byzantine times. At a larger scale, this information is related to that provided by older and newer excavations in other parts of the site, providing us with an urban scale framework for the insertion of the data coming from the excavations in the GBD and surrounding areas.

This framework could be very rapidly sketched as follows (Figure 5.2). The first human settlement in the area should be recognised on the top of the hill of Profitis Elias, immediately northward from the site. Recent excavations date it between the 9th and the 8th centuries BC. This first central place, presumably born by synoecism from dispersed settlements in the southern Mesarà Plain, was soon encircled by walls (just some part of which is actually identified on the terrain), and, in the 6th century BC extended to enclose the nearby hill of Agios Ioannis, which became the place of the acropolis of Greek Gortyn.[16] The Greek city was situated on the top and the southern slope of the acropolis and extended towards the alluvial plain of the Mitropolianos River. The *agora* was located very close to the exit of the river from the deep gorge that separates the Agios Ioannis hill from the adjacent hill. The overall image is of a quite small city, apparently not defended by walls and not extending into the plain. The southern limit of the city seems to be indicated by the Temple of Pythian Apollo, built in the 5th century BC, whose location was probably quite isolated in the plain.[17]

This temple itself was probably the focal point of the expansion of the city in Hellenistic times, when a large sanctuary complex was built in the area immediately east of it. The complex included a stadium for agonistic rituals and a series of buildings, an alignment which was the basis for further development of the Roman city.[18]

Gortyn became a Roman city after the conquest of Crete by Q. Caecilius Metellus in 67 BC (the *polis* of Gortyn was among the major supporters of the Roman expedition), but became a proper capital city only between the 1st and the 2nd centuries AD, when the monumental backbone of the Roman city was established. The urban area was greatly expanded towards the South and East, and the total extent of the city reached perhaps 150–180 hectares. The road network was organised around a main axis running from East to West, and the grid of porticoed streets was filled with the monuments that usually characterised a Roman provincial capital: temples, large baths, theatre, amphitheatre, stadium, and hippodrome. The Roman city had two focal points in the topography of power: the area of old Greek *agora*, and the seat of the *praetorium* located in the very centre of the Roman urban expansion in the plain. A special role in the setting of Roman Gortyn was played by the water system: an aqueduct some 15 kilometres long captured the water from the springs at the base of Mount Ida and brought it to the city. As result, the

58 *Enrico Zanini*

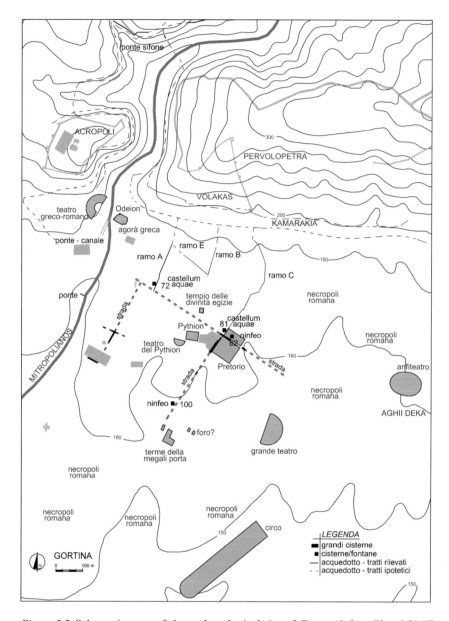

Figure 5.2 Schematic map of the archaeological site of Gortyn [after Giorgi 2016].

entire urban fabric was 'flooded' by water, used to feed at least two very large bath complexes, three *nymphaea* and, of course, the private houses. The amount of water captured was so large that it is very possible that it was also used for agricultural needs, transforming the plain to the south of the city itself into a place very suitable for intensive farming.[19]

The earthquake of 365 AD hit the city severely, however. Some large monuments were destroyed and abandoned (among them the *stadium* and the theatre connected with the shrine of Pythian Apollo,[20] while some others were promptly reconstructed. That was the case, for instance, of the *Praetorium* which was rebuilt around 383 AD. This reorganisation of urban fabric coincided with the impact of Christianisation on public spaces in the 5th century,[21] to which period has to be dated the construction of the first phase (at least) of the episcopal basilica of Mitropolis, with the related baptistery, and two other minor churches located in the same area.[22]

The 6th century seems to qualify as a very positive moment in Gortyn's urban history: the road network was restored; the same goes for the aqueduct, whose pipeline coming from the mountain was restored as well, whilst the urban distribution system registered a large renewal with the establishment of a dense network of open air *lacus* and covered reservoirs provided with fountains for public access to spring water.[23] One of the main protagonists of this urban renewal seems to have been the archbishop Vetranius, whose name is recorded on a mosaic inscription on the floor of the episcopal basilica at Mitropolis, while his monograms were found on some marble capitals coming from the church of Saint Titus (where maybe they have been reused) and from elsewhere.[24]

The 6th century represented the last well-documented moment in Gortyn's urban history until recent excavations. On that base of knowledge, the picture was drawn as one of progressive decay, maybe arrested for a while just in the age of Heraclius, when a series of acclamations to this emperor and his family were inscribed on four columns on the façade of a nymphaeum located just in front of the *praetorium*. To the age of Heraclius were assigned also the re-building of the *praetorium* itself and the new fortification of the ancient acropolis on the hill of Agios Ioannis, but in both these cases the archaeo-logical evidence seems not to be fully conclusive.[25]

On the basis of this pre-existing knowledge – and being aware that this is a somewhat complicated product of more than 100 years of archaeological investigations, using deeply different methodologies in excavating different areas – Gortyn appears to us as a sort of 'shifting city'. Born on the tops of hills, the city was based in Greek times on the top, the slope and the base of the Agios Ioannis or Acropolis hill; it expanded into the plain largely in Roman times, and retreated towards the Mitropolianos River in Late Antique to Early Byzantine times. It goes without saying that this image of shifting is mainly based on the information we have about the monumental backbone and/or the architectural carapace of the city itself. So it is the *city of monuments* that moves from the hill towards the plain and back to the river valley. But this city of monuments does not necessarily coincide with the *city of men*, to be understood as the places where the population of Gortyn actually lived and performed their everyday activities.

But in the case of Gortyn we can affirm that we are decidedly lucky, because the well-preserved urban water system I have just referred to provides us with an invaluable tool to better see the city of men. It has to be underlined

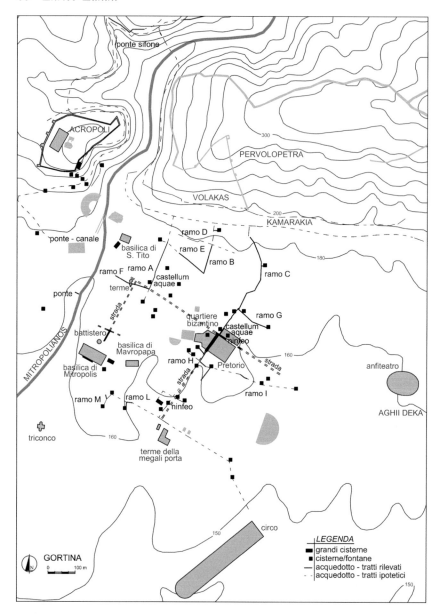

Figure 5.3 Schematic map of the archaeological site of Gortyn, showing the remains of the Roman and Early Byzantine urban water system [after Giorgi, 2016].

that the archaeological site of Gortyn hosts the best preserved and most easily readable urban water system in the whole Early Byzantine world (Figure 5.3). As I said before, the line of the aqueduct was built up in Roman times, but around the middle of the 6th century AD the spring water distribution system inside the city was completely reorganised. Some 55 reservoirs/fountains were built, distributing water all around the city. Now, since we can presume that the reservoirs and fountains were located very close to the places where the people that needed to use the water lived, we can use them as archaeological evidence to draw a map of the city of men in the 6th century.[26] But it is really interesting to see that our city of men just partially coincides with the city of monuments. The city of monuments seems to be a shifting one, whilst the city of men seems to be a more static one. In my mind, this should be an important *caveat* for any archaeological discussion on the image of Gortyn in Early Byzantine times, and a *caveat*, moreover, for a reflection about the concrete basis of our contemporary ideas about the ancient city in general.

The early Byzantine District in context

The brief excursus on the history and topography of Gortyn enables us to appraise how luckily located the relatively small excavations of the GBD project are: very close to the politico-administrative centre of the Roman and Late Antique city (the *Praetorium* complex) and at the intersection point of at least two images of the 'shifting' city. It is worth noting that I have no merit in this respect: since, at the time the position of our excavation was established, we were not yet aware of these trends at Gortyn. The location was decided just on the basis of an agreement between the director of SAIA and the Greek authorities about the opportunity to reunify the two areas traditionally excavated by Italian archaeologists in this part of the city (the Pythian temple excavated by Federico Halbherr at the end of 19th century and the *Praetorium* complex, excavated by a series of Italian archaeologists at different times during the 20th century).[27] As the result of this decision, we were able to excavate between 2001 and 2011 (although in the last four years the excavation was suspended, due to economic difficulties) a largely 'casual' sample of approximately 2,000 square metres. It qualifies as very representative of the whole district (being near to the 50% of the total extent), with the opportunity to match our data with the other dataset coming from the old and new excavations made in western part of the same district by other Italian teams (Figure 5.4).[28]

But very different is the numeric value of our sample when matched with the total physical extent of ancient, Late Antique and Early Byzantine Gortyn. Two thousand square metres are more or less just 0.12% of the total inhabited surface, which should be another important *caveat* for our idea of extracting general information about the history of the whole city from so small an archaeological sample.

Fortunately, however, our perception could be a bit more optimistic if we examine our sample also from a qualitative point of view. Our casual and lucky sample is directly linked with the two main urban infrastructures – the street grid and the water-supply system – that were restored or renewed in Early Byzantine times. So it is conceivable that we can extract

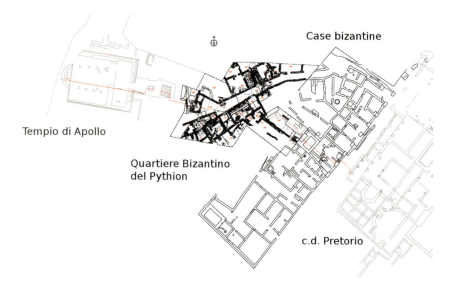

Figure 5.4 The Byzantine District of Gortyn and previously excavated monuments.

more general information about the city in examining the evolution over time of the relationship between our district and those infrastructures. This would be – at least theoretically – a way to connect the small-scale information we recover from our micro-stratigraphical excavation with the main lines of transformation of urban fabric in the last centuries of Gortyn's life.

Streets and water-supply will be henceforth the two main lines of our story: the two main archaeological witnesses of the transformation in the relationship between the people living and working in Early Byzantine Gortyn and the city as a whole. Said simply, we believe that if one really wants to see the *city of men*, instead of, or inside, *the city of monuments*, one should follow the streets to see the men as they move around the spaces of the city; and one should follow the water to see the men as they stay for living and working in their everyday places.

The street going across the GBD was clearly the topic of our investigation since the very beginning of our excavation (Figure 5.5). We identified the street already in the first field season and it became rapidly clear that it was the axis around which the space and the life of our district were organised. Our street is clearly a 'new' element in the scenery of ancient Gortyn, since its alignment differs from previous ones, both the Greek one (marked in our area by the shrine of Apollo) and the Roman one (marked instead by the *Praetorium* complex). Moreover, its birth date is clearly defined by the break-line of the earthquake of 21st July 365 AD. So it is a street belonging to the 'new' Late Antique city that was born after that catastrophe. At the urban scale, the new street had probably a 'natural' origin, starting as a simple path

Figure 5.5 The Byzantine District of Gortyn (GBD) seen from the south.

to cross over the landscape of ruins, connecting the main colonnaded street of ancient Gortyn (the one running east-west immediately north of the *Praetorium* complex) with the southern urban districts located near the river, which was probably densely populated, as testified by the presence of some important churches built during the century after the earthquake. At a more limited scale – the one of this part of the urban fabric – the new-born path marked an important new borderline between a completely abandoned area towards the west (the Pythian temple and related theatre) and a quickly renewed area towards the east, where the *Praetorium* complex was rapidly reorganised, as stated by a series of monumental inscriptions.

At the even smaller scale of our district, the new path marks the starting point of a very interesting phenomenon of *spatial asynchrony* between adjacent areas that characterised our district for some centuries, until the end of the human settlement in this part of the city. Different locales, including areas located in very close proximity, evolved in strikingly different ways during the same period; thus our term 'spatial asynchrony'. From the end of the 4th century, and mainly in the 5th century, the path – and immediately afterwards the street that replaced it – marks the borderline between a virtually abandoned or poorly used area, located north-west of the street, and another area, located immediately south-east of the street, where life rapidly restarted with the building up of some small houses and/or workshops.

64 *Enrico Zanini*

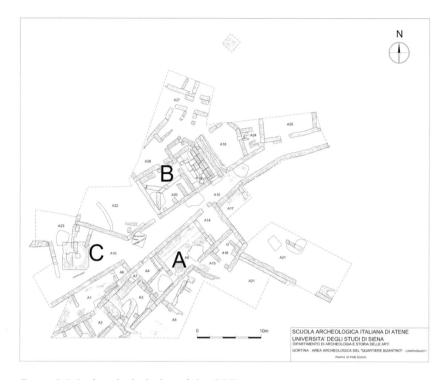

Figure 5.6 Archaeological plan of the GBD.

The causes of this spatial asynchrony are obviously complex, being connected with phenomena operating at different scales. An excellent example could be represented by a small sanctuary we had the opportunity to excavate just beside our street (Figure 5.6, C). The building was probably built in the 2nd or 3rd century AD as part of the Roman reorganisation of the temple of Pythian Apollo. It was physically connected with the shrine itself, as a small additional place of worship, perhaps to be identified as a *manteion*. This small building shared obviously the fate of the main temple and the related theatre. It was abandoned well before the earthquake and probably transformed into a small stable to shelter sheep or goats, in the same way as the nearby theatre, where the scenic building was transformed into a stable for horses, and the *cavea* was converted into a place for craft activities. After the definitive collapse of its roofing during the earthquake, our small building was converted, between the 4th and the 5th centuries AD, into a rubbish dump, where the refuse from the houses and workshops rebuilt on the opposite part of the street was collected.

The spatial asynchrony we have just described seems to continue in the 6th century: the area north-west of the street remained probably poorly used (but the investigation in this sector has to be completed), whilst the opposite area shows a radical renewal very probably connected with the *floruit* of the entire

Figure 5.7 The large building south of the street, seen from the east.

city at which I have already hinted (Figure 5.6, A). In this part of our excavated area, around the mid-6th century, the small houses built and transformed between the end of the 4th and the mid-5th centuries were reorganised into one single very large rectangular building, overlooking directly the street to one side which opened on the other side onto a large open area, maybe a garden or a courtyard. Our first ideal reconstruction sees the building as a 25-metres-long unitary complex, distributed on two floors (a large staircase being found in one room), with the circulation of people inside it ensured by a series of doors opening on the eastern courtyard (Figure 5.7). It is difficult to say whether our building was a single house in itself or was instead part of a larger and more articulated complex. In both the cases, however, the topographical relationship between our building and one – or even two – of the reservoirs/fountains erected as a part of the new urban water supply established around the mid-6th century seems quite sure.

Until now, we do not have a sure interpretation for our large building though. It consists of a series of rooms without any clear differentiation, the only one with a definite character being the northern one, which could have been a kitchen, provided with a fireplace and a long and narrow underground reservoir-shaped structure, maybe used for storage of food. The overall impression is that our building could constitute a utilitarian part of a larger complex, probably having its more important section overlooking the main

66 *Enrico Zanini*

street running West of the *Praetorium* complex. In this case, the relationship with the reservoirs or fountains would be even more interesting. At least judging from the better preserved examples, the reservoirs or fountains were located not along the streets or on the crossroads, but preferably within courtyards connected with one or more houses. This opens a space to reflecting about the reasons that determined this choice. If the reservoirs or fountains were products of a restoration and/or reorganisation of urban water distribution, their location could reflect a 'new' idea of public service, with the water not distributed following an abstract topographical model, but rather assigned to concrete population foci. Whether those foci could coincide with the residences of eminent citizens with their surrounding dependencies remains of course a matter of speculation.

The GBD over time

The landscape of the city in the mid-6th century which we have rapidly sketched on the basis of the archaeological data recorded in GBD contexts saw a dramatic change already between the last decades of 6th century and the early 7th century. And in this case too, the change was in the direction of a larger asynchrony in the reshaping of spaces in the two adjacent parts of the district.

A first major change intervened in the large building south-east of the street. Some small interventions (the blocking of some doors with rough masonry; opening of new passages between the rooms) radically changed the organisation of living and working spaces inside the building. The originally unitary building was divided into at least three small units, each of them formed of just one or two rooms. The doors that formerly connected each room with the eastern courtyard were blocked and new doors were opened on the opposite side, connecting the new units with the street running across the district.

The archaeological assemblages related with this phase seem to fit well with the overall image of a dramatic change of the socio-economic landscape in this part of the urban fabric. We found many traces of artisanal activities, the most readable of them being connected with the fabrication of iron knives or agricultural tools with goat horn handles, or with the production of chalk from alabaster. We found also many traces of a simple everyday life, such as at least two small hearths of a type that survived until very recently in the traditional lifestyle of the Cretan countryside. This homogeneous image was however in sharp contrast with some other finds that sound unexpected: several coins, some high-quality pottery, some pieces of personal adornment (clearly of military origin), even a lead seal. In particular, in a small room of the earlier building, now presumably converted into a stable, an assemblage of freshly discarded pottery contained several nearly complete imported vessels.

With this contradictory image in mind, we approached the excavation on the north-west side of the street, looking for a parallel path of transformation in the urban fabric, but our expectations were completely dismissed because the asynchrony became self-evident, taking the shape of a very large and relatively luxurious building erected around the beginning of the 7th century AD. Unfortunately, our investigation was stopped in 2011 before we were able to complete the excavation of the building, but the work we did makes us confident about the first interpretation that we can offer here.

We are dealing with a newly built, large edifice, erected presumably in the first decades of the 7th century, as attested by the stratigraphic relationship between the foundation trenches of its perimeter wall and the different levels of the street (Figure 5.6, B). The building is characterised by very large rooms distributed around an open courtyard elegantly paved with large, reused, slabs. It had two storeys and very probably faced with its most important and representative part onto the large colonnaded street that runs immediately to the north; being the street directly connected with the *Praetorium* area, and hence probably representing the most important point of 'display' for the public or private owner of our mansion.

The section of the building that we have excavated until now represents therefore the back part of a large edifice, probably destined to practical domestic functions. Nevertheless, the entrance connecting the internal courtyard to the street has some 'monumental' character, with a very large main door whose threshold is made from a reused lintel, and paving slabs quite similar to those we can see from this time in Gortyn, for instance in the renewed *Praetorium* or in the remade pavement of the episcopal basilica at Mitropolis (Figure 5.8).

Figure 5.8 The large building north-west of the street seen from the south.

68   *Enrico Zanini*

The overall impression is that we are dealing with a building that was in some way connected with public use, otherwise owned by a wealthy member of the urban upper class. Both the hypotheses seem to be compatible with the finding, among the ruins of the collapsed roof, of a marble slab with an engraved circular monogram. Until now, we were not able to properly solve the monogram, but its typology claims for it a date at the end of 6th or (better) beginning of the 7th century AD, and a relevant public office and name which are hidden within the complicated lettering.

Another very interesting archaeological indicator is represented by the water-supply. Our building is the first of those excavated until now in Gortyn, at least to my knowledge, that was served by a sort of 'private' water system. A large drain collected rainwater falling through a sort of *impluvium* onto the paved courtyard, with the rest of the rainwater coming directly from other areas of roofing. The presence of a cistern at the end of the drain could be supposed but it has not been archaeologically established yet. A second pipeline, made with reused amphorae and *tubuli*, was probably connected with the drainage system coming from the roofing. Once it emerged from the building, the pipeline ran under the street, carrying some water towards a sewer expressly built in the body of the street. It is still unclear, even though probable, that this second drainage functioned also as a latrine. In this case, we would have a large human waste-disposal system that would require an adequate interpretation.

In both the cases – whether public or private property – the circumstance that both the amphorae pipeline and the drain/sewer were installed into the body of the street suggests the possibility that in this moment the street itself was in some way privatised by the personal of public authority that owned the mansion. This would solve the apparent conundrum posed by the discrepancy between the poor quality of building and high quality of finds we have seen on the opposite side of the street.

The hypothesis we are working on currently is that we could be dealing with something resembling a medieval *insula* of the type we can see in Italian cities of the 10th–11th centuries: a main private building overlooking the main colonnaded street of the city, with a rear part destined to practical duties, opened with a quite monumental back-door entrance onto the old district's street. The street itself would become a sort of private elongated courtyard, where some artisanal activities took place. We find at least one hearth for cooking and traces of various activities. On the same courtyard opened the new small houses on the south-east of the old street, where people, activities, and perhaps animals connected with the owner of the principal house took their places.

Further towards the east, in the area once occupied by the garden or courtyard of the 6th-century building, we do not have yet any trace of intensive use. The image is that of an 'urban hole' between two much more intensified areas: one towards the west (our large building) and one, presumably, towards the East, overlooking the other major street. In this area some burials were found. The archaeological investigation was unable to produce a precise dating, but a 7th-century chronology appears highly probable. The overall image is not one of an abandoned area with some scattered poor burials. On the contrary, we seem to be looking at a well-organised small burial place, with relatively high-quality tombs.[29]

On the whole, the image that our excavation has produced for the 7th century seems to be in accordance with the idea of a 'multi-focal' city or, maybe better, a city with different densities. Inside the city, we presume, the people are not distributed in a more or less homogeneous way; rather, they are concentrated into smaller topographical units, originated by the presence of a public authority or a prominent citizen (a member of the world of *possessores* or *potentiores* frequently cited by literary sources?), or even simply by the presence of one 'vital' facility like spring water, still provided by the network of reservoirs or fountains, still fed by the aqueduct, albeit progressively in a crisis of maintenance.

The image of a large private building designed to be virtually independent from the unreliable feeding of the public aqueduct seems to fit well into this scenario. And that impression seems to be confirmed by the finding of a further developed and dense network of small surface channels cut into the upper stratigraphic levels in that area. It seems that from the second half of the 7th century onwards and until the final collapse of the roofs, perhaps in the late 8th century, every single drop of rainwater was carefully collected to be ducted to the main drain-system.

The last Gortyn under some collapsing roofs

The final phase of life in our district was sealed by a general roofing collapse, to be connected evidently to one of the earthquakes that frequently devastated Crete and are well attested by literary sources. Due to the known difficulty in dating 8th-century pottery assemblages in the absence of definite typological sequences and without the aid of the virtually disappeared coinage, it is quite impossible to say in which part of the 'long' 8th century this collapse occurred. More important is maybe trying to understand the reasons why this earthquake – evidently not the first in the city's history – marked a definitive break in the occupancy of this part, at least, of the city itself.

The traces to be followed in our research are evidently concealed under the roof's collapse, so it is worth describing in a little detail the archaeological assemblages we found, proceeding from the periphery towards the centre of our '*insula*'. Three important circumstances have to be remembered: (1) the final collapse was not instantaneous. As far I know, no people were ever found killed by fallen roofs in the different parts of the city, but it was rapid, as attested by the presence of some animals under the ruins. (2) Some of the rooms, mainly the peripheral ones, were virtually stripped of their furniture and abandoned before the collapse itself. (3) We have not excavated the properly residential part of the central building, so our image is indirectly

70 *Enrico Zanini*

generated by the objects in place and the refuse that we found in the 'intermediate' area between the core and the periphery of our *insula*. In other words, the archaeological dataset we are dealing with cannot be read through the lenses of any sort of Pompeian premise. We have to be aware that we are dealing with an image that is at the same time complex and altered by many factors; an image that deserves to be decoded and interpreted within the scenery of a city at the end of its life.

Looking at the most peripheral parts of our *insula*, the image looks controversial: the eastern courtyard or garden is maybe still used as a burial place and the last burials we can see could be classified as related to high social class. Conversely, the building between the garden and the street-courtyard seems to be nearly ruined. Some walls collapsed or were deliberately destroyed to open paths for livestock; some rooms were converted into open spaces, partially covered by canopies; the old kitchen of the large building of Justinianic age was still standing and covered by a solid roof, but it was converted into a single-room small house, arranged with a wooden mezzanine, where humans and animals shared a common space – a typology of small rural house with a long history in Crete, spanning from the 8th century BC until maybe the 19th century AD.

The collapsed roof of this small house sealed a situation of abandonment: no pottery or furniture in place, the space completely emptied with just some bones of slaughtered livestock accumulated on the earth floor.

Beyond the street transformed into an elongated courtyard, the spaces of the main building revealed a more dynamic situation. Under the ruins of the roof and the first floor, a large room at ground level is revealed to have been used as a cellar, where some 20 amphorae were preserved at the moment of the collapse. We are unable to determine if the amphorae were full or empty at the moment of the earthquake, but their presence alone testifies that the house was not completely abandoned. The same image derives from the finds in the slab-paved courtyard, where the collapse of the portico squashed four or five goats or sheep, evidently hosted into a small stable installed in a corner of the portico itself (Figure 5.9).

On the whole, the image seems to be of a markedly rural ambiance, and this is confirmed by the circumstance that a part of the slab-pavement of the old 'monumental' rear entrance of the main house shows signs of continued use by heavy animals, probably livestock. In such a rural context, the image offered by the sparse finds appears quite different, however. The private or public owner of the mansion was very probably still a member of the urban aristocracy, whatever this term could mean in the middle of the 8th century AD or so.

The marble slab with the unsolved monogram had perhaps belonged to an ancestor of the present owner, but, imagining that it was still exposed, its mere presence was probably read as a symbol of the past, and perhaps the present, authority of the family. This image is corroborated by the presence, among the ruins of the paved courtyard, of a *saltsario*, a chafing dish made in

Figure 5.9 Finds sealed under the collapsed roofs of the large building north-west of the street (*ca.* 8th century).

Glazed White Ware, produced at Constantinople, probably by the very beginning of the 8th century. This kind of luxurious tableware is, at least for the present, relatively rare outside Constantinople itself, and its presence in our Gortynian context could mean we are dealing with a man or a group of people that had still direct contacts with the capital city (Figure 5.10).

The amphorae kept in the cellar belong to a now quite well known typology of containers attested mainly in the Cretan countryside. The owner of the cellar did not use imported wine or oil, but the basis of his wealth was clearly in the surrounding countryside. And this wealth was not necessarily small, because 20 amphorae of wine are a not contemptible indicator of economic welfare, when compared with the hard times we are dealing with. Therefore, from this point of view, the large 8th-century house of the GBD could be reasonably assumed to be one of the possible paradigms of urban life in this era. The scenario is to some extent a contradictory one: the urban fabric is largely dissolved, with the empty spaces largely prevailing over the used ones, but some fundamental part of the ancient urban organisation remained alive.[30]

Speaking about the city of monuments, at least four main items seem to survive: (1) the churches (although we cannot say anything about them from our 'observatory', the continuity has to be presumed); (2) the backbone of the street network, which proves to be clean and not invaded by encroachment,

72 Enrico Zanini

Figure 5.10 A 'luxurious' Constantinopolitan tableware and its 'rural' context.

The 'Byzantine District' of Gortyn (Crete)   73

with the main houses overlooking it; (3) the backbone of the water supply, although in a progressively worsening condition; (4) the general idea of an organised city, witnessed at the best by the presence of the fortified acropolis.

Speaking about the city of people, the image is that of a place where some form of social hierarchy still survives: the owner of our mansion being probably a local lord, but one still in an economic and social position to stay in contact with the sphere of Constantinople, and using that marble monogram to publicly represent and self-represent some form of 'power'.

The earthquake acted probably as a catalyst in this process: after the extensive disruption of the city's backbones, the local aristocracy had not the economic resources and the political will to re-organise some form of civic life. From its side, the State administration was not in a condition – and probably had not any real interest – to sustain a possibly extensive urban restoration.

Coming to the end

The archaeological information we were able to retrieve from the contexts of the GBD allows us to follow the rapid and deep transformation in the urban fabric between the mid-6th and the 8th centuries AD and to envisage the socio-economic transformation that was the engine for this. The close relationship, both topographical-functional and social, between the houses of our district and the main urban infrastructure (streets grid and water-supply system) strengthens the hypothesis that this path of transformation could be applied to the city as a whole.[31] But the answer we have produced is just related to the first – and the simpler – of our questions: that one related with the way in which Early Byzantine Gortyn came to its end. Much more complicated is to answer the question 'why' the city disappeared. In this case, I believe our answer should be searched for once again in the reciprocal relationship between the local long-term micro-ecology and the Mediterranean short-term macro-economy.

The history of Late Antique Gortyn, since the devastating earthquake of 21st July 365 and until the mid-6th century, could be read in terms of the impact of the Mediterranean macro economy. The rebirth of the city after that earthquake, and maybe at some other times during the seismic cluster that affected Crete during the 5th and 6th centuries,[32] was strictly connected with the interest that the central administration attached to the role of the island and its capital city within a Mediterranean framework. After the division between the eastern and western part of the Roman Empire, Crete was, mainly in the first half of 6th century, a pivot in the structuring of the Early Byzantine Mediterranean. Despite the island and its capital city being rarely mentioned in literary sources, we have a clear image of the importance assigned to Crete from the very high position the archbishop of Gortyn held in the lists of subscribers at the Ecumenical Councils. But this scenario changed rapidly in the last decades of the same 6th century, when the Empire was facing increasing difficulties on many different fronts: the loss of the central role of the Mediterranean involved necessarily the interest the Empire had for Crete. There is no other way, at least in my mind, to explain the sudden decline we can see in the local economy, and in the absence of any real change in the economic structure of Crete. The island remained virtually self-sufficient, but lost its role in exporting goods. There is a steep drop in the distribution of Cretan amphorae in the Mediterranean, and in Crete's role as a pivot of commercial relationships between the southern Mediterranean and Greece.

The decline of the Mediterranean macro-economy involved a progressive re-emerging of the role of the local micro-economy. What we can see in our district is precisely this: a progressive localisation of production and consumption and decline of imported goods, paralleled by a progressive disappearance of the distinction between city and countryside (e.g., the mobility of people from the country towards the city, ruralisation of urban behaviours), paralleled by a progressive localisation of power.

The progressive reshaping of the multifocal city is the main archaeological witness of this complex phenomenon. Ancient/Late Antique/Early Byzantine Gortyn progressively dissolved into a cluster of small units centred around a specific 'facility' (e.g., the reservoirs of the aqueduct, progressively perceived as 'artificial' springs), and/or around a place of power (a church, the seat of a public power, a private residence of a powerful citizen); these urban sub-units being connected by the surviving, and in some manner maintained, backbone of the street system.

In parallel with the worsening of the Early Byzantine Empire between the 7th and the 8th centuries, the insularity of Crete became more and more a negative factor, until the final collapse of the city and its 'dissolution' into the local micro-ecology.[33] Eradicated from its Mediterranean context, Gortyn lost its role of point of contact between the local scale and the Mediterranean scale. Consequently, it lost its character as a node of intensification of the human settlement pattern of central Crete, closing a history that started some eight centuries before, when the Romans choose Gortyn as the place to manage the interaction between Crete and the rest of the Roman Mediterranean world.

This intimate connection between the fate of Gortyn and the changing framework of the Roman, Late Antique, and Early Byzantine Mediterranean is underlined by the evidence of the Byzantine 'reconquest' of Crete in 961. After that, Gortyn was not only forgotten in its role of ancient capital city and metropolitan seat, but also was neither fully reoccupied nor reintegrated with a proper role as a city. And it was the same for the rest of the ancient Roman cities across the southern part of Crete. After 961, the new capital city of Crete was Candia (Heraklion) and all the new important cities were placed across the northern part of the island. This is, at least in my opinion, a very interesting image of the change of the Byzantine world, from a Mediterranean one to an Aegean one, and of the role of Crete, from the pivot of the old world to the southern bastion of the new one.[34]

Notes

1 The Gortyn Byzantine District archaeological project is carried out jointly, and funded, by the Dept. of History and Cultural Heritage of the University of Siena and the Italian Archaeological School at Athens, with the permission of the Greek national authorities. Additional funding is yearly granted by the Italian Ministry of Foreign Affairs and International Cooperation. In 2011, the project received a research grant from Dumbarton Oaks too.
2 Loseby 2009; Zavagno 2009; Christie and Augenti, 2012; Dey 2015; Decker 2016.
3 Mundell Mango 2006.
4 Bouras 2002.
5 Brandes 1999; Saradi 2006.
6 Zanini 2003; Purcell 2005; Crow *et al.* 2016.
7 Zanini 2013a.
8 Zanini 2015.
9 Hordern and Purcell 2000: 96–101.
10 Hordern and Purcell 2000: 88–122.
11 Zanini 2013b.
12 The 'Gortyna Byzantine District'.
13 Di Vita 2010.
14 Di Vita 2000; Lippolis 2014.
15 Zanini 2009.
16 Allegro 1991.
17 Allegro 2004.
18 Lippolis 2005.
19 Giorgi 2007a; Pagano 2007.
20 Bonetto *et al.* 2009.
21 Baldini Lippolis and Vallarino 2012.
22 Baldini Lippolis 2002.
23 Giorgi 2007b.
24 Farioli Campianati, 2004; Sythiakakis Kritsimalli.
25 De Tommaso 2000; Perna 2012.
26 Giorgi 2016.
27 Zanini 2004.
28 Zanini 2004; Zanini *et al.* 2006; Zanini *et al.* 2009; Zanini and Giorgi 2002; Zanini and Giorgi 2003.
29 Di Vita 1986.
30 Baldini *et al.* 2012.
31 Baldini *et al.* 2012.
32 Stiros 2001.
33 Veikou 2010.
34 Zanini 2013a.

References

Allegro, N. (1991), 'Gortina, l'abitato geometrico di Profitis Ilias', in D. Musti, ed., *La Transizione Dal Miceneo all'Alto Arcaismo. Dal Palazzo Alla Città.* Rome: 321–330.
Allegro, N. (2004), 'Gortina al momento della conquista romana: il dato archeologico', in *Creta Romana E Protobizantina. Atti del congresso internazionale.* Padova: 531–556.
Baldini, I., Cosentino, S., Lippolis, E., Sgarzi, E., and Marsili, G. (2012), 'Gortina, Mitropolis e il suo episcopato nel VII e nell'VIII secolo. Ricerche preliminari', *Annuario Della Scuola Archeologica in Atene E Delle Missioni Italaliane in Oriente* 90: 239–310.

76 Enrico Zanini

Baldini Lippolis, I. (2002), 'Architettura protobizantina a Gortina: la basilica di Mavropapa', *Creta Antica* 3: 301–320.

Baldini Lippolis, I., and Vallarino, G. (2012) 'Gortyn: from the City of the Gods to Christian City', in T. Kaizer, A. Leone, E. Thomas, and R. Witcher, eds., *Cities and Gods: Religious Space in Transition*. Leuven/Paris/Walpole, MA: 103–116.

Bonetto, J., Ghedini, F., Bressan, M., Francisci, D., Falezza, G., Mazzocchini, S., and Schindler Kaudeka, E. (2009), 'Gortyna di Creta, Teatro del Pythion. Ricerche e scavi 2007–2010', *Annuario Della Scuola Archeologica in Atene E Delle Missioni Italiane in Oriente* 87: 1087–1098.

Bouras, C. (2002), 'Aspects of the Byzantine City, Eighth–Fifteenth Centuries', in A. Laiou, ed., *The Economic History of Byzantium*. Washington, DC: 497–528.

Brandes, W. (1999), 'Byzantine cities in the seventh and eighth centuries – different sources, different histories?' in G.-P. Brogiolo, and B. Ward-Perkins, eds., *The Idea and Ideal of the Town between Late Antiquity and the Early Middle Ages*. Leiden/Boston/Köln: 25–57.

Christie, N., and Augenti, A. (2012), *Vrbes extinctae: archaeologies of abandoned classical towns*. Farnham/Burlington.

Crow, J., Lopez Quiroga, J., Ivanišević, V., and Zanini, E. (2016), 'The Byzantine City and the archaeology of the third millennium', in *Proceedings of the 23rd International Congress of Byzantine Studies Belgrade, 22–27 August 2016*. Beograd: 63–143.

De Tommaso, G. (2000), 'Settore B. La Basilica del Pretorio', in A. Di Vita, ed., *Gortina V*, Padova: 285–383.

Decker, M. (2016), *The Byzantine Dark Ages*. London.

Dey, H.W. (2015), *The Afterlife of the Roman City*. Cambridge.

Di Vita, A. (1986), 'Atti della scuola 1986–1987', *Annuario Della Scuola Archeologica in Atene E Delle Missioni Italiane in Oriente*, 64–65: 435–534.

Di Vita, A. (2000), 'Gortina', *Rendiconti Dell' Accademia Nazionale dei Lincei, Classe di Scienze Morali, Storiche, E Filologiche* 11: 639–669.

Di Vita, A. (2010), *Gortina di Creta quindici secoli di vita urbana*. Rome.

Farioli Campanati, R. (2004), 'La basilica di Mitropolis a Gortina: tipologia e articolazione degli spazi liturgici', in *Creta Romana E Protobizantina*, Padova: 637–650.

Giorgi, E. (2007a), 'L'approvvigionamento idrico di Gortina di Creta in età romana', *Annuario Della Facolta di Lettere E Filosofia Dell'Università di Siena* 28: 1–28.

Giorgi, E. (2007b), 'Water technology at Gortyn in the 4th-6th century A.D.: transport, storage and distribution', in L. Lavan, E. Zanini, and A. Sarantis, eds., *Technology in Transition A.D. 300–650* (Late Antique Archaeology 4). Leiden/Boston: 287–320.

Giorgi, E. (2016), *Archeologia dell'acqua a Gortina di Creta in età protobizantina*. Oxford.

Horden, P., and Purcell, N. (2000), *The Corrupting Sea. A Study on Mediterranean History*. Oxford.

Lippolis, E. (2005), 'Il tempio del Caput Aquae e il tessuto urbano circostante: campagna di scavo 2005', *Annuario Della Scuola Archeologica in Atene E Delle Missioni Italaliane in Oriente* 83: 625–648.

Lippolis, E. (2014), 'L'archeologia degli Italiani a Creta: gli scavi di Gortina. Formazione, sviluppo e trasformazioni di una grande polis dell'Egeo', *Forma Urbis* 19: 1–56.

Loseby, S. (2009), 'Mediterranean Cities', in P. Rousseau, ed., *A Companion to Late Antiquity*. Oxford: 139–155.

The *'Byzantine District' of Gortyn (Crete)* 77

Mundell Mango, M. (2006), 'Action in trenches: a call for a more dynamic archaeology of early Byzantium', in E. Jeffreys, ed., *Proceedings of the 21st International Congress of Byzantine Studies. London, 21–26 August 2006*. Aldershot: 83–98.

Pagano, M. (2007), 'Ricerche sull'acquedotto e sulle fontane romane e bizantine di Gortina (Creta)', *Creta Antica* 8: 325–400.

Perna, R. (2012), 'L'acropoli di Gortina: la Tavola "A" della carta archeologica della citta di Gortina', *Ichnia, Collana del Dipartimento di Studi Umanistici, serie seconda*, 6. Macerata.

Purcell, N. (2005), 'Statics and dynamics: ancient Mediterranean urbanism', in B. Cunliffe, and R. Osborne, eds., *Mediterranean Urbanization, 800–600 BC*. London: 249–272.

Saradi, H. (2006), *The Byzantine City in the Sixth Century. Literary Images and Historical Reality*. Athens.

Stiros, S. (2001), 'The AD 365 Crete earthquake and possible seismic clustering during the fourth to sixth centuries AD in the Eastern Mediterranean: a review of the historical and archaeological data', *Journal of Structural Geology* 23: 545–562.

Sythiakakis Kritsimalli, V. (n.d.), 'Τα αρχιτεκτονικά γλυπτά του Αγίου Τίτου της Γόρτυνας και η συμβολή τους στη χρονολόγηση του μνημείου', in *Papers of the XIth International Congress of Cretan Studies*. Greece.

Veikou, M. (2010), 'Urban or rural? Theoretical remarks on the settlement patterns in Byzantine Epirus (7th-11th centuries)', *Byzantinische Zeitschrift* 103: 171–193.

Zanini, E. (2003), 'The urban ideal and urban planning in Byzantine new cities of the sixth century A.D.', in L. Lavan, and W. Bowden, eds., *Theory and Practice in Late Antique Archaeology* (Late Antique Archaeology 1). Leiden/Boston: 196–223.

Zanini, E. (2004), 'Lo scavo nel "quartiere bizantino" di Gortina. Il contesto metodologico dell'avvio di una ricerca', in *Bisanzio, La Grecia E l'Italia, Atti Della Giornata Di Studi in Onore Di Mara Bonfioli (Roma 22/11/2002)*. Rome: 145–159.

Zanini, E. (2009), '"Un gruppo di (povere) case di tarda epoca": centoquattro anni di letture di una testimonianza archeologica gortinia', *Annuario Della Scuola Archeologica in Atene E Delle Missioni Italiane in Oriente* 86: 697–704.

Zanini, E. (2013a), 'Creta in età protobizantina: un quadro di sintesi regionale', in D. Michaelides, P. Pergola, and E. Zanini, eds., *The Insular System in the Early Byzantine Mediterranean: Archaeology and History*, B.A.R. International Series 2523, Oxford: 173–190.

Zanini, E. (2013b), 'L'VIII secolo a Gortina di Creta e qualche idea sulla fine della città antica nel Mediterraneo', in R. Martorelli, ed., *Settecento-Millecento Storia, Archeologia E Arte Nei "secoli Bui" Del Mediterraneo*, Cagliari: 177–206.

Zanini, E. (2015), 'Il dissolversi della figura. La fine della città antica in una prospettiva mediterranea di lungo periodo', in A. Quintavalle, ed., *Medioevo: Natura e Figura*, Milano: 113–128.

Zanini, E., Costa, S., Giorgi, E., and Triolo, E. (2009), 'Indagini archeologiche nell'area del quartiere bizantino del Pythion di Gortyna: quinta relazione preliminare (campagne 2007–2010)', *Annuario Della Scuola Archeologica in Atene E Delle Missioni Italiane in Oriente* 87: 1099–1129.

Zanini, E., and Giorgi, E. (2002), 'Indagini nell'area del "Quartiere Bizantino" di Gortyna: prima relazione preliminare (campagna 2002)', *Annuario Della Scuola Archeologica in Atene E Delle Missioni Italiane in Oriente* 80: 918–938.

78   *Enrico Zanini*

Zanini, E., and Giorgi, E. (2003), 'Indagini nell'area del "Quartiere Bizantino" di Gortyna: seconda relazione preliminare (campagna 2003)', *Annuario Della Scuola Archeologica in Atene E Delle Missioni Italiane in Oriente* 81: 913–945.

Zanini, E., Giorgi, E., and Vattimo, E. (2006), 'Indagini nell'area del "Quartiere Bizantino" di Gortyna: quarta relazione preliminare (campagne 2005–2006)', *Annuario Della Scuola Archeologica in Atene E Delle Missioni Italiane in Oriente* 84: 889–914.

Zavagno, L. (2009), *Cities in transition, urbanism in Byzantium between late antiquity and the early Middle Ages (500–900 A.D.)*, B.A.R. International Series, Oxford.

6 Maritime Routes in the Aegean (7th–9th Centuries)
The Archaeological Evidence

Natalia Poulou-Papadimitriou

To the memory of my father Michalis Poulos, who lived his life sailing the seas.

As early as the 4th century the Aegean Sea and its islands were, thanks to Constantinople, one of the political and economic *foci* of the Mediterranean.[1] Three centuries later the situation had worsened dramatically for Byzantium. The period from the 7th until the 9th centuries corresponds to the transformation of the Eastern Roman Empire into the Byzantine state. During this period important changes in the Empire's frontiers and size took place, particularly after the East Syria, Palestine, and Egypt, which provided many of the agricultural goods – fell to the Arabs in the 640s. By the end of the 7th century the erstwhile province of *Africa Proconsularis* had passed into Arab occupation too. The presence of the Arabs in the Mediterranean, and in the Aegean in particular, created conditions which imposed major changes in important sectors of the administration, defence, the character of commerce, and the security of communications.[2]

As written sources shed little light on this particular period of Byzantine history, archaeological evidence plays a most important role. It is imperative to study in depth the extent to which evidence of material culture helps our understanding and interpretation of this period. In the process, the question will be examined whether archaeological evidence, corroborated by written sources, illustrates the nature and extent of maritime activity in the Aegean from the 7th to the 9th centuries. At this point, one must note that, until about twenty years ago, archaeological research on this transitional period of Byzantium had produced only scarce evidence. But in recent years, more and more scholars have been working on this subject. Their publications gradually add to our knowledge.[3]

The archaeological evidence presented in this chapter comes in its majority from research in the Aegean islands. Crete is included, despite actually being a distinct case. Because of its geographical situation, Crete, after the mid-7th and until the 9th centuries, was the southern frontier of the Byzantine Empire, bordering the Aegean islands. This situation renders Crete a very important island for the control of maritime traffic, especially during this period, when the Arabs arrive at the heart of the Aegean. The study will deal

DOI: 10.4324/9781003429470-8

80 *Natalia Poulou-Papadimitriou*

Figure 6.1 Map of Byzantine sites: 1. Constantinople, 2. Corinth, 3. Aigina, 4. Kythera, 5. Melos, 6. Santorini, 7. Herakleion, 8. Gortyn, 9, Itanos, 10. Pseira and Mochlos, 11. Yassi Ada, 12. Cyprus, 13. Cos, 14. Philippi, 15. Chios, 16. Lipsoi, 17. Samos, 18. Islands in Argolid Gulf, 19. Rhodes, 20. Amorgos, 21. Anafi, 22. Kydonia/Chania, 23. Eleutherna (Satellite image courtesy of Visible Earth, NASA; adapted by author).

in particular with small establishments on the Cretan coasts and on the islets close to the same, and their character.[4] These provide us with important data, which assist the understanding and interpretation of finds from further Aegean sites (Figure 6.1). Objects presented in this chapter have been excavated at sites dated between the 7th and the 9th centuries: the evidence of pottery and metal objects such as belt buckles is discussed, and reference made to the significance of coins recovered, as well as of lead seals.

The ceramic evidence

Starting with pottery, it is vital to observe at the outset the major importance of its study and publication for the interpretation of the activities and everyday life of inhabitants of a site. Among ceramic categories of this period, the discussion focusses on Glazed White Wares (=GWW),[5] and amphorae.

Glazed white ware I and II (Hayes' Saraçhane typology)

The earliest ceramics with a white fabric and a lead glaze started being produced in Constantinople or its wider region during the middle of the 7th

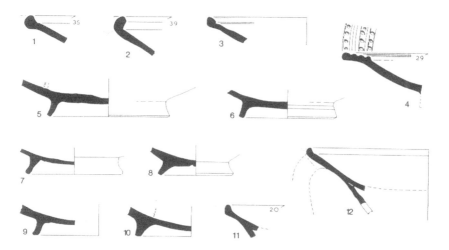

Figure 6.2 Glazed White Ware I from Saraçhane (With acknowledgements to Hayes, 1992).

century.[6] This is regarded as the Byzantine pottery of the capital *par excellence* (Figure 6.2). The first two groups, following Hayes typology from Saraçhane excavations (GWW I and early products of GWW II), date to the 7th/8th and 9th centuries. However, these early examples are fragile and very readily fragmented, and so can quite easily escape notice. Nonetheless, the category is significant for the dating of archaeological contexts of this period.

Where has such material been found? Sherds of Glazed White Ware I have been found in Corinth (in a layer of the third quarter of the 7th century),[7] Aigina,[8] Kythera (in a layer of the late 7th and 8th centuries),[9] Melos and Santorini.[10] It has been recovered also on several sites in Crete: some GWW I and early GWW II sherds appeared during the study of the ceramic material from the excavation of Agios Petros, near the coastal fortifications of Herakleion (Byzantine Chandax)[11]; in Gortyn, sherds of GWW I have been found in a layer of the late 7th/8th centuries[12]; a vessel of GWW I was unearthed in Agia Galini, along with three *folles* of Constans II minted in 643/4, 645/6, or 646/7 – this provides a *terminus post quem* and a date in the second half of the 7th century.[13] In contrast to what has been argued concerning the continuity of habitation at Itanos, the pottery published from this site dates to the early 8th century and shows that life at this site, at the very eastern end of Crete, went on, despite the Arab threat, at least until the first half of the 8th century.[14]

Finally, GWW I sherds have been found in the small settlement on the Pseira islet, just off the north coast of Crete towards the east, in a layer of the 8th century.[15] Moreover, this pottery has been found in the Yassi Ada shipwreck (Figure 6.3a, 6.3b) (with *follis* of Heraclius, *terminus post quem*: 625/626),[16] Cyprus (7th and 8th centuries), and Carthage in the west (the sherds there being dated shortly before 698).[17] A few examples have been

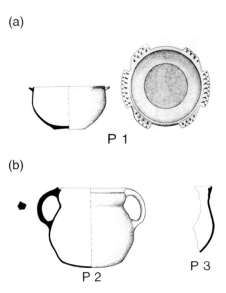

Figure 6.3 (a) Glazed White Ware I from Yassi Ada (With acknowledgements to Bass, 1982). (b) Glazed White Ware I from Yassi Ada (With acknowledgements to Bass, 1982).

found too in areas of Asia Minor.[18] Recovery of Glazed White Wares outside Constantinople, especially during the early phase of its production (7th–8th centuries), undoubtedly attests to contacts that the capital had with the largest peripheral cities, like Corinth, Gortyn, or Carthage. Beyond these, its recovery in sites of small size and of minor importance – according to the present data, such as Melos, Kythera, Pseira, Agia Galini, or Itanos – is a matter which deserves attention and can lead to interesting developments.

The few sherds of this pottery found in the Aegean were not necessarily objects of commerce, but could be mislaid personal possessions of traders. Their recovery, however, can still define the maritime routes which, during the 7th and 8th centuries, seem to have connected Constantinople with large port cities. In their journeying ships made stops at several islands and islets. The discovery of these vases in these small islands could point to the location of safe havens for the ships at that time.

Amphorae

If Glazed White Wares may indicate contacts between the two regions, then recovery of transport vessels constitutes the incontestable proof for these contacts.

Recent research into the time period from the 4th until the 7th centuries has provided revealing evidence for amphora-production centres, maritime routes and, as a consequence, the commercial relations between regions.[19]

However, for the 7th–9th centuries, comparable information on the production centres and typology of amphorae is scarce, and what does exist is of very recent recovery. During the past 15 years Greek and foreign archaeologists, who specialise in the Byzantine period, have been studying pottery systematically, using various scientific analytical processes that investigate fabrics and pottery workshops. Thus informed, they have proceeded to ask the right questions and have received, in return, interesting answers. Moreover, underwater archaeological investigations have provided important data on transport vessels of that period.[20]

It is well known that throughout the first half of the 7th century, the large pottery production centres continue to turn out those types of vessels that we have come to call 'international', since they carried agricultural produce throughout the entire Mediterranean, including, of course, the Aegean.[21] This exchange of goods over long distances continued largely unaltered until the middle of the 7th century. Indeed the activities of important regions such as Syria, Palestine, Egypt, and Tunisia expanded: their agricultural produce, 'packaged' in amphorae, travelled from one side of the Mediterranean to the other.[22] This picture changes around the middle of the 7th century because of the rise of Islam. From then on, significant changes in the Empire's frontiers, and thus size, took place; particularly so in the East, which provided many of these agricultural goods. Excavations reflect these territorial changes. This is as true for the ceramics as for other material classes – the territorial losses saw the loss of established production centres. New ones took their place; others increased their output; and a fresh suite of ceramics is the result.

Many of the amphorae from the wider Mediterranean production centres are no longer present in the Aegean.[23] At the same time (in the early 7th century), the so-called 'LRA1 imitations' take centre stage, although the production of LRA1 proper continues throughout the 7th century in Cyprus.[24] The LRA 1 'imitations' have the same elongated shape as their forerunners, but employ different clays. Three pottery production centres of this type of amphora have been found in Kardamaina on the island of Cos. Two of them are identified by pottery wasters.[25] In the third workshop the kiln has been preserved, and is dateable to the mid-7th century.[26] By the late 8th century appeared the amphorae that belong to Hayes' type 45 (the so called 'survivals' of type LRA 1): they too always keep to an elongated shape, but they are made carelessly and their fabrics use a significant variety of clays. Their production goes on through all the 8th and 9th centuries. Vessels of this type have been found in Saraçhane (in present-day Istanbul), at Philippi, at Ierissos in the Chalkidike, in Emporio on Chios, at Herakleion in Crete, as well as on the small islet of Pseira off its north coast.[27] The pottery workshop unearthed on the island of Lipsoi produced transport vessels which belong early in the repertoire of this group of amphorae (Hayes' type 45) (Figure 6.4).[28] An important source for these transport vessels is the cargo ship that was wrecked in the 9th century at Bozburun in Turkey (Figure 6.5).[29] Moreover, during the 8th and the 9th centuries the ovoid amphorae appear (Figure 6.6).[30]

84 *Natalia Poulou-Papadimitriou*

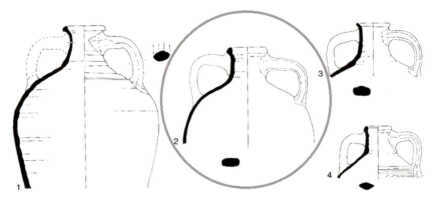

Figure 6.4 Amphora from Saraçhane, type Hayes 45 (With acknowledgements to Hayes (1992); adapted by author).

Figure 6.5 Amphora from Bojburun shipwreck. Type Hayes 45/survival of LRA1 (https://nauticalarch.org/projects/bozburun-byzantine-shipwreck-excavation/).

Figure 6.6 Ovoid amphora from the excavation at Pseira (author created).

What most characterises this period, however, is the abundance of almost globular-shaped amphorae. So far as typology is concerned, a new type or, more precisely, a new family of transport vessels with common morphological characteristics, appeared during the 7th century (Figure 6.7a, 6.7b).[31] These vessels have been found at several sites and in contexts that also date beyond the 7th century. They comprise the characteristic amphorae of 7th- and 8th-centuries levels in all of the sites where pottery has been studied. They have been found at Saraçhane in Constantinople, in Philippi, in Thessalonike, at Thasos, Samos and Chios, on the Yassi Ada shipwreck, at Melos, Corinth, Aegina and Kythera.[32] Globular amphorae from three

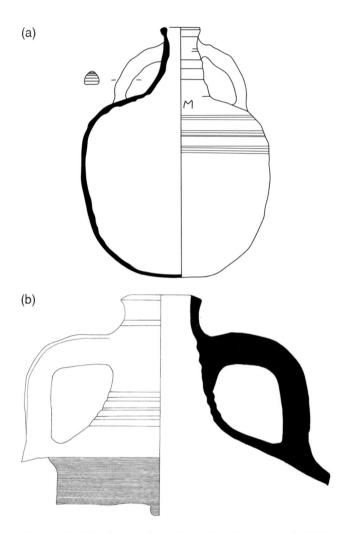

Figure 6.7 Globular amphora from Eupalinos tunnel (With acknowledgements to Hautumm (1981); adapted by author). (b) Globular amphora from Cos (author created with Sophia Didioumi, 2010).

different production centres have been unearthed in Kardamaina on the island of Cos.[33] Examples exist from very many sites on Crete as well: Eleutherna, Herakleion, Knossos, Gortyn, in the settlement of Agia Galini in the south coast, but also at the settlement of Priniatikos Pyrgos in the Gulf of Mirabello on the northeast coast, on the islet of Mochlos, and finally again on the small island of Pseira.[34]

In the materials of the 8th century we can distinguish the globular amphorae from those that now have a more elongated and ovoid shape below, but still retain the globular upper part of the body. This vessel type (i.e., the ovoid amphorae) is predominant during the 9th century (Figure 6.6).[35] Examples of such in Crete come from the modern town of Moires not far from Gortyn, from the island of Pseira and from Itanos.[36] A part of the shipwreck cargo at Bozburun consisted of this type of amphorae, while a similar transport vessel, dated to the 8th–9th centuries, has been found during the excavations at the Theodosian Harbour at Yeni Kapı.[37]

Regarding the globular amphorae, it was remarked above that they also appear outside the Aegean as the staple transport vessel for this period: in Byzantine Italy, Asia Minor, Cyprus, North Africa, Egypt, but also Syria under the Arabs, with which Byzantium appears to retain trading contacts.[38] All of these globular amphorae are strikingly homogenous in form. Small differences do occur in the shape of the handles, neck, and rim, calling for sub-classification into different types. However, what is most striking is the large variety of fabrics.[39]

The study of these amphorae not only outlines their typological developments, but offers insights into the way agricultural produce was ordered and transported, all at the behest of the state. Globular amphorae, accordingly, became the main transport vessel from the late 7th into the 8th centuries across the Empire and in areas in contact with the same: a sort of ceramic *koine* results.[40] This widespread phenomenon suggests that something more than just imitation of a successful shape is responsible (as argued earlier for LRA2): perhaps new ship types and changes in the system of handling of the material, all under a revised protocol of state control, played an effective role too.[41]

Changes also occurred in the organisation of pottery production: these amphorae were not produced by just a few large centres, but in many smaller workshops located at several sites around the Aegean, the smaller islands, as well as Crete and Cyprus and Byzantine Italy, as was suggested as early as 2001.[42] The 7th-century pottery workshop and kiln in Cos, which produced globular amphorae, is the very first example to be excavated and published in the Aegean.[43] Among Pseira's material are examples that were produced in the wider district of Mochlos, just up the coast from the small island.[44]

From the 7th century onwards the new realities imposed changes on institutions and, to a smaller or greater extent depending on the region, on agricultural production and, consequently, on commerce. The various imported amphorae found at any specific site suggest trade contacts between this site and the outside. They also indicate a need to re-organise production on a different basis from previous ones. The Aegean, Crete, Cyprus, as well as Asia Minor, had now to produce those goods that were previously imported from distant provinces that were no longer part of the Empire (i.e., Syria, Egypt, and North Africa-Tunisia). Each region capable of agricultural production had to meet its needs in one or more goods and export its surplus, if any, to Constantinople, to military bases and to regions deficient in these particular goods.[45] The Yassi Ada shipwreck (*terminus post quem*: 625/626) provides an eloquent example: during its last voyage, the ship collected amphorae from many different sites, as indicated by their various shapes and fabrics.[46]

All of this then demonstrates not merely the continuance of trade from the late 7th into the 9th centuries, but even its enhancement within and without the borders of Byzantine control. The *communis opinio* is in error. Both written sources and archaeological evidence combine to illustrate the robustness of trade in the 8th century.[47]

Archaeological evidence for state organisation and dignitaries' mobility

Belt buckles – lead seals – coins

Other than the amphorae, which continue to be produced and to circulate during the 8th and 9th centuries, excavations have also produced bronze belt buckles, lead seals, and coins.

It is well known by now that bronze belt buckles were manufactured during the period under study (i.e., from the early 7th into the 9th centuries) in workshops within the Empire's boundaries[48] (Figure 6.8a–6.8d). During the last 15 years information about their typological and chronological development has increased, so that now these accessories not only inform us about the dressing habits of the Byzantines, but also constitute important relative chronological evidence for the archaeological contexts in which they

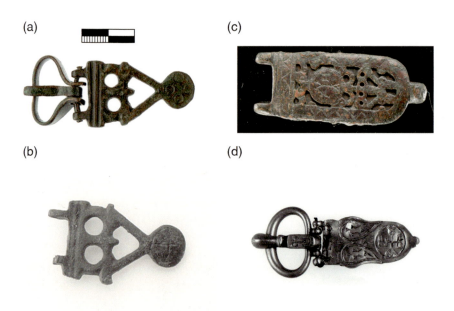

Figure 6.8 (a) Bronze belt buckle, Messara plain (author created, 2005). (b) Bronze belt buckle, Pseira island (author created, 2005). (c) Bronze belt buckle from Herakleion (author created, 2008). (d) Golden belt buckle from Crete (Ashmolean Museum), from 'Les plaques-boucles byzantines de l'île de Crète (fin VIe-IXe siècle)' by the author (2005).

are found. Their stylistic variety in combination with the material used for their production (iron, copper alloy, silver, or gold) argue that belt buckles were used by different groups in the population. Examples in precious metals are two gold belt buckles: one was found in southwest Crete in 1909 which is now in the collection of the Ashmolean Museum, Oxford, whilst the second one is from Kratigos, Mytilene, now in the collection of the Byzantine Museum, Athens.[49] The officers who wore these splendid buckles would have received them from the hands of the Emperor himself in a special ceremony, as proof of the important titles which they had received.[50]

Excavations at Early Byzantine sites like Corinth, Athens, the islets in the Gulf of the Argolid, the islands Kythera, Samos, Rhodes, Amorgos ('Pyrgos', Agia Triada), and Delos, the sites in Crete like Herakleion, Chersonesos, Gortyn, Eleutherna, and the islet of Pseira, but also sites such as Anemourion and Amorion in Asia Minor, have recovered a variety of buckle types (very simple or more ornate)[51] (Figure 6.8a–6.8d). It is possible to conclude that some of these accessories were possibly used by dignitaries of the administration and the army. Their recovery is consequently important, because they constitute valuable evidence for the organisation of the state and the mobility of its dignitaries.[52]

Finds such as the lead seals confirm again the mobility of dignitaries, or more precisely their documents, as well as the state's organisation. Lead seals belonging to officials responsible for taxation, for example, constitute important evidence not only for the movement of goods in the Aegean and Crete but primarily for the control exercised by the state on the commercial transactions.[53]

The seals demonstrate the presence of *kommerkiarioi* (κομμερκιάριοι) and other officers charged with tax collection, already at the end of the 7th century, on the islands of the Aegean and Crete.[54] These governmental agents were responsible for keeping transport and exchange under state inspection. The island of Amorgos looks as though it housed a regular naval station.[55] Lead seals of the 7th century show that *kommerkiarioi* controlled taxation in the Cyclades, as they mention their *apothēkai* (ἀποθῆκαι), or state warehouses (687/689 and 696/697).[56] It is interesting that a seal of the 8th century (713/714) mentions the *genikos kommerkiarios Ioannis* (γενικός κομμερκιάριος Ἰωάννης) associated with the *apothēkē* of the *Aigaion Pelagos* (ἀποθήκη Αἰγαίου Πελάγους).[57] Moreover, seals of the 8th century mention the *vasilika kommerkia* (βασιλικά κομμέρκια), such as those of Melos (730/731), the islands of the *Aigaion Pelagos* (734/735?), and the *dioikisis* of Melos (διοίκησις Μήλου), along with Thera, Anaphe, Ios, and Amorgos (738/739).[58]

Among the published lead seals there are many important ones for the history of the administration in the island of Crete during the 8th and 9th centuries[59]: inscribed seals mention the *apothēkē* (688/690 and 694–696) as well as the *vasilika kommerkia* of Crete (τῶν βασιλικῶν κομμερκίων Κρήτης) (730–741).[60] Moreover, three seals – two of them found during excavations, the other one a confiscation – are important for the direct or indirect

90   *Natalia Poulou-Papadimitriou*

connection of Crete with the capital during the 8th and 9th centuries. The lead seal of the emperor Tiberios III (698–705) – confiscated in Herakleion but found in the wider area of Messara – is the very first imperial seal found in Crete[61]; and the seal of Baanes *patrikios, magistros,* and *komes* [of the imperial Opsikion] 'Βαάνη, πατρικίῳ μαγίστρῳ καί κόμιτι [τοῦ θεοφυλάκτου βασιλικοῦ Οψικίου]', dated to the first half of the 8th century, which came to light at Priniatikos Pyrgos, Mirabello Bay,[62] testify to the close relations of the island with Constantinople. It must be emphasised that the *komes* of Opsikion was one of the most important military commanders, responsible for north-western Anatolia as well the capital.[63]

The third lead seal belonged to a dignitary connected with the imperial court, who held the functions of *vestitor* and that of *protonotarios* ('Ιωάννη βεστίτορι καί πρωτονοταρίῳ τοῦ βασιλικοῦ σακελλίου): dated between the late 8th and the mid-9th centuries, it was found on the eastern slope of the acropolis of Knossos.[64] This seal is significant for understanding the Cretan administrative history before the Arab invasion as well as for the continuity of life at Knossos – with the necessary administrative organisation and closest relations to the central government.[65] It seems then that Knossos – or at least the hill with the acropolis – continued to be inhabited[66] at the same time that Khantax/Herakleion was a fortified town.[67] On the other hand all these seals show that Crete was integrated into the administrative system of the Empire during the transitional period.

Of 8th-century date is one more lead seal, found on the island of Kythera, during the excavation of the site of Agios Georgios sto Vouno.[68] This seal belonged to an officer Baanes (distinct from the *patrikios* Baanes mentioned above). His title of από ἐπάρχων is usually attributed to the officers who generally oversaw public workshops or who were responsible for the collection of trade tariffs.[69] The mobility of the officers is also demonstrated by the seals, which have turned up on many of the islets in the Gulf of the Argolid and date chiefly to the 8th century.[70]

These classes of finds discussed above express vividly the mobility of state officials in the Aegean and Crete throughout the 7th, 8th, and 9th centuries. They also reveal the care of the central administration for the secure transfer of essential products, and also the control of manufacture in a period when the shipping routes were dangerous due to the presence of the Arabs.

Concerning the currency, it is known that the 7th-century coins, particularly the *folles* of Heraclius and Constans II, clearly outnumber those from the 8th and early 9th centuries.[71] It has been argued that 7th-century coins' circulation and usage went on well beyond their issue, possibly well into the 8th century.[72] The example of Agios Georgios on Kythera is instructive: whilst eight coins of Heraclius and ten of Constans II came to light – many of them clipped and carelessly struck – not a single coin of the 8th century was recovered. But there is other 8th-century material there, in the shape of two lead seals and an important amount of pottery. Items relevant to activity there in the 9th century involve again pottery, and also a *follis* of Leo V (date of issue 813–820). One may observe then that, despite the lack of coins, the rest of the archaeological material provides ample evidence to support activity at Agios Georgios sto Vouno throughout the 8th and 9th centuries, whilst at the same time links are confirmed to have existed with the Aegean and Constantinople.[73] This is corroborated by archaeological finds across the Aegean and Crete.[74]

Maritime routes in the Aegean: islands, coastal settlements, havens, and anchorages: some case studies

At this point it is of interest to summarise the case studies concerning some of the sites where the archaeological evidence was found and so better determine their character (Figure 6.1).

1 Excavations and/or survey research on the islands and islets of the Gulf of the Argolid have provided interesting archaeological evidence of belt buckles and lead seals dated from the 7th to 8th centuries. Moreover, architectural remains and pottery dated to the same period were found in all these places.[75] The link to the neighbouring coast must have been unbroken and of foremost importance ensuring uninterrupted activity on all these islands.[76]

2 Aghios Georgios sto Vouno is a minor site on the east coast of Kythera (Figure 6.9a–6.9c). During the 7th century, a fortified settlement with a water cistern was situated on the hill top. Small-sized constructions are also set on the south slopes. All these architectural remains were constructed in the 7th century and remained in use during the 8th century too, as attested by the *folles* of Heraclius and of Constans II, as well as by pottery found during the excavation. This settlement carried on its activity during the 8th and 9th centuries. The 8th-century lead seal and the *follis* of Leo V (813–820), as well as pottery from the same layers, comprise the archaeological evidence for activity at this specific site for the period under study. This complex seems to work as a point of control for the harbours of Palaiopolis and Avlemon/ Agios Nikolaos. At the same time from the hill top it is possible to oversee almost the whole seascape between Crete and Kythera; in a sense, then, also the access from the western Mediterranean into the Aegean. It should be emphasised that during the period examined, the route to the West was of utmost importance to the Byzantines.[77]

3 On the other side of the Aegean the fortified settlement of Emporio, on its peninsula in south-east Chios, is dated to the reign of Constans II.[78] In Samos the fortification of a part of the ancient town, namely the low hill found right next to the harbour, dates from the 7th century as well.[79] During the same period (the mid-7th century) there was created, on the top of Mount Ampelos (Lazaros), a fortified settlement,[80] which probably func- tioned as a permanent watch-post for the wider maritime area (Figure 6.10a, 6.10b). The amphorae found on Samos (in excavations in the Heraion,

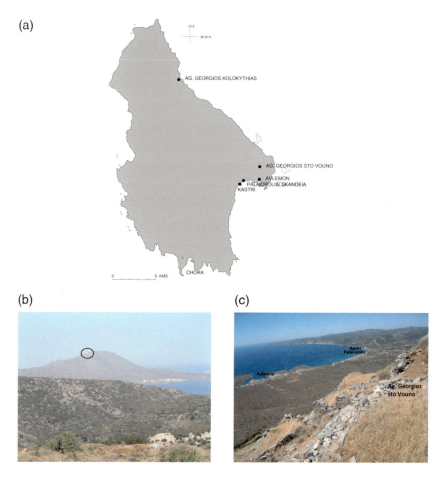

Figure 6.9 (a) The island of Kythera (author created). (b) Agios Georgios sto Vouno and Palaiopolis (Photograph by the author). (c) Agios Georgios sto Vouno and Palaiopolis (Photograph by the author).

Pythagoreion, and Eupalinos Tunnel, as well surface finds from the fortified settlement of Lazaros) date from the mid-7th and the 8th centuries, and some of them are probably of local manufacture. These vases carried goods produced in Samos in the same period.[81]

4 As we have already noted, Crete, was, after the mid-7th and until the 9th century, the southern border of the Byzantine Empire. This situation rendered Crete a very important island for the control of maritime traffic, especially during this period, when the Arabs arrive at the heart of the Aegean. The value that the central government put on strengthening the island is shown by the fact too that parts of the major cities – inland, like Gortyn and Eleutherna or coastal, like Herakleion and Kydonia/Chania – were walled in the 7th

Figure 6.10 (a) Pseira Island (Photograph by the author). (b) Pseira Island (Photograph by the author).

century, whilst simultaneously life outside the walls of the city went on (e.g., around Gortyn and Eleutherna).[82] Activity in those cities as well in Knossos and Chersonesos continued on throughout the 8th and in some cases at least into the start of the 9th century. The new element is that these cities are now fortified.

94   *Natalia Poulou-Papadimitriou*

5 The end of the 7th century found small settlements and coastal facilities in full swing in Crete. The Pseira island settlement, endowed with a water reservoir, is set on the south part of the islet, overlooking the small safe anchorage below (Figure 6.11a, 6.11b). This cove still attracts small boats in cases of bad weather conditions, due to the lack of a safe harbour on the Cretan coast opposite. The main phase dates to the late 7th and the 8th centuries, while archaeological evidence suggested that human activity continued through the 9th century. Pseira served as an anchorage for the Byzantine ships and the ceramic material reflects contacts with many areas in the Aegean and with Constantinople.[83] These small islands acted as reference points for ships on their journeying in the Aegean, exactly as did the islet of 'Ta Christiana' in the voyage of the Byzantine fleet to Crete in 949.

6 In the same area of Crete (i.e., the north-east coast), on the peninsula of Priniatikos Pyrgos, near the modern village of Kalo Chorio, an Early Byzantine settlement has been unearthed, whose main phase is dated to the 8th and 9th centuries. Although the excavations in the area are in progress, an interesting case study is the identification of small rectangular spaces excavated on the rocky peninsula, as storage units. This identification was corroborated by the finding of trade amphorae, a lead seal that show state control over this installation, and a *miliaresion*, a rare find in the 8th century. More precisely, the recovery in this same layer of a lead seal belonging to an official of the 8th century, as well as the *miliaresion* [of Leo III and Constantine V (720–741)],[84] substantiate the suggestion, already put forward, that, despite the Arab raids, or even in view of them, the central authority enhanced its contacts with Crete through the 8th century, creating safe berthing areas and arranging full command over agricultural produce and the movement of goods. These coastal sites were able to act as points of entry for produce to and from the mainland: they played an important role in the transport of produce and in maritime communications.[85]

Conclusion

The facts, already set forth, enable the following conclusions to be made. The Byzantines knew that the Aegean was vital to them. In the Archipelago new conditions were created by the strong Arab presence. It is exactly this change in the *status quo* that forced the central government to redesign the control mechanisms of production and the collection of taxes, while at the same time protecting the passages between the islands of the Aegean and strengthening every harbour, bay or even cove, which was useful in ensuring a safe journey, and the docking and the supply of the mercantile and military fleets.

These islands and coastal areas were not by any means detached from the mainland, but remained in direct contact with it, comprising indeed a vital part of it, for instance even the islets of the Argolic Gulf. We believe that

Figure 6.11 (a) Pseira island: the cistern (Photograph by the author). (b) Mochlos, Loutres: the cistern (Photograph by the author).

96   *Natalia Poulou-Papadimitriou*

these could not have supported a human presence for any length of time without there being a direct connection and communication with that part of the Peloponnesian coast directly opposite to them. Not only the important ports but also minor gulfs or bays on islets, fitted out to provide shelter even for the smallest number of ships, were protected; small-scale settlements were founded, each equipped with water cisterns. Some of these islands and islets were used as naval stations for the Byzantine fleet, such as those of 'Ta Christiana' and 'Dia', on the path of the fleet's sailing to Crete against the Arabs, according to the *Stadiodromikon* in 949.[86]

The majority of these settlements continued to exist not only through the 7th but also into the 8th and the 9th centuries. The scarcity of coin evidence among the finds is compensated for by the systematic study of pottery from this period (7th–9th centuries), which is essential for the dating of the sites.

Furthermore, the archaeological evidence indicates that the state could and did control maritime routes, whether commercial or military, even at this troubled time when the Arab threat was omnipresent. It was exactly because of the Arab threat that the Byzantines took care to reinforce the defence of Crete and the Aegean islands. They knew that every safe harbour or small gulf could prove useful in case of need. Also, it seems that the central government took care, gradually between the 7th and the 9th centuries, to organise a system for controlling and storing produce (e.g., seals with reference to specific warehouses, storage areas in coastal areas), and managing product distribution. Agricultural production was so important that specific documents were issued and officials were sent to the provinces for *in situ* inspection and organisation. Aside from the well-sized cities of the period under study, such as Corinth or Gortyn, material evidence has been recovered from small coastal settlements, which were until recently considered to have been abandoned at the time. These coastal sites must have served as gateways for produce moving to and from the mainland, whilst at the same time playing a vital role in the transferral of material and in maritime communication.

Material evidence from the above-mentioned areas suggests relative ease of movement on the Aegean sea-routes during the 7th, 8th, and 9th centuries, that is to say, contact between the centre and the periphery. The historical circumstances related to the 7th and to the 8th centuries differ considerably, however.

In the mid-7th century, Constans II clearly attached importance to the western provinces of the Empire, attending in person to the creation of safe passages for the fleet through the Aegean Sea; Emporio in Chios being a typical case in point. At the same time the central government took care to reinforce places of observation for the control of the sea routes, Agios Georgios sto Vouno on Kythera being one such. Many other fortified sites, as well watch-posts, dated to the 7th century onwards have been excavated in the Aegean and in Crete.[87]

The 8th century and the reign of Leo III (commencing with the siege of Constantinople by the Arabs in 717 AD), lead to immediate action being taken by the emperor, formation of the theme of the *Kibyrrhaiotai* being part of it. Meanwhile he reinforced coastal sites and passages in the Aegean, particularly in the Cyclades and on the island of Crete. Crete in particular seems in the 8th century to have enjoyed a close and even privileged relationship with the central authority, as is attested by the archaeological finds (fortified enclosures, lead seals, coinage, buckles, pots). The date of the creation of the theme of Crete (θέμα Κρήτης), before the Arab conquest or not, is a topic that has been extensively discussed among researchers, who have expressed opposing views.[88] But whatever the view that will be finally proven correct, the fact is that in the 8th century, the care on the part of the central government to strengthen and protect the Aegean created new conditions on the island and boosted activity in the urban centres and the coastal facilities.

In the same period, the state made clear its intention and its ability to take control of commerce and exchanges: the recovery of the lead seals of *kommerkiarii, apothēkai,* and *vasilika kommerkia* in several Aegean sites – a few of which, such as Anaphi, right in the middle of the Archipelago – provide substantial proof. The identification of specific areas in coastal locations as being for storage (warehouses) points in this direction. Furthermore it is within the organisation of a better control of the flow of produce that the new family of globular amphorae should find its place, vases which are used *par excellence* for the transfer of goods to all the corners of the Empire.

One should always bear in mind that the Aegean was in fact the heart of the Empire, and that ensuring safe passage through it constituted a prerequisite for the safety of the capital itself. Archaeological evidence, constantly updated, will further illustrate the maritime routes through the Aegean islands during this transitional period of Byzantium.

Notes

1 Wickham 2005: 780.
2 Haldon 1990: 97–99; Haldon 1995; Brandes 1999: 25–57; Brubaker and Haldon 2011; Wickham 2005.
3 Hayes 1992; Kingsley and Decker 2001; Sanders 2004: 163–194; important here too are the *BAR International Series LRCW 1–4, Archaeology and Archaeometry,* 2003, 2007, 2010, 2014; for the island of Kythira during this period, the maritime routes and the ceramic evidence, cf. Poulou-Papadimitriou 2013: 25–266; Gabrieli, Jackson, and Kaldelli 2007: 791–801.
4 Professor Zanini has worked on Gortyn: his findings are presented in this same volume.
5 Glazed White Ware is the Constantinopolitan ware in a white fabric with glaze, first produced in Constantinople during the 7th century.
6 Hayes 1992: 12–34; Poulou-Papadimitriou 2020: 365–375.
7 Slane and Sanders 2005: 273–280, Fig. 11.4-1.
8 Felten 1975: 74–76, nos. 151–158, pl. 20, Fig. 28.
9 Poulou-Papadimitriou: 2013: 87–92.
10 Sanders, 1996, 148; Dafi 2005: 272.
11 Poulou-Papadimitriou, forthcoming. For the excavation, cf. Borboudakis 1968: 427–429. For the results of the recent excavation in the early Byzantine fortifications in Herakleion, see Sythiakaki, Kanaki, and Bilmezi 2015: 395–410.

98 Natalia Poulou-Papadimitriou

12 Di Vita 1993: 351–355; Zanini *et al.* 2015: 565–574.
13 Vogt 1994: 68, 72; Sidiropoulos 1994: 75–78. The GWW I piece from Agia Galini was published as a cooking pot; in the drawing, the vessel was restored with two small lug handles. See Vogt 1994: 68. With the permission of the excavator, I. Gavrilaki, archaeologist in the EFA of Chania, I have examined the vessel and found that it is a glazed ceramic, with hard, light grey clay and a greenish, matt glaze on the inner surface and the rim. It is a vase which had two relatively large handles, similar to that published by the excavations of Saraçhane and ranked by the excavator in the GWWI category. This vessel is thus imported from Constantinople. Cf. Poulou-Papadimitriou 2011: 394–395. For the same sorts of vessels from Saraçhane, see Hayes 1992: 18, Fig. 38.1-2.
14 Xanthopoulou 2015: 585–593, and esp. 585–586; Xanthopoulou *et al.* 2014: 811; Poulou-Papadimitriou and Nodarou, 2014: 876–877. It has been argued that the town of Itanos did not survive after the first decades of the 7th century: see Tsigonaki 2009: 172–174.
15 Poulou-Papadimitriou 2001: 238–240, Figs. 7–8; Poulou-Papadimitriou 2011: 394, Fig. 11a, b.
16 Bass 1982: 165–167, Figs. 8–9, P1-P4.
17 For Cyprus and Carthage, see Hayes 1980: 375–380 and especially 375–379.
18 Böhlendorf-Arslan 2004: 97–99.
19 Peacock and Williams 1986; Reynolds 1995; Bonifay 2004; Eiring and Lund 2004; Pieri 2005; cf. also *LRCW* 1–4 (Oxford 2005, 2007, 2010, 2014).
20 See note 3; important for the typology of transport vessels dated from the transitional period are the finds from the shipwrecks of Yassi Ada and Bozburun, as well as those from the excavation at Yeni Kapı, Istanbul, cf. Bass 1982; Hocker, Yamini, and Yamini 1998: 3–13; Pekin *et al.* 2007: 260–269; for the shipwrecks, cf. Kocabaş, 2008.
21 See note 19; Poulou 2017: 195–200.
22 Poulou 2017: 195–200, with bibliography.
23 Some types, like LRA 4 and LRA 5/6 from Palestine, no longer reach the regions surrounding the Aegean, whilst others, such as LRA3, have fallen out of production by the beginning of the 7th century, cf. Bezeczky 2010: 351–358, for LR3 amphorae see 355.
24 Armstrong 2009: 163–164; Demesticha 2003: 473–474; on imitations of LRA 1, cf. *Poulou-Papadimitriou and Nodarou 2014*: 875. In this earlier study we had considered the amphora from Lipsoi workshop as LRA 1 *imitations*. We tend to believe now that these vessels date later and are characterised as belonging to the Hayes' 45 type (*survivals* of LRA 1, cf. present study).
25 In the excavation at the Aghia Theotita basilica, amphorae wasters and moulds for clay lamps are evidence for the existence of a pottery workshop: see Diamanti 2010. In the basilica of Presbyter Photeinos (Πρεσβυτέρος Φωτεινός), dated from mid-5th to the second half of 7th centuries, there are indications for the production of amphorae: Brouscari 2011.
26 Poulou-Papadimitriou and Didioumi 2010: 741–749.
27 Hayes 1992: 73, type 45, Fig. 58.16; Poulou-Papadimitriou, forthcoming; for examples from Veria, Chalkidice, Emporio, Herakleion, and Pseira, cf. Poulou-Papadimitriou and Nodarou 2014: 875.
28 Papavasileiou, Sarantidis, and Papanikolaou 2014: 159–168.
29 Hocker, Yamini, and Yamini 1998: 5, Fig. 3, Class 1.
30 Poulou-Papadimitriou and Nodarou 2014: 874–875; Poulou 2017: 200.
31 Poulou-Papadimitriou 2014: 138–140; Poulou 2017: 207.
32 Hayes 1992: 66–73, Figs. 23.3–13, 25.1; for examples from Greece cf. Poulou-Papadimitriou 2001: 243–248; Poulou-Papadimitriou 2013: 116–118; Poulou-Papadimitriou and Didioumi 2010: 743–744; Poulou-Papadimitriou, forthcoming.

33 For the production centres of the island of Cos, cf. notes 25, 26; Poulou-Papadimitriou and Didioumi 2010: 741–749; Poulou-Papadimitriou and Didioumi 2015: 401–418; Didioumi 2014: 169–180.

34 See note 23; for Priniatikos Pyrgos, cf. Klontza-Jaklova 2014: 135–142; cf. also the communication of Tzavella: 2015.

35 Poulou-Papadimitriou and Nodarou 2014: 874–875.

36 For Pseira, Moires, and Herakleion, cf. Poulou-Papadimitriou and Nodarou 2014: 874–875; Poulou-Papadimitriou 2011: 400–406, Figs. 18–20; for Itanos, cf. Xanthopoulou 2015: 585–593.

37 Hocker, Yamini, and Yamini 1998: 5, Fig. 3, class 4; an amphora of the same type, dated in the 8th–9th centuries, has been presented in the Archaeological Museum of Istanbul in the exhibition with the finds from excavations in the city during the construction of the Marmaray and Metro Projects (June 2009).

38 Poulou-Papadimitriou 2001: 246; Poulou-Papadimitriou and Didioumi 2010: 743–744; Poulou-Papadimitriou and Nodarou 2014: 874.

39 The results of the petrographic analysis of the globular amphorae from Pseira, for example, are most telling in this regard. Out of the 20 identified examples, 15 have a different clay composition. Of these, five were made locally on Crete: see Poulou-Papadimitriou and Nodarou 2014: 873–883; Poulou 2017: 203; the remaining examples originate from other Aegean sites. The same diversity was noted, though on a greater scale, in other Cretan sites (i.e., Gortyn, see Portale and Romeo 2001: 260–410) as well as in Saraçhane: Hayes 1992: 66–67, 71–73; Yassi Ada: Bass 1982: 157–165, Figs. 8.4, 8.5, 8.6; Van Doorninck 1989: 247–253, Figs. 1, 2; S. Antonino di Perti: Murialdo 2001: 286–295, pls. 17–19; and Crypta Balbi: Sagui, Ricci, and Romei 1997: 36–38, Figs. 2.4, 2.5, 2.6.

40 Poulou-Papadimitriou 2001: 247; Poulou-Papadimitriou 2018: 39.

41 Poulou-Papadimitriou 2018: 39.

42 Poulou-Papadimitriou 2001: 247. I had first expressed such an opinion at the conference '*The Dark Ages of Byzantium*' in May 1999.

43 For production centres on the island of Cos, cf. notes 25 and 26.

44 Poulou-Papadimitriou and Nodarou 2014: 875–876.

45 Poulou 2017: 204–205.

46 Bass 1982: 157–165, Figs. 8.4, 8.5, 8.6; Van Doorninck 1989: 247–253, Figs. 1, 2; see also Poulou, 2017: 206.

47 The 8th-century *Vita of Pangratius of Taormina* (a saint of the 1st century AD) talks of traders (πραγματευταί) sailing between Sicily and Jerusalem, and mentions, as items of import to Sicily, carpets from Asia, olive oil from Crete, incense and wine from the islands cf. Laiou 2002: 697–770 and especially 708, n. 50.

48 Poulou-Papadimitriou 2005: 687–704, with bibliography.

49 Poulou-Papadimitriou 2005: 695, 697–698, Fig. 11; Touratsoglou and Chalkia 2008: 116–117. This belt buckle from Kratigos is dated in the 6th–7th centuries by Touratsoglou and Chalkia. We are in favour of a date from the 7th century onwards.

50 Kazanski and Sodini 1987: 80, Fig. 11; Werner 1984: 21.

51 For examples from all these sites, see Poulou-Papadimitriou 2005: 687–704, with bibliography. Recent research in Herakleion has uncovered two more examples published in Poulou-Papadimitriou 2008: 155, Fig. 4, 5, 5a. In the Archaeological Museum of Heraklion, there are some 16 Byzantine belt buckles, coming from the wider region of the Messara. These finds were confiscated by the police force in 2000: see Poulou-Papadimitriou 2005: 692. For the examples found in Rhodes see Nika 2014: 333–358. Two belt buckles were uncovered during the excavation of 'Pyrgos' at Agia Triada on Amorgos: cf. Marangou 2005: Figs. 58.3, 66.6-7, on 59, 67. These bronze belt buckles, of Corinth and of Bologna types, constitute

100   *Natalia Poulou-Papadimitriou*

evidence for the mobility and the presence of dignitaries in the island of Amorgos during the 7th and the 8th centuries. For the seven bronze belt buckles uncovered on Delos – one of them of Corinth type (8th-century) – see Deonna 1938: 239, pl. 77, no. 638, 296, Figs. 366-67, pl. 88, nos. 758-63.

52 Poulou-Papadimitriou 2005: 703–704.
53 Montinaro 2013: 351–538; Haldon 2012: 99–122. See also Brandes 2002.
54 For the sources of this period, see Leontsini 2017.
55 Touratsoglou 1999: 351–352.
56 Zacos and Veglery 1972: 126–128, no. 42.5; Montinaro 2013: nos. 39, 96, on 457, 482. See also Cosentino 2013: 65–76 and especially 72.
57 Montinaro 2013: 495, no. 129; Zacos and Veglery 1972: no. 213, on 162, Table 17; Nesbitt and Oikonomides 1994: no. 40.23.
58 Zacos and Veglery 1972: no. 242, on 192, 194, Table 34, no. 249, on 162, Table 17 and on 192, Table 34.
59 Tsougarakis 1990: 143–144; Touratsoglou, Koltsida-Makri, and Nikolaou 2006: 49–68; Starida 1984: 45–51.
60 Zacos and Veglery 1972: no. 189, on 166, 190, Table 19, 33; Ragia 2011: 99–108. It is interesting that the lead seal that referred to the *apotheke* of Asia, Karia, Lykia, Rhodes and Chersonesos is proposed to mean the Chersonesos of Crete, cf. Brandes 2002: 536–537, no. 129; this proposition is accepted by Montinaro 2013: 460, no. 44, 477, no. 84. See also Haldon 2012: 112–113.
61 Touratsoglou, Koltsida-Makri, and Nikolaou 2006: 50, no. I.1
62 Lead seal of 8th century: +Βαάνῃ, πατρικ(ίῳ) μαγίστρ(ῳ) κ(αί) κόμιτ(ι) [τοῦ θεοφυλάκτου βασιλικοῦ Οψικίου] cf. Hayden and Tsipopoulou 2012: 578–579, no. 3i, Fig. 5 (after Professor Werner Seibt).
63 Touratsoglou, Koltsida-Makri, and Nikolaou 2006: 50, no. I.1.
64 Dunn 2004: 139–146.
65 Dunn 2004: 143–144.
66 Dunn 2004: 144; Touratsoglou, Koltsida-Makri, and Nikolaou 2006: 52–53, nos. 4–7, four seals of late 7th/8th centuries with the mention of πόλεως Κνωσοῦ; Sidiropoulos 2004b: 651–653.
67 Poulou-Papadimitriou 2011: 385.
68 Penna 2013: 421, 427, 452, n. 1, 5; Poulou-Papadimitriou 2013: 168–177.
69 Penna 2013: 427.
70 Avramea 1997: 99; on the islands of Spetses, Dokos, Daskalio, Korakonisi, Chinitsa, and Plateia were found 21 lead seals of Byzantine dignitaries.
71 Nikolaou 2004: 298–300; Nikolaou 2010: 78–80; Poulou-Papadimitriou 2018: 34.
72 Haldon 2012: 112, with previous bibliography.
73 Poulou-Papadimitriou 2013: 168–177.
74 Dunn 2004: 145; Sidiropoulos 2004a: 193–223.
75 Personal observations, after visiting the islets of Gulf of Argolis during the summers of 2012 and 2014.
76 On this subject, see also Nikolaou 2004: 301–302; Armstrong 2009: 177.
77 Poulou-Papadimitriou 2013: 25–266 and especially 46–57: 160–191.
78 Hood 1989: 7–8.
79 For this information, I thank the former Director of the 27th Ephorate of Byzantine Antiquities, Mrs Olga Vassi.
80 Tsakos 1979: 13; Poulou-Papadimitriou 1985: 161–165.
81 Poulou-Papadimitriou 1985: 164, pl. 142.a,b; Poulou-Papadimitriou and Nodarou 2014: 874, 876. On the Heraion finds, cf. Kienast *et al.* 2017: 125–212.
82 See the present article, and Poulou, forthcoming.
83 Poulou-Papadimitriou and Nodarou 2007: 755–766; Poulou-Papadimitriou 2011: 387.

Maritime Routes in the Aegean (7th–9th Centuries) 101

84 For the lead seal see above and note 47; for the coin, cf. Sidiropoulos 2012: 13; Klontza-Jaklova 2014: 40.
85 Poulou-Papadimitriou 2014: 141.
86 Constantinus Porphyrogenitus, *De cerimoniis aulae byzantinae,* I.Reiske, ed., 2 vols, Bonn, 1829–1830: II, 45 (p. 678).
87 Poulou-Papadimitriou 2018, 40.
88 Tsougarakis 1988: 164–178; Kountoura-Galaki 2017. Recently, Brubaker and Haldon suggested also that the creation of the theme of Crete could be placed before the Arab conquest: cf. Brubaker and Haldon 2011: 761–762, n. 132.

ABBREVIATION: *LRCW 1,2,3,4* = *Late Roman Coarse Wares[1/2/3/4], Proceedings of the [] International Conference on Late Roman Coarse Wares, Cooking Wares and Amphorae in the Mediterranean: Archaeology and Archaeometry*

References

Armstrong, P. (2009), 'Trade in the East Mediterranean in the 8th Century', in M. Mango, ed., *Byzantine Trade, 4th-12th Centuries*, Farnham: 157–178.

Avramea, A. (1997), *Le Péloponnèse du IVe au VIIIe siècle: changements et persistances*. Byzantina Sorbonensia 15, Paris.

Bass, G. (1982), 'The pottery', in G. Bass and H. Van Doorninck, eds, *Yassi Ada I, A Seventh Century Byzantine Shipwreck*, College Station, Texas: 155–188.

Bezeczky, T. (2010), 'Trade connection between Ephesus and Adriatic region', *Histria Antiqua* 19: 351–358.

Böhlendorf-Arslan, B. (2004), *Glasierte byzantinische Keramik aus der Türkei*, 3 vols. Istanbul.

Bonifay, M. (2004), *Études sur la céramique romaine tardive d'Afrique*. B.A.R. International Series 1301, Oxford.

Borboudakis, E. (1968), 'Δοκιμαστική ανασκαφή Αγίου Πέτρου των Ενετών Ηρακλείου', *Archaiologikon Deltion* 23, *Chronika*: 427–429.

Brandes, W. (1999), 'Byzantine cities in the seventh and eighth centuries – different sources, different histories?', in G. Brogiolo and B. Ward-Perkins, eds., *The Idea and Ideal of the Town between Late Antiquity and the Early Middle Ages*, Leiden: 25–57.

Brandes, W. (2002), *Finanzverwaltung in Krizenzeiten. Untersuchungen zur byzantinischen Administration im 6.-9. Jahrhundert*. Forschungen zur byzantinischen Rechtsgeschichte 25, Frankfurt am Main.

Brouscari, E. (2011), *Συμβολή στην ιστορία και την αρχαιολογία της Κω κατά την παλαιοχριστιανική περίοδο: η βασιλική του πρεσβυτέρου Φωτεινού*, unpublished PhD thesis (University of Athens).

Brubaker, L., and Haldon, J. (2011), *Byzantium in the Iconoclast Era c. 680–850: a History*. Cambridge.

Cosentino, S. (2013), 'Mentality, technology and commerce: shipping amongst the Mediterranean Islands in Late Antiquity and beyond', in D. Michaelides, P. Pergola and E. Zanini, eds., *The Insular System of the Early Byzantine Mediterranean. Archaeology and History*, B.A.R. International Series 2523, Oxford: 65–76.

Dafi, E. (2005), *Thera and the Southern Aegean from Late Antiquity to Early Byzantium: pottery, production and sea-routes*, unpublished PhD thesis, The University of Birmingham.

Demesticha, S. (2003), 'Amphora Production on Cyprus during the Late Roman Period', in Ch. Bakirtzis, ed., *Actes du VIIe Congrès international sur la céramique médiévale en Méditerranée, Thessaloniki, 11–16 Octobre 1999*, Athens: 469–476.

102 *Natalia Poulou-Papadimitriou*

Deonna, W. (1938), *Le mobilier délien*, Exploration archéologique de Délos XVIII, Paris.

Diamanti, C. (2010), *Εντόπια παραγωγή και εισαγωγή αμφορέων στην Αλάσαρνα της Κω (5ος – 7ος αι.)*. Athens.

Didioumi, S. (2014), 'Local pottery production in the Island of Cos, Greece from the Early Byzantine period: a preliminary report', in N. Poulou-Papadimitriou, E. Nodarou, and V. Kilikoglou, eds., *Late Roman Coarse Wares 4: Late Roman Coarse Wares, Cooking Wares and Amphorae in the Mediterranean: Archaeology and Archaeometry. The Mediterranean Market without Frontiers (Thessaloniki, April 2011)*, B.A.R. International Series 2616, Oxford: 169–180.

Di Vita, A. (1993), 'Gortyna', *Annuario della scuola archeologica in Atene* 66–67 (1988–1989): 351–355.

Dunn, A. (2004), 'A Byzantine fiscal official's seal from Knossos excavations and the archaeology of Dark-Age cities', in M. Livadiotti and I. Simiakaki, eds., *Creta Romana e Protobizantina, Atti del Congresso Internazionale, Iraklion 23–30 settembre 2000*, vol. I, Padua: 139–146.

Eiring, J., and Lund, J. (2004), Transport amphorae and trade in the eastern Mediterranean. *Acts of the International Colloquium at the Danish Institute at Athens, September 26–29, 2002*, Monographs of the Danish Institute at Athens 5, Athens.

Felten, F. (1975), 'Die christliche Siedlung', in H. Walter, ed., *Alt-Ägina*, I.2, Mainz: 55–80.

Gabrieli, R., Jackson, M., and Kaldelli, A. (2007), 'Stumbling into the darkness: trade and life in post-Roman Cyprus', in M. Bonifay and J.-C. Tréglia, eds., *Late Roman Coarse Wares 2, Proceedings of the 2nd International Conference on Late Roman Coarse Wares, Cooking Wares and Amphorae in the Mediterranean: Archaeology and Archaeometry. (Aix-en-Provence-Marseille-Arles, 13th-16th April 2005)*, B.A.R. International Series 1662, Oxford: 791–801.

Haldon, J. (1995), *Byzantium in the Seventh Century. The Transformation of a Culture*, 2nd edition, Cambridge.

Haldon, J. (2012), 'Commerce and exchange in the seventh and eighth centuries. Regional trade and the movement of goods', in C. Morrisson, ed., *Trade and Markets in Byzantium*, Dumbarton Oaks Byzantine Symposia and Colloquia, Washington, DC: 99–122.

Hautumm, W. (1981), *Studien zu Amphoren der spätrömischen und frühbyzantinischen Zeit*. Bonn.

Hayden, B., and Tsipopoulou, M. (2012), 'The Priniatikos Pyrgos project: preliminary report on the rescue excavations of 2005-6', *Hesperia* 81: 507–584.

Hayes, J. (1980), 'Problèmes de la céramique des VIIème-IXème siècles à Salamine et à Chypre', in M. Yon, ed., *Salamine de Chypre. Histoire et archéologie. État des recherches*, Colloques internationaux du CNRS 578, Paris: 375–387.

Hayes, J. (1992), *Excavations at Saraçhane in Istanbul 2: The Pottery*. Princeton.

Kingsley, S., and Decker, M., eds. (2001), *Economy and Exchange in East Mediterranean during Late Antiquity*. Oxford.

Hocker, F., Yamini, S., and Yamini, G. (1998), 'Bozburun Byzantine shipwreck excavation: the final campaign 1998', *The International Nautical Archaeology Quarterly* 25.4: 3–13.

Hood, S. (1989), 'Introduction', in M. Balance *et al.* eds., *Excavation in Chios 1952–1955: Byzantine Emporio*, BSA Supplementary Volume 20, Oxford: 7–8.

Kazanski, M., and Sodini, J.-P. (1987), 'Byzance et l'art "nomade": remarques à propos de l'essaie de J. Werner sur le dépôt de Malaja Pereščepina (Pereščepino), *Revue archéologique* 1987/1: 71–90.

Kienast H., Moustaka, A., Grobschmidt, K., and Kanz, F. (2017), 'Das archaïsche Osttor des Heraion von Samos. Bericht über die Ausgrabungen der Jahre 1996 und 1998, *Archäologische Anzeiger*: 125–212.

Klontza-Jaklova, V. (2014), 'The Byzantine sequences at Priniatikos Pyrgos: preliminary observations on ceramic chronology and architectural phasing', in B. Molloy and C. Duckworth, eds., *A Cretan Landscape through Time: Priniatikos Pyrgos and its Environs*, B.A.R. International Series 2634, Oxford: 135–142.

Kocabaş, U., ed. (2008), *The 'Old Ships' of the 'New Gate' in Yenikapı'nın Eski Gemileri, Yenikapı Shipwrecks* 1. Istanbul.

Kountoura-Galaki, E. (2017), 'The Formation of the Isaurian Administrative Network: the Example of the Naval Theme of Kibyrrhaiotai and of Crete', *Graeco-Arabica* 12: 97–128.

Laiou, A. (2002), 'Exchange and trade, seventh-twelfth centuries', in A. Laiou, ed., *The Economic History of Byzantium: From the Seventh through the Fifteenth Century*, vol. 2, Dumbarton Oaks Studies 39, Washington, DC: 697–770.

Leontsini, M. (2017), 'The Byzantine and Arab navies in the southern Aegean and Crete: shipping, mobility and transport (7th-9th c.)', *Graeco-Arabica* 12: 171–234.

Marangou, L. (2005), *Αμοργός* II. *Οι αρχαίοι πύργοι*, Βιβλιοθήκη της εν Αθήναις Αρχαιολογικής Εταιρείας 239, Athens.

Montinaro, F. (2013), 'Les premiers commerciaires "byzantins"', in C. Zuckerman, ed., *Constructing the Seventh Century, in TM* 17: 351–538.

Murialdo, G. (2001), 'Le anfore di transporto', in T. Mannoni and G. Murialdo, eds., *S. Antonino: un insediamento fortificato nella Liguria bizantina*, Collezione di Monografie preistoriche ed archeologiche XII, Bordighera/Florence: 255–296.

Nesbitt, J., and, Oikonomides, N., eds. (1994), *Dumbarton Oaks: A Catalogue of the Byzantine Seals at Dumbarton Oaks and in the Fogg Museum of Art*, II. *South of the Balkans, the Islands, South of Asia Minor*. Washington, DC.

Nika, A. (2014), 'Χάλκινες πόρπες από τη Ρόδο. Εξαρτύματα ένδυσης φοιδεράτων ή Βυζαντινών?, in P. Triantafyllidis, ed., *σοφία άδολος. Τιμητικός τόμος για τον Ιωάννη Χρ. Παπαχριστοδούλου*, Rhodes: 333–358.

Nikolaou, Y. (2004), 'Numismatic circulation in the Aegean Islands during the seventh century', in G. Livadas, ed., *Festschrift in Honour of V. Christides, in Graeco-Arabica* 9–10: 291–309.

Nikolaou, Y. (2010), 'Συμβολή στη νομισματική κυκλοφορία των νησιών του Αιγαίου κατά τον 7ο αι. Ο "Θησαυρός" Χίος/1998', in P. Tselekas, ed., *Το νόμισμα στα νησιά του Αιγαίου, νομισματοκοπεία, κυκλοφορία, εικονογραφία, ιστορία: πρακτικά συνεδρίου της Ε' Επιστημονικής Συνάντησης, Μυτιλήνη, 16–19 Σεπτεμβρίου 2006*, vol. I, in *Οβολός* 9, Athens: 77–93.

Papavasileiou, E., Sarantidis, K., and Papanikolaou, E. (2014), 'A ceramic workshop of the Early Byzantine period on the Island of Lipsi in the Dodecanese (Greece): a preliminary approach', in N. Poulou-Papadimitriou, E. Nodarou and V. Kilikoglou, eds., *Late Roman Coarse Wares 4: Late Roman Coarse Wares, Cooking Wares and Amphorae in the Mediterranean: Archaeology and Archaeometry. The Mediterranean Market without Frontiers (Thessaloniki, April 2011)*, B.A.R. International Series 2616, Oxford: 159–168.

104 *Natalia Poulou-Papadimitriou*

Peacock, D., and Williams, D., 1986, *Amphorae and the Roman Economy: An Introductory Guide.* Longman, London, New York.

Pekin, A., *et al.* (2007), Gün Işığında İstanbul'un 8000 Yılı: *Marmaray, Metro, Sultanahmet Kazıları.* Kentlerin Kralicesi İstanbul 9, Istanbul.

Penna, V. (2013), ' Ἡ μαρτυρία τῶν νομισμάτων καὶ τῶν σφραγίδων', in G. Sakellarakis, ed., Κύθηρα, Τὸ μινωικό ιερό κορυφής στον Άγιο Γεώργιο στο Βουνό, 3. Τα ευρήματα, Archaeological Society at Athens 282, Athens: 419–462.

Piéri, D. (2005), *Le commerce du vin oriental à l'époque byzantine (Ve – VIIe siècles). Le témoignage des amphores en Gaule,* Bibliothèque Archéologique et Historique 174, Beirut.

Portale, E., and Romeo, I. (2001), 'Contenitori da trasporto', in A. di Vita, ed., *Gortina V. 3, Lo scavo del Pretorio (1989–1995) I Materiali,* Monografie della Scuola archeologica in Atene 12, Padua: 260–410.

Poulou, N. (2017), 'Transport amphorae and trade in the Aegean from the 7th to the 9th century AD: containers of wine or olive oil?', *BYZANTINA* 35: 195–216.

Poulou, N. (forthcoming), 'Philippi in transition: gradual development or crisis and recovery?', in S. Friesen *et al.*, eds., *Philippi, from Colonia Augusta to communitas christiana: Religion and Society in Transition, 7–10 July 2015,* Leiden.

Poulou-Papadimitriou, N. (1985), *Samos paléochrétienne: l'apport du matériel archéologique,* unpublished PhD thesis, University of Paris.

Poulou-Papadimitriou, N. (2001), –'Βυζαντινή κεραμική από τον νησιωτικό χώρο και από την Πελοπόννησο (7^{ος} – 9^{ος} αι.): μία πρώτη προσέγγιση', in E. Kountoura-Galakis, ed., *Οι σκοτεινοί αιώνε ςτου Βυζαντίου (7^{ος} – 9^{ος} αι.),* Ινστιτούτο Βυζαντινών Ερευνών, Διεθνή Συμπόσια 9, Athens: 231–226.

Poulou-Papadimitriou, N. (2005), 'Les plaques-boucles byzantines de l'île de Crète (fin VIe-IXe siècle)', in *Mélanges Jean-Pierre Sodini,* in *Travaux et Mémoires* 15: 687–704.

Poulou-Papadimitriou, N. (2008), 'Στιγμές από την'ιστορία του'Ηρακλείου. Από την πρωτοβυζαντινή εποχή έως την περίοδο της οθωμανικής κυριαρχίας (7^{ος}-19^{ος} αι.)', in A. Ioannidou-Karetsou, ed., *Ηράκλειο. Η άγνωστη ιστορία της αρχαίας πόλης,* Heraklion: 149–201.

Poulou-Papadimitriou, N. (2011), 'Τεκμήρια υλικού πολιτισμού στη βυζαντινή Κρήτη: από τον 7^{ο} έως το τέλος του 12^{ου} αιώνα', in E. Kapsomenos, M. Andreadaki-Vlazaki, and M. Andrianakis, eds., *Πεπραγμένα Ι' Διεθνούς Συνεδρίου (Χανιά 2006), Α, Στρογγυλή Τράπεζα, 1. Μεσοβυζαντινή Κρήτη:* 381–447.

Poulou-Papadimitriou, N. (2013), 'Άγιος Γεώργιος στο Βουνό. Η βυζαντινή και η πρώ῎ιμη ενετική περίοδος', in G. Sakellarakis, ed., *Κύθηρα, Τὸ μινωικό ιερό κορυφής στον Άγιο Γεώργιο στο Βουνό, 3. Τα ευρήματα,* Library of the Archaeological Society at Athens 282, Athens: 26–266.

Poulou-Papadimitriou, N. (2014), 'Θαλάσσιοι δρόμοι στο Αιγαίο κατά την πρωτοβυζαντινή περίοδο: η μαρτυρία της κεραμικής', in N. Zarras and M. Stefanakis, eds., *Αρχαιολογία και Τέχνη στα Δωδεκάνησα κατά την Ύστερη Αρχαιότητα,* Ευλιμένη 2, Rethymnon: 127–152.

Poulou-Papadimitriou, N. (2018), 'The Aegean during the "Transitional Period" of Byzantium: the archaeological evidence' in J. Crow & D. Hill, eds., *Naxos and the Byzantine Aegean: insular responses to regional change,* Athens: 29-50.

Poulou-Papadimitriou, N. (2020), 'Εφυαλωμένη κεραμική με λευκό πηλό από την Κωνσταντινούπολη (GWW I-II/7ος-9ος αιώνας): Η διάδοση στον αιγαιακό χώρο', in P. Kalogerakou *et al.*, eds., Κυδάλιμος. Τιμητικός Τόμος για τον Καθηγητή Γεώργιο Στυλ. Κορρέ. AURA SUPPLEMENT 4: vol. 3, 365–375.

Poulou-Papadimitriou, N. (forthcoming), *Η κεραμική από την παλαιά ανασκαφή του Αγίου Πέτρου των Δομινικανών στο Ηράκλειο.*

Poulou-Papadimitriou, N., and Didioumi, S. (2010), 'Nouvelles données sur la production de l'atélier protobyzantin à Kardamaina (Cos - Grèce)', in S. Menchelli, S. Santoro, M. Pasquinucci, and G. Guiducci, eds., *Late Roman Coarse Wares 3, Late Roman Coarse Wares, Cooking Wares and Amphorae in the Mediterranean: Archaeology and Archaeometry, Comparison between western and eastern Mediterranean*, B.A.R. International Series 2185, vol. 2, Oxford: 741–749.

Poulou-Papadimitriou, N., and Didioumi, S. (2015), 'Two pottery workshops in the island of Cos (Greece)', in F. Thuillier and É. Louis, eds., *Tourner autour du pot … Les ateliers de potiers médiévaux du Ve au XIIe siècle dans l'espace européen*, Caen: 401–418.

Poulou-Papadimitriou, N., and Nodarou, E. (2007), 'La céramique protobyzantine de Pseira: la production locale et les importations. Étude typologique et pétrographique', in M. Bonifay and J.-C. Tréglia, eds., *Late Roman Coarse Wares 2, Proceedings of the 2nd International Conference on Late Roman Coarse Wares, Cooking Wares and Amphorae in the Mediterranean: Archaeology and Archaeometry. (Aix-en-Provence-Marseille-Arles, 13th-16th April 2005)*, B.A.R. International Series 1662, Oxford: 755–766.

Poulou-Papadimitriou, N., and Nodarou, E. (2014), 'Transport vessels and maritime routes in the Aegean from the 5th to the 9th c. AD. Preliminary results of the EU funded 'Pythagoras II' project: the Cretan case study', in N. Poulou-Papadimitriou, E. Nodarou, and V. Kilikoglou, eds., *Late Roman Coarse Wares 4: Late Roman Coarse Wares, Cooking Wares and Amphorae in the Mediterranean: Archaeology and Archaeometry. The Mediterranean Market without Frontiers (Thessaloniki, April 2011)*, B.A.R. International Series 2616, Oxford: 876–877.

Ragia, E. (2011), 'The geography of the provincial administration of the Byzantine Empire (ca. 600–1200): I. 2. Apothekai of the Balkans and of the Islands of the Aegean Sea (7th-8th c.)', *Byzantinoslavica* 69: 86–113.

Reynolds, P. (1995), *Trade in the Western Mediterranean, AD 400–700: the Ceramic Evidence*. B.A.R. International Series 604, Oxford.

Sagui, L., Ricci, M., and Romei, D. (1997), 'Nuovi dati ceramologici per la storia economica di Roma tra VII e VIII secolo', in G. Demains d'Archimbaud, ed., *La céramique médiévale en Méditerranée. Actes du 6e congrès de l'AIECM 2, Aix-en-Provence (13–18 novembre 1995)*, Aix-en-Provence: 35–48.

Sanders, G.D.R., (1996), 'Two *kastra* on Melos and their Relations in the Archipelago', in P. Lock and G.D.R. Sanders, eds., *The Archaeology of Medieval Greece*, Oxbow Monograph 59, Oxford: 147–177.

Sanders, G.D.R. (2004), 'Problems in interpreting rural and urban settlement in southern Greece, AD 365–700', in N. Christie, ed., *Landscapes of Change: Rural Evolutions in Late Antiquity and the Early Middle Ages*, Aldershot: 163–193.

Sidiropoulos, K. (1994), 'Τα νομίσματα', *Κρητική Εστία* 4: 75–78.

Sidiropoulos, K. (2004a), 'Νομισματική ιστορία της ρωμαϊκής και πρωτοβυζαντινής Κρήτης (67 π.Χ.-827 μ.Χ.): Testimonia et Desiderata', in M. Livadiotti and I. Simiakaki, eds., *Creta Romana e Protobyzantina, Atti del Congresso Internazionale, Iraklion 23–30 settembre 2000*, vol. 1, Padua: 193–223.

106   *Natalia Poulou-Papadimitriou*

Sidiropoulos, K. (2004b), 'Κνωσός, Colonia Iulia Nobilis Cnosus, Μακρυτοιχος: Τα νομισματικά ίχνη της ιστορίας', in N. Gigiourtakis, ed., *Το Ηράκλειο και η περιοχή του. Διαδρομή στο χρόνο*, Herakleion: 635–671.

Sidiropoulos, K. (2012), 'Numismatic finds from Priniatikos Pyrgos: major gains from minor capital', in *Fieldwork and Research at Priniatikos Pyrgos and Environs 1912–2012, A Conference, Athens, 1–2 June 2012*, Athens: 13.

Slane, K., and Sanders, G.D.R. (2005), 'Corinth: late Roman horizons', *Hesperia* 74: 243–297.

Stallman, C. (1986), *The Life of Saint Pancratius of Taormina*, unpublished PhD thesis Oxford University.

Starida, L. (1984), 'Βυζαντινά μολυβδόβουλλα από το Ηράκλειο Κρήτης', *Αμάλθεια* 15: 45–51.

Sythiakaki, V., Kanaki, E., and Bilmezi, X. (2015), 'Οι παλαιότερες οχυρώσεις του Ηρακλείου: μια διαφορετική προσέγγιση με βάση τα νεότερα ανασκαφικά δεδομένα', in P. Karanastasi, A. Tzigkounaki, and X. Tsigonaki, eds., Αρχαιολογικό Έργο Κρήτης 3, Πρακτικά της 3ης Συνάντησης. Rethymnon.

Tsakos, K. (1979), 'Συμβολή στην παλαιοχριστιανική και πρώϊμη βυζαντινή μνημειογραφία της Σάμου', *Αρχαιολογική Εφημερίς*: 11–25.

Tsigonaki, C. (2009), ' Ίτανος. Ιστορία και τοπογραφία μιας παράκτιας θέσης της ανατολικής Κρήτης κατά την πρωτοβυζαντινή περίοδο', in O. Gratziou and C. Loukos, eds., *Ψηφίδες. Μελέτες Ιστορίας, Αρχαιολογίας και Τέχνης στη μνήμη της Στέλλας Παπαδάκη-Oekland*, Herakleion: 159–174.

Touratsoglou, I. (1999), 'εν οστράκω θαλασσίω...Ο Θησαυρός της Αρκεσίνης Αμοργού', in N. Stampolidis, ed., *Φως Κυκλαδικόν. Τιμητικός τόμος στη μνήμη του Νίκου Ζαφειρόπουλου*, Athens: 351–352.

Touratsoglou, I., and Chalkia, E. (2008), *Ο Θησαυρός της Κρατήγου Μυτιλήνης*. Athens.

Touratsoglou, I., Koltsida-Makri, I., and Nikolaou, Y. (2006), 'New lead seals from Crete', *Studies in Byzantine Sigillography* 9: 49–68.

Tsougarakis, D. (1988), *Byzantine Crete: From the 5th Century to the Venetian Conquest*. Athens.

Tsougarakis, D. (1990), 'The Byzantine Seals of Crete', in N. Oikonomides, ed., *Studies in Byzantine Sigillography* 2, Washington, DC: 137–152.

Tzavella, E. (2015), 'Πρινιάτικος Πύργος, ένα λιμάνι της ανατολικής Κρήτης. Οι μαρτυρίες των αμφορέων της μεταβατικής περιόδου (7ος-9ος αι.): μία πρώτη προσέγγιση', in *8th Scientific Meeting of the Greek Committee of Byzantine Studies, Athens, 16–18 December 2015*: 78.

Van Doorninck, F. (1989), 'The cargo Amphoras on the 7th century Yassi Ada and 11th century Serçe Limani shipwrecks: two examples of a reuse of Byzantine Amphoras as transport jars', in V. Déroche and J.-M. Spieser, eds., *Recherches sur la céramique byzantine*, BCH, Supplément XVIII, Paris: 247–257.

Vogt, C. (1994), 'Πρωτοβυζαντινή κεραμική από την Αγία Γαλήνη', *Κρητική Εστία* 4: 39–75.

Werner, J. (1984), *Der Grabfund von Malaja Pereščepina und Kuvrat, Kagan der Bulgaren*. München.

Wickham, C. (2005), *Framing the Early Middle Ages. Europe and the Mediterranean, 400–800*. Oxford.

Xanthopoulou, M. *et al*. (2014), 'Local coarse wares from Late Roman Itanos (East Crete)', in N. Poulou-Papadimitriou, E. Nodarou, and V. Kilikoglou, eds., *Late*

Roman Coarse Wares 4: Late Roman Coarse Wares, Cooking Wares and Amphorae in the Mediterranean: Archaeology and Archaeometry. The Mediterranean Market without Frontiers (Thessaloniki, April 2011), B.A.R. International Series 2616, Oxford: 811–817.

Xanthopoulou, M. (2015), ' Ένας αμφορέας της όψιμης πρωτοβυζαντινής περιόδου από την Ίτανο', in P. Karanastasi, A. Tzigkounaki, and X. Tsigonaki, eds., *Αρχαιολογικό Έργο Κρήτης, Πρακτικά 3ης Συνάντησης*, Rethymnon: 585–593.

Zacos, G., and Veglery, A. (1972), *Byzantine Lead Seals*, vol.1, Parts 1–3. Basel.

Zanini, E., Stefano, C., Giorgi, E., and Triolo, E. (2015), 'The excavation of the Early Byzantine District near the Pythion in Gortyn (field seasons 2011–2013): an image of the end of the Mediterranean city', in P. Karanastasi, A., Tzigounaki, and X. Tsigonaki, eds., *Αρχαιολογικό Έργο Κρήτης, Πρακτικά 3ης Συνάντησης*, Rethymnon: 565–574.

7 The 7th-Century Restoration of the Acheiropoietos Basilica and Its Significance for the Urban Continuity of Thessalonike during the 'Dark Age'

Konstantinos T. Raptis

Dedicated to the loving memory of my wife,
Maria Kakagia

The Acheiropoietos basilica (Figure 7.1), which, on the basis of recent studies, was originally founded in the last decade of the 5th or the first decade of the 6th century, during the reign of Anastasius I, fits more than any of the Thessalonian monuments to the standardised Early Byzantine ecclesiastical architecture, comprising – in its present state – a typical example of the three-aisled timber-roofed basilica with narthex and galleries.[1] Despite the typological inalterability throughout its 15-century history, the building suffered several devastations due to seismic impact, each one followed by a restoration project, characterised by the architectural vocabulary of the corresponding period. Based on evidence concerning the structural phases of the basilica, which were re-documented during a recent consolidation project,[2] it seems that apart from the late 5th century structure, preserved mainly in the ground floor level of the basilica, the building maintains in its present state traces of five major reconstructions along with minor repairs.[3]

The present chapter traces the alterations that were applied in the architectural design of the basilica during its first large-scale restoration that followed the partial ruination of its upper structure due to a natural disaster. This chapter also explores the function of the several annexes which were added to the main building, and at the same time attempts to comprehend the role that Acheiropoietos basilica had during the 7th and the 8th centuries, a period lacking written sources regarding this ecclesiastical building, despite its apparent significance for the Thessalonian episcopal see.

The first rehabilitation of the basilica is observed with difficulty, since its masonries have been largely substituted during sequential Byzantine and Ottoman restorations. However, the examination of building materials, masonry characteristics and architectural sculptures used in certain parts of the monument, which – until now – have been considered as remains of the primary structure, establishes the following:

Based on the chronology suggested for the foundation of the building, the Ionic impost capitals of the galleries, made with Proconnesian marble, had been dated

DOI: 10.4324/9781003429470-9

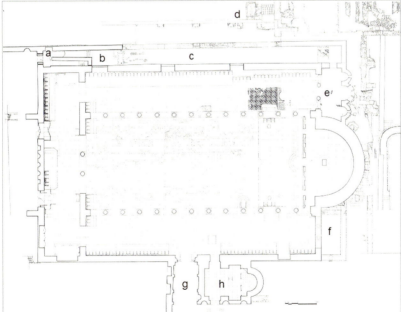

Figure 7.1 Acheiropoietos basilica: view from the southeast (above); plans (below).

in the middle or the third quarter of the 5th century.[4] By examining the same capitals – given the provenance of their material – in the context of the typological evolution of the Ionic impost capitals of the Constantinopolitan workshops,[5] it turns out that only three of them – one restored on the easternmost column of the north gallery[6] and two formerly located in the courtyard of the monument,[7] and therefore none among them on its original place – belong to the first group of the type with the volutes projecting, even slightly, from the lateral sides of the impost,[8] which is generally dated in the second half of the 5th until the beginning of the 6th century. Thus, these three capitals may be attributed to a phase synchronous with the architectural sculptures of the nave colonnades.[9] On the contrary, the 12 capitals of the south gallery (Figure 7.2b–o) belong to numerous simplified

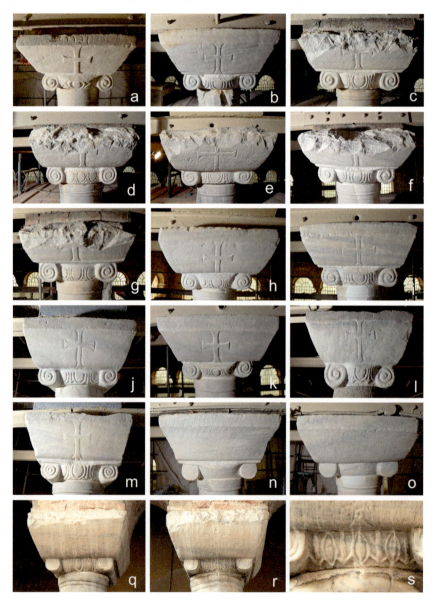

Figure 7.2 Ionic impost capitals: (a) restored at North Gallery Arcade, (b–o) in situ at South Gallery Arcade, (q–s) in situ at northeast tribelon.

The 7th-Century Restoration of the Acheiropoietos Basilica   111

variations of the second group of Ionic impost capitals with closed contour, the main characteristic of which is the diminished – compared to the impost – Ionic part.[10] These 12 capitals can be furthermore subcategorised on the basis of either the mediation or the absence of a listel that corresponds to a diminished abacus between the rather schematic echinus and the impost. Probably prefabricated in standardised size, these capitals, which individually may be dated from the first half until the end of the 6th or the beginning of the 7th century, comprise a multifarious set used during either a restoration, or possibly the primary addition of the gallery arcades during a phase posterior to the foundation of the basilica.[11]

A differentiation in the structure of the south gallery arcade is also observed. The brickwork mortar-joints, unlike those of the ground floor level *opus mixtum,* are uneven to the thickness of the bricks; usually wider and irregularly shaped joints are made with more reddish mortar due to an increase of the ceramic aggregates.[12]

Furthermore, the masonries that were evidently built simultaneously with the foundation of the basilica are limited at both the external walls and the nave arcades at the ground-floor level: a horizontal masonry joint can be traced between the first and the second phase slightly below the level of the gallery timber-floors. Thus the masonries that can be attributed with certainty to the primary construction of the basilica are not extended in any case to the gallery level, suggesting that the galleries maintained until nowadays belong to a subsequent structural phase of the monument.[13]

To the evidence indicating either an early remodelling or even the subsequent addition of the galleries and the clerestory, the imposts used on the pilasters of the gallery arcades can be added. They differ from the corresponding ground-floor sculptures in both the form of the relief crosses adorning their faces, and the fact that they are made on marble slabs cut from inscribed Roman sarcophagi.[14]

Such inconsistency of the sculptural decoration is also observed at the tribelon (Figure 7.3) opened to the eastern wall of the north aisle, forming the entrance to a Middle Byzantine annex, distorted in the 20th century (Figure 7.1e).[15] The simplified Ionic impost capitals of this tribelon, both set on a mismatched pair of columns, are characterised by the imbalance of the Ionic part and the impost, as the first corresponds just to 1:4 of the total height.[16] The above ratio in conjunction with the absence of the diminished abacus between the Ionic part and the impost, the extremely schematic volutes and the coarsely malformed *ovoli* that decorate the truncated echinus suggest – if compared with a late 6th–7th century Ionic Impost capital from Saraçhane – a 7th-century dating.[17]

Additionally the structure of these tribelon arches does not resemble the arches of the nave arcades, while their materials differ from the ones used in the tribelon responds, which seem to be formed by the widening of a pre-existing opening – possibly of an original doorway, as it has already been suggested.[18] The arch of this opening is partially maintained behind the marble pilaster that forms the north respond of this second-phase tribelon.[19]

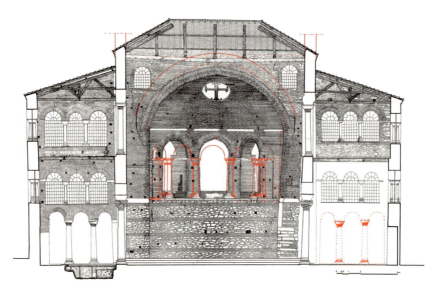

Figure 7.3 Cross-section looking east (with, in red, the hypothetical reconstruction of the 7th-century apse and southeast tribelon).

As seen by the building materials and the texture of the mortar used in the certain phase, along with the tribelon arches the overhead triple-light window was remodelled, with mortar similar to the one used in the gallery arcades.

A tribelon of analogous dimensions was formed during the same period on the corresponding wall of the south aisle (Figure 7.3), attesting a symmetrical conformation on either side of the presbytery apse during that early restoration of the basilica, while auxiliary, probably non apsidal, chambers were synchronously added outside these *tribela,* thus flanking the presbytery apse (Figure 7.1e–f).[20] However, their architectural form can only be implied,[21] since the north, rectangular, and probably without apse, annex was eventually replaced by the mid-Byzantine chapel with tripartite sanctuary which, even though distorted, is maintained today at the east end of the north aisle. The corresponding south annex was entirely destroyed during Late Byzantine or early Ottoman years.

A longitudinal two-storey annex, 36 metres long and two metres wide, was synchronously attached along the north side of the basilica (Figure 7.1c). Its exterior north wall was probably articulated with a row of brick-built piers with inserted marble colonettes: an architectural arrangement typologically, morphologically and also statically similar to that of the lateral colonnades at the 7th century basilica of St. Demetrius. On the basis of evidence left on the north wall of the basilica, the ground level of this portico was covered with a barrel vault, while its upper story had a lean-to timber roof.[22] This portico, which communicated through multiple doors with the north aisle and the northeast auxiliary chamber, also gave access to the basilica from a large pre-existing building at the north (Figure 7.1d), which in the same period sustained extensive repairs.

At the same time the earthquake-damaged, small and square in plan, northwest annex with a use so far undetermined, was replaced by a longitudinal brick-built barrel-vaulted ramp-way (Figure 7.1a) that gave access to the galleries from neither the narthex nor the exonarthex, but through an intermediate vestibule (Figure 7.1b), from both the north aisle and the newly built north portico, which communicated with a residential building to the north (Figure 7.1c).[23]

The impact that the same natural disaster had on the west and south parts of the basilica cannot be documented, as large parts of the narthex and the south aisle were rebuilt in subsequent, Ottoman and modern, phases. However, at the same period the south monumental propylon of the basilica, leading to Acheiropoietos from the main Decumanus of the city, was re-modelled. The second-phase propylon (Figure 7.1g), constructed after the devastation of its predecessor in the space that occurred between two pre-existing walls,[24] is formed by four pairs of marble pilasters, which by means of a blind arcade on each side bear a barrel vault (Figure 7.4a–b).[25] Based on the masonry characteristics, the construction of this vaulted structure may be synchronous or slightly subsequent to the gallery remodelling, but prior to another sequential Byzantine restoration of the basilica.

The only evidence offering chronological criteria are the eight pilaster capitals (Figure 7.4c–j). Identical per pair, they are made with white, coarse-grained marble, and may be discerned in three subgroups. The four – finer in sculptural terms among them – that form the two central pairs are quite similar as far as the accurate execution of both the symmetrical seven-lobed acanthus leaves and the secondary ornamental motifs is concerned (Figure 7.4e–h). Another pair differs in the formation of the parietal, wide, lobes of the acanthus leaves with four or five leaf-tips each, which form irregular negative motives, and the development of ribbon-like helixes, under the abacus (Figure 7.4c–d). The recently uncovered, roughest pair of capitals was certainly sculpted for this particular edifice by a less sophisticated craftsman. Due to their placement, adjacent to the marble doorframe, they are less wide; each bears two, irregularly formed, acanthus leaves with malformed fantail-like lobes, supplemented by an awkwardly formed, linear sprout covering the space between the central acanthus leaf and the doorframe (Figure 7.4i–j). Despite their differences these pilaster capitals have been dated as a set from as early as the third quarter of the 5th until the middle of the 6th century.[26] The latter could be convincing only for the four symmetrically arranged ones. It seems that the schematic execution and the rather malformed fantail-like lobes of the less elaborate acanthus leaves, which probably imitate ineffectively the acanthus archetypes of the Early Byzantine imposts of the nave, establish a 7th-century date for the set.[27]

The newly-built vaulted propylon cancelled the west doorway of the adjacent apsidal chamber, also restored during the same period with a barrel

Figure 7.4 South propylon: (a) the doorframe, (b) the east blind arcade, (c–j) marble pseudo-pilaster capitals.

vault (Figure 7.1h), and identified as either a diaconicon[28] or baptistery,[29] which – hereafter accessed only from the interior of the south aisle[30] – was probably altered in terms of use.[31]

All the aforementioned annexes, namely the north portico, the northeast *pastoforion*, the apsidal south chamber as well as the east end of the south aisle, and the exonarthex of the basilica, were synchronously re-paved with medium-sized irregularly shaped marble slabs.[32] Probably along with this floor renewal, the formerly known drainage conduit was incorporated in the floor of the south apsidal chamber.[33]

Based on the aforementioned evidence, the Acheiropoietos basilica was probably erected without galleries,[34] which were added to the basilica during its first – among many – structural restoration after the apparent devastation of its upper structure by an earthquake. Thus instead of the rehabilitation of the high, statically inadequate, clerestory of the first phase, the basilica was redesigned with extended galleries. The lateral galleries copied in lower proportions the longitudinal arched colonnades of the ground floor, whereas the western gallery – based on the mosaic found on the north front of the south arcade towards the central aisle[35] – can be reconstructed as an open wide hall overlooking the nave; most probably fenced with a simple barrier of marble parapets, instead of an arched colonnade.[36] Based on architectural evidence, the Western Gallery extended up to the western façade, occupying the upper floor over both the narthex and the exonarthex.[37] The clerestory with two-light windows, developed on both sides of a three-light one, would have also been extended over the Western Gallery to the exterior wall that formed the western facade of the basilica (Figure 7.5).[38]

Even though, during the first restoration of the basilica the five-light window of the sanctuary apse, with four marble mullions, remained unaltered, the semidome, probably severely cracked by the same natural disaster, was extensively restored. Based on evidence documented during the last consolidation of the monument, the second-phase semidome was larger than the maintained one, which was probably reconstructed during an Ottoman, 15th century restoration of the monument (Figure 7.3).[39]

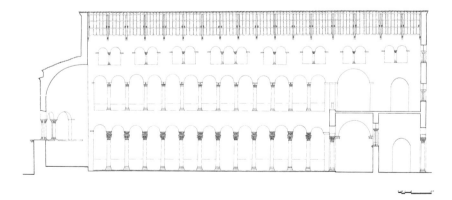

Figure 7.5 Longitudinal section looking north; hypothetical reconstruction of the 16th century phase with galleries and clerestory.

116 *Konstantinos T. Raptis*

The architectural sculptures used in the repairs and additions to the basilica offer a *terminus post quem* in the late 6th – or even the early 17th – century for the construction of the galleries, and in the 17th century for the peripheral additions, and along with the inference that this extended restoration of the basilica was probably imposed by a seismic devastation of the structure, point to the notorious – according to the narration of the Miracles of St. Demetrius[40] – early 7th-century earthquakes as the cause of the entire restoration project.

Having in mind the urban insecurity and the economic crisis of the 7th century, what were the factors that motivated a monumental restoration of the basilica, especially since this phase is characterised not only by the rehabilitation of its devastated parts but also by the addition of extended galleries, the rebuilding of the pre-existing annexes and the addition of new, extended, ones? These alterations of the basilica cannot have been carried out at once. Probably only the rehabilitation of the main building with the addition of the galleries, necessary for the reopening of the building to the congregation was performed immediately after the earthquake, leaving the rest to the years following, according to the needs of the Thessalonian see.

I suggest that, after the disastrous series of earthquakes that shook Thessalonike during probably the third decade of the 7th century, Acheiropoietos, maintaining almost untouched the ground floor level including its sculptural decoration, was the least ruined among the four great churches of the city. Moreover, since both the five-aisled episcopal basilica, which is the predecessor of Hagia Sophia,[41] and the palatial Rotunda probably present discontinuity in this period,[42] Acheiropoietos was, along with the church of the patron saint Demetrius,[43] the only one that was, monumentally and to such an extent, restored during the period in question. Therefore, from the mid-7th century and mainly due to the severe ruination of the neighbouring Early Byzantine episcopal basilica, under Hagia Sophia church, which was hereafter limited to its sanctuary area,[44] Acheiropoietos gained the role of the cathedral, accommodating also the offices of the episcopate. That probably demanded the architectural conformity of the basilica to late 6th- and early 7th-century liturgical innovations introduced after 574,[45] as well as the addition of galleries to host special services or events, associated with the presence of the bishop, the ecclesiastical hierarchy and representatives of the imperial court,[46] as well as the addition of extended annexes to host the administrative services of the significant Thessalonian episcopal see.

Thus, apart from the rehabilitation of the main building with the addition of extended galleries,[47] *pastoforia* probably now flanked the presbytery apse. The addition of the barrel-vaulted ramp-way assisted the, probably restricted to the congregation, access to the galleries, and the longitudinal north portico ensured the communication of the interior of the basilica with both the offices and the administrative services of the episcopate, which were probably hosted in the upper storey of the northern annexes, and the residence of the archbishop at the also restored building at the north of the basilica.

The 7th-Century Restoration of the Acheiropoietos Basilica   117

Furthermore the rebuilding of the monumental south propylon into a barrel vaulted corridor continued the immediate access from the *Leophoros*, while the use of the adjacent apsidal annex was probably altered from diaconicon to a small – though convenient after the proclamation of infant baptism – baptistery, whose existence is probably alluded to in the homily that archbishop Leo, the Mathematician (or Philosopher), delivered in the church in 842.[48]

The Acheiropoietos probably hosted the services of the episcopate till the middle or the third quarter of the 8th century, when, after the erection of Hagia Sophia church,[49] the cathedral returned to its original base, emphasising with its Constantinopolitan cross-domed architectural form the rule of Byzantine imperial Christianity over the ecclesiastical affairs of Illyricum,[50] which had been under Papal jurisdiction until 732.[51]

Notes

1 Raptis 2016a: III, 749; Raptis 2017a: 113; Raptis 2017b: 46; Raptis forthcoming-a.
2 Raptis and Zombou-Asimi 2013.
3 Raptis and Zombou-Asimi 2011: 449–463; Raptis 2016a: III, 749–750.
4 Kautzsch 1936: 167; Farioli–Olivieri 1964: 172; Vemi 1989: 18–19, 130–132, n. 121–122, 123–124, 126.
5 Zollt 1994: 275–276, 299–301.
6 Vemi 1989: 132, n. 124; Fig. 2a.
7 Vemi 1989: 130–131, n. 121–122.
8 Zollt 1994: 275–276 Gruppe 1.
9 Raptis 2016a: III, 570–573; Raptis forthcoming-b.
10 Vemi 1989: 131, n. 123; Raptis, 2016a: III, 574–578; Raptis forthcoming-b.
11 Raptis 2016a: III, 580; Raptis 2016b: 487–488; Raptis 2018: 88; Raptis forthcoming-b.
12 Raptis 2016a: II, 478–486.
13 Raptis 2016a: III, 754–756.
14 Raptis 1999: 226–229; Raptis 2016a: III, 605–615; Raptis forthcoming-b.
15 A reconstruction of this Middle-Byzantine annex is suggested by G. Velenis (Velenis 2003: 37ff).
16 Vemi 1989: 132, n. 126; Raptis 2016a: III, 578–579; Raptis forthcoming-b; Fig. 2q-s.
17 Zollt 1994: 46, n. 99.
18 Pelekanidis 1949: 20.
19 Raptis 2016a: II, 378–379.
20 Theocharidou 1986: 144; Raptis 2016a: III, 769.
21 From the structural phase under examination only the north external wall of the northeast chamber remains, carefully jointed with the northeast corner of the north aisle. The similar southern annex is evidenced by the eastward expansion of the foundation of the south wall and the disruption of the outer wall of the apse at the assumable junction with the eastern masonry of the southeast annex.
22 Raptis and Zombou-Asimi 2011: 458; Raptis 2016a: II, 424–430.
23 Raptis and Zombou-Asimi 2011: 458; Raptis, 2016a: II, 424–430.
24 Kleinbauer 1984: 241–257, 255.
25 Raptis 2016a: II, 412–417.

118   *Konstantinos T. Raptis*

26 Kautzch 1936: n. 241; Farioli-Olivieri 1964: 142–143; Sodini 1984a: 220.
27 Raptis 2016a: III, 596–603; Raptis forthcoming-b.
28 Orlandos 1964–1965: 362; Sodini 1984b: 464–465.
29 Pelekanidis 1949: 24; Xynggopoulos 1941–1952: 478–481.
30 Xyngopoulos 1941–1952: 481.
31 Raptis 2016a: 418–423.
32 Asimakopoulou-Antzaka 1998: 284–286, n. 18.1–2.
33 Xyngopoulos 1941–1952: 481.
34 Raptis 2016a: 764–768; Raptis 2017a: 112–113; Raptis 2018: 88; Raptis forthcoming-a.
35 Nalpantis 2013: 124–125; Raptis 2014: 106–107; Raptis 2016a: III, 726–727.
36 Fourlas 2012: I, 226; Raptis 2016a: III, 767–768.
37 Raptis 2016a: III, 767–768.
38 Raptis 2016a: III, 768.
39 Raptis 2016a: III, 768, 785–786; Raptis forthcoming-a.
40 Lemerle 1981: 104–110.
41 Mentzos 1981: 201–221; Theocharidou 1994: 34–39.
42 Velenis 2003: 51ff.
43 Mentzos 2012: 82–103; Bauer 2013, *passim*.
44 Mentzos 1981: 205; Marki 1997: 61.
45 Ćurčić 2010: 212; Popović 1979: 277–278.
46 Raptis 2018: 88. Regarding the problem of the existence – or not – of galleries above the lateral aisles of the Early Byzantine Basilicas of the Illyricum, and their function, see Raptis 2018.
47 The re-dating of the south gallery arcade to the second quarter or the middle of the 7th century creates another chronological problem, since its intrados are decorated with mosaics until now considered synchronous to the mosaic decoration of the ground floor arcades; both dated in the second half of the 1st century. Though, based on structural and historical criteria, the gallery mosaic decoration could not be prior to the midline of the 7th century and posterior of the first half of the 8th century, since after the erection of Hagia Sophia domed church the focus turned on the new Thessalonican cathedral. The mural, both mosaic and painted, decoration of Acheiropoietos basilica has been recently revised by the author (Raptis 2014: 109–112).
48 Laurent 1964: 281–302.
49 Velenis 2003: 70–71. Regarding the construction of Hagia Sophia cross-domed church during the third quarter of the 8th century see Velenis 1997: 70–77 and Velenis 2003: 70–71.
50 Cormack 1977: 35.
51 Anastos 1957: 14–31.

References

Anastos, M. (1957), 'The transfer of Illyricum, Calabria and Sicily to the Jurisdiction of the Patriarchate of Constantinople in 732–733', in *Sylloge Byzantina in onore di Silvio Giuseppe Mercati*, Rome: 14–34.
Asimakopoulou-Atzaka, P. (1998), *Τα ψηφιδωτά δάπεδα της Θεσσαλονίκης*. Thessaloniki.
Bauer, F.A. (2013), *Eine Stadt und ihr Patron: Thessaloniki und der Heilige Demetrios*. Regensburg.
Cormack, R. (1977), 'The arts during the Age of Iconoclasm', in A. Bryer and J. Herrin, eds., *Iconoclasm: Papers Given at the* 9th *Spring Symposium of Byzantine Studies*, Birmingham: 35–44.

The 7th-Century Restoration of the Acheiropoietos Basilica 119

Ćurčić, S. (2010), *Architecture in the Balkans from Diocletian to Süleyman the Magnificent*. New Haven and London.

Farioli-Olivieri, R. (1964), 'I capitelli paleobizantini di Salonicco', *Corsi di cultura sull'arte ravennate e bizantina* XI: 132–177.

Fourlas, B. (2012), *Die Mosaiken der Acheiropoietos-Basilika in Thesssaloniki. Eine vergleichende Analyse dekorativer Mosaiken des 5. Und 6. Jahrhunderts*. Berlin.

Kautzsch, R. (1936), *Kapitellstudien. Beiträge zu einer Geschichte des Spätantiken Kapitelles im Osten vom Vierten bis ins Siebente Jahrhundert*. Berlin/Leipzig.

Kleinbauer, W.E. (1984), 'Remarks on the building history of the Acheiropoietos church at Thessaloniki', in *Actes du Xe Congrès International d'Archéologie Chrétienne*, vol. II, Thessaloniki/Vatican City: 241–257.

Laurent, V. (1964), 'Une homélie inédite de l'archevêque de Thessalonique, Léon le Philosophe, sur l'Annonciation (25 mars 842)', in *Mélanges Eugène Tisserant*, vol. II, Vatican City: 281–302.

Lemerle, P. (1981), *Les plus anciens recueils des Miracles de Saint Démétrius et la pénétration des Slaves dans les Balkans*, vol. II. Paris.

Marki, E. (1997), 'Ἡ Ἁγία Σοφία και τα προσκτίσματά της μέσα από τα αρχαιολογικά δεδομένα', in *Θεσσαλονικέων πόλις – Γραφές και Πηγές 6000 χρόνων* 1: 54–61.

Mentzos, A. (1981), 'Συμβολή στην έρευνα του αρχαιότερου ναού της Αγίας Σοφίας Θεσσαλονίκης', *Μακεδονικά* 21: 201–221.

Mentzos, A. (2012), 'Hagios Demetrios', in A. Mentzos, ed., *Impressions: Byzantine Thessalonike through the Photographs and Drawings of the British School at Athens*, Thessaloniki: 82–103.

Nalpantis, D. (2013). 'Fragment of wall mosaic', in A. Drandaki, D. Papanikola-Bakirtzi, and A. Tourta, eds., *Heaven and Earth: Art of Byzantium from Greek Collections*, Athens: 124–125.

Orlandos, A. (1964–1965), 'Ἡ από του νάρθηκος προς το ιερόν μετακίνησις του διακονικού εις τας ελληνιστικάς βασιλικάς', *DChAE* 4: 353–372.

Pelekanidis, S. (1949), *Παλαιοχριστιανικὰ μνημεῖα Θεσσαλονίκης: Ἀχειροποίητος, Μονὴ Λατόμου*. Thessaloniki.

Popović, V. (1979), 'La signification historique de l' architecture religieuse de Tsaritchin Grad', *Corsi di Cultura sull' Arte Ravennate e Bizantina* XXVI: 249–311.

Raptis, K. (1999), 'Παρατηρήσεις επί ορισμένων δομικών στοιχείων της Αχειροποιήτου', *Το Αρχαιολογικό Έργο στη Μακεδονία και στη Θράκη* 13: 226–229.

Raptis, K. (2014), 'The mural decoration of Acheiropoietos basilica revisited', in M. Rakocija, ed., *Proceedings of the XII International Symposium "Niš and Byzantium"*, Niš: 101–114.

Raptis, K. (2016a), *Αχειροποίητος Θεσσαλονίκης. Αρχιτεκτονική και γλυπτός διάκοσμος*, vol. I-III, unpublished PhD thesis, Aristotle University of Thessaloniki.

Raptis, K. (2016b), 'The sculptural decoration of Acheiropoietos basilica (Thessaloniki) re-evaluated under the light of a recent architectural analysis of the monument', in D. Dželebdžić and S. Bojanin, eds., *Proceedings of the 23rd International Congress of Byzantine Studies, Thematic Sessions of Free Communications*, Belgrade: 487–488.

Raptis, K. (2017a), 'Αχειροποίητος Θεσσαλονίκης: επανεξετάζοντας την αρχιτεκτονική και την οικοδομική ιστορία της πρωτοβυζαντινής βασιλικής', in *Abstracts of the 37th Symposium of Byzantine and Post-Byzantine Archaeology and Art: "Tribute to Charalambos Bouras"*, Athens: 112–114.

120   Konstantinos T. Raptis

Raptis, K. (2017b), 'Αρχιτεκτονικά έργα του Αναστασίου Α΄ στη Θεσσαλονίκη', in *Abstracts of the International Symposium in Honour of Emeritus Professor George Velenis*, Thessaloniki: 46.

Raptis, K. (2018), 'Remarks about the existence of galleries above the lateral aisles of the Early Byzantine basilicas of the Illyricum; a theorem to be either proved or contradicted', in *Abstracts of the XVII International Congress of Christian Archaeology "Frontiers. The Transformation and Christianization of the Roman Empire between Centre and Periphery"*, Utrecht/Nijmegen: 88.

Raptis, K. (forthcoming-a), 'The building history of Acheiropoietos basilica reconsidered', in M. Rakocija, ed., *Proceedings of the XVII International Symposium "Niš and Byzantium"*. Niš.

Raptis, K. (forthcoming-b), 'The sculptural decoration of Acheiropoietos basilica (Thessaloniki) re-evaluated in the light of a recent architectural analysis of the monument', in *Archaeology of a World of Changes. Selected Papers on Late Roman and Early Byzantine Archaeology from the 23rd International Congress of Byzantine Studies, B.A.R. I.S.* Oxford.

Raptis, K. and Zombou-Asimi, A. (2011), 'Αχειροποίητος Θεσσαλονίκης: παρατηρήσεις και σκέψεις σχετικά με την οικοδομική ιστορία και την αποκατάσταση της παλαιοχριστιανικής βασιλικής', in A. Stefanidou, ed., *Εν χώρω τεχνήεσσα, Τιμητικός Τόμος για την Ξ. Σκαρπιά-Χόιπελ*, Thessaloniki: 449–463.

Raptis, K., and Zombou-Asimi, A. (2013), 'The consolidation and restoration project of Acheiropoietos basilica in Thessaloniki', in M. Koui, F. Zezza, and P. Koutsoukos, eds., *Proceedings of the 8th International Symposium on the Conservation of Monuments in the Mediterranean Basin*, vol. I, Athens: 411–428.

Sodini, J.-P. (1984a), 'La sculpture architecturale à l époque paléochrétienne en Illyricum', in *Actes du Xe Congrès International d'Archéologie Chrétienne*, I, Thessaloniki/Vatican City: 207–298.

Sodini, J.-P. (1984b), 'Les dispositifs liturgiques des basiliques paléochrétiennes en Grèce et dans les Balkans', *Corsi di Cultura sull'Arte Ravennate e Bizantina* XXXI: 441–473.

Theocharidou, K. (1986), 'Acheiropoietos basilica, Thessaloniki: early Byzantine additions to the 5th-century building and their liturgical function (preliminary report)', in *Abstracts of Short Papers of the 17th International Byzantine Congress*, Washington, DC: 344–345.

Theocharidou, K. (1994), *Η αρχιτεκτονική του ναού της Αγίας Σοφίας στη Θεσσαλονίκη*. Athens.

Velenis, G. (1997), 'Η χρονολόγηση του ναού της Αγίας Σοφίας Θεσσαλονίκης μέσα από τα επιγραφικά δεδομένα', in *Θεσσαλονικέων πόλις – Γραφές και Πηγές 6000 χρόνων* 3: 70–77.

Velenis, G. (2003), *Μεσοβυζαντινή ναοδομία στη Θεσσαλονίκη*. Athens.

Vémi, V. (1989), *Les chapiteaux ioniques à imposte de Grèce à l' époque paléochrétienne*, BCH Supplément 17, Paris/Athens.

Xyngopoulos, A. (1941-1952), 'Περὶ τὴν Ἀχειροποίητον Θεσσαλονίκης', *Μακεδονικά* 2: 472–487.

Zollt, Th. (1994), *Kapitellplastik Konstantinopels von 4. bis 6. Jahrhundert n. Chr., Asia Minor Studien* 14. Bonn.

8 Some Remarks on the 'Dark Age' Architecture of Hagia Sophia, Thessalonike[*]

Sabine Feist

The Church of Hagia Sophia in Thessalonike is one of the central monuments of Byzantine ecclesiastical architecture during the so-called Transitional Period, and it is the only well-preserved example in modern Greece.[1] In spite of – or rather because of – its significance for developments during the Transitional Period, the church's architecture, its classification, and its date have remained controversial.[2] This chapter aims to dispel some of the controversies around the Hagia Sophia during the Transitional Period, particularly concerning the church's original appearance and its relation to its huge predecessor basilica.

The domed church, which probably served as the city's cathedral, had several predecessors on the same spot: a Roman bath and two successive Late Antique basilicas.[3] Basilica (A) had three aisles and was probably built around the year 400. Basilica (B) can be reconstructed as a huge five-aisled basilica, which was terminated by a projecting semi-circular apse in the East, and by a narthex and an atrium in the West (Figure 8.1). This huge Basilica (B), usually dated to the 5th century,[4] fitted well into Thessalonike's Late Antique urban landscape, which was characterised by basilical churches.

The present, much smaller, domed church replaced the huge Late Antique basilica at some later date (Figure 8.1). There are numerous different datings for the erection of the new church, which range from the 4th/5th to the 8th centuries.[5] However, the monograms of emperor Constantine VI, his mother Eirene, and the archbishop Theophilos in the bema-mosaics are our only tangible indications for dating, which suggest the erection of the domed church in the last quarter of the 8th century. Apart from the dating, also the reason for the replacement of Thessalonike's largest basilica by a much smaller domed church is uncertain. As in many other cases of the Transitional Period, an earthquake is supposed to have been responsible for the basilica's destruction and the erection of the new church.[6] However, the incorporation

---

[*] This chapter is based on the author's master's thesis *Die Sophienkirche in Thessaloniki. Kritische Bestandsaufnahme ihrer Architektur und Besprechung der gegenwärtigen*. I am grateful to Armin Bergmeier, Albrecht Berger, and Nikolaos Karydis for advice and discussion.

DOI: 10.4324/9781003429470-10

122 *Sabine Feist*

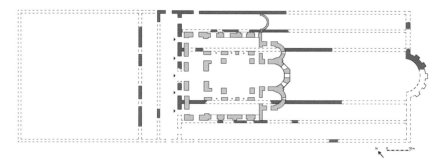

Figure 8.1 Plan of Hagia Sophia, Thessaloniki (basilica and domed church). S. Feist (based upon Theoharidou 1988: Fig. 2, Pl. I; Hadjitryphonos 1998-1999: Eik. 3b).

of older parts of the basilica into the new church speaks against this hypothesis. Maybe we have to think of new explanatory models like the non-availability of timber for the basilicas' wooden roofs or an intended dissociation of the cathedral's architecture from Thessalonike's other churches.

The present church has a cruciform naos that is extended by corner compartments on the ground and the gallery level. The naos is surrounded by a kind of ambulatory made up of narthex, lateral aisles, and galleries. Arcades on columns and piers divide these lateral spaces from the church's core. At the ground floor level, a projecting tripartite sanctuary with semi-circular apses on the interior and a polygonal main apse on the exterior terminates the church in the East. The apse's side chambers neither extend as far as the aisles' exterior walls nor do they have a gallery story.[7]

Because the present-day Hagia Sophia is the result of various building phases, the reconstruction of the original domed church has always been central to scholarship.[8] Kalliopi Theoharidou, who presented the most recent detailed investigation of the church, examined the different building materials in order to identify its original state. According to her, the limestone-brick masonry entirely belongs to the domed church's first building phase while the gneiss-brick masonry is the result of a second phase.[9] This classification disregards two important aspects:

1 It is well known that gneiss was used for the foundation of the domed church,[10] which unquestionably belongs to the initial building phase.
2 Limestone as well as gneiss is part of a shared type of masonry with alternating bands of brick and stone in which the measurements of bricks and joints are identical.[11]

Therefore, gneiss cannot act as an indicator for a subsequent building phase any longer and all masonry consisting of alternating bands of brick and stone – both limestone and gneiss – has to be considered as integral parts of the

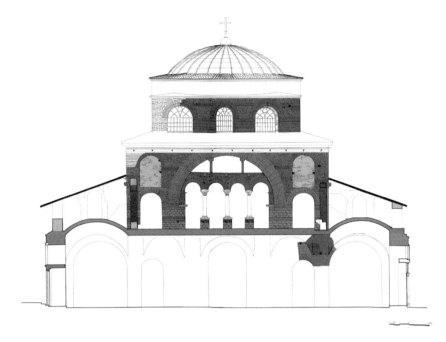

Figure 8.2 Reconstruction of the transverse section of Hagia Sophia (domed church). S. Feist (based upon Theoharidou 1988: pl. V).

church's original state. Beside the entire ground floor this new classification of the church's original masonry comprises most parts of the galleries' exterior and interior walls.[12] The embedded consoles in the galleries' interior walls and the masonry traces in the eastern walls of the lateral galleries indicate the original roof slope. Lean-to roofs are the most probable solution for the upper floors' initial state (Figure 8.2).[13]

Despite this new classification of the domed Hagia Sophia's original masonry, its original state shows some irregularities on the ground floor level as well as on the level of the galleries. These peculiarities are due to the contradictory treatment of the remains of the church's predecessor Basilica (B), which – unlike the Roman bath and Basilica (A) – was partly maintained. On the one hand, contact between old and new structures was strictly avoided at ground level. For this reason the new church was built on top of new independent foundations.[14] These new foundations caused a shifting of axes visible in the apse's side chambers' entrances, which are not located in the aisles' centre but have been moved next to the eastern corner piers. Not only these entrances but also discharging arches in the side chambers' eastern exterior walls are located above the old foundations to avoid contact between the previous basilica and the new domed church (Figure 8.1).[15] On the other hand, and contrary to the separation of old and new structures at ground level, the domed church's walls above ground incorporated parts of its basilical predecessor.

Figure 8.3 Fragments of the basilica's narthex in front of the domed church's west façade. U. Peschlow.

Apart from the common use of *spolia* – namely the reuse of limestone and gneiss as building material and the reuse of Late Antique architectural sculpture – at the Hagia Sophia in Thessalonike large parts of the basilica's narthex were maintained and were incorporated into the new domed church.[16] The hypothesis of the integration of the older basilical narthex is likely for the following reasons: Some fragments of the eastern wall of the basilica's narthex are preserved about 70 centimetres in front of the domed church's west façade (Figure 8.3).[17] Built with gneiss and brick, they run parallel to the church and rise higher than its floor. Although these structures are in a poor condition today, photographs from the 1970s testify a former connection between the fragmentary wall and the church's west façade (Figure 8.4). Neither the two windows nor the masonry above these connectors belong to the Hagia Sophia's initial state however.[18] They replaced the original rectangular recesses, which extended into the gallery floor of the domed church's west façade.[19] By setting the basilica's nave pilasters into these recesses, the Late Antique narthex and the new church from the Transitional Period were connected at two points (Figure 8.1).[20] In addition to these archaeological evidences, the maintenance of the basilical narthex would also explain the lack of decoration on the west façade of the domed church.[21] Furthermore, the examination of iconographic and written sources is indicative of a long-lasting connection between these two structures: in the 11th century, four of the six openings in today's western façade were decorated with fresco paintings.[22] Given the absence of traces of window and door jambs, the paintings had to be protected against weather by another structure – probably the basilica's narthex or at least its remaining

Figure 8.4 Detail of the fragments of the eastern wall of the basilica's narthex in front of the domed church's west façade that testify a former connection between the structures. U. Peschlow.

eastern wall.[23] Moreover, Symeon of Thessalonike mentions a μεγάλου νάρθηκος in his Hypotyposis.[24] If this refers to the old basilical narthex it must have been kept intact until the early 15th century.[25] Altogether it therefore seems probable that the Late Antique basilical narthex was maintained and was incorporated into the much smaller church and that it served as its exonarthex.

The maintenance and incorporation of the earlier narthex did not only leave traces on the church's exterior but also in its interior. The most affected areas include the Hagia Sophia's new (eso)narthex as well as its western gallery, which are closely connected with each other. Only the northern pendentive dome of the vaults of the esonarthex belongs to the original state.[26] Its southern counterpart, a cross vault, originates from a later structural alteration.[27] Nevertheless, it can be surmised that a pendentive dome originally covered this bay, too.[28] A subsequent alteration must also be assumed for the three central esonarthex vaults. After investigating the corresponding upper

Figure 8.5 Western gallery of Hagia Sophia, looking south. S. Feist.

floor level, it is obvious that this central area was raised at a later date because the vaults are cut into the western gallery's stylobate (Figure 8.5).[29] But what did the modified central esonarthex's areas look like originally? Cross vaults must be ruled out because the original vaults sprang from the same height as the present-day vaults do.[30] A central barrel vault, however, has not been proposed yet (Figure 8.2). A barrel vault would not only have sprung from the same height as today's vaults do, but the western gallery would also have had the same floor level as the lateral ones.

Nonetheless, because of the original pendentive domes on both sides of the esonarthex, the corresponding upper floor level – namely both western corner bays – must have been about 120 centimetres higher than the remaining gallery floor level (Figure 8.2). This irregularity can be explained as a result of the galleries' accessibility: today the Hagia Sophia's upper floor can be reached via the bell tower, which does not belong to the church's original state, as is testified by its masonry and by a joint between tower and church (Figure 8.6).[31] Originally, access to the galleries must have been granted by another way. It is probable that the old basilica's narthex not only served as the domed Hagia Sophia's exonarthex, but that also the church's upper floor was accessible through it. The higher cross vaults at both ends of the western gallery provided a corresponding floor level that connected the upper floor of the old narthex with the gallery level of the new domed church.[32] Hence the galleries' floor level in the exonarthex – and thus the basilica's entire upper floor – must have been about 120 centimetres higher than the new domed

Figure 8.6 Bell tower of Hagia Sophia, view from west. S. Feist.

church's gallery storey. It is likely that not only the corner bays' floor level was elevated, but that also their roof was higher and, thus, independent from the roof of the lateral galleries.

Probably the different floor levels of old and new church did not only affect the upper floor's corner bays of the domed Hagia Sophia but also its western gallery. While the lateral galleries are nearly identical, the interior wall of the western gallery is elevated: here the columns rest upon 120 centimetre-high pedestals and the springing of the arches as well as the consoles are 90 centimetres higher than those in the lateral galleries (Figures 8.5, 8.7). Scholarship

Figure 8.7 Galleries of Hagia Sophia (photo taken from the northern gallery, looking southwest). S. Feist.

has produced several reconstructions for the western gallery's original roofing system but there is no general agreement yet.[33]

Despite the deviation in the western gallery, the church's interior can be perceived as a unity. This homogeneity is achieved by the equal height of all cross-arms as well as by the unbroken continuity of convex cornices across all galleries – including those in the western part (Figure 8.7). In the north and south these convex cornices mark the springing of the arches of the galleries' interior walls.[34] Even though the springing of the arches in the western gallery is about 90 centimetres higher than the lateral ones, the convex cornices continue also in this area at the lower level (Figure 8.7). An additional second flat cornice that is located 90 centimetres higher marks the springing of the western arches (Figure 8.8).[35] Therefore, a contemporary beholder could not perceive any striking irregularity within the church.

In conclusion, three main assumptions can be made:

1 The rebuilding of the Hagia Sophia shows a marked determination to preserve and incorporate predecessor structures.
2 Contact between the old and new structures has been reduced to a minimum.
3 The re-use of older structural elements has not visibly affected the coherence of the new interior.

These features are not only characteristic for the rebuilding of Hagia Sophia of Thessalonike during the Transitional Period, but also for several other churches from the wider Byzantine Empire. The Hagia Sophia in Thessalonike

'Dark Age' Architecture of Hagia Sophia, Thessalonike 129

Figure 8.8 Northern column of the western gallery. S. Feist.

must, thus, be regarded as emblematic of a more widespread approach to Late Antique ecclesiastical architecture during the Transitional Period.

Notes

1 For a comparative study of Byzantine architecture from the Transitional Period or 'Dark Age' see the author's published PhD thesis, Feist 2019.
2 The most important scholarly works are (in chronological order): Texier and Pullan 1864: 154–158; Wulff 1903: 35–52; Diehl *et al.* 1918: 117–149, pl. XXXV-XLIX; Kalligas 1935; Theoharidou 1988 = Theoharidou 1994; Theoharidou 1992; Mentzos 2009. Theoharidou's Greek monograph contains better illustrations and updated footnotes and bibliography. Furthermore footnotes 27, 29, 57,

130 *Sabine Feist*

and 338, the figures 7 and plate 40a, as well as the fourth appendix including plates 44–55, are added.

3 Excavation reports are published in: Kalligas 1936, 1938, 1939, 1940, 1941–1944; Pelekanides 1941–1952, 1960, 1961–1962 and Drosoyanni 1963. For the bath see also Adam-Veleni 2003: 157–159. For the Late Antique basilicas see also Mentzos 1981; Theoharidou 1988: 9–13; Hadjitryphonos 1998–1999: 104–106; Kazamia-Tsernou 2009: 340–344; Mentzos, 2009: 87; Ćurčić 2010: 61, 105.

4 5th century: Pelekanides 1961–1962: 256; Hattersley-Smith 1996: 144; Mentzos 2009: 87; and Ćurčić 2010: 61. 4th century: Theoharidou 1988: 10.

5 4th/5th century: Diehl *et al.* 1918: 130. 6th century: Texier and Pullan 1864: 154; Strzygowski 1901: 157, and Wulff 1914: 386. 7th century: Laurent 1895: 431–433; Theoharidou 1988: 155–157; Ousterhout 2001: 4, 10, and Ćurčić 2010: 61. 8th century: Kalligas 1935: 65; Buchwald 1969: 43; Janin 1975: 409; Mango 1975: 165; Krautheimer 1986: 295; Cormack, 1980–1981: 122–123, and Ruggieri 1991: 261.

6 Theoharidou 1988: 156; Mentzos 2009: 87; Ćurčić 2010: 204.

7 For detailed plans see Theoharidou 1988: pls. I-XI.

8 Different building phases are for example discussed by: Diehl *et al.* 1918: 118–130; Kalligas 1935: 22; Theoharidou 1988: 35–52; Ćurčić 2010: 259.

9 Theoharidou 1988: 126–131.

10 Theoharidou 1988: 137.

11 For the measurements see Theoharidou 1988: Table II. The change of building materials might also be caused by trivial reasons: if the limestone-brick masonry consists of reused material its source might have been exhausted. Furthermore gneiss is a local product and consequently cheaper than limestone.

12 The upper parts of the side galleries' lateral exterior walls, parts of the side galleries' east and west exterior walls, and the entire exterior wall of the west gallery originate from subsequent alterations (Theoharidou 1988: 49–52, pls. VIII-XI). Furthermore the upper parts of the church's exterior walls (including apse and side chambers) were elevated at some later date to support a new roofing system (Theoharidou 1988: 51).

13 Lean-to roofs have already been suggested by Wulff 1903: 39, 105, Figs. 4–5; Pelekanides 1955: 398–403, Fig. 1, and Mango 1975: 165. Kalligas 1935: 17, 20 proposes supporting pillars instead of a roof truss that would have blocked the upper windows. For gallery roofs without a truss (as it is shown in the reconstruction: Fig. 2) see Choisy 1899: 530–531 and Orlandos 1952: 139, Figs. 100, 118. Due to Theoharidou's distinction of limestone and gneiss masonry (see above) she considers the galleries' consoles as well as the roof slope as part of a subsequent alteration (Theoharidou 1988: 53). For the first phase she proposes cross-vaulted galleries instead (Theoharidou 1988: 53–59 (lateral galleries), 59–63 (west gallery), Figs. 20–22). Her reconstruction of the church's original state disregards the masonry's unity on the one hand, on the other hand it remains unclear how the cross vaults should have been supported. (Theoharidou 1988: Fig. 20). Diehl *et al.* 1918: 121, and Mentzos 2009: 94, for example, argue against galleries in the Hagia Sophia's original state.

14 Theoharidou 1988: 137.

15 Theoharidou 1988: 10.

16 For the reuse of architectural sculpture see Mentzos 1981: 216–219; Theoharidou 1988: 112–124, and Ćurčić 2010: 105. Wulff 1903: 50, and Kautzsch 1936: 142–143 argue against the reuse of the capitals. For the maintenance of the narthex, see Theoharidou 1988: 64–68, and Ćurčić 2010: 258.

17 Theoharidou 1988: 10, 125–126.

18 This has been proven by the removal of the plaster of the western wall in the 1940s and 1970s (Pelekanides 1955: 398, 401; Theoharidou 1988: 35, 66).

'Dark Age' Architecture of Hagia Sophia, Thessalonike 131

19 Theoharidou 1988: 66.
20 Theoharidou 1988: 65.
21 Theoharidou 1988: 66.
22 Pelekanides 1955: 407; Cormack 1980–1981: 113.
23 Although Kalligas and Pelekanides did not establish a connection between the surviving basilical narthex and the domed church, they already proposed a protective structure (Kalligas 1941–1944: 48; Pelekanides 1955: 401–402).
24 Darrouzès 1976: 72, ft. 17 seems to be the only reference to the Hypotyposis (Folio 20v: 'εἰς τὸν ἐπάνω τῆς βορείου πύλης τοῦ μεγάλου νάρθηκος ναὸν τοῦ Σωτῆρος.')
25 Darrouzès 1976: 72 equates the "great narthex" with the church's atrium.
26 Theoharidou 1988: 40, 169.
27 Kalligas 1935: 16; Theoharidou 1988: 44.
28 Kalligas 1936: 116; Theoharidou 1988: 59–62. Janin 1975: 410 considers the northern pendentive dome as a subsequent alteration.
29 Theoharidou 1988: 44.
30 This has been proven by an investigation of the narthex's masonry (Theoharidou 1988: 60).
31 The bell tower's date is uncertain. Its erection in Turkish times has been proposed by Wulff 1903: 42; Kalligas 1935: 14–15, and Theoharidou 1988: 16–18.
32 The galleries might have been accessible by wooden staircases from these higher corner bays.
33 Kalligas 1935: 17 proposes a lean-to roof supported by pillars for the western gallery's original state. According to him the pillars have rested upon three small square bases recognisable on old photographs. Pelekanides 1955: 399–401, Fig. 1, suggests a western gallery without floor, roof and exterior wall. Theoharidou 1988: 59–63, Fig. 20, proposes cross vaults. The complicated roofing system of the church's western gallery cannot be discussed in detail in this chapter. Nonetheless, the elevation of the western corner bays as well as of the interior wall of the western gallery might argue for only one unified roof in this area.
34 Theoharidou 1988: 112–113, Fig. 33.2.
35 Theoharidou 1988: 112–113, Fig. 33.4.

References

Adam-Veleni, P. (2003), 'Thessaloniki: history and town planning', in D. Grammenos, ed., *Roman Thessaloniki*, Thessaloniki.

Buchwald, H. (1969), *The church of the Archangels in Sige near Mudania*. Vienna.

Choisy, A. (1899), *Histoire de l'architecture*, I. Paris.

Cormack, R. (1980–1981), 'The apse mosaic of S. Sophia at Thessaloniki', *DChAE* 10: 111–135.

Ćurčić, S. (2010), *Architecture in the Balkans: From Diocletian to Süleyman the Magnificent*. New Haven.

Darrouzès, J. (1976), 'Sainte-Sophie de Thessalonique d'après un rituel', *REB* 34: 45–78.

Diehl, C. *et al.* (1918), *Les monuments chrétiens de Salonique*. Paris.

Drosoyanni, F. (1963), 'Μεσαιωνικά Μακεδονίας', *ArchDelt* 18 (B2), 235–242.

Feist, S. (2019), *Die byzantinische Sakralarchitektur der Dunklen Jahrhunderte*. Wiesbaden.

Hadjitryphonos, E. (1998–1999), 'Ἡ εικόνα, το περιεχόμενο και οι επεμβάσεις στο χώρο γύρω από την Αγία Σοφία Θεσσαλονίκης', *Μνημείο και περιβάλλον* 5: 97–129.

132 Sabine Feist

Hattersley-Smith, K. (1996), *Byzantine public architecture between the fourth and early eleventh centuries AD. With special reference to the towns of Byzantine Macedonia.* Thessaloniki.

Janin, R. (1975), *Les églises et les monastères des grands centres Byzantins (Bithynie, Hellespont, Latros, Galèsios, Trébizonde, Athènes, Thessalonique)*. Paris.

Kalligas, M. (1935), *Die Hagia Sophia von Thessalonike.* Würzburg.

Kalligas, M. (1936), Άνασκαφικαί έρευναι εἰς τόν ἐν Θεσσαλονίκη ναόν τῆς Ἁγίας Σοφίας', *PraktArchEt* 91: 111–118.

Kalligas, M. (1938), Άνασκαφικαί έρευναι εἰς τόν ἐν Θεσσαλονίκη ναόν τῆς Ἁγίας Σοφίας', *PraktArchEt* 93: 67–75.

Kalligas, M. (1939), Άνασκαφικαί έρευναι εἰς τόν ἐν Θεσσαλονίκη ναόν τῆς Ἁγίας Σοφίας', *PraktArchEt* 94: 73–84.

Kalligas, M. (1940), Άνασκαφικαί έρευναι εἰς τόν ἐν Θεσσαλονίκη ναόν τῆς Ἁγίας Σοφίας', *PraktArchEt* 95: 23–27.

Kalligas, M. (1941–1944), Έργασίαι εἰς τόν ναόν τῆς Ἁγίας Σοφίας τῆς Θεσσαλονίκης, *PraktArchEt* 96-99: 44–52.

Kautzsch, R. (1936), *Kapitellstudien. Beiträge zu einer Geschichte des spätantiken Kapitells im Osten vom vierten bis ins siebente Jahrhundert.* Berlin.

Kazamia-Tsernou, M. (2009), *Μνημειακή τοπογραφία Θεσσαλονίκης. Οι ναοί Α': 4ος – 8ος αιώνας.* Thessaloniki.

Krautheimer, R. (1986), *Early Christian and Byzantine architecture*, 4th edition. London.

Laurent, J. (1895), 'Sur la date des églises St. Démétrius et Ste. Sophie à Thessalonique', *BZ* 4: 420–434.

Mango, C. (1975), *Byzantinische Architektur.* Stuttgart.

Mentzos, A. (1981), 'Συμβολή στην έρευνα του αρχαιότερου ναού της Αγίας Σοφίας Θεσσαλονίκης', *Makedonika* 21: 201–221.

Mentzos, A. (2009), 'Il problema della prima fase', in R. Farioli Campanati, ed., *Ideologia e cultura artistica tra Adriatico e Mediterraneo orientale (IV-X secolo). Il ruolo dell'autorità ecclesiastica alla luce di nuovi scavi e ricerche. Atti del convegno internazionale, Bologna – Ravenna, 26-29 November 2007*, Bologna: 87–98.

Orlandos, A. (1952), *Η ξυλόστεγος παλαιοχριστιανική βασιλική της μεσογειακής λεκάνης. Μελέτη περί της γενέσεως, της καταγωγής, της αρχιτεκτονικής μορφής και της διακοσμήσεως των χριστιανικών οίκων λατρείας από των αποστολικών χρόνων μέχρις Ιουστινιανού*, Βιβλιοθήκη της εν Αθήναις Αρχαιολογικής Εταιρείας 35, Athens.

Ousterhout, R. (2001), 'The architecture of iconoclasm', in L. Brubaker, and J. Haldon, eds., *Byzantium in the iconoclast era (ca. 680–850). The sources*, Aldershot: 3–36.

Pelekanides, S. (1955), Νέαι έρευναι εἰς τήν Ἁγίαν Σοφίαν Θεσσαλονίκης καί ἡ ἀποκατάστασις τῆς ἀρχαίας αὐτῆς μορφῆς', *Πεπραγμένα τοῦ Θ' Διεθνοῦς Βυζαντινολογικοῦ Συνεδρίου* 1955: 398–407.

Pelekanides, S. (1941-1952), 'Χριστιανικά κιονόκρανα μέ ἀνεμιζόμενα φύλλα', *Makedonika* 2: 167–178.

Pelekanides, S. (1960), 'Μεσαιωνικά Μακεδονίας', *ArchDelt* 16 (B2): 222–230.

Pelekanides, S. (1961–19620), 'Μεσαιωνικά Μακεδονίας', *ArchDelt* 17 (B2): 253–256.

Ruggieri, V. (1991), *Byzantine religious architecture (582–867): its history and structural elements.* Rome.

Strzygowski, J. (1901), 'Die Sophienkirche in Saloniki. Ein Denkmal, das für die Wissenschaft zu retten wäre', *OC* 1: 152–158.

'Dark Age' Architecture of Hagia Sophia, Thessalonike   133

Texier, C., and Pullan, R. (1864), *L'architecture Byzantine. Ou recueil de monuments des premiers temps du christianisme en Orient précédé de recherches historiques et archéologiques*. London.

Theoharidou, K. (1988), *The Architecture of Hagia Sophia, Thessaloniki. From Its Erection up to the Turkish Conquest*, B.A.R., International Series 399. Oxford.

Theoharidou, K. (1992), 'The structure of Hagia Sophia in Thessaloniki from its construction to the present', in R. Mark, and A. Çakmak, eds., *Hagia Sophia from the Age of Justinian to the Present*, Cambridge: 83–99.

Theoharidou, K. (1994), *Η αρχιτεκτονική του ναού της Αγίας Σοφίας στη Θεσσαλονίκη. Από την ίδρυσή του μέχρι σήμερα*. Athens.

Wulff, O. (1903), *Die Koimesiskirche in Nicäa und ihre Mosaiken nebst den verwandten kirchlichen Baudenkmälern. Eine Untersuchung zur Geschichte der byzantinischen Kunst im 1. Jahrtausend*. Strasbourg.

Wulff, O. (1914), *Altchristliche und byzantinische Kunst 2. Die byzantinische Kunst von der ersten Blüte bis zu ihrem Ausgang*. Berlin.

Part 3

Urban and Rural Revival

9 Bridging the *Grande Brèche*

Rethinking Coins, Ceramics, Corinth, and Commerce in the Centuries Following AD 500

G. D. R. Sanders

A few years ago, I outlined the problems facing archaeologists working with 5th through 7th-century material in Southern Greece.[1] Although largely negative, there were some points of light in prospect. I represented our current understanding of latest Antiquity in southern Greece as something of a Potemkin village; a portrayal of urban and rural archaeology that scholars wanted to see rather than what really was. This unhappy mirage was generated by the inductive imposition of historical events on the later archaeology mainly by preoccupied Classicists. For instance, we were told that the Athenian lamp makers ceased glazing their lamps and the Athenian sculpture workshops closed after the Herulian sack in AD 267. At Corinth we hear that 'the last quarter of the 4th century was a period of destruction and decline … In 395 the invading Goths under Alaric delivered the coup de grace to this unhappy period'. One authority wrote that the buildings of the Early Christian period after Alaric 'bear the marks of material dilapidation, artistic decline and civic hopelessness'.[2] The last nails in this cultural coffin at Corinth were hammered in by the Slavs.

My pessimism about these outdated perspectives on Late Antiquity has recently turned to optimism with the appearance of a new generation of scholars who appreciate Byzantine archaeology in a novel fashion. Many are not trained as historians or art historians, let alone as Classicists or Byzantinists, but rather as archaeologists. They take an altogether more systematically scientific approach to their work, focusing on what the earth yields rather than the weight of received orthodoxy. More and more, I am seeing stratigraphy, potsherds, and faunal, human and vegetal remains replacing chronicles, earthquakes, and invaders as primary resources for understanding the period. Like northern European and Italian archaeologists, this new generation is digging by single contexts in large open areas, rather than in Kenyon-Wheeler boxes. They are, moreover, thinking outside of the box. In the Northeast Peloponnese, this change has come about because leaders like Professor Timothy Gregory and Doctor Dimitri Athanassoulis have promoted the work of competent younger scholars who are participating in an open discussion of issues thereby moving the field inexorably forward.

DOI: 10.4324/9781003429470-12

138   *G. D. R. Sanders*

In Central Greece the problems we faced understanding the countryside between 500 and 800 arose from a lack of data from Corinth itself. This situation has changed somewhat since the publication of four horizons from Corinth dated conventionally by fine ware imports, lamps, and associated coins.[3] The presentation of these assemblages has influenced the thinking of archaeologists working with material elsewhere in the northeast Peloponnese. These include Jenni Hjohlman, who was introduced to Horizon 4 on a visit to Corinth when researching her doctoral dissertation on the pottery from Pyrgoudhi in the Berbati valley,[4] Mark Hammond, whose own dissertation on pottery from the Panayia Field at Corinth was overseen by both the authors,[5] Yannis Lolos and Elli Tzavella working with survey material at Sikyon,[6] and Chris Cloke for his dissertation on the Nemea Survey pottery.[7]

If setting the archaeological record straight has played its part, the history we relied on has been shown by Ilias Anagnostakis and Anthony Kaldellis to have been art. They read the *Chronicle of Monemvasia* as an adaption of Pausanias and the story of Basil I and the widow Danielis as a version of Solomon and the Queen of Sheba to show that the history of the period should not be taken entirely at face value.[8]

With the terrible spectre of the Slavs tamed, the 7th century in southern Greece now appears relatively healthy. As Bill Caraher said on a drive up to a remote 7th-century hilltop site in the Western Argolid Regional Project area '[Fifteen years ago the claim of 7th century material seemed preposterous] but now, if a survey project does not have 7th-century material, someone is doing something wrong'.[9] So far, we have succeeded in pushing the onset of the Dark Ages later, and this has been achieved simply by publishing assemblages conventionally. More can be done by critically appraising the quality of the archaeology which produced the scholarship on which we have relied, for instance how past archaeologists understood coins in the excavated record and how this has shaped pottery chronologies. Recent work at Corinth has shown how a more rigorous and holistic approach to contexts can produce significant shifts even in extensively published and well-established areas such as Hellenistic pottery.[10]

Since Corinth has been so important for producing pottery sequences and chronologies, it seems logical too to reconsider why material of the 6th to 11th centuries is so poorly represented in the extensive areas excavated to date; can this be a real gap in a city known to have been extant even if a shadow of its former self? If the city reconfigured itself in Late Antiquity, as we know Athens did, then it is possible that we have missed the monuments of this half millennium. Finally, a better understanding of who had pottery may lead to an insight as to why material culture in these centuries is so poorly known. The object of this essay is not to solve problems but, like its earlier form,[11] to provoke discussion and reflection so that we may understand the nature of the problems better.

The 'Cult of the Coin'

Regrettably, coins are the foundation of archaeological chronology for the period in question. Pottery, the commonest artefact found during excavation and in surface survey, is usually dated by the latest coins in a context without giving much consideration to the condition of the coin and how long it had been in circulation before it was lost.[12] In fact, the chronology of John Hayes' monumental *Late Roman Pottery* (*LRP*) is so deeply entrenched in the archaeological psyche that archaeologists in Late Roman levels almost automatically turn to it to date their contexts before consulting their own coins and stratigraphy. This approach does not encourage periodic testing of Hayes' assertions and tends to perpetuate the status quo.

Coins of the 5th century are frustrating for many reasons. The commonest 5th-century coins found are *minimi* or *nummi*, small coppers with a theoretical value of 7,000–7,200 to the gold *solidus*.[13] A majority of them, down to the Anastasian reforms in 498, are only 8 to 11 mm in diameter and on average weigh 0.9 grams. They are consequently quite difficult objects to see in excavated earth. Excavations prior to World War II at Corinth and the Athenian Agora employed several hundred workmen, wielding large pick-axes in extensive areas under minimal supervision (Figure 9.1). At peak efficiency in the Athenian Agora, in 1939, a daily average of 215 workers were employed who in 18 weeks moved 56,000 tonnes of earth. That is an average

Figure 9.1 Excavation at the Athenian Agora. Removal of the 'Burnt Layers' June 23, 1933. Site Notebook H'-5-43, p. 865, Agora image 2012.34.1153. Note the wooden apparatus in the background. This is the conveyor belt which carried the excavated earth to the dump. Agora Archives.

140 G. D. R. Sanders

of 14.5 tonnes per man per week, or about 2.4 tons a day.[14] To put this in perspective, a time and motion study at Corinth in 2004 estimated that the workmen removed about 1 m^3 (ca. 1.7 tons) of plough zone per person in a seven-hour working day. Working at this speed in the era when most of the contexts used by Hayes for *LRP* were excavated, the ability to recover pottery and coins was very poor. At Corinth, sieves were rarely and selectively used until the 1990s. These were shaker sieves with a 10 mm mesh that required two men to operate and, as a consequence, were expensive to deploy. Obviously, *nummi* were not systematically recovered. In fact the recovery rate of all material culture, even in relatively modern excavations, is not good.

Today, at least at Corinth, all contexts are partially sieved and many are sieved 100% with a mesh of a few millimetres.[15] The effect on recovery rates has been dramatic and is measurable. In 5th and 6th-century contexts, obviously digging very carefully, between 90% and 95% of the *nummi* are recovered in the sieve. It is difficult to believe that many Mediterranean excavations achieved anything like a 5 to 10% rate of *nummus* recovery, let alone in the Athenian Agora excavations of 1930s.

The problem with 5th-century *nummi* is compounded by their fabric. From ca. 404/408 until at least the reign of Anastasius I (491–518) *nummi* in the eastern provinces were made from a bronze alloy with a high lead content. Coins that were in frequent use became so worn as to be illegible and when buried, the lead oxidises and deteriorates. On the evidence of four hoards from Sardis, Barbara Burrell concludes that ' … in the fifth century probably half of the coins circulating were unmarked, unidentifiable as legal tender at all, and included a large proportion of old coins as well … '.[16]

Early in the reign of Anastasius I the *nummus* rapidly declined in weight. These coins are also often illegible, indeed some were not even struck and yet they still circulated. Anastasius reformed the coinage in 498 with the introduction of the *follis*, worth 40 *nummi*, with sub-divisions of half, quarter, and eighth *follis* coins in addition to the *nummi* with a value of 1/23,040 of a gold *solidus*.[17] A second reform in 512 increased the size of the *follis* and increased the value of a *nummus* to 1/11,520 of a gold *solidus*.[18] Notwithstanding the reforms, hoard evidence from Greece demonstrates that *nummi* were not demonetised and continued to circulate.[19] Indeed these small denominations continued to be struck up to the end of Justinian I's reign when the follis began to decline in size and the *nummus*' place as petty coinage was taken by *dodecanummia* and *pentanummia*.[20] For instance, over half of the 225 coins in the Blue Cigarette Box Hoard of the mid-6th century were illegible *nummi*, and the legible coins included 18 of the very small, light coins of Anastasius.[21] The mid-6th century '1937 Bath Hoard' at Corinth had 387 coins of which 185 were illegible; there were also 92 of Anastasius and only six coins of Justinian.[22] These and other central Greek hoards of the period make it clear that old coins remained in circulation for very long periods.

The longevity of coins is poorly understood however. Examination of coins in hoards and shipwrecks indicates that while some coins were lost within months of their issue, the majority saw extended circulation, even several decades, before deposition. Coins are also extremely resilient. Many context finds, like a proportion of the pottery in a given deposit, are re-deposited as survivors. Together, circulation and re-deposition account for the disturbing statistic from Portchester in England that only about 5% of the coins in a context dated within 20 years of the latest pottery and almost 50% were minted forty or more years before.[23] In other words, one has to find a large number of coins in a deposit to be sure of finding even one that offers a reasonable terminus date for the deposition of the accompanying material culture.

Evidence that this pattern of older coins in a deposit is not just random re-deposition of older coins, but reflects the continued use of old coins, comes from the wider Peloponnese, where Callegher compares coin usage in city and countryside. During the 6th century, 4th, and 5th centuries coins continued to circulate along with illegible coins and locally struck *nummi*, and they are even found in hoards down to the end of the 6th century.[24]

Given these observations, it is easy to imagine that in situations, such as the Athenian Agora excavations of the 1930s, if tiny coins of Anastasius I, Justin I, and Justinian were not recovered, or were illegible or were unstruck, then contexts of the 6th century have been mistakenly dated by their associated legible coins to the reigns of Zeno (474–91), Leo I (457–74), Marcian (450–7), or even earlier. It seems that excavators, like Henry Robinson, studying Athenian Agora contexts from early excavations considered 'only those coins sufficiently well preserved to be included in the Agora catalog of coins' because 'so many were corroded as to be wholly illegible; still more were in a condition which permitted no more than a partial identification'.[25] As a result, they are almost certainly biasing their chronology towards the 5th century when a 6th-century date is highly likely. The belief in coin dating as traditionally practised certainly tends to chronological conservatism. To illustrate the point, I need to digress from the subject period by several hundred years and briefly discuss lessons learned from the excavation of Frankish Corinth.

Between 1986 and 1997 a large green field site south of the museum was opened and excavated down to the floor levels that preceded the abandonment and collapse of several large late medieval units. The latest coins on the floors were many of the later 13th and early 14th centuries struck for rulers of the Principality of Morea down to 1313. Coin dating the excavation suggested that the end of this part of Corinth came about as the result of either an earthquake or earthquakes in the first two decades of the century or a Catalan raid in 1312.[26] All the pottery found in pits, fills, and on floors was, obviously, late 13th to early 14th century.

When I re-engaged in the study of the period, a short article on the northern Italian *tessere mercantile* (jetons) from Corinth caught my attention.[27] Several of the published jetons were found in the excavation in question. One, in a stone built pit under the floor and hearth of one room and under the roof and wall collapse, was struck for the Giovanni Sercambi and

142   G. D. R. Sanders

Nicolao di Bartolomeo Vanni society in Lucca. Giovanni was born in 1348 and did not inherit his father's estate until he was in his 30s.[28] This context dates the construction of the unit at least 60 and more likely 80 years after our archaeological interpretation of the coin profile suggested that it had been abandoned. Lest this seems an aberration, there are at least ten good deposits now dated either by late 14th-century *tessere* or by late 14th- to 15th-century mould-blown glass with the same pottery profile. To say that this revelation has upset the status quo is an understatement. What we had understood to be 12th and 13th-century Corinth is now Renaissance Corinth! Furthermore, it indicates that the coins now offer a narrative that was previously difficult for most Classical archaeologists to believe.

The reason why all the 'lost' coins were in pre-destruction contexts was because they were not lost but merely not recovered because they had lost any monetary value. When they circulated as cash, each represented an hour's labour and could purchase up to two kg of wheat, enough to feed a family of four for a day.[29] In the mid-14th century, they were replaced by Venetian coins and became obsolete. Closer examination of contexts and pottery of the 13th century and earlier 14th century, re-dated to account for the new information, strongly suggests that changes in coinage at Corinth demonetised ca. 1210, 1225, and 1267 also led to the non-retrieval of the old modules. Effectively the *terminus post quem* is not the date of their issue, but of their demonetisation.

This powerful example of the way we use coins to date contexts has great significance for the interpretation of coin finds in contexts of other periods. For instance, if there is a significant number of coins in a context, were they really 'lost' or were they obsolete? In the case of Late Roman contexts, were large numbers of associated 5th-century and a few 6th-century *nummi* indicative of a third quarter of the 6th-century date when the *pentanummus* became the smallest denomination circulating? Similarly, are several *penta-nummi* in a context indicative of a third quarter of the 7th-century context, when 20 *nummi* coins became the smallest denomination minted? This bears on the actual date of the African Red Slip form 104.15 dated AD 580–585 cited above (n. 12) that came from a context with ten coins of Justin II and one of Tiberius II and other significant Late Roman 'coin dated' pottery contexts, the most significant of which by far is discussed below.

The chronology of the Late Roman pottery

Pottery experts are usually not also numismatists at they seem to have a poor comprehension of coins and their circulation and few actually look at the coins in the contexts they are studying. Personally, I like to look at every coin in the contexts I am studying because sometimes attributions may have changed since the catalogued identification was made. It is possible that even illegible coins can be given a range of dates based on fabric, size, or weight. For instance, *nummi* of the mid-5th century are remarkably homogenous in size and weight but *nummi* of Anastasius I (and later emperors) are

Bridging the Grande Brèche   143

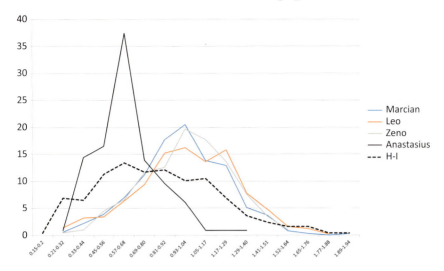

Figure 9.2 Diameter and weight of *nummi* based on an unscientific sample taken from Burrell 2007, the Athenian Agora and Corinth collections.

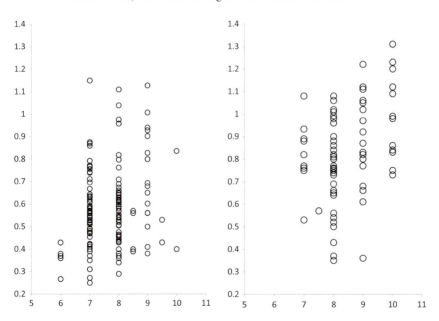

Figure 9.3 Coins of Anastasius I (left) and Zeno (right) charted by diameter (x) and weight (y).

significantly smaller and lighter (Figure 9.2, Figure 9.3). The bottom line is that coins that are less than or equal to 0.8 grams in weight or less than or equal to 7mm in diameter are probably coins of Anastasius or later emperors (Figure 9.3). In fact, the lighter, the later.

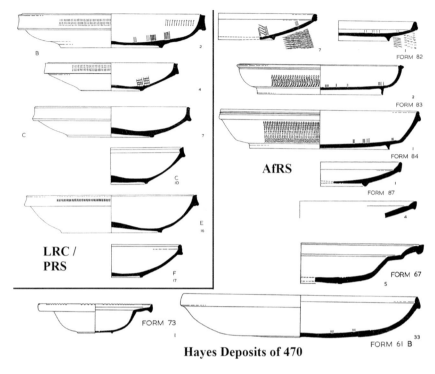

Figure 9.4 Phocean Red Slip (PRS) and African Red Slip (AfRS) in 'the deposits of *c.* 460–75', from Hayes 1972.

An example is the contexts Hayes repeatedly describes in *LRP* as 'the deposits of *c.* 460–75',[30] crucial for understanding Late Roman C and African Red Slip fine wares. These deposits are important for establishing the chronology of AfRS Forms 61A, 63, 64, 66, 67, 68, 73, 82, 83, 84, 85, 87, 91, LRC Forms 2 and 3B, 3C, 3E, 5, 8, and both Athenian lamps and their imitations (Figure 9.4, Figure 9.5). Hayes dated the pottery as contemporary with what he considered the latest coins ('with coins down to Leo I' 457–74) without allowing for any extended use of the coins in question. When one collects the dispersed *Athens Agora* xxxii individual pieces together, one sees that his date for each piece has become more nuanced over time and that occasional late 5th and early 6th-century shapes of pottery have infiltrated 'the deposits of *c.* 460–75', and that there are also several residual pieces. Deposit H-I 7–8:1 in particular has morphed from being a precisely dated deposit into a dumped fill or fills that contains pottery dating from ca. 400 to the early 6th century. Methodologically this is a bit unsettling because the 'deposit' he used to define the third quarter of the 5th century in *LRP* is no longer what it was originally purported to be, and yet continues to define the third quarter of the 5th century.

More unsettling still is to look at the 'coins down to Leo I' in Deposit H-I 7–8:1 of the Agora of Athens. In fact, there were 1,482 coins of which the latest,

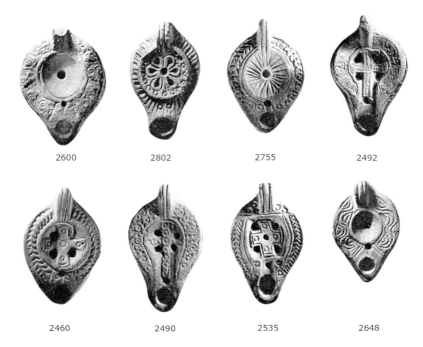

Figure 9.5 Type XXVIII lamps and one Type XXXI lamp (no. 2490) in 'the deposits of *c*. 460–75', from Perlzweig 1961.

one of Constans II, 12 Medieval, and one Ottoman are certainly contaminated from later undetected strata (Figure 9.6). There were also 201 illegible coins simply listed as 'Vandal' but which more recent research has shown are regional official issues, for instance of 'monogram' and other *nummi* of the 5th and 6th centuries.[31] Of the 21 identified 'Vandal' coins, two belonged to Justinian and these suggest that a significant proportion of the unidentified examples continued the sequence down to the mid-6th century. There were also two coins of Baduila (549–52), and probably one of Justin I.[32] One each of Baduila and Justinian came from the burnt layer and another of each ruler came from the stratum immediately above. Hayes may have considered these to be contaminations like the medieval and later coins but here it is important to note that the overall statistics for the coins in 'the deposits of c. 460–75' are remarkably similar to those for mid-6th century hoards (Figure 9.7), for instance, two from Corinth.[33]

Knowing now about non-retrieval and non-recording of 6th-c *nummi*, the presence of these mid-6th century coins makes Hayes's assertion that these strata are dated by 'coins down to Leo I' difficult to substantiate. Indeed, his assertion that deposit I-J 9:1 'with early 6th century coins' and AfRS forms 82.7, 88, 89/90, 93b, 96/97/99A and PRS forms 3F, 3 small, 7 and 9 (Figure 9.6) that he initially dated to the early 6th century suggesting that the pottery might be rather earlier,[34] casts further doubt. The coins were two of Anastasius and one of Justinian

146   *G. D. R. Sanders*

Greek	62	Marcian 450-457	17
Pre-Constantine	10	Leo I 457-474	14
Roman 4th century	104	Roman late 4th and 5th century	232
Constantine I 306-33 A.D.	4	Roman 5th century	33
Constantius II 323-361 A.D.	27	"Vandal"	201
Constantius Gallus 325-354 A.D.	1	Justin I 518-527	1
Julian I 355-363 A.D.	4	Justinian I 527-5 A.D.	2
Valens 364-378	9	Baduila 549-552 A.D.	2
Valentinian I 364-75	4	Illegible	74
Gratian 375-383 A.D.	3	Not a coin	21
Theodosius I 379-395	28	Disintegrated	171
Maximus I 383-388	1	Constans II, 641-66 A.D.	1
Flavius Victor 383-388	1	Alexius I	3
Valentinian II 383-392	20	Anon Class XI follis	2
Arcadius 395-408	40	Manuel I, 1143-1180 A.D.	5
Honorius 395-423 A.D.	33	William Villehardouin 1245-62	1
Theodosius II 408-450 A.D.	31	Antoine Venier 1382-1400 A.D.	1
Valentinian III 425-455	5	Turkish	1
Total Constantine to Valentinian III	315		

Figure 9.6 Coins from 'the deposits of *c.* 460–75'.

Hoard	No. coins	% legible	Latest	% legible 40+ years older than latest
Mattingly 1931	478	76	Justinian x 1	99.7
Edwards 1937	742	45	Justinian x 1	99.7
Deposits of *c.* 460-75	1080	49	Baduila x 2	99.1

Figure 9.7 A comparison of the coins in 'the deposits of *c.* 460–75' with two hoards.

I, and may indicate that his revised date of ca. 520–540 is rather closer to the mark,[35] but he persists in dating the individual pieces to 'early 6th century' or ca. AD 500–525 (Hayes 2009, 229 no. 1118, 230 no. 1134, 231 nos. 1138 and 1143, 232 no, 1152),[36] as they had been in *LRP*.[37] At Corinth an almost complete PRS form 3C bowl was recently found in a mid-6th century context with coins of Anastasius and Justin I while *LRP* form 84.1, a complete bowl from Corinth that Hayes dated mid- to late 5th-century by the associated pottery was actually found nearby and probably from the same phase of deposition as the 3C bowl, was stratified over a context with a coin of Justin II (565–74).[38] I suggest that there is ample evidence to suggest a much later date for the pottery and lamps (Figure 9.7) in 'the deposits of *c*. 460–75' and that these should be ca. 525 to 575+. It gives one good reason to re-examine the dating evidence for contexts at Antioch, Abu Mena, Elephantine, Carthage, Marseilles, and, obviously, Corinth.

In dating deposits at Corinth thought to be of the first half of the 5th century (Assemblage 1) and of the second half of the 5th century to as late as the beginning of the 6th century (Assemblage 2), Slane and Sanders relied on the evidence of the canonical fine ware chronology laid out in *LRP* and *Agora XXXII* rather than the coins found with the pottery. Our Assemblage 1 had a coin of Marcian and another identified as either Leo I or Zeno.[39] Although Kathleen Slane does not agree, based on these coins, and sieved contexts excavated under my direction, rather than un-sieved contexts excavated between 30 and 80 years ago, I would now argue that our Assemblage 1 was deposited after the third quarter of the 5th century and would now date our Assemblage 2, which resembles 'the deposits of *c*. 460–75' to the mid-6th century.

This proposal has potentially tremendous implications. If correct, it will drag earlier 5th-century material into the 6th century and move 6th-century pottery well into the 7th century, a period for which we have far fewer coins. In this light, one late 6th to early 7th-century context from the Athenian Agora is worth considering. Hayes illustrated substantially preserved fine wares including PRS form 10A, and AfRS form 99.[40] Although he mentions a coin found with later pottery illustrated,[41] he seems to consider the coins with the PRS form 10A and AfRS form 99C to be insufficient in light of the 'established' dates. The pots were found in the make-up of a floor in a room with two coins of Constans II (641–668).[42]

It would also mean that historical non-events, such as the 551 Corinth earthquake (see below), the Slavic invasion, and our reliance on fuzzy coin dating, need to be replaced in our thinking by a closer understanding of depositional processes, stratigraphy and historical processes. Even so, my conclusions do not yet help much at Corinth. Even with these new potentially 6th-century deposits, the city seems to have been in transition, even decline, from the mid-6th century onwards, unless this is a mirage produced by the topographical focus of the excavations for over a century. To this we now turn.

The fortifications and location of Byzantine Corinth

Since 1896, the American excavations at Corinth have concentrated on the area of the Roman Forum with less extensive excavations in the Theatre, the Odeum, the Asklepieion, the Gymnasium area, the Demeter Sanctuary, and the Cenchreae Gate basilica. Until the 1970s, several generations of archaeologists assumed that the Forum lay over the Greek agora and that the overlying medieval market place was a direct descendant of its Greek and Roman function. When Timothy Gregory turned his attention to the Late Roman

148 G. D. R. Sanders

fortification wall, he thought that he had found traces of evidence south and west of the Forum. These led him to believe that the 'Epistyle Wall' in the Gymnasium excavation area was part of the northern line of the fortifications and his plan of the walls reasonably has the Forum at its centre.[43] Gregory's Late Roman city had about 7 kilometres of defences enclosing some 180 hectares, ten times the size of Late Roman Athens or Sparta, which were both only about 16 to 20 hectares in extent. My interest in the walls was sparked by a rescue excavation 100 metres east of the Forum area in 1985, which revealed a five-metre-high section of wall and a rectangular tower 450 metres south of its expected line (Figure 9.8).[44] This wall artificially terraced the natural cliff

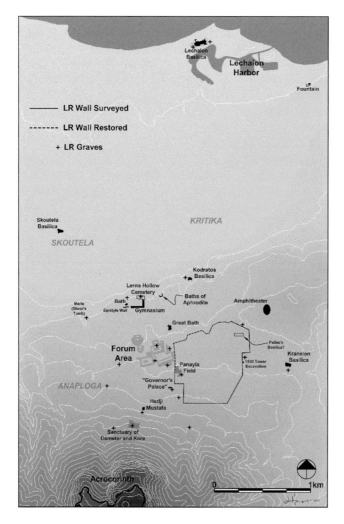

Figure 9.8 Map of Late Roman Corinth from Acrocorinth to Lechaion by James Herbst. Corinth Archives.

between the upper and lower plateaux of Corinth. Its construction technique suggests that a section of wall standing on the rock-cut terrace immediately to the east of the Julian Basilica, was part of the western line of the city wall and not of the 'Metropolitan Church'.[45]

Where visible, the known sections of this wall are built of *spolia* facing a core of slaked lime cement and rubble (Figure 9.9). It is almost four metres

Figure 9.9 An excavated portion of the city wall at Kraneion showing the core, robbed outer face and tombs built against the outer face.

Photo: author.

150   *G. D. R. Sanders*

thick and was originally probably about six or more metres high. Its massive construction and its linear nature made the monument an obvious target for remote sensing. In order to resolve the questions which had arisen, Corinth Excavations collaborated with Dr Michael Boyd and the Fitch Laboratory of the British School at Athens to undertake a resistivity survey to trace its line. Part of the design was to chase the wall, starting with the visible sections and then working along the line. In order to confirm or to negate the existence of a more extensive enceinte, we also sought evidence from large areas where the wall's existence was hypothesised. Between 2000 and 2005 we surveyed a total area of about 8 ha in search of the wall, out of our total geophysical coverage at Corinth of 13 ha. This extensive coverage revealed definite stretches totalling some 800m on its eastern, southern, and western sides, including several key points where the wall turns. Survey in the areas where the line of the wall was predicted by Gregory west and north of the forum, however, produce negative results. The 'Epistyle Wall', moreover, has a completely different construction with no trace of lime mortar. According to our survey Corinth's Late Roman wall was about 3.2 km long and enclosed an area of about 53 ha. It completely excluded the Roman forum and most of the western and northern sections of the earlier Roman city.

The wall's construction closely resembles that of another huge fortification, the trans-Isthmian wall, also recorded and described in detail by Professor Gregory.[46] This monument, the Hexamilion, is even larger, and stretches almost eight kilometres from coast to coast following, where possible, the geological marine terraces (Figure 9.10). It originally had about 150 towers spaced between 50 and 60 metres apart. Several sections of the trans-isthmian wall have now been cleared and consolidated. The two faces are also built of *spolia* and the core is of slaked lime cement and rubble. Whoever caused these walls to be constructed commandeered enough *spolia* for about 170,000 m^2 of facing and 170,000 m^3 of slaked lime and rubble for the core. This could only have come from the public and more substantial private buildings of Roman Corinth and Isthmia. At Perachora, for instance, the burnt edge of the kiln used to slake limestone and marble members from the sanctuary of Hera can be easily traced a few metres south of the temple. The construction of the walls of this new Corinth and the Hexamilion must have caused the almost complete demolition of the old Corinth and its sanctuaries. It was either a renewal after some disaster, a deliberate *damnatio memoriae* by replacing pagan city and monuments with Christian monuments, or both.

To date Corinth's fortifications, Gregory consulted the meagre 1930s excavation record of short sections of the wall east of the modern village. Late 4th-century coins and lamps in the layers physically cut by the wall suggested a *terminus post quem* ca. 400 and he considered its construction to have been in reaction to the barbarian incursions of the late 4th century rather than the Justinianic date proposed by others. He dated the Hexamilion to the same period and the attested building works under Justinian in the mid-6th century were, therefore, simply refurbishments. Since Gregory's appraisal, the chronologies of

Figure 9.10 Sebastian Ittar's 1802 plan of the west side of the Isthmus showing the Hexamilion wall and the Roman canal cuttings. Note the seaside fortress and outwork which also appear on the Morosini map of 1670. Corinth Archives.

various categories of archaeological material have been reappraised and the 4th-century lamps are now considered to continue well into the 5th century and later.[47] One context at Isthmia crucial for the dating of the wall contains an African Red Slip form 73A bowl dated by Hayes to ca. 420–475 and indicated that the new lamp chronology is closer to reality.[48] The bowl is of a type found in 'the deposits of *c.* 460–75' discussed above. My later chronology for this material would therefore place the construction of the wall in the mid-6th century.

In the case of the city wall at Corinth, we have no saved pottery by which to date its construction. A coin of Justin I was found at a depth of 2.1m below the top of the wall in a narrow trench (Trench E) on its west (interior) side, over a metre below the top of the foundations (Figure 9.11).[49] This and the few other late coins recovered were dismissed by Dorothy Hill as insignificant in the light of the overwhelming number of larger, earlier legible coins.[50] Gregory also has his doubts about the value of these latest coins, which he suspected were intrusions or the result of later robbing.[51] When excavating the wall, Carpenter and Hill noted stratigraphy in their drawn sections but

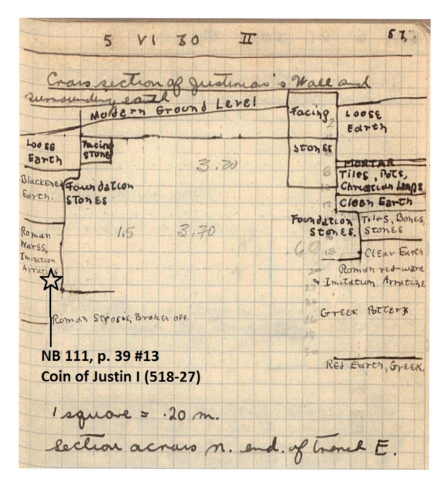

Figure 9.11 Section through the city wall (Site Notebook 111, p. 52) showing coin relative to the top of the foundations. Corinth Archives.

certainly did not dig stratigraphically. Even so, the coin of Justin I in the foundations facilitates a mid-6th rather than an early 5th-century date.

At the northeast of the enceinte, Demetrios Pallas undertook a small excavation from which he recovered a huge Late Roman Corinthian column capital. This, he thought, could only have belonged to a basilica even larger than the Lechaion basilica and, on the basis of style, he thought it to be rather later. Although we now believe the Lechaion basilica to be mid-6th century, even Pallas's late 5th-century date for the capital tends to suggest that the wall is later than Gregory proposed. The basilica had burials associated with it suggesting that it originally stood outside the city and the eastern line of the new city wall appears to have been laid out to incorporate the basilica within the new city. Furthermore, the earliest burials in the forum are late 6th century and these suggest that it was no longer forbidden to bury here because it now lay outside the new city.

The construction style of the wall and monuments excavated by the Byzantine Ephoreia within its circuit are consistent with recently excavated monuments in the Panayia Field, such as a small bath building and a structure immediately to the south of it, which are demonstrably later 5th-century.[52] Confirmation or refutation of this hypothesis will come when the present study of the material culture from these Ephoreia excavations is complete, but a Justinianic date now seems likely. We know from other interventions, for instance at Antioch, that Justinian was capable of completely moving a city and rebuilding on a smaller scale after wholesale destructions. We also know that Procopius records that Justinian built the fortifications after a plague and an earthquake had much reduced Corinth's population.

The earthquake and Lechaion

The earthquake and plague in question are that of ca. 522 of which Procopius writes in his *Anecdota* 'And earthquakes destroyed … Corinth … And afterwards came the plague as well … which carried off about one-half of the surviving population'.[53] Following this 'He [Justinian] also rendered secure all the cities of Greece … renewing their circuit walls in every case. For they had fallen into ruin long before, at Corinth because of terrible earthquakes which had visited the city'.[54]

Notwithstanding this explicit literary evidence, a later event has stuck in the minds of most academics writing about Corinth largely because Pallas ascribed the destruction of the Lechaion basilica to another earthquake that occurred in 551/2.[55] Writing of this event in the *De Bellis*, Procopius adds a list of areas affected in Boeotia and Achaia.[56] Since Corinth was the principal city of the Achaia, its omission from the list almost certainly means the city was not affected. The event seems to have had its epicentre between Nafpaktos and Itea about 90 km from Corinth and, given the evidence of historical earthquakes in the region, most seismologists now seriously doubt that such a distant event can have had any effect on Corinth.[57] Nonetheless, a group of German geographers have suggested that the earthquake caused a tsunami that destroyed Olympia, 22 km inland and 30m above sea level.[58]

Based on cores and a consideration of beach rock formations at Lechaion, one of the authors of this somewhat surprising, historically significant but undocumented disaster has suggested that a tsunami resulting from the same earthquake destroyed the Lechaion basilica and buried it in sand.[59] This interesting and well-presented interpretation contradicts an almost contemporary study published by a team of Greek and French coastal geomorphologists who have a keen grasp of archaeological site formation.[60] It is not appropriate to anticipate publication of an excavation that I supervised next to the artificial island in the inner harbour of Lechaion in October 2017 but I

Figure 9.12 Lechaion Harbour. A marks the location of the basilica, B the island monument, and CC the gravel hills. Corinth Archives.

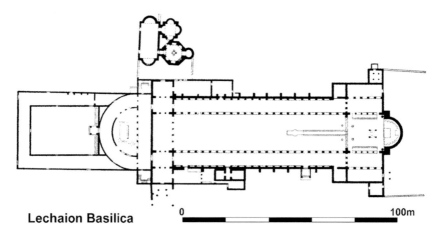

Figure 9.13 Lechaion Basilica. Corinth Archives.

can say that it presented an extremely lucid depositional history of the harbour fills, including an event that destroyed the island monument between ca. 50 and 125 AD, probably during the reign of Vespasian.[61] The results led me to examine to the basilica more closely with both the German and Greek/French publications in hand (Figures 9.12 and 9.13).

It is clear the sand layer thought to have been deposited against the north wall of the basilica pre-existed the basilica. In my informed opinion, it was created along with the two taller hills to the east and the sand bar between them and the basilica, when dredging the outer harbour after the earthquake of ca. 522 lifted the land relative to sea level making it unnavigable. It is clear the sand was dug away to build the north wall of the basilica because the poured rubble and lime mortar foundations are visible below the neatly finished superstructure of the two rooms north of the Prothesis at a low level. These foundations are dug into the sand. One of these rooms has a blocked door to an annex physically bonded to it on its north side and, while the southern exterior end west wall of this structure is partially finished, an ascending line of unfinished walling is witness to the fact that the north end of this wall was partially dug into and built against the sand. Indeed, the threshold of its exterior door is at the level of the top of the sand hill.

Relevant to the construction date is the coin of Justin I found in a fill of tightly pressed soil at a depth of about 1m below the paving at the west end of the south aisle. This layer was covered with a thin layer of black soil and another layer of packed soil. It seems quite clear that the basilica was built after the earthquake of ca. 522.[62] There can be no real doubt that the basilica was destroyed by an earthquake but based on the contents of the grave of Thomas the Presbyter immediately south of the apse, this took place sometime after 600.[63] The pottery from Corinth in *LRP* dated there before 551 belongs to houses on the south side of the basilica that co-existed with the monument.

It is now clear that all the areas excavated by the American School over the past 120 years lie outside the rediscovered Late Antique wall. Logically the perceived decline of Corinth after the 6th century is more to do with the mistaken assumption that we were digging within heart of the city rather than outside the walls. The date of these walls has been an ongoing discussion and resolving the date and destruction caused by the earthquake has helped reduce ambiguities. I now believe that, in addition to our simplistic treatment of coins and contexts, there are complex broader economic reasons for the visibility and invisibility of material culture in the transition between antique and medieval both in Corinth and southern Greece in general.

The economy of Corinth

In recent years, there has been an increasing volume of research on wealth distribution in past societies. Nearly all of this refers to the economic model proposed by Thomas Malthus (1766–1834) who observed that the world had finite resources, so an increase in population led to a decrease in average wealth. Relative poverty led, in turn, to a declining population and an increase in average wealth. This cycle was only broken with the Industrial Revolution in England and subsequently in other industrialised nations. The exceptional case of England is accounted for by its widespread maritime trade

156   *G. D. R. Sanders*

and a burgeoning of the number of families with an income two or more times subsistence level.

Subsistence level income is defined as sufficient to pay taxes, etc., and to feed and clothe oneself. At any time the vast majority of the world's population has lived either at or close to subsistence. Walter Scheidel and Steve Friesen suggest that for an individual in the Roman Empire a subsistence income was the wheat equivalent (W.E.) of 390 kg *per annum* and that the 'optimistic' to 'pessimistic' range of the Empire's population living at or below this level was from 65% to 82%.[64] Branko Milanovic further developed his own research to suggest that there were regional differences in *per capita* income and that, at the time of the death of Augustus, the average *per capita* income of peninsular Italy was 2.14 times subsistence and that of the Aegean world was only 1.30. By AD 300, these regional figures had converged and the average income of the Italian peninsula was 1.35 times subsistence and continued to decline. In contrast, the Aegean world's average income only began to decline after AD 600 and the Levant remained stable at about 1.30 to 1.45 throughout the 700 years covered by his study.[65] Milanovic also highlights differences in wealth distributions between city and countryside (Figure 9.14). Taking the Byzantium empire ca. AD 1000 as his example he estimates the numbers of people living on different incomes to suggest that there was a large wealth gap between urban and rural populations. About 99% of those engaged in agriculture lived on an income at or near subsistence whereas only about 10 to 20% of the urban population did.

My own estimate for subsistence for Corinth is based on the annual income of sharecroppers working the land of the Ottoman landlord Kiamel Bey before the Greek War of Independence. After allowing for seed, paying tax and other smaller amounts, a family retained half of the remainder, about 790 kg of mixed wheat and barley *per annum*.[66] This they supplemented with small amounts of meat, for example from poultry, wild vegetables, pulses, and fruit. When Corinth was a thriving city, the income distribution of the population probably resembled Milanovic's non-agricultural estimate. With a

Agricultural	Av. income (N)	%	Non-agricultural	Av. income (N)	%
Tenants, Wage earners Slaves Smallholders	3.5 to 3.8	99	Marginals	3.5	10-20
			Workers Soldiers	6 to 6.5	30-40
Large landholders	20	1	Traders craftsmen	12	34-57
			Nobility	350	3-6

Figure 9.14 After Milanovic 2004: 31, table 7. Byzantium *c.* 1000, income in nomismata.

Bridging the Grande Brèche   157

rapid contraction of its population and a decline in trade, as happened after 146 BC, after the mid-6th century and in the 15th century, Corinth became a fair sized agricultural town with a wealth distribution somewhere between Milanovic's agricultural and urban population. The difference between the two profiles is the estimated 99% of the population living at or close to subsistence in the agricultural economy and the 10 to 20% at or close to subsistence in the urban economy. What kind of material culture can we expect those living at or close to subsistence to have possessed?

Pottery is usually considered by archaeologists to be universal and to have been the common utensil of the poorest echelons of society. This is not backed up by the evidence. A cooking pot or pitcher costs two or three hours of labour.[67] This may seem inexpensive, but, given the great poverty of people living at subsistence, and the short lifespan of such pots in daily use, about three months, buying pottery makes little economic sense. Copper or iron, when readily available, was relatively expensive costing a few days of labour for pieces the equivalent size of their ceramic counterparts. On the other hand, the useful life of a metal pot is several generations since it can be repaired constantly and eventually recycled. It is, moreover, hygienic and heats its contents far more rapidly. The penetration of metal into the households of the poorer echelons of society is amply demonstrated by the packs of common soldiers on Trajan's column. Each carried a metal *patera* and olla, the price of which was almost certainly deducted from the soldiers' pay. Pottery found in excavation and survey would, therefore, seem to be a marker of those with incomes measured in multiples of subsistence, in Milanovic's scheme, large landowners and the urban traders, craftsmen and nobility.

One lesson we have learned from Greece's recent economic problems and austerity measures is that the urban wage earner is poorer and can afford to buy fewer non-essentials but it is the white-collar workers who have taken the most serious cuts in income, having been subjected to much greater taxation. They are often property rich and cash poor leaving them struggling either to pay property tax and, in a difficult market, to sell unwanted properties. In essence, the austerity measures have seen a contraction in the number of Greeks with surplus wealth and an overall increase in the ranks of the poor. More serious population and economic setbacks, such as those experienced in the 6th and 7th centuries must have had more dramatic effects.

Corinth experienced a rapid transformation when its new city wall was constructed in the mid-6th century (see above). It also suffered considerable setbacks in the second quarter of the 6th century some of which affected large parts of the Mediterranean hinterland. It seems likely that these events briefly enriched the poorest echelons of society until a protracted economic recession set in contracting the average income, empire-wide.

In ca. 522 there was an earthquake that resulted in considerable damage and loss of life at Corinth. It was an event sufficiently large that Procopius mentions it not once but twice and, from what I have witnessed, through tectonic uplift it transformed the navigable inner harbour of Lechaion into a

158   *G. D. R. Sanders*

shallow lagoon and required the dredging of the outer harbour to render it useable again. Later, there was a global event, now identified as the eruption of Ilopango in El Salvador, dated by tree ring sequences in a tree killed by the ash fallout to AD 535, that led to temporary global cooling, unseasonal weather, crop failure and famine in the year 535/6.[68] Procopius relates in his *De Bellis* that 'during this year a most dread portent took place. For the sun gave forth its light without brightness ... and it seemed exceedingly like the sun in eclipse, for the beams it shed were not clear'.[69] Tree rings, ice cores, and chronicles tell us that this was an event that affected the entire planet. Some think that the Justinianic plague beginning in 541/2 was a direct consequence.[70] This plague, according to Procopius (see above), killed half of those at Corinth who survived the recent earthquake. The pandemic continued sporadically into the 8th century, revisiting populations to kill those with no resistance, born after the previous manifestations.[71]

The effect of these events on Corinth must have been devastating initially but the city's location and economy were sufficient to maintain urban lifestyles. The construction of the Hexamilion and new city walls, building within the new city and the refurbishment of Lechaion must have had an immediate positive impact on the local economy. Evidence from contexts of later 6th and 7th centuries indicates that Corinth continued to flourish and imported North African and Phocaean fine wares and the contents of amphorae from the eastern Mediterranean.[72]

Studies of pre- and post-plague economies in Western Europe in the 14th century provide a scenario for what may have happened to the economy of the northeast Peloponnese after 541/2. For instance, in England wages of farm labourers and builders increased dramatically, beginning immediately after the plague year 1348–9, thereby increasing their purchasing power by 50% and, with the population continuing to decline over the following century, the purchasing power of their wages increased to 250% of pre-plague levels.[73] The aftermath saw the decline of serfdom, the rise in the use of hired labour and a change from direct cultivation of estates managed by the owner to a system in which land was rented to tenants at low rents. It was an era in which successful landless peasant farmers potentially could become landed yeomen. In the commercial sector, there was greater competition for fewer customers, which changed their business practices. It is entirely possible that the agricultural population experienced similar benefits after the first major (i.e., 'Justinianic') wave of mortality, and maintained them, along with continued population decline, into the 7th century.

If in the previous centuries, land holdings had been concentrated in the hands of large landholders, these landowners employed slaves and more or less tied labour, had greater access to markets, and sought to make themselves independent of tradesmen and fees by acquiring mills, potteries, and even boats. It was a period of high-income inequality, when nearly all the agricultural population lived at or close to subsistence. In the post-plague decades, the purchasing power of the agricultural population increased in part because their labour was at a premium. Under these circumstances, many large landowners probably sought to divest themselves of parcels of land for which they could not find cultivators. Farm labourers could then potentially, in time, acquire a parcel of land, others such as urban merchants and tradesmen with the means, could diversify their investments by buying property and the reorganisation of the army in the 7th century established an army manned by soldiers supported by land grants. The latter did not cultivate the land themselves; they received a share of rent from the cultivators equivalent to three or four times subsistence. Changes such as these transformed the agricultural income profile from 99:1 to something more like 79:20:1. The newly established 20% had surplus income to buy non-essential objects and perhaps this explains why imported red wares and wine amphorae, especially in coastal regions, become more common in the rural archaeological record.

By analogy with the Black Death and its aftermath, the effects of the Justinianic plague may have lasted about 250 years. The real income was therefore highest in the mid-7th century but thereafter declined reaching the early 6th century low by the end of the 8th century. In terms of wealth distribution, therefore, the decline in rural archaeological visibility should begin ca. 700, becoming almost invisible ca. 800. Corinth and its hinterland, however, should be different. Although the hinterland had a diminished urban market to supply, the city still functioned as a political, ecclesiastic, military, and economic hub.

Despite excavating in the wrong places and having made several errors of interpretation, we do have some sense of what kind of material we might find within the walls of the new city from the very rare deposits found outside the walls. Tenth and 11th-century ceramic forms can be seen to have evolved from Late Roman shapes. One of the latest African Red Slip forms, a pedestal plate, evolved into the plain pedestal plates of the Middle Byzantine period. Similarly, Late Roman Amphora 2 became the typical clunky Middle Byzantine amphora type, and the Late Roman fruit amphora also recognisably survived.[74] In addition to these, there is an array of incised, gouged, matt painted, and burnished ceramics and thin-walled cooking wares with silver mica, and clunkier cooking pots with gold mica. Handmade pottery is uncommon.

Conclusions

Written five decades ago, *LRP* is a masterpiece that has served scholars working across a huge geographical area from Elephantine in the southeast to the Crimea in the northeast, and from Ireland in the northwest to Southern Spain in the southwest. In many ways, this book was a navigational map which charted the murky waters of Late Antique archaeology making it more grounded in scientific reason than guesswork. Nevertheless, *LRP* was a product of its time, when coin dating was universally accepted, barbarians

160 G. D. R. Sanders

were held to be thorough when sacking cities and earthquakes were believed to be of Biblical proportions. The material available for study came from excavations which, by today's standards, was ropey at best and artefact recovery was worse than poor. Archaeology has changed and so must our ideas about Late Antiquity. If one looks holistically at the centuries following AD 500 at Corinth it becomes clear that the narratives of scholars who have focused on their specialist fields are based on a narrow perspective and that these narratives are not resilient. Reconsidering coin circulation and why coins are found in the archaeological record demands that we adjust pottery chronologies accordingly rather than tinkering with the status quo as the tendency has been in the past. Doing so extends the evidence for a healthy if faltering economy well into the 7th century and probably beyond. Instead of doom and gloom, the Dark Age can be cast as period of gradual economic decline and an equally slow but steady recovery. In better light, the Grande Brèche is an apophenic delusion. It is not the terrible chasm it seemed when cast in dark shadows but a valley in economic time which material culture, commerce, and the economy traversed to reach the Middle Byzantine high ground beyond.

Notes

1 Sanders 2004.
2 Broneer 1954: 159.
3 Slane and Sanders 2005.
4 Hjohlman 2002.
5 Hammond 2015.
6 Lolos 2011; Tzavella *et al.* 2014.
7 Cloke 2016.
8 Anagnostakis and Kaldellis 2014.
9 Caraher, *pers. comm.* 2017.
10 James 2018; Sanders *et al.* 2014a; Sanders *et al.* 2014b.
11 Sanders 2004.
12 Hayes 1972. Hayes does not discuss his approach to using coins, but following up references to the pieces from the Athenian Agora indicates that he generally dates the material with the latest coins. For instance, Hayes 1972: 165–166 dates AfRS Form 104 from ca. 530 to the mid-7th century; Form 104 #13, dated ca. 550, is from a deposit 'with coins to Justinian and possibly Baduila'. Form 104 #15, dated 580–585, came from a context (Burnt Area at 53/Δ) with ten coins of Justin II and one of Tiberius II; and Form 104 #22, dated as late as the mid-7th century, came from a context (p. 169) with coins to ca. 660.
13 Stipulated by a law, Novel 16.2 of Valentinian III in 445.
14 Shear 1933: 454; Shear 1940: 261.
15 Sanders *et al.* 2017: 15–19.
16 Burrell 2009: 169.
17 Bijovsky 2013: 185–188.
18 Bijovsky 2013: 188.
19 Burrell 2007: 253–254.
20 Bijovski 2013: 181–182.
21 Walker 1978: 45–47.

Bridging the Grande Brèche   161

22 Harris 1941: 145.
23 Crummy and Terry 1979: 50–51.
24 Bijovski 2013: 173–174; Callegher 2005: 225–235.
25 Robinson 1959: 1.
26 Williams 2003.
27 Saccocci and Vanni 1999. This abstention from post-Classical material became an obligation: that I should concentrate on material dating before the foundation of Constantinople.
28 Saccocci and Vanni 1999: 235.
29 Small 1989: 388, Table 1.
30 Hayes 1972: 116, 131–144, 337–342.
31 Thompson 1954: 3.
32 Agora notebook H'-I, p.112, coin of March 9th in 4/ME, 'burnt layer': 'Baduila, King of Ostrogoths 549–552 AD'; p.171, coin #23 of March 17th in 16–40, MH-ΞE, 58 (2.60–3.20); above burning, 'Baduila, King of Ostrogoths 549–552 A.D.'; p. 508–510, coin #of May 4th, 'Vandal head of Justinian I 527–565 A.D.', and p. 706, coin #9 of May 31st, 'Justinus I 518–527' from dump which, from where they were excavating that day, was probably in 12/MB lowest layer above Classical floor, or in 25/ME burnt layer.
33 Mattingley 1931; Edwards 1937.
34 Hayes 1972: 131.
35 Hayes 2009: 299.
36 Hayes 2009: 229 no. 1118, 230 no. 1134, 231 nos. 1138 and 1143, 232 no. 1152.
37 Athenian Agora notebook E-I-bis-72, p. 134–135 #25 Anastasius I; Athens Agora notebook, p. 154bis -156bis #7 Anastasius I, and p. 134–135 #2 Vandal coin with head of Justinian I.
38 C-2007–33, PRS Form 3C: latest coins in the layer below Coins 2007–159 and 2007–157, Anastasius I, and Coin 2007–158, probably Justin I. When numismatist Orestes Zervos says 'probably' one can generally take it as 'almost certainly'. Hayes 1972: 132–133, C-1965–13 AfRS Form 84.1, Corinth notebook 264, p. 168 and Coin 1965–388, Corinth notebook 264, p. 181.
39 Slane and Sanders 2005: 250.
40 Hayes 2003: 530–531, Figs. 6 and 7. Hayes 2008: 88, no. 41.
41 Hayes 2003: 531, Fig. 11.
42 P33377 to 33379, with coins 397, 399 and 402 in Lot PP116.
43 Gregory 1979: 265.
44 Unfortunately, the records for this Ephoreia excavation are no longer available and I have lost the photograph that I took. The excavation was 75m S15°of the Ottoman tekke next to Tassos' Hotel and tavern, and 125m due east of the apse of the Panagia church.
45 Scranton 1957: 9–11.
46 Gregory 1993.
47 Karivieri 1996; Slane and Sanders 2005: 282.
48 Wohl 1981: 121; Hayes 1972: 123–124.
49 Corinth notebook 111, 39 #13; initially identified as Anastasius I, but the reference to Wroth 1886: 32 #135 (the example actually appears on p. 3), indicates that the monogram is one that is now attributed to Justin I by Adelson and Kustas, 1964: 191 #242–71.
50 Corinth notebook 111, p.144.
51 Gregory 1979: 269.
52 Athanasoulis et al. 2010: 172–177; Sanders 1999.
53 Procopius, Anecdota: 18.41–44.
54 Procopius, De Aedificiis: 4.2.23.

162   G. D. R. Sanders

55 Pallas 1966: 159, 161, 166–167; Pallas 1967: 158, 161.
56 Procopius, *De Bellis*: 8.16–25.
57 Ambraseys and Jackson 1990; Ambraseys 1994.
58 Vott *et al.* 2011; Koster *et al.* 2011.
59 Hadler *et al.* 2011.
60 Minos-Minopoulos *et al.* 2013; Kolaiti *et al.* 2017. Eleni Kolaiti was kind enough to also send me a copy of her archaeological notes in which she discusses the continued use of the site of the basilica after its alleged destruction by tsunami.
61 https://www.theguardian.com/science/2017/dec/14/new-underwater-discoveries-in-greece-reveal-ancient-roman-engineering
62 Minos-Minopoulos *et al.* 2013: 1771, Fig. 2.
63 Slane and Sanders 2005: 291.
64 Scheidel and Friesen, 2009: 83–84.
65 Milanovic 2004: 4–12.
66 Sanders 2014: 111–113.
67 Sanders 2014: 15.
68 Dull *et al.* 2010.
69 Procopius, *De Bellis*: 3.14.
70 Keys 2000.
71 Stathakopoulos 2004: 139–41.
72 Slane and Sanders 2005: see Assemblages 3 and 4.
73 Clark 2001: 99–100.
74 Slane and Sanders 2005: see #4–16.

References

Primary Sources

Procopius, *Anecdota*, H.B. Dewing, trans. (1935) Cambridge, Mass.
Procopius, *De Aedificiis*, H.B. Dewing, trans. (1935) Cambridge, Mass.
Procopius, *De Bellis*, H.B. Dewing, trans. (1935) Cambridge, Mass.

Secondary Sources

Adelson, H.L., and Kustas, G.L. (1964), 'A sixth century Hoard of Minimi from the Western Peloponnese', *American Numismatic Society Museum Notes* 11: 159–205.
Anagnostakis, I., and Kaldellis, A. (2014), 'The textual sources for the Peloponnese, A.D. 582–959: Their creative engagement with Ancient Literature', *GRBS* 54: 105–135.
Ambraseys, N. (1994), 'Material for the investigation of the seismicity of Central Greece', in P. Albini and A. Moroni, eds., *Materials of CEC Project; Review of Historical Seismicity in Europe* (http://emidius.irrs.mi.cnr.it/RHISE/home.html).
Ambraseys, N., and Jackson, J. (1990), 'Seismicity and associated strain of central Greece between 1890 and 1988', Geo*physical Journal International* 101: 663–708.
Athanasoulis, D., Athanasoula, M., Manolessou, E., and Meleti, P. (2010), 'Σύντομη επισκόπηση της αρχαιολογικής έρευνας μεσαιωνικών καταλοίπων Κορίνθου', *Πρακτικά του Η΄ Διεθνούς Συνεδρίου Πελοποννησιακών Σπουδών*: 167–170.
Broneer, O. (1954), *Corinth I.iv. The South Stoa and Its Roman Successors*. Princeton.
Bijovsky, G. (2013), *Gold Coin and Small Change: Monetary Circulation in Fifth–Seventh Century Byzantine Palestine*, Polymnia: Numismatica antica e medievale. Studi 2. Trieste.

Burrell, B. (2007), 'A Hoard of Minimi from Sardis and the currency of the fifth century C.E.', *Revue Numismatique* 163: 235–282.

Burrell, B. (2009), 'Small Bronze Hoards at late fifth century C.E. Sardis', in N. Cahill, ed., *Love for Lydia: A Sardis Anniversary Volume Presented to Crawford H. Greenewalt, Jr.: Archaeological Exploration of Sardis; Report 4*, Cambridge, MA/London: 159–169.

Callegher, B. (2005), 'La circulation monétaire à Patras et dans les sites ruraux environnants (VIe-VIIe siècle)', in J. Lefort, C. Morrisson, and J.-P. Sodini, eds., *Les villages dans l'Empire byzantin (IVe-XVe siècle), Réalités Byzantines 11*, Paris: 225–253.

Clark, G. (2001), 'The Long March of History: Farm Laborers' Wages in England 1208-1850', *NajEcon Working Paper Reviews* (http://www.dklevine.com/archive/refs4625018000000000238.pdf).

Clark, G. (2016), 'Microbes and markets: Was the black death an economic revolution?', *Journal of Demographic Economics* 82 (2): 135–165.

Cloke, C. (2016), *The Landscape of the Lion: Economies of Religion and Politics in the Nemean Countryside (800 B.C. to A.D. 700)*, unpublished PhD thesis, University of Cincinnati.

Crummy, P., and Terry, R. (1979), 'Seriation problems in urban archaeology', *Pottery and the Archaeologist*, Institute of Archaeology Occasional Publication 4, London: 49–60.

Dull, R., Southon, J., Kutterolf, K., Freundt, A., Wahl, D. and Sheets, P. (2010), 'Did the TBJ Ilopango eruption cause the AD 536 event?', *American Geophysical Union Fall Meeting Abstracts* 13: 2370.

Gregory, T. (1979), 'The late Roman fortification wall at Corinth', *Hesperia* 48: 264–280.

Gregory, T. (1993), *Isthmia V. The Hexamilion and the Fortress*. Princeton.

Edwards, K. (1937), 'Report of the coins found in the excavations at Corinth during the years 1930–1935', *Hesperia* 6: 241–256.

Hadler, H., Vött, A., Koster, B., Mathes-Schmidt, M., Mattern, T., Ntageretzis, K., Reicherter, K., Sakellariou, D., and Willershäuser, T. (2011), 'Lechaion, the Ancient Harbour of Corinth (Peloponnese, Greece) Destroyed by Tsunamigenic Impact', in *Proceedings of the 2nd INQUA-IGCP-467 International Workshop on Active Tectonics, Earthquake Geology, Archaeology and Engineering*. Corinth.

Hammond, M. (2015), *Late Roman Ceramics from the Panayia Field, Corinth (Late 4th to 7th C.): The Long-Distance, Regional and Local Wares in Their Economic, Social and Historical Contexts*, unpublished PhD thesis, University of Missouri at Columbia.

Harris, J. (1941), 'Coins found at Corinth', *Hesperia* 10: 143–162.

Hayes, J. (2008), *Agora XXXII. Roman Pottery: Fine-Ware Imports*. Princeton.

Hayes, J. (2003), 'Rapports régionaux: Grèce', in Ch. Bakirtzis, ed., *VIIe Congrès Internationale sur la Céramique Médiévale en Méditerranée*, Athens: 35–44.

Hayes, J. (1972), *Late Roman Pottery*. London.

Hjohlmann, J. (2002), *Farming the Land in Late Antiquity: The Case of Berbati in the Northeast Peloponnese*. Stockholm.

James, S. (2018), *Corinth VII.7. Hellenistic Pottery: The Fine Wares*. Princeton.

Karivieri, A. (1996), *The Athenian Lamp Industry in Late Antiquity*, Papers and Monographs of the Finnish Institute at Athens V. Helsinki.

164   G. D. R. Sanders

Keys, D. (2000), *Catastrophe: An Investigation into the Origins of the Modern World*. New York.

Kolaiti, E., Papadopoulos, G., Morhange, C., Vacchi, M., Triandafyllou, I., and Mourtzas, N. (2017), 'Palaeoenvironmental evolution of the Ancient Harbor of Lechaion (Corinth Gulf, Greece): Were changes driven by human impacts and gradual coastal processes or catastrophic tsunamis?', *Marine Geology* 392: 105–121.

Koster, B., Reicherter, K., Vött, A., and Grützner, C. (2011), 'The evidence of tsunami deposits in the gulf of Corinth (Greece) with geophysical methods for spatial distribution', in *Proceedings of the 2nd INQUA-IGCP-467 International Workshop on Active Tectonics, Earthquake Geology, Archaeology and Engineering*. Corinth.

Lolos, Y. (2011), *Land of Sikyon: Archaeology and History of a Greek City-State*. Hesperia Supplements 39, Princeton.

Mattingly, H. (1931), 'A Late Roman Hoard from Corinth', *Numismatic Chronicle ser.* 5.2: 229–233.

Milanovic, B. (2004), 'An estimate of average income and inequality in Byzantium around year 1000', *World Bank – Development Research Group (DECRG)*, University of Maryland 13 Jan 2005 (36 pages). SSRN: https://ssrn.com/abstract= 647764.

Minos-Minopoulos, D., Pavlopoulos, K., Apostolopoulos, G., Dominey-Howes, D., and Lekkas, E. (2013), 'Preliminary results of investigations of possible ground deformation structures on the Early Christian Basilica, Ancient Lechaion Harbour, Corinth, Greece', *Bulletin of the Geological Society of Greece* 47: 1769–1778.

Pallas, D. (1966), 'Ἀνασκαφή Βασιλικῆς ἐν Λεχαίω', *Praktika tes Archaiologikes Etaireias*: 144–170.

Pallas, D. (1967), 'Ἀνασκαφική ἔρευνα ἐν Λεχαίω', *Praktika tes Archaiologikes Etaireias*: 137–166.

Perlzweig, J. (1961), *Agora VII. Lamps of the Roman Period. First to Seventh Century after Christ*. Princeton.

Robinson, H. (1959), *Agora V. Pottery of the Roman Period: Chronology*. Princeton.

Saccocci, A., and Vanni F. (1999), 'Tessere mercantili dei secc. XIII-XV dagli scavi della Missione americana a Corinto', *Rivista Italiana di Numismatica e Scienze Affini* 100: 201–242.

Sanders, G.D.R. (1999), 'A Late Roman Bath at Corinth: Excavations in the Panayia Field, 1995–1996', *Hesperia* 68: 441–480.

Sanders, G.D.R. (2004), 'Problems in interpreting rural and urban settlement in Southern Greece, AD 365-700', in N. Christie and S. Scott, eds., *Landscapes of Change: Rural Evolutions in Late Antiquity and the Early Middle Ages*, Aldershot: 163–193.

Sanders, G.D.R. (2014), 'Landlords and tenants: Sharecroppers and subsistence farming in Corinthian historical context', in S. Friesen, S. James and D. Schowalter, eds., *Corinth in Contrast: Studies in Inequality*, Leiden: 103–125.

Sanders, G.D.R. (2016), *Recent Finds from Ancient Corinth: How Little Things Make Big Differences*, Tenth Babesch Byvanck Lecture, Leiden.

Sanders, G.D.R., James, S., Carter Johnson, A., Tzonou-Herbst, I., Herbst J., Anastasatou N., and Ragkou K. (2017), *Corinth Excavations Archaeological Manual*. Grand Forks, North Dakota.

Sanders, G.D.R., James, S., Tzonou-Herbst, I., and Herbst, J. (2014a), 'The Panayia field excavations at Corinth: The Neolithic to Hellenistic phases', *Hesperia* 83: 1–79.

Sanders, G.D.R., Miura, Y., Kvapil, L. (2014b), 'A re-examination of some of the South Stoa Wells at Corinth', in P. Guldager Bilde and M. Lawall, eds., *Pottery, Peoples and Places. Study and Interpretation of Late Hellenistic Pottery*. Aarhus.

Scheidel, W., and Friesen, S. (2009), 'The size of the economy and the distribution of income in the Roman Empire', *JRS* 99: 61–91.

Scranton, R. (1957), *Corinth XVI. Medieval Architecture in the Central Area of Corinth*. Princeton.

Shear, T. (1933), 'The campaign of 1932', *Hesperia* 2: 451–474.

Shear, T. (1940), 'The campaign of 1939', *Hesperia* 9: 261–307.

Slane, K., and Sanders G.D.R. (2005), 'Late Roman Horizons', *Hesperia* 74: 243–297.

Small, C. (1989), 'The builders of Artois in the early fourteenth century', *French Historical Studies* 16: 372–407.

Stathakopoulos, D. (2004), *Famine and Pestilence in the Late Roman and Early Byzantine Empire: A Systematic Survey of Subsistence Crises and Epidemics*. Aldershot.

Thompson, M. (1954), *The Athenian Agora, II: Coins from the Roman through the Venetian Period*. Princeton.

Tzavella, E., Trainor, C., and Maher, M. (2014), 'Late Roman Pottery from the Sikyon Survey Project: Local production, imports, and urban evolution (4th–7th C. AD) (Greece)', in N. Poulou-Papadimitriou, E. Nodarou and V. Kilikoglou, eds., *LRCW 4 Late Roman Coarse Wares, Cooking Wares and Amphorae in the Mediterranean. Archaeology and Archaeometry. The Mediterranean: A Market without Frontiers*, Oxford: 91–102.

Vött, A., Fischer, P., Hadler, H., Handl, M., Lang, F., Ntageretzis, K., and Willershäuser, T. (2011), 'Sedimentary burial of Ancient Olympia (Peloponnese, Greece) by high energy flood deposits – The Olympia Tsunami Hypothesis', in *2nd INQUA-IGCP conference*, Corinth, Greece, http://www.geo1.uni-mainz.de/Dateien/20110711_Corinth_2011_Abstract_Voett_et_al_Olympia_accepted(3).pdf Accessed 30 July 2018.

Walker, A. (1978), 'Four AE coin hoards in the collection of the American School of Classical Studies at Athens', *Hesperia* 47: 40–48.

Williams, C.K. (2003), 'Frankish Corinth', in C.K. Williams, and N. Bookidis, eds., *Corinth: Results of Excavations Conducted by the American School of Classical Studies at Athens, vol. XX. Corinth, The Centenary (1896–1996)*, Princeton: 423–434.

Wohl, B. (1981), 'A deposit of lamps from the Roman Bath at Isthmia', *Hesperia* 50: 112–140.

Wroth, W. (1911), *Catalogue of the Coins of the Vandals, Ostrogoths and Lombards, and of the Empires of Thessalonica, Nicaea and Trebizond in the British Museum*. London.

10 Byzantine Butrint vis-à-vis 'Dark Age' Athens

A Ceramic Perspective

Joanita Vroom

Introduction

This chapter deals with some new finds of Early and Middle Byzantine ceramics and some novel, perhaps for some quite surprising, thoughts they instigate on the 'Dark Ages' and the following centuries in some urban centres in the eastern Mediterranean.[1] It concerns recently excavated or re-covered (meaning: re-discovered in storage rooms) archaeological finds from two major urban centres in this region: Athens (Greece) and Butrint (Albania). The ceramic finds discussed here date from the Early Byzantine ('Dark Age') and Middle Byzantine periods, broadly ranging from the 7th to the 12th/early 13th centuries.

In order to understand the wider context and importance of these finds, I will first give an introduction of my research project at Leiden University into the material culture of four major coastal towns in the eastern Mediterranean from Early Byzantine to Ottoman times.[2] This perspective allows me to take you on a 'grand tour' along some of the post-classical nodal points in the developments of material culture in the Byzantine world, among them Butrint in Albania, Athens in Greece, Ephesus in western Turkey, and Tarsus in eastern Turkey (Figure 10.1).

In the second part of this chapter, I will discuss pottery finds from the two most western of these sites (Butrint and Athens), leaving the two Anatolian cities (Ephesus, Tarsus) for later publications.[3] The two western sites share many similarities, especially in their long history and richness of archaeological material. Butrint has been excavated in the last 20 years, and much of the Late Roman and Byzantine material from the site has already been studied and (partly) published.[4] In the case of Athens, the extremely productive Agora excavations stretch over the last 80 years, but the majority of the Byzantine and Ottoman finds have yet remained unstudied, posing quite some challenges for us when we recently were given the opportunity to start their diagnosis and analysis. Yet, already the first years of research on the Post-Classical pottery from the Agora ex-cavations have proven that there is much potential indeed for further research.[5]

DOI: 10.4324/9781003429470-13

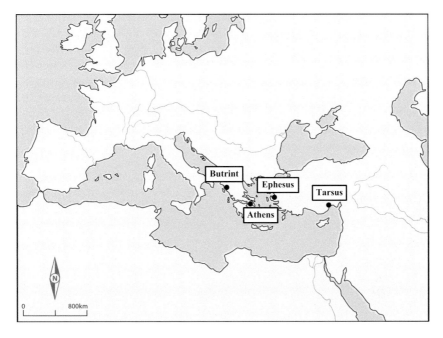

Figure 10.1 Map with the four key urban sites of the VIDI research project (J. Vroom).

Here, it is my aim to discuss some of the preliminary results of our study of the until now mostly unknown Early and Middle Byzantine pottery from Butrint and Athens. I will set out to understand these finds against the background of the economic and social conditions of Butrint and Athens during these periods, and in the framework of the habitation history and spatial organisation of these two urban centres.

The research project

For the Leiden project, I have chosen to study in more detail the material culture from four coastal urban sites due to their geographical location, their long history of occupation and the variety of socio-economic and political phenomena that they experienced.[6] That is to say, two urban centres (Athens and Ephesus) are situated in the core region of the Byzantine and Ottoman Empires, one on the western coast and the other on the eastern coast of the Aegean (Figure 10.1). The other two sites are located in the peripheries of both Empires: Butrint on the western frontier is affected by its proximity to Medieval Italy, while it also participates in the economic and political networks that interconnect the western Balkans.[7] Tarsus, on the other hand, becomes a crossroad of Byzantine, Arab, and Crusader cultures, and the material coming from the excavations highlights the cross-cultural interaction between the Christian and the Islamic world.[8]

168 Joanita Vroom

The best part of any research is to have a wonderful dataset at one's disposal, which offers new possibilities for the study of changing production and distribution systems, of changing cooking and eating habits, of changing habitation history and organisation of space. We employ a multidisciplinary approach in our study, combining archaeological artefacts, written sources, and pictorial evidence as sources of information. However, emphasis is placed on the study of ceramics (in combination with other archaeological sources of information) as indicators of production, distribution, and consumption patterns, of economic conditions and of social change – themes which I touched upon in my earlier publications.[9] Advocating for the use of pottery beyond a simple dating tool, we explore changes in their shape, use, and distribution in relation to socio-economic developments. The pottery analysis tries to shed light on contacts both with neighbouring sites and rural settlements in the hinterland as well as with production centres around the Mediterranean.

In order to make sense out of thousands of sherds of different fabric, shape, decoration, function, and provenance that come from four different sites and span over 13 centuries of use, we record everything systematically in our database that has been designed specifically for the needs of this project. The database is also connected to ArcGIS software that allows us to create distribution maps of ceramics, and study the location of pottery in relation to the location of other artefacts at the four sites within our research project.

Butrint

The first case-study in this chapter concerns the coastal site of Butrint in southwestern Albania, near the border with Greece (Figure 10.1). Situated opposite the island of Corfu and opposite Apulia in southern Italy (across the Adriatic Sea), Butrint serves as a metaphorical bridge between East and West – between Byzantium and the Latin world – and especially with Italian trading centres in the Adriatic region such as Otranto, Brindisi, and Venice.[10] Since 1994 large-scale excavations have taken place under direction of the Albanian Institute of Archaeology in Tirana and Professor Richard Hodges of the University of East Anglia (the current director of the American University at Rome), and I would like to thank them for allowing me to study and publish their material.

Butrint is a multi-period site on a peninsula, surrounded by the so-called Vivari Channel, and it was inhabited in various forms from Archaic times onwards with a peak in the Roman and Byzantine periods. During the recent years of excavation, thousands of Medieval and Post-Medieval ceramic finds were recorded from various parts of the site, and we are currently studying them in great detail. These include finds from the Well of Junia Rufina, the Baptistery, the Triconch Palace, the Acropolis, the Forum, and the Western Defences.[11]

On the other side of the Vivari Channel, south of the peninsula, are two more excavations carried out by the British-Albanian team with pottery finds of later periods. These include the Triangular Fortress and the Roman-period suburb on the Vrina Plain.[12] In this last place the remains of a 9th- to

10th-century Byzantine building were recovered, constructed in the ruins of a 5th-century basilica complex, as well as contemporary industrial activity (including a pottery kiln) next to the building.[13]

Presently, I first focus on the Early Byzantine ceramic finds from just one part of Butrint; that is to say, from two towers in the so-called Western Defences.[14] The towers are located on the western side as part of the defensive wall that protected the lower part of the town. Recent excavations produced here spectacular finds of the Early Byzantine period roughly dated from the (late) 7th to 9th centuries, or the so-called Dark Ages in Byzantine history – a period which is still very much *terra incognita* in this part of the Mediterranean.[15]

The Western Defences

The Western Defences comprise a circuit wall 106m long, enforced by three towers, two rectangular, and one horseshoe-shaped. The western fortifications should be dated to the late 5th century based on the archaeological finds and their architecture.

Somewhere in the 8th to early 9th centuries a fire seemed to have started on the ground floor of both rectangular towers, which caused the collapse of their upper floor and roof. All the material inside the two towers was sealed by the collapsed material. The walls of the towers did not collapse, and the tallest point that they survive is 9 meters (see Figure 10.2 for a reconstructed drawing of Tower 1).

Tower 1 yielded, smashed beneath the debris of the burnt rafters and the roof tiles, a large collection of glass (including 69 goblets, window glass, and cullet found in a restricted area), an intriguing metal object and a range of very broken Early Byzantine pots.[16] Intriguingly, a small *lekythos* of the 4th century BC was also among the Early Byzantine finds, brought no doubt from the city's ancient cemetery and in re-use during Early Medieval times by people perhaps with antiquarian interests.[17]

The Early Byzantine pottery finds from the two towers were the first assemblages in Albania to have ever been found in 'Pompeian conditions' to date. It was therefore suggested by the excavators that the collapses in both towers could not have been coincidental and probably took place at the same time. According to the excavators, the collapse was caused by an intentional fire, perhaps even connected to tension in the city such as possible revolt and even an attack or siege.[18]

However, a closer study of the ceramic assemblages of the two towers points to differences in their chronology. For example, the date of the pottery finds from one tower have been now dated to the 7th–8th centuries, and those from the other tower to the late 8th and early 9th centuries.[19] So, we must be careful with the interpretation of this material.

The ceramic finds in both towers consist, among others, of a variety of small globular amphorae, coarse wares, heavy utility vessels (such as large storage jars), plain and painted light utility vessels, and table wares. If we

Figure 10.2 Butrint, Western Defences, reconstructed drawing of Tower 1 (W. Euvermans).

look at the function of the pottery finds, it is clear that amphorae and coarse wares are dominant in both towers and in all four trenches, whereas table wares play hardly any role and are only represented by a few examples. But we must also keep in mind the missing artefacts in any archaeological record, so in this case perhaps table wares were made in more perishable materials such as wood or leather.

Tower 1

In an effort to better understand the possible function of Tower 1, an attempt has been made to reconstruct its interior just before the collapse (Figure 10.3). The towers were very complex deposits to excavate and in many cases it

Figure 10.3 Butrint, Western Defences, reconstructed drawing with finds in the interior of Tower 1 (W. Euvermans).

proved very difficult to distinguish between pots that were located on the ground floor and were smashed when the upper floor/floors collapsed, and material that came down from the upper stories, especially because so much material was moved and used in the post-fire occupation layers. Overall, we distinguished on the ground floor a large concentration of imported amphorae and a variety of other vessel types in smaller quantities. Combining field notes and photos and putting together hundreds of sherds, we have now reconstructed around 24 complete and half-complete vessels and have been able to estimate the possible location of 14 in Tower 1.[20]

The amphorae of the ground floor were concentrated in the south-eastern corner of Tower 1 (Figure 10.3). The glass finds were also placed close to the door. From the way they were found they must have been contained in a basket or some type of box that did not survive in the archaeological record. One chafing dish and a cooking pot were found close to the hearth in the centre of the ground floor. Two tall bottle-shaped vessels were found towards the east wall and some small jugs closer to the door. The metal object, which was found in the collapse layers of both towers, was probably part of a mechanism for opening a trap door between the ground and first floors. An identical mechanism has been found, for instance, inside a contemporary tower at Amorium in Turkey.[21]

The number and variety of pottery found in the interior of both towers, as well as the predominance of household wares of an utilitarian nature suggest that Tower 1 was used as a dwelling in which storing of goods, preparation of food, and cooking were all taking place (Figure 10.3). This tower might have been associated with some minor industrial activity because of the presence of the recycled glass.[22] Apart from getting a better typology and chronology for pottery finds in this region, the tower context also permits a new view on economic activity, domestic life, and oversea contacts in Butrint during Early Byzantine times.

Athens

In Athens, the second site for study within our research project, we aim to explore similar themes as in Butrint. Here we are, for instance, working on the spatial distribution of the material culture in the Athenian Agora during Byzantine, Crusader, and Ottoman times, in combination with the organisation and use of space and the function of buildings.

We are currently studying Byzantine to Ottoman finds from excavations in the Athenian Agora ran by the American School of Classical Studies from the 1930s onward, with special attention to the later ceramics. I would therefore like to thank Professor John Camp, director of the Athenian Agora excavations of the American School of Classical Studies at Athens, as well as his team in the Agora, for helping us to cooperate in studying and publishing the later material from the excavations in the ancient Agora of Athens.

On Figure 10.4 one can distinguish a plan of the Athenian Agora at the height of its development during Late Antiquity, with the Stoa of Attalos marking the eastern border of the Agora. The line on the Stoa of Attalos and its area below approximately shows the Late Roman fortification wall of Athens, built in the 4th century and also known as the 'Post-Herulian' wall (Figure 10.4).

Until now the general view has been that the area of the ancient Agora, which was mostly left outside the Late Roman fortification wall of Athens, was largely abandoned and neglected from the 7th until the 9th centuries. All in all, 'Dark Age'/Early Byzantine Athens has sometimes been portrayed as a small and insignificant settlement with only regional significance.[23] However, already during the first study seasons of taking a closer look at the Byzantine to Ottoman finds from the Agora excavations, this traditional view seems untenable.

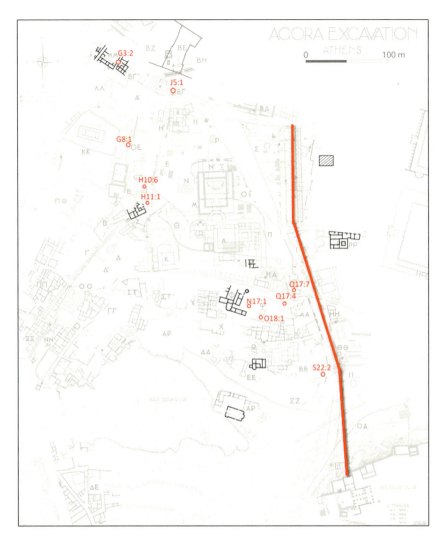

Figure 10.4 Athens, map of the 'Dark Age' wells in the Agora; the line (on the right) marks the Late Roman fortification wall (J. Vroom, E. Tzavella and ASCSA).

'Dark Age' Athens

From 2010 onwards we focused on the study of the material dated in the 7th–9th centuries in the Agora, a period not well understood and understudied at Athens. Although our work is still in an initial stage, we can already see evidence for different types of activities including habitation, industry, and public spaces outside the 4th-century Late Roman wall, contrary to prior beliefs. We are also discovering great differences in the type and

174 *Joanita Vroom*

intensity of occupation in different sections of the Agora per period. These differences argue against the idea of a uniform pattern of occupation characterising the entire area of Athens in the course of 13 centuries.

Considering the difficulties in recognising Dark Age/Early Byzantine material and in distinguishing sherds of the 7th and 8th centuries, for example, we were hoping to find some basic types of pottery that reached Athens or were made locally between the 7th and 9th centuries to help us establish a basic typology and chronology and follow the development of specific types of vessels in those centuries.[24] In other words, we needed to start from closed deposits, preferably with complete pots and clear stratigraphy, similar to what we had in Butrint. So we went back to the notebooks, to descriptions, photographs of artefacts and looked for anything suspicious, either because it was labelled as 'Dark Age' or, 7th century or later, or anything that was dated between Late Roman and Middle Byzantine times.

Our work began with the study of wells which we recognised as of the Dark Age/Early Byzantine period, and from there we expanded in contexts from buildings, burials, and open spaces. For every section included in our study, we were also noting the quantity, type, and distribution of coins, so we can think more about the relation of pottery and coins found in the Agora in the future.[25]

We started with the study of several wells that were not only well stratified, but also contained diagnostic finds and even complete pots (Figure 10.4). These wells were located in the north-western part of the Agora (G3:2 and J5:1), in the centre of the Agora (G8:1, H10:6 and H 11:1.2, which was the well with the largest assemblage), and close to the Late Roman fortification wall, most of these outside it (Q 17:4, Q 17:7, N17:1, O18:1 and S22:2). The separated locations of these wells made sure that we would deal with deposition of 7th- to 9th-century material in very different areas of the Agora, both close to and far away from the Late Roman 'Post-Herulian' wall. We are planning to publish the well H 11:1.2 data in full detail in a forthcoming publication,[26] but the study of the other wells is still work in progress which will continue in the coming seasons.

A Dark Age well

Attention is given here towards the pottery and other finds from one particular well. This is the one with the largest ceramic assemblage, found as well H 11:1 in Section Z of the Agora (Figure 10.5). The number and variety of complete pots found in this well have provided a great guide to recognise Late Roman-Early Byzantine to Middle Byzantine material in other contexts in the area of the Agora and the base for a typology and chronology of local and imported wares at Athens.

The well is 12 meters deep and contains pottery, building materials such as tiles and stones, parts of inscriptions, one bronze lamp and 11th-century coins. Its initial phase of use was between the 7th and 9th centuries, and then

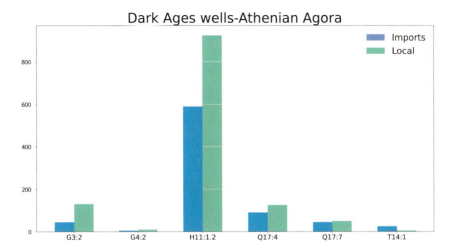

Figure 10.5 Athens, percentages of local, imported, and unknown ceramic finds from various 'Dark Age' wells in the Agora (J. Vroom, E. Tzavella).

it was abandoned. In the 11th century, the well was reused after some remodelling on its upper part. The pottery found inside the well represents three successive periods of use in the area of the Agora: 'Late Roman-Early Byzantine', 'Early Byzantine', and 'Middle Byzantine'. The pottery is found in a stratigraphic sequence, with Middle Byzantine pottery found in the upper layers and the Late Roman-Early Byzantine vessels towards the bottom of the well.

There is a variety of vessel shapes found in the well from small jugs and bowls to amphorae, cooking pots and a large basin. The majority of the amphorae comes from the lower parts of the well and consequently also from the earlier periods, whereas the tableware are found exclusively in the upper part and thus in the Middle Byzantine layers. In the middle and lower layers, that is to say, from 6 meters down there are some recognisable shapes of the Early Byzantine period such as a 7th-/8th-century globular amphora type known from excavations in Italy and Northern Africa.[27] Together with these amphorae, there were also amphora-derivatives of well-known Late Roman types, such as the Late Roman 1 amphora or the Palestinian carrot-shaped amphora with small differences in shape.[28] Jugs with a flat base were further present in those contexts, and these ones have also been found in other Dark Age/Early Byzantine wells in the Athenian Agora that we studied in the past years.

By looking at the probable provenance of the pottery found in well H 11.1 in relation to their date we can already trace some changes in the contacts of Athens in three successive periods. Thus, in the Late Roman-Early Byzantine period, Athens participated in a large economic network that expands from Gaza to Sinop to Crete and southern Italy.[29] In the subsequent Early

176   *Joanita Vroom*

Byzantine period, the trade connections represented by the pottery finds are more limited, covering only production centres in the Aegean. At the same time, economic relations with southern Italy are maintained, and local production continued. Finally, in the Middle Byzantine period, local production has increased significantly, while small numbers of sherds came from different areas of the Aegean.

Other parts in the Agora

Apart from the finds from the wells, we studied material found at nearby locations. It concerns here mostly pottery discarded in pits as well as goods stored in large storage jars (*pithoi*), often dug in the ground and located close to architectural remains that were probably in use in Early and Middle Byzantine times. From previous publications we know that during the Middle Byzantine period the whole area of the Agora was filled with private houses. Their plans were simple, with a group of modest rooms surrounding a courtyard.[30]

The lively activity in this period seems to be underlined by the large numbers of pits, wells, and *pithoi* found on various floors of the Middle Byzantine houses.[31] In fact, various types of glazed and unglazed pottery as well as of *pithoi* were, for instance, used in these dwellings.[32] The quantity of these last containers for the storage of oil and grain appears to highlight the practice of storing agricultural products from the Athenian hinterland in town dwellings during Middle Byzantine times.

The number and variety of complete vessels (especially cooking pots) found in wells, pits, and cisterns have allowed us to start creating newly revised typologies and chronological sequences of local and imported wares in 7th- to 9th-century Athens and beyond. The rediscovery of this material in the storage rooms of the Agora excavations also raises new questions about the topography and the nature of activities in Athens during the Early Byzantine to Middle Byzantine periods. In forthcoming study seasons we hope therefore to expand our research to the study of contexts from houses, open spaces, and burials in order to explore the variety of activities in the Agora district.

Conclusion

This initial research revealed sections with large amounts of Early Byzantine material, especially pottery but also glass, metal objects, standing buildings, road levels, burials, and coins, underlining the use of space in the so-called Dark Ages. In the end, our research on the Dark Age/Early Byzantine phases in both cities aims at a better understanding of the economy, administration, and living conditions in towns during the 7th to the 9th centuries. Based on the analysis of the finds, we examine how towns transformed in the course of these centuries, how they differ from Late Roman towns, and how they contribute to the evolution of urban centres in the Middle Byzantine period.

But to do this successfully, we insist on working towards a better understanding of this period's material culture. In the case of ceramics, emphasis must be placed on recognising and correctly dating material of the 7th to 9th centuries. In this chapter, I would like to draw your attention to the difficulties in differentiating the small shape differences between Late Roman and Early Byzantine pottery even if we are dealing with complete pots in closed contexts, let alone when we are dealing with small fragmented body sherds from survey material. Only when we have a good handle on this period's material culture can we really understand the impact of political and economic changes in urban life, and appreciate the role of the Dark Age/Early Byzantine and the subsequent Middle Byzantine period in the evolution of Byzantine culture.

It is fair to conclude that the first years of our research project have shown that our chosen line of approach to the material culture of the Byzantine to Ottoman periods is fruitful and exciting. Nevertheless, we would like to emphasise that there are no easy answers in archaeology, and certainly not in our field of research. Especially the Dark Ages in Byzantine history remain a problematic period, and progress here is a matter of hard and careful work.

However, we think we have now achieved for the first time a clearer picture of the Dark Age/Early Byzantine period and the start of the Middle Byzantine period in some major urban centres in Greek lands. Our data for Butrint and Athens show substantially more continuity of habitation from Late Antiquity onwards than was known before. Interesting as this is in itself, it is perhaps above all an important message for the next generations of archaeologists. If there is any prediction to be made about the future course of archaeology in these regions, it seems quite certain that we will be facing more and more Byzantine layers in contemporary and forthcoming excavations, and that we can really contribute to the knowledge about the past of Greek lands when we keep 'digging for the Byz'.[33]

Notes

1 Periodisation used in the present article is according to the pottery chronology (and nor according to the chronology routinely used by many historians); thus as follows: 'Late Roman' means the period from the 4th to the mid-7th centuries; 'Early Byzantine' is the mid-7th to late 9th centuries, and therefore is synonymous to 'Dark Age'; 'Middle Byzantine' is the early 10th to late 12th/early 13th centuries. The text of this contribution was already submitted in October 2014 and has not been revised since.

2 The VIDI research project at Leiden University with the title '*Material Culture, Consumption and Social Change; New Approaches to Understanding the Eastern Mediterranean during Byzantine and Ottoman Times*' was carried out with a small team, including a post-doctoral researcher, some guest researchers and a few undergraduate and graduate students; see for more information, http:// archaeology.leiden.edu/reserach/neareast-egypt/byzantine-ottoman. I would like to thank the Netherlands Organisation of Scientific Research (NWO) for awarding me with a VIDI research grant for the years 2010–2015.

178 *Joanita Vroom*

3 See Vroom 2019a; Vroom 2015; Vroom and Fındık 2015; Bağcı 2015.
4 See, for instance, Reynolds 2004; Vroom 2004; Reynolds and Vaccaro 2013; Vroom 2013a.
5 See for earlier publications on the later ceramics found in the Athenian Agora, Waagé 1933; Frantz 1938; Frantz 1942; Frantz 1961: figs. 19, 21, 23–33, 36–40, 61–62; Frantz 1988.
6 Vroom 2013b.
7 E.g., Vroom 2004; Vroom 2006; Vroom 2008.
8 Bağcı 2015; see also Haldon and Kennedy 1980; Redford 1998.
9 E.g., Vroom 2003; for more articles on these subjects, see www.academia.edu/JoanitaVroom.
10 Vroom 2012a.
11 E.g., Gilkes *et al.* 2002; Vroom 2004; 2006; 2008; 2012a; 2012b; 2013a; Hodges and Vroom 2007.
12 E.g., Vroom 2006; Vroom 2019b.
13 E.g., Bowden and Hodges 2012; Greenslade 2013; Greenslade and Hodges 2013.
14 Hodges *et al.* 2009: 320.
15 Vroom 2011.
16 Jennings 2010.
17 Hodges 2008: 65.
18 Hodges and Kamani 2009; Kamani 2011; Kamani 2013.
19 Vroom 2012b; Vroom and Kondyli 2015.
20 Vroom 2012b: 295.
21 Harrison *et al.* 1993:161 and fig. 3.
22 We know, for instance, of well-known examples of industrial activities within a tower such as the case of a smithy in the Sadovsko Kale, a village in Bulgaria; see Curta 2004: 159.
23 E.g., Frantz 1938: 429; Frantz 1988: 117–122; Kazanaki-Lappa 2002; see also Ch. Bouras 2010: 33–35, for the shrinking of Byzantine Athens.
24 See Hayes 2003: figs. 7, 8, 10, and 11; Vroom 2011: figs. 4a–b.
25 In the meantime, Dr Pagona Papadopoulou joined our team to restudy the later coins from the Athenian Agora, next to the recent work done by Dr Julian Baker on Late Medieval coin hoards in the Agora. See about the problematic relation between coins and pottery, Papadopolou 2015.
26 See for more detailed information, Vroom, Tzavella and Papadopoulou (forthcoming).
27 See, for instance, Vroom 2014: 60–61.
28 See in general for these amphora types, Reynolds 2005: plate 15; Vroom 2014: 52–53.
29 Vroom and Kondyli 2015: figs. 21 and 24.
30 Frantz 1961: fig. 34.
31 Shear 1997; Camp 2007.
32 Frantz 1961: fig. 35.
33 Vroom 2013b: 79–80.

References

Bağcı, Y. (2015), 'A new look on Medieval ceramics from the old Gözlükule excavations in Tarsus: A preliminary presentation', *X Congresso internacional. A cerâmica medieval no Mediterraneo, 22 a 27 outubro 2012, Silves*, Silves: 627–636.
Bouras, Ch. (2010), *Βυζαντινή Αθήνα 10ος-12ος αι.* Athens.

Bowden, W., and Hodges, R. (2012), 'An "ice age settling on the Roman empire": Post-Roman Butrint between strategy and serendipity', in N. Christie and A. Augenti, eds., *Urbes Extinctae: Archaeologies of Abandoned Classical Sites*, Aldershot: 207–242.

Camp, J. McK. (2007), 'The Athenian Agora: Excavations of 1989–1993', *Hesperia* 76: 627–663.

Curta, F. (2004), *The Making of the Slavs. History and Archaeology of the Lower Danube Region, c. 500–700*. Cambridge.

Frantz, A. (1938), 'Middle Byzantine pottery in Athens', *Hesperia* 7: 429–467.

Frantz, A. (1942), 'Turkish pottery from the Agora', *Hesperia* 11: 1–28.

Frantz, A. (1961), *The Middle Ages in the Athenian Agora*. Princeton, N.J.

Frantz, A. (1988), *Late Antiquity A.D. 267–700. The Athenian Agora: Results of Excavations Conducted by the American School of Classical Studies at Athens*, vol. XXIV. Princeton, N.J.

Gilkes, O., Crowson, A., Hodges, R., Lako, K., and Vroom, J. (2002), 'Medieval Butrint: Excavations at the Triconch Palace 2000 and 2001', *Archeologia Medievale* 29: 343–353.

Greenslade, S. (2013), 'The Vrina Plain settlement between the 1st–13th centuries', in I.L. Hansen, R. Hodges, and S. Leppard, eds., *Butrint 4. The Archaeology and Histories of an Ionian Town*, Oxford: 123–164.

Greenslade, S., and Hodges, R. (2013), 'The aristocratic *oikos* on the Vrina Plain, Butrint c. AD 830–1200', *Byzantine and Modern Greek Studies* 37: 1–19.

Haldon, J., and Kennedy, H. (1980), 'The Arab-Byzantine frontier in the eighth and ninth centuries: Military organisation and society in the borderlands', *Zbornik Radova Vizantoloskog Instituta* 19: 79–116.

Harrison, R.M., and Christie, N., *et al.* (1993), 'Excavation at Amorium: 1992 interim report', *Anatolian Studies* 43.

Hayes, J.W. (2003), 'Rapports régionaux: Grèce', in 'De Rome à Byzance; de Fostat à Codoue; Évolution des faciès céramiques en Mediterranée (Ve-IXe siècles)', in Ch. Bakirtzis, ed., *VIIe Congrès international sur la céramique médiévale en Méditerranée, Thessaloniki, 11–16 Octobre 1999*. Athens.

Hodges, R. (2008), *The Rise and Fall of Byzantine Butrint*. London/Tirana.

Hodges, R., and Kamani, S. (2009), 'Assedio e devastazione, un brano di storia a Butrinto', *Archeologia Viva* 137: 60–63.

Hodges, R., Kamani, S., Logue, M., and Vroom, J. (2009), 'The sack of Butrint, c. AD 800', *Antiquity* 83: 320 (http://antiquity.ac.uk/projgall/hodges).

Hodges, R., and Vroom, J. (2007), 'Late Antique and Early Medieval ceramics from Butrint, Albania', in S. Gelichi and C. Negrelli, eds., *La circolazione delle ceramiche nell'Adriatico tra tarda antichità ed altomedioevo*, Mantua: 375–388.

Jennings, S. (2010), 'A group of glass ca. 800 A.D. from tower 2 on the Western Defences, Butrint, Albania', in J. Drauke and D. Keller, eds., *Glass in Byzantium – Production, Usage, Analyses*, Mainz: 225–235.

Kamani, S. (2011), 'Butrint in the mid-Byzantine period: A new interpretation', *BMGS* 35.2: 115–133.

Kamani, S. (2013), 'The Western Defences', in I.L. Hansen, R. Hodges, and S. Leppard, eds., *Butrint 4. The Archaeology and Histories of an Ionian Town*, Oxford: 245–256.

Kazanaki-Lappa, M. (2002), 'Medieval Athens', in A. Laiou *et al.*, eds., *The Economic History of Byzantium. From the Seventh through the Fifteen century*, Washington, D.C.: 639–646.

180   *Joanita Vroom*

Papadopolou, P. (2015), 'Coins and pots: Numismatic and ceramic evidence in the archaeology and economic history of the Middle Ages', in J. Vroom, ed., *Medieval and Post-Medieval Ceramics in the Eastern Mediterranean – Fact and Fiction. Proceedings of the First International Conference on Byzantine and Ottoman Archaeology, Amsterdam, 21–23 October 2011*, Turnhout: 199–226.

Redford, S. (1998), *The Archaeology of the Frontier in the Medieval Near East: Excavations at Gritille, Turkey (Archaeological Institute of America, Monographs New Series 3)*. Boston.

Reynolds, P. (2004), 'The Roman pottery from the Triconch Palace', in R. Hodges, W. Bowden and K. Lako, eds., *Byzantine Butrint: Excavations and Survey 1994–99*, Oxford: 224–269.

Reynolds, P. (2005), 'Levantine amphorae from Cilicia to Gaza: A typology and analysis of regional production trends from the 1st to 7th centuries', in J. Ma. Gurt i Esparraguera, J. Buxeda i Garrigós and M.A. Cau Ontiveros, eds., *LRCW 1. Late Roman Coarse Wares, Cooking Wares and Amphorae in the Mediterranean. Archaeology and Archaeometry (BAR I.S. 1340)*. Oxford.

Reynolds, P., and Vaccaro, E. (2013) 'Roman pottery: In-phase and residual material', in A. Sebastiani *et al.*, 'The Medieval church and cemetery at the Well of Junia Rufina', in I.L. Hansen, R. Hodges and S. Leppard, eds., *Butrint 4. The Archaeology and Histories of an Ionian Town*, Oxford: 226–234.

Shear, T.L. Jr. (1997), 'The Athenian Agora: Excavations of 1989–1993', *Hesperia* 66: 495–548.

Vroom, J. (2003), *After Antiquity. Ceramics and Society in the Aegean from the 7th to the 20th Centuries. A.D. A Case Study from Boeotia, Central Greece*, Archaeological Studies Leiden University 10, Leiden.

Vroom, J. (2004), 'The Medieval and Post-Medieval fine wares and cooking wares from the Triconch Palace and the Baptistery', in R. Hodges, W. Bowden and K. Lako, eds., *Byzantine Butrint: Excavations and Survey 1994–99*, Oxford: 278–292.

Vroom, J. (2006), 'Corfu's right eye: Venetian pottery in Butrint (Albania)', in M. Guštin, S. Gelichi and K. Spindler, eds., *The Heritage of the Serenissima. The Presentation of the Architectural and Archaeological Remains of the Venetian Republic. Proceedings of the International Conference Izola – Venezia 4 - 9.11.2005*, Koper: 229–236.

Vroom, J. (2008), 'Dishing up history: Early Medieval ceramic finds from the Triconch Palace in Butrint', *Mélanges de l'Ecole française de Rome – Moyen Âge* 120-2: 291–305.

Vroom, J. (2011), 'The other "Dark Ages": Early Medieval pottery finds in the Aegean as an archaeological challenge', in R. Attoui, ed., *When Did Antiquity End? Archaeological Case Studies in Three Continents (BAR I.S. 2268)*, Oxford: 137–158.

Vroom, J. (2012a), 'From one coast to another: Early Medieval ceramics in the southern Adriatic region', in S. Gelichi and R. Hodges, eds., *From One Sea to Another. Trading Places in the European and Mediterranean Early Middle Ages, Proceedings of the III International SAAME Conference – Comacchio 27th–29th March 2009*, Turnhout: 375–413.

Vroom, J. (2012b), 'Early Medieval pottery finds from recent excavations at Butrint, Albania', in S. Gelichi, ed., *Atti del IX congress internazionale sulla ceramica medievale nel Mediterraneo. Venezia, Scuola Grande dei Carmini, Auditorium Santa Margherita, 23–27 novembre 2009*, Florence: 289–296.

Vroom, J. (2013a), 'The Medieval and Post-Medieval pottery finds', in A. Sebastiani *et al.*, 'The Medieval church and cemetery at the Well of Junia Rufina', in I.L. Hansen, R. Hodges and S. Leppard, eds., *Butrint 4. The Archaeology and Histories of an Ionian Town*, Oxford: 234–240.

Vroom, J. (2013b), 'Digging for the "Byz". Adventures into Byzantine and Ottoman archaeology in the eastern Mediterranean', *Pharos* 19.2: 79–110.

Vroom, J. (2014), *Byzantine to Modern Pottery in the Aegean. An Introduction and Field Guide* (2nd rev. ed.). Turnhout.

Vroom, J. (2015), 'The glass finds' and 'The small finds', in S. Ladstätter, ed., *Die Türbe in Artemision. Ein frühosmanischer Grabbau in Ayasuluk/Selçuk und sein kulturhistorisches Umfeld*, Vienna: 313–328, 329-343.

Vroom, J. (2019a), 'Medieval Ephesus as a production and consumption centre', in P. Magdalino and S. Ladstätter, eds., *Ephesus from Late Antiquity to the Later Middle Ages*, Vienna: 229–254.

Vroom, J. (2019b), 'The Medieval and Post-Medieval pottery finds from the Vrina Plain excavations', in S. Greenslade, ed., *Butrint 6: Excavations on the Vrina Plain, vol. II: The Finds*, Oxford: 1–14.

Vroom, J., and Fındık, E. (2015), 'The pottery finds', in S. Ladstätter, ed., *Die Türbe in Artemision. Ein frühosmanischer Grabbau in Ayasuluk/Selçuk und sein kulturhistorisches Umfeld*, Vienna: 205–311.

Vroom, J., and Kondyli, F. (2015), '"Dark Age" Butrint and Athens: Rewriting the History of Early Byzantine towns', in J. Vroom, ed., *Medieval and Post-Medieval Ceramics in the Eastern Mediterranean – Fact and Fiction. Proceedings of the First International Conference on Byzantine and Ottoman Archaeology, Amsterdam, 21–23 October 2011*, Turnhout: 317–342.

Vroom, J., Tzavella, E., and Papadopoulou, P. (forthcoming), 'Hearth of Darkness. New research on finds from a well in the Athenian Agora, ca. 7th to 10th centuries', *Hesperia*.

Waagé, F.O. (1933), 'Excavations in the Athenian Agora. The Roman and Byzantine pottery', *Hesperia* 2: 279–328.

11 The Defences of Middle Byzantium in Greece (7th–12th Centuries)

The Flight to Safety in Town, Countryside, and Islands

Nikos D. Kontogiannis and Michael Heslop[1]

Introduction

Among Byzantinists, fortifications are still a relatively little-studied subject.[2] It is usually acknowledged that their character changed over the period under review in this chapter, as a consequence both of changing enemies faced by the Empire along its borders and of internal socio-economic conditions. In this chapter, following a brief historical survey, we focus on three groups of fortifications representing distinctive defence patterns. Analysis of these groups could, in our opinion, provide examples and patterns valid in other regions, potentially yielding a more comprehensive perspective on Byzantine fortifications in Greece.

Research has approached the defenses of Byzantium over the years through a number of viewpoints: as part of wider fortification and tactical patterns,[3] as part of regional and historical topography,[4] as examples of landscape features and aesthetic statements,[5] or, more recently, as meta-physical entities – holy lands – in the Byzantine mentality.[6]

The fortifications of Byzantine Greece have been included in multiple studies by various scholars. When grouping the monuments according to the historical period in which they were built or used, one obviously has to accept the dates proposed by the most recent fieldwork on the site; this however may be considerably changed by future research.

In presenting a brief overview of relevant material from Greece, it is apparent that the 5th and 6th centuries saw the deployment of efforts to endow the Balkan provinces, including Greece, with fortifications of various sizes and forms, many of which could have been initiated and funded by central authorities.[7] Among city walls could be mentioned Traianoupolis, Didymoteichon, Anastasioupolis (later Peritheorion), Komotini, Maroneia, Kitros, Maximianoupolis (later Mosynopoulis), Philippoi, Amphipolis, Rentina, Thessalonike, Dion, Kastoria, and Servia in northern Greece;[8] Nikopolis in Epiros;[9] Melivoia and Platamonas, in Thessaly;[10] Athens in central Greece;[11] Patra, Corinth, Epidauros, Sparta, Monemvasia, and Tigani in the Peloponnese;[12] and Anavatos in Chios[13] (see Figure 11.1 for these and later place-names). They co-existed with numerous smaller forts

DOI: 10.4324/9781003429470-14

The Defences of Middle Byzantium in Greece (7th–12th Centuries) 183

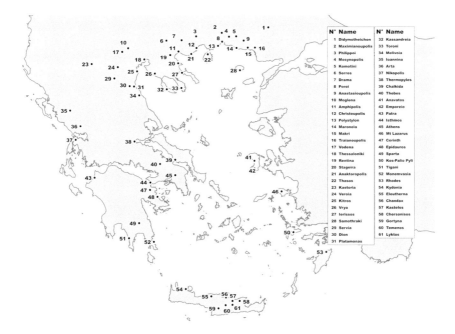

Figure 11.1 5th–12th-century fortifications.

scattered in the countryside and on the littoral,[14] as well as a number of linear/cluster fortifications in the tradition of Roman *limes* in the areas of Anastasioupolis, Thermopyles/Dhema, Isthmos, and Kassandreia.[15]

These walls are found in all forms (from long walls and monumental city enclosures to citadels and isolated hill forts) and cover practically the whole land, serving as a matrix which Middle Byzantium used, restructured or abandoned and rediscovered, according to its needs and the changing nature of its enemies. They exhibit various masonry styles from the all-brick and *opus mixtum* to ashlar and re-used spolia facades. Some of them show a high degree of sophistication in regard to the defensive features they employ, pointing to the presence of a technologically advanced army. Equally diverse are the interpretations proposed for their erection, with the all-Justinian attribution gradually receding as scholarship advances.

By the 7th and 8th centuries, Byzantine Greece faced adverse realities and a host of new enemies (the Slavs on the mainland, and the Arabs in the Aegean).[16] How many of the previous fortifications were still used, by whom and as part of which organisation remains unclear. The mention of the Byzantine castle of Ashab al baqar in the Arab translation of a Christian source has led to lively discussions and multiple contestants (such as Neapoli-Voies, Elaphonisos, Paulopetri or Paliokastro Voion in Lakonia, Damalas and Dokos in Troizenia, Kythera or Antikythera), though without any conclusive data.[17] At present, it seems that the state or its local officials

184   *Nikos D. Kontogiannis and Michael Heslop*

initiated only a handful of new fortification projects, all within the framework of ad hoc military needs. Coastal and island areas received small forts, walls around a restricted settlement and/or a fortified citadel: Polystylon (former Abdeira), along with large-scale additions at Thessalonike in northern Greece;[18] Emporeio in Chios and Mt Lazarus in Samos;[19] Tigani in the Peloponnese;[20] the city of Rhodes;[21] and Kydonia (modern Chania), Eleutherna, Chandax (modern Herakleion), Lyktos, Chersonisos, and Gortyna in Crete.[22] In one or two cases, such as Rhodes and Kydonia, masonry with ancient, re-used material that imputes a monumental aspect, and the presumed presence of sophisticated features (regularly spaced towers, outer walls and moats), point to a level of technology which can be perceived as continuing 5th–6th-century practices.

The 9th century seems to have been a very different era in the military history of the empire. In Asia Minor a distinct pattern of reinforcing the main military bases can be discerned, as in the cases of Ancara and Nicaea.[23] This was probably not a response to an immediate threat, but rather the consequence of extensive available resources that allowed the reorganisation on the basis of a more stable and secure environment. A similar process could also be upheld for Greece, where the formation of new Themes (ca. 800) has been interpreted as the gradual re-assertion of central authority and establishment of imperial control.[24] It coincided with the end of the process that transformed the Late Antique cities to Byzantine *kastra*.[25] Among the few fortifications, or parts of them, that can be ascribed to this period can be cited Poroi, Thessalonike, Servia, and perhaps Christoupolis (modern Kavala) in northern Greece.[26] Written sources and material evidence confirm the continued or recurring use of others, such as Didymoteichon and Mosynopolis in northern Greece;[27] and Emporio in Chios.[28] Also attributable to this period are hebes and Chalkida (see below).

The ensuing period of the Macedonian Era (10th–11th centuries) was a period of continuous military expeditions and successful campaigns, when Byzantines are said to have stormed castles and walled cities in their conquering wars, the culminating point of this process in the Balkans being the annexation of Bulgaria.[29] Obviously, the state's interest was focused on the defenses of the newly acquired territories and on those sites related to battlefields, all the while that military bases far from the lines of fire were maintained.

In Byzantine Greece, reconquered Crete exhibits a number of new fortifications, several of which were short-lived. Examples include Kastelos and Temenos, which were erected after the conquest of the island in 961, as well as the slightly later rebuilding of the Chandax walls.[30] On the mainland, and especially on its northern coastline, various military works were instigated; examples include Maroneia, Christoupolis, Vrya, Samothraki, Philippoi, Rentina, Stageira, Thessalonike, and Servia.[31] Furthermore, a number of fortifications are mentioned in the written sources and seem to have been used during this period, for example Komotini, Didymoteichon, Mosynopolis,

The Defences of Middle Byzantium in Greece (7th–12th Centuries)   185

Polystylon, Kitros, Drama, Serres, Moglena, Vodena, Veroia, Kastoria, Thasos, Makri, Toroni, and Ierissos in northern Greece;[32] a group of coastal forts on the peninsula of Chalkidiki, along with the linear walls of both Chalkidiki and Kassandreia;[33] Platamonas in Thessaly;[34] Anavatos in Chios;[35] and Acrocorinth in Peloponnese.[36]

The Comnenian state, covering the late 11th and the 12th centuries, was a political entity that differed significantly in its social and military structure, both from its predecessor and, of course, from what came after. The general impression is that Byzantium in this period relied for its defence on the presence of multilateral armies that depended on a grid of strong fortifications. Indeed, castle-building was a fundamental factor in its survival and was strongly promoted by the central authority.[37]

The material remains in Constantinople and Asia Minor have been a subject of research, with an emphasis on the evolution of technology initiated by the introduction and use of the counterweight trebuchet under the Comnenian dynasty.[38] The various enemies confronted in the Balkans and the Aegean islands led to the strengthening and re-use of many, if not all, previous fortifications. However, apart from references to the existence and use of fortresses in written sources (such as Arta and Ioannina in Epiros;[39] Platamonas in Thessaly;[40] and Moglena and Kastoria in northern Greece[41]), only a small amount of architectural data on specific cases exists, such as Maroneia, Rentina, Thessalonike, and possibly Anaktoropolis in northern Greece;[42] the city of Rhodes and Palio Pyli at Kos in the Dodecanese;[43] and Tigani in the Peloponnese.[44] More substantial remains, tentatively dated to the period of Manuel Komnenos (1143–1180), have been recognised in Acrocorinth.[45]

Fortifying the Middle Byzantine *Kastra*: Thebes and Chalkida

When moving away from this general framework and focusing on specific case studies, a great deal of interpretative skill is required in order to counterweight the insufficient historic sources, along with the diverse and fragmentary nature of the physical evidence. The three cases examined below, present differences when it comes to their size, geography, function, and preservation; yet, they were chosen in the hope that each one could represent a pattern of defence which, allowing for local conditions, was repeatedly encountered throughout the Greek mainland and insular territory.

The first case focuses on the fortified cities, the kastra, of Boeotia. The area (Figure 11.2) experienced a series of major events such as raids, plagues, and earthquakes.[46] From the 9th century onwards, the city of Thebes became the administrative and military capital of the Theme of Hellas, seat of its head (the *strategos*).[47] It housed both the local land aristocracy and thriving industrial production, namely the silk manufacturing workshops.[48] The civic centre was situated on the Kadmeia hill, a place that was continuously inhabited from prehistory onwards. The city extended also beyond the Kadmeia hill, with a

186 *Nikos D. Kontogiannis and Michael Heslop*

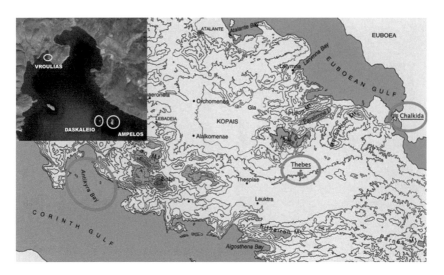

Figure 11.2 Boeotia with inset of Antikyra Bay.

number of suburbs and cemeteries/parochial churches, which yielded variably Early Byzantine (5th–6th centuries) and Middle Byzantine (11th–12th centuries) material. However, based on present data, it is impossible to be definitive on patterns of settlement expansion or retraction.

Kadmeia was naturally fortified and retained enclosure walls from various periods going back to Mycenean times.[49] Based on rescue excavations and dispersed remains on the fringe of the hill, it appears that the medieval enclosure was a simple curtain wall with regularly spaced rectangular towers. Most of its surviving parts were built by reusing ancient blocks with broken bricks at the joints. Some others have small stones set in rough courses, while a single stretch of wall is built with a more decorative, if not distinctive, mid-Byzantine façade (Figure 11.3). Yet, in all cases it is hard to pinpoint a date for a continuously reused complex without further field-work; attributions range from Justinian in the 6th to the Catalans in the 14th century.[50]

The regional authorities of Thebes communicated with the central government of Constantinople through the naval station of Euripos, present-day Chalkida, where also the Theme flotilla was stationed.[51] This was a town that was transferred from its former position in the bay of Aghios Stephanos to the east coast of the Euripos Straits, a control post and necessary stopping point for all shipping travelling in the medieval Aegean. More effective control of the Straits, proximity to Thebes and a smaller defensible site may account for the decision to transfer the town. Based upon the latest evidence, occupation at the old site dates from the first half of the 8th century, while the earliest material from the new site dates from the second half of the 9th century.[52]

Figure 11.3 Walls of Kadmeia, Thebes.

The Byzantine walls are mentioned in relation to a failed siege of the city by a certain Amir of Tarsus, ca. 880.[53] The relevant passage describes how walls and towers surrounded the city which had been prepared for the expected attack by the strategos of Hellas (from Thebes), who gathered all his available forces. The defenders used a number of weapons, such as Greek fire, stone, and arrow-throwing catapults, and succeeded in repulsing the main attack on the land front, where there was also a moat surrounding the city.

This mid-Byzantine enclosure has been revealed in a number of rescue excavations, and lay at the core of the walls that surrounded the town until they were taken down at the end of the 19th and early 20th century.[54] They enclosed a trapezoidal area, whose three sides were aligned with the coastline, while the fourth, slightly concave side faced the Euboean mainland. It was again a linear curtain with rectangular towers at almost identical intervals, protected, as noted, from the mainland by a moat. The wall had a thickness of ca. 3.50 m and was constructed with a mortared rubble core and facings of large ashlar porous, and to a lesser extent, marble blocks, many of which were reused material from older buildings. These features were attested both in the excavated parts and at the sole surviving section, indicating a consistency and regularity which points to a single building scheme (Figure 11.4).

The common features observed in the walls of Thebes and Chalkida and their complementary role in the imperial administration of Byzantine Greece point to a centrally controlled plan for defending these towns. This was probably implemented at the time of the reorganisation of the Theme of Hellas, at the end of the 8th or in the early 9th century. Both fortifications may have undergone alterations or later repairs right up till the end of Byzantine rule in 1204, a hypothesis corroborated by the archaeological finds

Figure 11.4 Walls of Chalkida.

for 12th-century Chalkida; however, more work is needed before decisive data is at hand.

Defending the countryside of Boeotia

The second case study of this chapter examines rural fortifications, i.e., smaller forts in naturally protected locations (coastal or inland) destined to ensure the safety of nearby population. When it comes to Middle Byzantine Boeotia, written sources and architectural remains present a picture of relative prosperity for an agricultural area where land was divided among, or jointly cultivated by, great landowners and flourishing villages. Included in

The Defences of Middle Byzantium in Greece (7th–12th Centuries)   189

the former can be counted public officials, such as Leo, the founder of Panagia Scripou at Orchomenos, and monasteries, chief among which was the Hosios Loukas foundation.[55] An outstanding village case study is the birthplace of Hosios Loukas, Kastorion (modern Thisvi), situated in south Boeotia; apparently, it was a small-size, yet dense, settlement with scattered parochial churches within its grid.[56]

In times of danger the rural population would either find refuge near or behind the walls of strong *kastra*, in this case Thebes (and perhaps Livadia),[57] or seek shelter in nearby locations, going backwards and forwards between mountainous locations and off-coast islands. Indeed, the *vita* of Blessed Luke, the 10th-century founder of the famous Hosios Loukas monastery, could be perceived as a testimony to the harsh realities faced by the people of the area during the 9th and 10th centuries with continuous flights to safety.[58] During the Hungarian raid of 943, Luke fled to the islet called Ampelos (Vine) just off Zaltsa[59] (see inset to Figure 11.2). Accompanied by numerous locals, he spent three years there. The place is described as a hard and arid piece of land.

Archaeological records, when available, can complement, alter, or readjust this picture. Although recent research on the islet of Ampelos did not produce any 10th-century remains, thus testing the veracity of the *vita*, it uncovered a small 6th-century settlement.[60] In fact, based on the presently known data, the settlement and defence pattern of south-west Boeotia can be reconstructed for the 6th and almost certainly for the ensuing 7th century. What came afterwards, however, must remain an object for future research.

The southwest part of Boeotia, where the plains of Thisvi and Thespiai adjoin the Gulf of Corinth, seems to have been an area of considerable activity during this period with settlements, probably on both sides of the Gulf as well as on a number of islets, that served a dual purpose of secure habitation for those who worked the land and of protecting and facilitating communications.[61] The presence of numerous, small-scale fortification works in the area (such as Thisvi /Kastorion, Chostion/Chorsiai, Mavrovouni, Palaiokastro/Siphai, Thespiai, Agios Konstantinos/Kastri, and Plataiai) reveals what was perhaps a centrally directed programme in the face of the perilous conditions that prevailed in the 6th and 7th centuries.[62] To the above-mentioned military installations, can be added two more, until recently, little-known cases.

These two small forts, one on a rocky coastal outcrop and the second on an off-shore islet, served as checkpoints, guard stations, and places of refuge for the neighbouring populations against menaces both from the mainland and the sea. They were almost certainly related to the wider military network observed in this area, though it is only possible to speculate about their exact function at present.

The coastal fort is located on the peninsula of Vroulias (Figure 11.5), just outside the port of the early Byzantine city of Antikyra, above the natural bay of Aghios Isidoros. A rubble wall survives that circumvents and uses the

Figure 11.5 Vroulias.

rock in order to isolate it from the surrounding area. Various buildings and cisterns on the abrupt slope to the sea attest to a more permanent use of the site by a restricted number of inhabitants. The main defenses are obviously directed towards the land, while at the same time overlooking and communicating with the sea. Although masonry is plain and indistinctive, all surface ceramics clearly date from the 6th and 7th centuries.

The islet fort, currently known as Daskaleio (Figure 11.6), lies some 200 m from Ampelos. Unlike Ampelos, its whole perimeter is surrounded by walls crowning the rocks that rise high above sea level. Surviving up to ca. 0.5 m above ground level, they are made with roughly cut stones alternating with

The Defences of Middle Byzantium in Greece (7th–12th Centuries) 191

Figure 11.6 Daskaleio.

bands of brick. The bricks are rectangular ceramic slabs used here intact in their original position, rather than broken or reused. This is a strong indication for an Early Byzantine date of construction. Across the middle of the islet runs a transverse wall made of well-hewn ashlar bricks which divides the area into two halves. What is more surprising is the existence of large cisterns in both halves, thus covering a substantial percentage of the surface. The surviving cistern of the western half is an underground vaulted structure, supported by large built pillars, and still plastered with hydraulic mortar. The cistern of the eastern half consists of two parallel barrel-vaulted chambers above ground. The walls are built with bands of rubble alternating with zones of bricks very similar to the walls, while the vaults are built entirely with bricks.

Daskaleio with its enclosure and cisterns, far more than Vroulias, is an outstanding and monumental construction, whose character seems to go beyond a simple guard-post for local navigation. The questions raised, such as the conditions that originated the building, the identity of its users, its period of use, and so on, must largely remain a subject for future research. It is, however, interesting that the islet has no port facilities, and only one slightly accessible side. Its construction features point to a single endeavour, and based on the size of the cisterns, it seems to have had the capacity to sustain a substantial population.

Next to the rudimentary Vroulias with its rubble masonries and small-scale buildings, which could easily be interpreted as a post for a local guard designed to defend neighbouring populations, Daskaleio certainly has the

192 *Nikos D. Kontogiannis and Michael Heslop*

allure of an important naval base, run by a higher military authority. In fact, these forts represent the potential variations that can be observed in small-scale regional fortifications. They were constructed in the transition period from Early to Middle Byzantium, and, despite the lack of physical evidence, could have been used periodically in the following centuries in the face of eminent danger.

Defending the Island of Kalymnos

The third case study focuses on the fortification pattern of Kalymnos, seen as a representative example of an Aegean insular community. Kalymnos, one of the Dodecanese islands, lies 2.5 km south of Leros, 12 km north of Kos and 22 km from the Turkish coast. It is split by three parallel mountain ranges, running east to west; the northern-most one joins a further range stretching to the north-west along a peninsula. Two fertile valleys, about 5 km apart, separate the mountain ranges, one leading from Pothia to Kantouni, and the other from the village of Vathy inland. A variety of anchorages are scattered around the island, of which Vathy was the most secure (Figure 11.2 shows most of the place names mentioned in the text).

Little is known about the history of the island under Byzantine rule. It is likely, however, that the island was subjected to Arab raids in the 7th, 8th, and 9th centuries, followed by Seljuk attacks, led by the Emir of Smyrna, in the late 11th century. It is probable that Kalymnos belonged to Leon Gabalas, the ruler of Rhodes, from 1204 onwards: the Nicaean Greeks recovered control over the island by the middle of the 13th century.

Rich in Hellenistic and Early Christian remains such as the magnificent church of Christ of Jerusalem, particularly in the area comprising the two valleys, Kalymnos contains a number of Hellenistic fortified sites, the most impressive of which is the fortress at Kastri, just inland from the northern port of Emboreio.[63] It is located on the edge of a huge cave in a high cliff.[64] The ancient fortresses of Empolas, Fylakeio, or Kastraki in the Vathy valley do not, however, seem to have been developed by the Byzantines in response to Arab attacks. Instead, coastal settlements positioned to facilitate trade and travel were abandoned until the end of the 10th century, and new fortified positions erected in more inaccessible, usually mountainous locations.

Although Vathy had the advantage of being the largest and most fertile valley on the island, it was vulnerable to attack once the dog-leg entrance to the harbour had been breached. Local legend suggests that the population deserted the valley and moved to two fortified areas. The most accessible of these was at Kastelli (Figure 11.7), a fortified settlement built on the rocky, conical hill of the Aspropountari promontory. This was at a point where the western coast of Kalymnos turns south to face the small island of Telendos. It was comprised of two sections; the first was an outer fortified bailey with the remains of houses, cisterns but no wells, gates, rectangular towers and walls down to, but not along the sea,[65] while the second section was an inner

Figure 11.7 Kastelli – general view from south.

stronghold built in the form of an acropolis at the top of the hill. Entrance to this inner portion was by means of a rock-cut staircase on a narrow ledge; additional towers supplemented a wall containing a large vaulted cistern.[66] Well-built in possibly two construction phases, the site has good sight lines for controlling the northern entrance to the straits separating Kalymnos from Telendos; it may have served as a land base for a nearby naval force.[67]

A serious earthquake in 554 is supposed to have severed Telendos from Kalymnos. Well-populated and fertile, with a small harbour, the Arab raids commencing in the second half of the 7th century compelled the inhabitants of Telendos to abandon their coastal settlement and take refuge at Aghios Konstantinos (Figure 11.8). Naturally defended on its southern, eastern, and western sides, this fortified settlement clings to the north-eastern side of Mount Rakhi at a height of 250 m.[68] Ruins remain of defensive walls, a small gateway, a guardhouse/watch-tower, a bulwark on a rocky outcrop, four large vaulted cisterns still coated with hydraulic plaster, a chapel, converted from the original basilica and a variety of different-sized houses, each with their own individual cistern; the settlement apparently lacked wells and indeed a cemetery. Approached up difficult, steep paths, with more than one way in and out, the remote location suggests that inhabitants must have felt very afraid to have selected it as their place of refuge. Views to the south and west are blocked by the tall cliffs of Mount Rakhi, though the sight lines to the north and east are superb, overlooking the channel between the two islands and Kastelli.

Aghios Konstantinos is also in sight of the third Byzantine fortified settlement in this area, Galatiani (Figure 11.9). Situated at a height of 589 m

Figure 11.8 Aghios Konstantinos – cisterns, bastions, and east wall.

above sea level, the concealed site is located on a small plateau, again with no wells, at the highest point of the north-western range of mountains on Kalymnos. Access from the village of Aginontas below is extremely difficult at present as the bottom of the path has been washed away. An easier, but still arduous, approach is along the ridges connecting Mount Galatiani to the top of the new road between Arginontas and Vathy. Similar in style to Aghios Konstantinos, the fortified settlement here consists of a gate, walls protecting the accessible sides, houses, and two large cisterns.[69] The sight lines from here are exceptional, covering views in all directions apart from the channel to the south, extending towards Leros to the north and Kos to the south.

Koutellas believes that all three fortified settlements described above, none of which have been excavated, would have been built in the middle of the 7th century, when the inhabitants of both Kalymnos and Telendos abandoned coastal villages and withdrew to more remote mountainous areas.[70] He also believes that these three settlements were in their turn desrted in the middle of the 10th century; this belief is based upon archaeological evidence supporting the resettlement of the eastern coast of Telendos at that time and the absence of any surface finds at Galatiani dating from after the 10th century. It is possible, though, that Kastelli was constructed later than the 7th century as it is so much better built than the other two sites;[71] it certainly is sited in a more useful strategic position than the other two locations.

The remaining Byzantine castle and fortified settlement are at Chorio, the old capital of Kalymnos. There is no documentary evidence to suggest that the site is pre-Hospitaller but Koutellas considers that the castle was originally

Figure 11.9 Galatiani – cistern and views of Kastelli and Aghios Konstantinos.

built in the 11th century, conceivably in reaction to raids by Seljuk pirates.[72] It was certainly a far larger settlement than any of the three sites discussed hereto and may have accommodated up to as many as 1500 people in an area of over 30,000 sqm. Constructed at the highest point of a slanting plateau rock, 255 m above sea level, the remains of the walls contain a gateway, drawbridge, towers and bastions, gun loops and arrow slits, while inside the walls are the remnants of houses, churches, and cisterns.[73] No Byzantine work appears to survive, but it is possible that the earthquake of 1493 destroyed any such evidence. The sight lines from the castle are not encompassing: views in directions other than to the south-west are effectively blocked.

Reconstructing interconnecting sight lines on the island is problematic as it is not clear which Hellenistic sites were used by the Byzantines for observation purposes (Figure 11.10). The Byzantines presumably maintained lookouts at Aghios Konstantinos and Galatiani after the settlements had been abandoned. Sight lines along the western coast run from Kastelli to the hill named Vigla[74] just to the north of Kantouni, from where a link could be made with the castle at Chorio and the dominant hill in the south-west corner of the island, namely Merovigli.[75] Connections with the eastern coast are more conjectural. There is another hill called Vigla above the mid-point of the coast, and it is possible that connections with Chorio might have been by way of, first, the point which later became the site of the monastery of Panagia Kyra Psili and, second, by way of the ridge above the Hellenistic site at Kastraki. In any case, the Byzantines would have undoubtedly installed the same comprehensive communication system as they had on the other islands

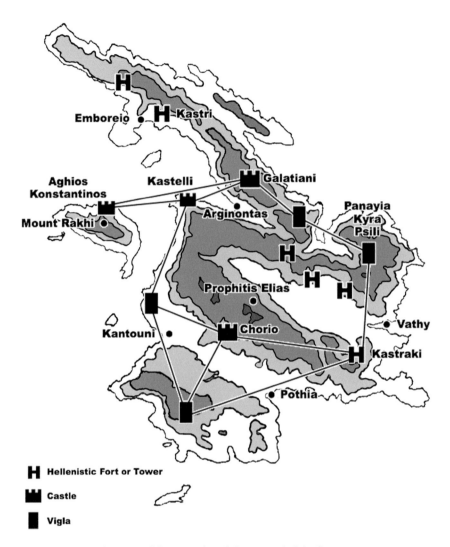

Figure 11.10 Kalymnos with Byzantine defences and sight lines.

under their control.[76] (Figure 11.11 illustrates how Kalymnos might have linked up with other Dodecanese islands.)

Conclusion

There are good reasons why the Byzantine fortifications of Greece have not yet received the attention they deserve. The evidence is ambiguous, lacking or hard to obtain; diverse types of masonry and hard-to-date patterns of materials' use and re-use; few documents or inscriptions and remote sites that are

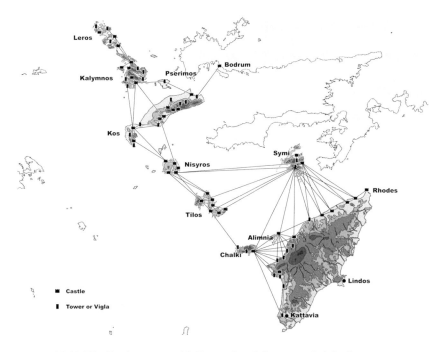

Figure 11.11 The Dodecanese with Byzantine defences and sight lines.

dispersed and expensive to study. Students have been reluctant to engage themselves with usually massive monuments that require, above all, extensive resources and a multidisciplinary approach. In fact, it appears that in each case, the method is adapted to the building.[77] Furthermore, research has to variably rely on a combination of tools, such as historical sources, architectural styles, military technology, archaeological finds (i.e., pottery from excavations and surface surveys), geophysical surveys, aerial photos, and so on.

The present chapter is an effort to present three diverse cases of fortifications occupied during the Middle Byzantine period. Their distinct character (civic, rural, and insular) may represent a pattern that facilitates study, even though in each case the fortifications appear to be the result of a dynamic interaction among multiple local factors that are hard to generalise. Nevertheless, in each case, we can detect the response of the local communities to the wider politics of the Empire. The *kastra* of Thebes and Chalcis represent the regional centres through which Byzantium controlled and safeguarded its administrative apparatus in the Greek territories of the empire. The south Boeotian forts provided a means to protect local provincial populations but also patrol the ever-important naval arteries of the empire. Finally, the islanders relied on interlinked fortifications that effectively secured their own safety while at the same time helping the Empire retain control.

198 *Nikos D. Kontogiannis and Michael Heslop*

Fighting against recurrent raiding armies or fleets of varying strength and different objectives, Byzantine Greece remained part of the Empire by channelling its forces into multiple fortification projects. These projects were adapted each time, both to the local potential and circumstances, as well as to the expected offenses. In the end, we must envisage fortifications as the visible remains of a society whose vitality was primarily directed towards self-preservation.

Notes

1 Nikos Kontogiannis is largely responsible for the first half of this chapter and Michael Heslop for the second half.
2 The only general and much-cited sources on the subject remain Foss and Winfield 1986, and Lawrence 1983. However, the relevant bibliography is constantly enriched with studies on both individual and a variety of fortifications in all parts of the Byzantine Empire. For an updated review of the Balkan fortifications, for example, see Ćurčić 2010.
3 Gregory 1995-1997, vol. 3.
4 Evgenidou 1997; Karagianni 2010.
5 Bakirtzis and Oraiopoulos 2001: 61–62.
6 Bakirtzis 2012: 139–158.
7 Avramea 1997: 60–63; Bowden 2003: 93–95; Bouras 2013: 49–53. For a wider Balkan perspective, see Curta 2006: 40–46.
8 Lawrence 1983: 184–185, 213; Evgenidou 1997: 29–32, 38, 40, 42, 46, 52, 75–76, 89, 102, 121–122, 138–140, 148–149; Velenis 1998: 107–127; Moutsopoulos 2001: 129–130; Koukouli-Chrysanthaki and Ch. Bakirtzis 2003: 18–21; Outserhout and Ch. Bakirtzis 2007: 89, 94–98; Petkos 2008: 9, 12–13; Petkos 2009: 20; Ćurčić 2010: 102, 138–139; Karagianni 2010: 118–119, 127, 148, 155, 186–187, 189–192, 198; Tsouris 2012: 571, 574, 581.
9 Lawrence 1983: 193–194; Chrysostomou and Kefallonitou 2001: 15, 20–23; Bowden 2003: 89–90; Zachos 2008: 150–157; Ćurčić 2010: 131; Chalkia 2013: 143, 146–147.
10 Loverdou-Tsigarida 2006:, 14–16; Sdrolia 2013: 11–15. Platamonas lies on the border between Thessaly and Macedonia.
11 Lawrence 1983: 193, 195; Bouras 2013: 171.
12 Lawrence 1983: 180, 217 (suggesting an 8th century date for Monemvasia); Ćurčić 2010: 126; Gkioles and P. Damoulos 2012: 192–193; Athanasoulis 2013: 196–197.
13 Kavvadia 2012: 241–242.
14 See below for examples from Boeotia. For various forts in northern Greece, see Karagianni 2010: 71–73, 105ff. For the fort of the island of Rho in the Dodecanese, see Antoniou 2012: 92–96.
15 Lawrence 1983: 193; Cherf 1984: 32–57; Gregory 1993; Evgenidou 1997: 164–165; Toska, D. Bitzikopoulos and M. Kamenidou 2005: 35–39; Karagianni 2010: 217–218; Tsouris 2012: 574, 580–581; Athanasoulis 2013, 198.
16 Curta 2006: 96–110; Bouras 2013: 58.
17 Zavvou 2012: 68–73.
18 Evgenidou 1997: 54; Velenis 1998: 127–132; Ćurčić 2010: 258; Karagianni 2010: 119–190; Tsouris 2012: 575, 581.
19 Lawrence 1983: 202; Ballance *et al.* 1989: 49–61.
20 Gkioles and Damoulos 2012: 193.

The Defences of Middle Byzantium in Greece (7th–12th Centuries) 199

21 Kollias 2000: 303–305; Manoussou-Ntella 2001: 20; Manoussou-Ntella 2012: 313–316; Michaelidou 2013: 245.
22 Tzompanaki 1996: 111–115; Tsigonaki 2012: 85–87, 93–94, 96–97, 99–100; Andrianakis 2012: 75–76, 81–86; Andrianakis 2013: 254.
23 Foss and Winfield 1986: 79–120 (Nicaea), 142–144 (Ancara).
24 Curta 2006: 111–118; Ćurčić 2010: 263.
25 Evgenidou 1997: 173–174; Bouras 2013: 58, 60.
26 Petkos 2009: 20; Ćurčić 2010: 277–278; Karagianni 2010: 139–140; Tsouris 2012: 574–576, 581.
27 Evgenidou 1997: 32, 46; Ousterhout and Bakirtzis 2007: 90.
28 Ballance et al. 1989: 73–81.
29 Curta 2006: 237–247.
30 Karpodini-Dimitriadi 1995: 176–178, 184–185, 196–197; Tzompanaki 1996: 120–132; Andrianakis 2012: 77–78; Andrianakis 2013: 256–257.
31 Lawrence 1983: 212–215; Evgenidou 1997: 40, 68, 76, 102, 144–146; Velenis 1998: 133–135; Moutsopoulos 2001: 131; Koukouli-Chrysanthaki and Bakirtzis 2003: 14, 85; Doukata-Demertzi 2008: 40–44; Petkos 2009: 20; Ćurčić 2010: 277–278, 294; Karagianni 2010: 127–128, 139, 148–149, 218–221; Tsouris 2012: 574–575, 581; Kourkoutidou-Nikolaidou 2013: 101.
32 Evgenidou 1997: 29, 39, 42, 46, 79, 86, 94, 133–134, 139; Ousterhout and Bakirtzis 2007: 90; Petkos and M. Paisidou 2009: 20–23; Karagianni 2010: 107–108, 110–112, 155–156, 185–186, 191–192, 206–207, 225–226; Tsouris 2012: 571, 573, 579–581; Petkos 2013: 105.
33 Toska, Bitzikopoulos and Kamenidou 2005–6: 40; Tsouris 2012: 579–580.
34 Evgenidou 1997: 152; Loverdou-Tsigarida 2006: 16; Tsouris 2012: 582.
35 Kavvadia 2012: 246–247.
36 Athanasoulis 2013: 204.
37 Birkenmeier 2002: 139–168, 182–187. Especially for Asia Minor, see Foss and Winfield 1986: 145–149; Foss 1996: 20–22.
38 Foss and Winfield 1986: 50–51; Chevedden 2000: 76–87; Decker 2013: 227–229.
39 Papadopoulou 2002: 105; Papadopoulou and A. Karamperidi 2008: 29, 143–145.
40 Loverdou-Tsigarida 2006: 16–17; Karagianni 2010: 195.
41 Evgenidou 1997: 135, 139; Karagianni 2010: 155–156.
42 Evgenidou 1997: 40, 82–83; Moutsopoulos 2001: 131; Ćurčić 2010: 370; Karagianni 2010: 128, 142–143 (with the various dates for Anaktoropolis); Tsouris 2012: 571, 577–579.
43 Kollias 2000: 306–307; Kontogiannis 2002: 81; Manoussou-Ntella 2001: 20–22; Manoussou-Ntella 2012: 316–317; Michaelidou 2013: 245.
44 Gkioles and Damoulos 2012: 193.
45 Athanasoulis 2009,
46 Koilakou 2013: 183–186.
47 For Byzantine Thebes and its topography, see Koder and Hild 1976: 270; Symeonoglou 1985: 156–157, 161; Louvi-Kizi 2002: 631–638 (with all previous bibliography and archaeological finds); and Koilakou 2013: 181–190.
48 Curta 2006: 277–278; Bouras 2013: 63; Koilakou 2013: 184–186.
49 Faraklas 1988, esp. 77–118.
50 Faraklas 1998: 58–69; Louvi-Kizi 2002: 631, 635; and Koilakou 2013: 189. For the defenses of Thebes during the fourteenth century, see Kontogiannis 2012a: 78–80.
51 Koder and Hild 1976: 156. For the topography and the material evidence of Middle Byzantine Euripos, see Kontogiannis 2012b: 30–35.
52 The former consists of an early 8th century lead seal (scheduled to be published by Niovi Bouza, who is thanked for the information), and the latter includes coins of Basil I (Kontogiannis 2012b: 33).

200　*Nikos D. Kontogiannis and Michael Heslop*

53　Kontogiannis 2012b: 31 (with references to the primary sources). The date of the siege is uncertain, and the various dates given by modern scholars vary from after 872/873 (Ševčenko (ed.) 2011: 210) to, or after, 883 (Decker 2013: 223; and Pryor and Jeffreys 2006: 620).

54　Kontogiannis 2012b: 32–33 with previous bibliography.

55　See http://kassiani.fhw.gr/boeotia/Forms/fLemmaBodyExtended.aspx?lemmaID= 12851 (entry: G. Vaxevanis, accessed 11/9/2014) and http://kassiani.fhw.gr/boeotia/ Forms/fLemmaBodyExtended.aspx?lemmaID=12862 (entry: Ch. Koilakou, accessed 11/9/2014)

56　Dunn 2006: 38–39, 51–53; http://kassiani.fhw.gr/boeotia/Forms/fLemmaBody Extended.aspx?lemmaID=14495 (entry:E.Voltiraki, accessed 11/9/2014)

57　For the attribution of sections of the Livadia castle to the Middle Byzantine period, see Mamaloukos and A. Kampoli-Mamaloukou 1999: 8.

58　Dunn 2006: 41–43.

59　Connor and Connor (eds.) 1994: ch. 50–51, pp. 80–83.

60　We would like to thank the excavators (P. Kalamara, S. Skartsis and G. Vaxevanis) for sharing this information.

61　Gregory 1992: 17–34; and Dunn 2006: 47. See also, Gregory 1984: 287–304 for the settlement on the Diporto islet. Veikou 2012: 177–188 has explicitly addressed the subject of off-shore island settlements.

62　Dunn 2006, 46–49 (with earlier bibliography); Vionis 2018: 146–147, 153–155.

63　These sites are well described by Mikhalis Koutellas, the local representative of the Greek Archaeological Service, in Koutellas 2006.

64　The site is described in Bean and Cook 1957: 130.

65　The design followed the instruction in the 6th century *Anonymi Strategikon* that 'the walls must not be built at the water's edge'; cited in Veikou 2012: 174.

66　The site has been decribed by Gerola 1914: 246–247; Spiteri 2001: 195 and Koutellas 2005: 66–67.

67　The nearest safe anchorage would have been at Emboreio.

68　Spiteri 2001, 197 and Koutellas 2005, 67–69, have also described this site, as has Deligiannakis 2016: 105–106.

69　Koutellas appears to have been the first person to appreciate the significance of the site; Koutellas 2005: 65–66. The church in the middle of the settlement is still used occasionally.

70　Koutellas 2006: 65. The years between 654 and 680 are usually regarded as the time of greatest insecurity in this period. Kollias also discusses Kastelli and Aghios Konstantinos and agrees with Koutellas' dating attribution: see Kollias 1994: 29–31.

71　Bean and Cook 1957: 132, report the story that Kastelli was said to have been founded by survivors from the destruction of the Vathy area in the 9th century.

72　The Aegean had become a Byzantine-dominated sea again following the recovery of Crete in 961.

73　Described by Gerola 1914, 244–245; Spiteri 2001, 190–193; Papavasileiou –and V. Karabatsos 1996: 197–208; and Koutellas 2000: 84–89.

74　The word *vigla* means lookout post. Some may have been fortified towers or *pyrgoi*, while in other cases the term *viglai* may only refer to positions, usually on a hill close to the coast, from which shipping movements could be seen.

75　Standing at a height of nearly 500 m above sea level.

76　See Pattenden 1983 for a description of the communication system.

77　In this respect it is interesting to note the very different methodologies followed by previous studies on Byzantine Fortifications, such as Foss and Winfield 1986; Foss 1985; Foss 1996; Gregory 1995. See also the relevant passages in Ćurčić 2010.

References

Andrianakis, M. (2012), 'I protovyzantini Akropoli ton Chanion' [The protobyzantine acropolis of Chania], in A. Kavvadia, and P. Damoulos, eds., *I ochyromatiki architektoniki sto Aigaio kai o mesaionikos oikismos Anavatou Chiou, Praktika Diethnous Synedriou, Chios 26–28 Septembriou 2008* [Military architecture in the Aegean and the medieval settlement of Anavatos-Chios, Proceedings of the International Congress, Chios, 16–18 September 2008]. Management Fund for Archaeological Projects Execution, Chios: 75–90.

Andrianakis, M. (2013), 'Herakleion in Crete', in J. Albani, and E. Chalkia, eds., *Heaven and Earth, Cities and Countryside in Byzantine Greece*. Ministry of Culture and Sports; Benaki Museum, Athens: 252–263.

Antoniou, G. (2012), 'I architektoniki tou Ochyrou sti niso Ro Dodekanisou'[The architecture of the Fort on the island of Rho, Dodecanese] in A. Kavvadia, and P. Damoulos, eds., *I ochyromatiki architektoniki sto Aigaio kai o mesaionikos olikismos Anavatou Chiou, Praktika Diethnous Synedriou, Chios 26–28 Septembriou 2008* [Military architecture in the Aegean and the medieval settlement of Anavatos-Chios, Proceedings of the International Congress, Chios, 16–18 September 2008]. Management Fund for Archaeological Projects Execution, Chios: 91–104.

Athanasoulis, D. (2009), *The Castle of Acrocorinth and Its Enhancement Project (2006–2009)*. Hellenic Ministry of Culture and Tourism; 25th Ephorate of Byzantine Antiquities, Ancient Corinth.

Athanasoulis, D. (2013), 'Corinth' in J. Albani, and E. Chalkia, (eds), *Heaven and Earth, Cities and Countryside in Byzantine Greece*. Ministry of Culture and Sports; Benaki Museum, Athens: 192–209.

Avramea, A. (1997), *Le Péloponnèse du IVe au VIIIe siècle, changements et persistances*, Byzantina Sorbonensia 15. Publications de la Sorbonne, Paris.

Bakirtzis, N. (2012), 'Ta teichi ton vyzantinon poleon: aisthitiki, ideologies kai symvolismoi' [The walls of the Byzantine cities: aesthetics, ideologies and symbolism], in T. Kiousopoulou, ed., *Oi Vyzantines Poleis (8os–15os aionas), Prooptikes tis ereunas kai nees ermineutikes proseggiseis* [The Byzantine cities (8th–15th c.), perspectives of research and new interpretative approaches]. Editions of the Philosophical Faculty of the University of Crete, Rethymno: 139–158.

Bakirtzis, N., and Oraiopoulos, Ph. (2001), *Dokimio gia tin ochyromatiki sto Vyzantio, o Voreioelladikos choros 4os–15os ai.*[Essay on the fortifications of Byzantium, the Northern Greek space 4th–15th c.]. Archaeological Receipts Fund, Athens.

Ballance, M., Boardman, J., Corbett S., and Hood, S. (1989), *Excavations in Chios 1952–1955, Volume 4 Byzantine Emporio*. The British School of Archaeology at Athens Supplement 20, Thames and Hudson.

Bean, G., and Cook, J. (1957), 'The Carian Coast III', *BSA* 52: 58–146.

Birkenmeier J. (2002), *The Development of the Komnenian Army 1081–1180, History of Warfare* vol. 5. Brill, Leiden.

Bouras, Ch. (2013), 'Byzantine cities in Greece', in J. Albani, and E. Chalkia, eds., *Heaven and Earth, Cities and Countryside in Byzantine Greece*. Ministry of Culture and Sports; Benaki Museum, Athens: 45–73.

Bouras, Ch. (2013), 'Byzantine Athens, 330–1453', in J. Albani, and E. Chalkia, eds., *Heaven and Earth, Cities and Countryside in Byzantine Greece*. Athens Ministry of Culture and Sports; Benaki Museum, 168–179.

202   *Nikos D. Kontogiannis and Michael Heslop*

Bowden, W. (2003), *Epirus Vetus, the Archaeology of a Late Antique Province.* Duckworth, London.

Chalkia, E. (2013), 'Nikopolis', in J. Albani, and E. Chalkia, eds., *Heaven and Earth, Cities and Countryside in Byzantine Greece.* Ministry of Culture and Sports; Benaki Museum, Athens: 140–155.

Cherf, W. (1984), *The Dhema Pass and Its Early Byzantine Fortifications*, Unpublished Ph.D. Thesis. Loyola University, Chicago.

Chevedden, P., (2000), 'The invention of the counterweight Trebuchet: A study in cultural diffusion', *DOP* 54: 71–116.

Chrysostomou, P., and Kefallonitou, F. (2001), *Nikopolis* [in Greek]. Archaeological Receipts Fund, Athens.

Connor, C., and Connor W., eds. (1994), *The Life and Miracles of Saint Luke of Steiris, Text, Translation and Commentary.* Hellenic College Press, Brookline, Mass.

Ćurčić, S. (2010), *Architecture in the Balkans from Diocletian to Suleyman the Magnificent.* Yale University Press, New Haven; London.

Curta, F. (2006), *Southern Europe in the Middle Ages, 500–1250*, Cambridge Medieval Textbooks. Cambridge University Press, Cambridge.

Decker, M. (2013), *The Byzantine Art of War.* Westholme, Yardley.

Deligiannakis, G. (2016), *The Dodecanese and the Eastern Aegean Islands in Late Antiquity, A.D. 300–700.* Oxford University Press, Oxford.

Doukata-Demertzi, S. (2008), *Paliochora Maroneias, i anaskafi tis palaiochristianikis vasilikis kai tou mesovyzantinou oikismou* [Paliochora of Maronoia, the excavation of the early Christian basilica and of the middle Byzantine settlement]. Ministry of Culture; 12th Ephorate of Byzantine Antiquities, Kavala.

Dunn, A. (2006), 'The rise and fall of towns, loci of maritime traffic, and silk production: The problem of Thisvi-Kastorion', in E. Jeffreys, ed., *Byzantine Style, Religion and Civilization, in Honour of Sir Steven Runciman.* Cambridge University Press, Cambridge: 38–71.

Evgenidou, D. (1997), *Kastra Makedonias kai Thrakis, Vyzantini Kastroktisia* [Castles of Macedonia and Thrace, Byzantine Castle building]. Adam, Athens.

Faraklas, N. (1988), *Thiva, mnimeiaki topografia tis archaias polis, meros A': oi ochyroseis* [Thebes, monumental topography of the ancient city, part A: the fortifications]. Editions of the University of Crete, Athens.

Foss, C. (1985), *Survey of Medieval Castles of Anatolia – 1 (Kütahya)*, B.A.R., International series 261. BAR, Oxford.

Foss, C. (1996), *Survey of Medieval Castles of Anatolia II: Nicomedia*, British Institute of Archaeology at Ankara Monograph 21. British Institute of Archaeology at Ankara, London.

Foss C., and Winfield, D. (1986), *Byzantine Fortifications, an Introduction.* University of South Africa, Pretoria.

Gerola, G. (1914), 'Monumenti Medievali delle Tredici Sporadi', *Annuario della regia Scuola Archeologica di Atene* 2: 169–356.

Gkioles, N., and Damoulos, P. (2012), 'Oi ochyroseis sto Vyzantino Kastro tis Mainis sto Tigani tis Mesa Manis' [The fortifications at the Byzantine Castle of Maini in Tigani of Mesa Mani], in A. Kavvadia, and P. Damoulos, eds., *I ochyromatiki architektoniki sto Aigaio kai o mesaionikos oikismos Anavatou Chiou, Praktika Diethnous Synedriou, Chios 26–28 Septembriou 2008* [Military architecture in the Aegean and the medieval settlement of Anavatos-Chios, Proceedings of the

The Defences of Middle Byzantium in Greece (7th–12th Centuries) 203

International Congress, Chios, 16–18 September 2008]. Chios Management Fund for Archaeological Projects Execution, 187–194.

Gregory, S. (1995–1997), *Roman Military Architecture on the Eastern Frontier*. A.M. Hakkert, Amsterdam.

Gregory, T. (1993), *Isthmia: Excavations by [UCLA] and [OSU] under the Auspices of [ASCSA]. Volume 5. The Hexamilion and the Fortress*. American School of Classical Studies at Athens, Princeton N.J.

Gregory, T. (1992), 'Archaeological explorations in the Thisbe Basin', in J. Fossey, ed., *Boeotia Antiqua II: Papers on Recent Work in Boiotian Archaeology and Antiquity*. J.C. Gieben, Amsterdam: 17–34.

Gregory, T. (1984), 'Diporto: an Early Byzantine Maritime Settlement in the Gulf of Corinth', *DChAE* 12: 287–304.

Karagianni, F. (2010), *Oi vyzantinoi oikismoi sti Makedonia mesa apo ta archaiologika dedomena (4os-15os)* [Byzantine Settlements of Northern Greece (Macedonia) through Archaeological Data]. University Studio Press, Thessaloniki.

Karpodini-Dimitriadi, E. (1995), *Kastra kai fortetses tis Kritis, eikones kai mnimes* [Castles and fortresses of Crete, images and memories]. Adam, Athens.

Kavvadia, A. (2012), 'O mesaionikos oikismos tou Anavatou ypo to fos tis neoteris archaiologikis ereunas' [The medieval settlement of Anavatos in the light of recent archaeological research]. in A. Kavvadia, and P. Damoulos, eds., *I ochyromatiki architektoniki sto Aigaio kai o mesaionikos oikismos Anavatou Chiou, Praktika Diethnous Synedriou, Chios 26–28 Septembriou 2008* [Military architecture in the Aegean and the medieval settlement of Anavatos - Chios, Proceedings of the International Congress, Chios, 16–18 September 2008]. Management Fund for Archaeological Projects Execution, Chios: 239–248.

Koder, J., and Hild, F. (1976), *Hellas und Thessalia*, Tabula Imperii Byzantini 1. The Austrian Academy of Sciences, Vienna.

Koilakou, Ch. (2013), 'Byzantine Thebes', in J. Albani, and E. Chalkia, eds., *Heaven and Earth, Cities and Countryside in Byzantine Greece*. Ministry of Culture and Sports; Benaki Museum, Athens: 180–191.

Kollias, E. (1994), 'Schediasma archaiologias kai technes tes Kalymnou, apo ta palaiochristianika chronia mechri to telos tes Ippotokratias (1522)' [Outline of the archaeology and art of Kalymnos from the Early Christian Era up to the end of the Rule of the Knights (1522)], in *Kalymnos – Ellenorthodoxos Orismos tou Aigaiou* [Kalymnos, Greek-Orthodox definition of the Aegean]. Holy Metropolis of Leros, Kalymnos and Astypalaia, Athens: 23–50.

Kollias, H. (2000), 'I palaiochristianiki kai vyzantini Rodos. I antistasi mias ellinistikis polis' [Early Christian and Byzantine Rhodes. The resistance of a Hellenistic city], in *Rodos 2,400 chronia, I poli tis Rodou apo tin idrisi tis mechri tin katalipsi apo tous Tourkous (1523), Diethnes epistimoniko synedrio Rodos, 24–29 Oktovriou 1993, Praktika*, Tomos B [Rhodes 2,400 years, the city of Rhodes from its foundation until the conquest by the Turks (1523), International scientific congress Rhodes, 24–29 October 1993, Proceedings, vol. II]. Ministry of Culture, Athens: 299–308.

Kontogiannis, N. (2002), *Mesaionika kastra kai ochyroseis tis Ko* [Medieval castles and fortifications of Kos], Municipalities of Antimachia and Pyli, Athens.

Kontogiannis, N. (2012a), 'Anichneuontas tin Katalaniki Voiotia: i amyntiki organosi tou Doukatou ton Athinon kata ton 14o aiona' [Retracing the Catalan Boiotia: the defensive organisation of the Duchy of Athens during the 14th century], in

204 *Nikos D. Kontogiannis and Michael Heslop*

I Katalano-Aragoniki kyriarchia ston Elliniko choro [Catalan-Aragonese domination in the Greek mainland]. Cervantes Institute, Athens: 67–109.

Kontogiannis, N. (2012b), 'Euripos-Negroponte-Eğriboz: material culture and historic topography of Chalcis from Byzantium to the end of Ottoman rule', *Jahrbuch der Österreichischen Byzantinistik* 62: 29–56.

Koukouli-Chrysanthaki, Ch., and Bakirtzis, Ch. (2003), *Philippoi* [in Greek]. Archaeological Receipts Fund, Athens.

Kourkoutidou-Nikolaidou, E. (2013), 'Philippi', in J. Albani, and E. Chalkia, eds., *Heaven and Earth, Cities and Countryside in Byzantine Greece*. Ministry of Culture and Sports; Benaki Museum, Athens: 101.

Koutellas, M. (2000), 'Ta Ippotika kastra tes Kalymnou' [The Hospitaller castles of Kalymnos], *Corpus* July 2000: 84–89.

Koutellas, M. (2006), *Kalymnos: History, Archaeology, Culture* (Municipality of Kalymnos: Kalymnos: Organization of Cultural Development of the Prefecture of Dodecanese).

Koutellas, M. (2005), 'Ta vyzantina kastra tes Kalymnou' [The Byzantine Castles of Kalymnos], *Corpus* June, 2005: 66–67.

Lawrence, A. (1983), 'A skeletal history of Byzantine fortifications', *BSA* 78: 171–227.

Louvi-Kizi, A., (2002), 'Thebes', in A. Laiou, ed., *The Economic History of Byzantium: From the Seventh through the Fifteenth Centuriesi*, Dumbarton Oaks Studies 39. Dumbarton Oaks, Washington, D.C.: 631–638.

Loverdou-Tsigarida, K. (2006), *To Kastro tou Platamona* [The castle of Platamona]. Archaeological Receipts Fund, Athens.

Mamaloukos, S., and Kampoli-Mamaloukou, A. (1999), *To kastro tis Livadeias, Istoria-architektoniki, Katalogos ekthesis* [The castle of Livadia, history – architecture, Exhibition catalogue]. Municipality of Livadeia, Athens.

Manoussou-Ntella, K. (2001), *Mesaioniki poli Rodou. Erga apokatastasis (1985–2000)* [Medieval city of Rhodes, restoration works (1985–2000)]. Management Fund for Archaeological Projects Execution, Rhodes.

Manoussou-Ntella, K. (2012), 'Mesaioniki Rodos, apo to vyzantino kastro sto Palati tou Megalou Magistrou' [Medieval Rhodes, from the Byzantine castle to the Palace of the Grand Master], in A. Kavvadia, and P. Damoulos, eds., *I ochyromatiki architektoniki sto Aigaio kai o mesaionikos oikismos Anavatou Chiou, Praktika Diethnous Synedriou, Chios 26–28 Septembriou 2008* [Military architecture in the Aegean and the medieval settlement of Anavatos-Chios, Proceedings of the International Congress, Chios, 16–18 September 2008]. Management Fund for Archaeological Projects Execution, Chios: 313–330.

Michaelidou, M. (2013), 'The city of Rhodes', in J. Albani, and E. Chalkia, eds., *Heaven and Earth, Cities and Countryside in Byzantine Greece*. Ministry of Culture and Sports; Benaki Museum, Athens: 240–251.

Moutsopoulos, N. (2001), *Rentina II. To Vyzantino kastro tis mygdonikis Rentinas. I ochyrosi kai i ydreusi tou oikismou* [Rentina II. The Byzantine castle of the Mygdonian Rentina. The fortification and the aqueduct of the settlement]. The Technical Chamber of Greece, Athens.

Outserhout, R., and Bakirtzis, Ch. (2007), *The Byzantine Monuments of the Evros/Meriç River Valley*. European Center for Byzantine and Post-Byzantine Monuments, Thessaloniki.

Papadopoulou, V. (2002), *I vyzantini Arta kai ta mnimeia tis* [Byzantine Arta and its monuments]. Archaeological Receipts Fund, Athens.

Papadopoulou, V., and Karamperidi, A., eds. (2008), *Ta vyzantina mnimeia tis Ipeirou* [The Byzantine monuments of Epirus]. Ministry of Culture; 8th Ephorate of Byzantine Antiquities, Ioannina.

Papavasileiou, E., and Karabatsos, V. (1996), 'To kastro ste Chora Kalymnou kai e anadeixe tou' [The castle in Chora of Kalymnos and its promotion], *Archaiologiko Deltio* 44–46 (1989–91): 197–208.

Pattenden, P. (1983), 'The Byzantine Early Warning System', *Byzantion* 53: 258–299.

Petkos, A. (2008), *Diocletianopolis, Guide of the Archaeological Site*. 11th Ephorate of Byzantine Antiquities, Veroia.

Petkos, A. (2009), 'Restoration of the monuments', in *Servia, a Byzantine Fortified City, Journeys in Space and Time*. Ministry of Culture; 11th Ephorate of Byzantine Antiquities, Veroia: 13–24.

Petkos, A. (2013), 'Berroia', in J. Albani, and E. Chalkia, eds., *Heaven and Earth, Cities and Countryside in Byzantine Greece*. Ministry of Culture and Sports; Benaki Museum, Athens: 104–113.

Petkos, A., and Paisidou, M. (2009), *Early Byzantine Pella – Byzantine Edessa, two key points on a history trail*. Ministry of Culture; 11th Ephorate of Byzantine Antiquities, Veroia.

Pryor, J., and Jeffreys, E. (2006), *The Age of the ΔPOMΩN, The Byzantine Navy ca 500–1204*. Brill, Leiden.

Sdrolia, S. (2013), *The Castle of Melivoia, Velika Agia*. 7th Ephorate of Byzantine Antiquities, Larissa.

Spiteri, S. (2001), *Fortresses of the Knightsi*. Book Distributors Ltd, Malta.

Symeonoglou, S. (1985), *The Topography of Thebes from the Bronze Age to Modern Times*. Princeton University Press, Princeton, N.J.

Ševčenko I., ed. (2011), *Theophanis Continuati Liber V Vita Basilii Imperatoris,* CFHB 42. de Gruyter, Berlin.

Toska, L., Bitzikopoulos, D., and Kamenidou, M., (2005–2006), 'Anaskafikes ereunes sto diateichisma tis Kassandreias' [Excavation research at the transverse wall of Kassandreia], *Dekati* 2: 34–41.

Tsigonaki, Ch. (2012), 'Poleon anelpistois metavolais: istorikes kai archaiologikes martyries apo ti Gortyna kai tin Eleytherna tis Kritis (4os-8os ai.)' [On the unbelievable changes of cities: historical and archaeological testimonies from Gortyna and Eleutherna in Crete (4th-8th c.)], in T. Kiousopoulou, ed., *Oi Vyzantines Poleis (8ος–15ος aionas), Prooptikes tis ereunas kai nees ermineutikes prosegiseis* [The Byzantine cities (8th–15th c.), perspectives of research and new interpretative approaches]. Editions of the Philosophical Faculty of the University of Crete, Rethymno: 73–100.

Tsouris, K. (2012), 'I amyntiki organosi ton Thrakikon kai Makedonikon akton apo ton 9o mechri ton 15o aiona'[The defensive organisation of the Thracian and Macedonian coasts from the 9th to the 15th century], in A. Kavvadia, and P. Damoulos, eds. *I ochyromatiki architektoniki sto Aigaio kai o mesaionikos oikismos Anavatou Chiou, Praktika Diethnous Synedriou, Chios 26–28 Septembriou 2008* [Military architecture in the Aegean and the medieval settlement of Anavatos-Chios, Proceedings of the International Congress, Chios, 16–18 September 2008]. Management Fund for Archaeological Projects Execution, Chios: 561–588.

206 *Nikos D. Kontogiannis and Michael Heslop*

Tzompanaki, Ch. (1996), *Chandakas, i poli kai ta teichi* [Chandax, the city and the walls]. Society of Cretan Historical Studies, Herakleion.

Veikou, M. (2012), 'Byzantine Histories, Settlement Stories: *Kastra,* "Isles of Refuge", "Unspecified Settlements" as in-between or Third Spaces, Preliminary Remarks on Aspects of Byzantine Settlement in Greece (6th–10th c.)', in T. Kiousopoulou, ed., *Oi Vyzantines Poleis (8os–15os aionas), Prooptikes tis ereunas kai nees ermineutikes prosegiseis* [The Byzantine cities (8th–15th c.), perspectives of research and new interpretative approaches], Editions of the Philosophical Faculty of the University of Crete, Rethymno: 159–206.

Velenis, G. (1998), *Ta teichi tis Thessalonikis apo ton Kassandro os ton Irakleio* [The walls of Thessaloniki from Kassander to Herakleios]. University Studio Press, Thessaloniki.

Vionis, A. (2018), 'Understanding Settlements in Byzantine Greece, New Data and Approaches for Boeotia, Sixth to Thirteenth Century', *DOP* 71, 127–173.

Zachos, K., ed. (2008), *Nikopoli, Apokaliptontas tin poli tis nikis tou Augoustou* [Nikopolis, discovering the city of Augustus' victory]. Management Fund for Archaeological Projects Execution, Athens.

Zavvou, E. (2012), 'Palaiokastro Voion. To vyzantino kastro Ashab al baqar?' [Palaiokastro Voion. The Byzantine castle Ashab al baqar?], in L. Souchleris, and S. Raptopoulos, eds., *O Panagiotis Velissariou, i romaiki kai vyzantini Peloponnisos, Praktika diimeridas eis mnimin tou archaiologou Panagioti Velissariou* [Panagiotis Velissariou, the Roman and Byzantine Peloponnisos, proceedings of the two-day conference in memory of the archaeologist Panagiotis Velissariou], I Archaiologia stin Peloponniso 1[Archaeology in the Peloponnese 1]). Archaeological Institute of Peloponnesian Studies, Municipality of Megalopoli: 68–73.

http://kassiani.fhw.gr/boeotia/Forms/fLemmaBodyExtended.aspx?lemmaID=12851 (entry: G. Vaxevanis, accessed 11/9/2014).

http://kassiani.fhw.gr/boeotia/Forms/fLemmaBodyExtended.aspx?lemmaID=12862 (entry: Ch. Koilakou, accessed 11/9/2014).

http://kassiani.fhw.gr/boeotia/Forms/fLemmaBodyExtended.aspx?lemmaID=14495 (entry: E.Voltiraki, accessed 11/9/2014).

12 The Demographic and Economic History of Byzantine Greece in the *Long Durée*

The Contribution of the Pollen Data

Adam Izdebski

Introduction

The purpose of this chapter is to provide a brief introduction to the palynological evidence that is available for the study of Byzantine Greece. Apart from offering an overview of all the existing pollen sites that contain information relevant to the vegetation history of this area during the last 2,000 years, this text also provides a short historical interpretation of the changes that the Greek landscapes underwent throughout the Byzantine era, as recorded by the pollen data. For the most part, and in particular as regards the interpretative section, this chapter discusses the results of a larger-scale quantitative analysis whose results have already been published in detail elsewhere.[1] However, as in this last chapter the historical interpretation deals with the entire Byzantine world, from the Balkans to Anatolia, it seems useful to offer a separate chapter that focuses solely on Greece and in this way provides a brief overview of what palynology and environmental history can contribute to the study of this part of the Byzantine world.

Therefore, after presenting the pollen sites from Greece, this chapter proceeds to describing briefly the method of analysis and the results we obtained for Central Greece and Macedonia. Finally, it focuses on the three major issues in the history of Byzantine Greece that probably benefit most from including the pollen evidence in the scholarly debates. The first one is the environmental aspect and the dating of the Late Antique economic and settlement expansion in Greece. The second 'historical' sub-section concerns the Middle Byzantine economic revival, and again the pollen data provide interesting information on the chronology and the scale of human exploitation of the natural environment. The last issue discussed here is the late medieval crisis, and in particular the impact of the Black Death on the society and economy of medieval Greece.

The pollen data for Byzantine Greece

The palynological data come from sedimentary cores extracted from water environments, such as lakes, for which there are more detailed introductions

DOI: 10.4324/9781003429470-15

to palynology in historical contexts.[2] Samples of sediments that accumulated over millennia contain pollen which was deposited in a lake at the time when a given layer of sediment was formed. The changing composition of pollen assemblages in subsequent samples reflects more or less directly the vegetation structure around the coring site at a given period of time; in particular, it allows us to trace its transformations over time. Since the total number of pollen grains counted in each sample differs from one sample to another, when interpreting the pollen data one must not focus on the change in the absolute numbers of pollen grains belonging to a particular plant or group of plants (i.e., to a pollen taxon). Instead, the interpretation should concern the share that a given pollen taxon has in the total pollen sum within a particular sample, which is always expressed in percentage values.

Although the European Pollen Database contains currently more than 30 pollen sites that are located in the modern Republic of Greece, only a minor part of all the existing palynological data can be used for the study of the last 2,000 years. This is due to the lack of precise and reliable chronologies for most of the sites; in order to build an age-depth model for a sediment core (from which pollen samples are taken) that would span the last 2,000 years, one needs at least one or two radiocarbon dates from this period or not much earlier, and preferably also an age estimate for the top of the core. Currently, such information is only available for 11 sites from the whole of Greece. The location of these sites is presented on Figure 12.1, while Figure 12.2 contains the information on their original publications and their most up-to-date age-depth models. These models were used for the creation of a palynological database of Byzantine Greece, which was later analysed with the numerical methods described in the following section.

The pollen sites in our database are divided into three categories according to their chronological quality, that is, the number of radiocarbon dates and the credibility of the surface age. The best sites, that belong to the first category, have at least two radiocarbon dates in total, with at least one falling into the last two millennia; a 'second category' site has at least one radiocarbon date for the entire core, not earlier than 500 BC; the worst sites are those whose youngest radiocarbon date is earlier than that, but still not earlier than 1500 BC. Luckily, there is only one site of this last type in our database, although – when compared to the most recently studied sites in Europe that tend to be provided with five or more radiocarbon dates – the majority of the Greek sites cannot be said to be particularly well-dated.

At this point, it is also worth noticing that the pollen sites available for the study of Byzantine Greece concentrate in two areas. The first one is the highlands that surround the Macedonian plain – this region, however, contains no site from the plain itself. The second group of sites is located on the coasts of Central Greece: Thessaly, Attica, Argolis, and Acarnania. While these sites are relatively well located in order to provide information on the economic activity of the local societies, they offer hardly any information about the processes taking place in the adjacent highlands.

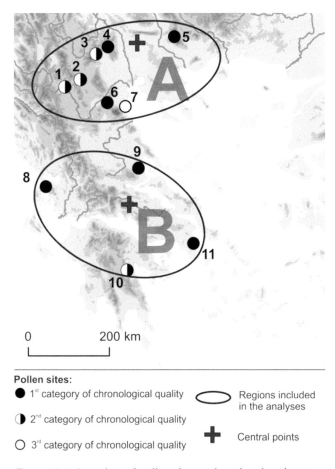

Figure 12.1 Location of pollen sites and analysed regions.

The analysis and its results

Our numerical analysis consists of three steps for which a full description has been published.[3] First, we had to create continuous time series out of the original pollen data that provide pollen percentage values only for specific years, which are those to which a particular sample is dated; we achieved that by *linear spline interpolation*. Second, we applied a standard filter used in econometrics to remove high-frequency fluctuations in time series, in order to remove at least part of the error inherent to our data (caused, for instance, by random events occurring at the time of sediment accumulation). Third, we aggregated our data into trends that represent changes in the vegetation structure on the regional level. For both Macedonia and Central Greece we defined central points that represent entire regions. For these two locations, we produced counterfactual trends in all the pollen taxa included in our database.

210   *Adam Izdebski*

	Site name	Latitude	Longitude	Chron. quality	Original publication	Age-depth model
				Macedonia		
1.	Orestias	40.500	21.250	2	Kouli & Dermitzakis 2010	Kouli & Dermitzakis 2010
2.	Khimaditis Ib	40.616	21.583	2	Bottema 1974	New model - Izdebski et al. 2015
3.	Mount Voras	41.020	21.910	2	Gerasimidis & Athanasiadis 1995	Gerasimidis et al. 2009
4.	Mount Paiko	41.052	22.275	1	Gerasimidis & Athanasiadis 1995	Gerasimidis et al. 2008
5.	Lailias	41.266	23.600	1	Gerasimidis & Athanasiadis 1995	Gerasimidis & Athanasiadis 1995
6.	Flambouro	40.259	22.171	1	Gerasimidis & Athanasiadis 1995	Gerasimidis & Panajiotidis 2010
7.	Litochoro	40.138	22.546	3	Athanasiadis 1975	EPD cal BP model by S. Panajiotidis
				Central Greece		
8.	Voulkaria	38.866	20.833	1	Jahns 2005	New model - Izdebski et al. 2015
9.	Halos	39.166	22.833	1	Bottema 1974	New model - Izdebski et al. 2015
10.	Lerna	37.500	22.583	2	Jahns 1993	New model - Izdebski et al. 2015
11.	Vravron	37.920	24.000	1	Kouli 2012	Kouli 2012

Figure 12.2 Pollen sites from Central Greece and Macedonia with data for the Byzantine period.

We computed these trends as weighted averages of the percentage values of the pollen taxa; these values were taken from all the sites included into a regional dataset. The weights reflect the differences among sites as regards their chronological quality, their geographical distance to the region's central point, and the time distance between the year for which the average value is being computed and the year of the original sample which is the nearest one in time to the year being computed. Whereas the weights for the chronological quality were given arbitrary values, the weights for the two distances are endogenous, i.e., they result from the actual structure of the data.

The results obtained for Central Greece and Macedonia are presented in this chapter on three diagrams. The first one (Figure 12.3) presents the changes in the proportionate share of cereal and olive pollen in the total pollen signal from both regions (olive only in Central Greece). These trends provide an indication of the intensity of human agricultural activity on the regional scale. The two other figures show the changes in the composition of forests and their relative importance within the entire regional landscape. Already for Antiquity the transformations of forest vegetation reflected very closely the economic activity of local populations.

The Demographic and Economic History of Byzantine Greece 211

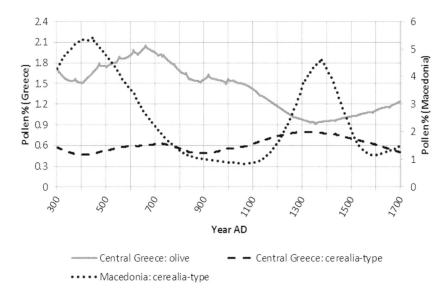

Figure 12.3 Key anthropogenic indicators in Central Greece and Macedonia.

Late Antiquity

When we compare the trends in cereal and olive pollen for Central Greece and Macedonia in Late Antiquity (ca AD 300–600), we see that despite the fact that within this period an agricultural expansion undoubtedly occurred in both regions, its duration in each of them was substantially different. Thus, in the highlands surrounding the Macedonian plain the period of the most intense cereal cultivation seems to date relatively early, that is AD 350–450. It is followed by an increase in pine pollen, which may suggest a secondary expansion of forest vegetation onto the cultivated land (while the cutting of oak that continues beyond AD 450 would be a sign of larger-scale wood-cutting) (Figure 12.2). In Central Greece, on the contrary, the relatively slow agricultural expansion continues beyond AD 450 and lasts until the end of the 7th century, which is visible in the trends of both cereals and olive; it is only after ca AD 700 that the tree vegetation recovers (Figure 12.4). The fact that in both regions we have evidence for a Late Antique expansion of the rural economy is not surprising, and it has already been noticed by archaeologists.[4] What is striking in this context is the relatively early end of this phase in the hills surrounding the Macedonian plain, which, however, may have to do with the lack of security experienced by the Northern Balkans from the 5th century onwards (Figure 12.4).

The Middle Byzantine revival

For this period, we again notice significant differences in the timing of the same phase in the settlement-economic history of both regions, that is, of the

212 *Adam Izdebski*

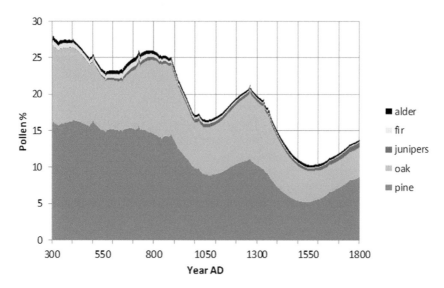

Figure 12.4 Key forest taxa in Central Greece.

Middle Byzantine revival.[5] It starts at least a century earlier in Central Greece (between AD 900 and 1000, first visible in the decrease of tree pollen, then in a rise of cereals). In the Macedonian highlands, the agricultural expansion does not start much before AD 1100, which again may have to do with the relative insecurity of this area, which formed the borderland between Byzantium and the Bulgarian state (Figure 12.3). Another difference between the two regions concerns the relative scale of cereal cultivation: whereas in Macedonia the highest values achieved in the Middle Ages reach only as high as the Late Antique climax, in Central Greece the medieval cereal cultivation seems to have exceeded the scale of the Late Antique cereal production. However, there is a substantial difference between the structure of the Late Antique and the medieval rural economies in this region: the relative importance of olive visibly declined after the 7th century AD. This phenomenon is characteristic for the entire Byzantine world, and may have to do with changes in the culturally-conditioned demand for olive oil once the ancient *polis* culture ceased to exist.

The Black Death

None of the diagrams leaves doubt that the 14th century saw a major reversal in the expansion of the agricultural economy visible throughout the previous centuries. In Macedonia, an abrupt change in the trends of both cereals and beech as well as pine can be dated to the middle of the 14th century (Figure 12.5). At this point, the values of cereal pollen decreased, while the secondary forests – beech and pine – started to expand. This coincides with

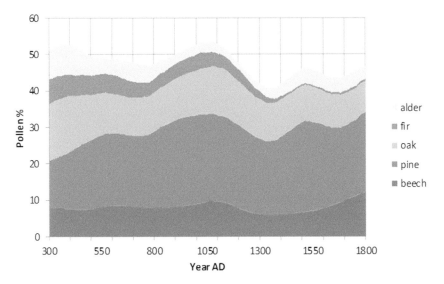

Figure 12.5 Key forest taxa in Macedonia.

the coming of the Black Death to Macedonia and Greece,[6] which is believed to have caused substantial damage to the population of Macedonia, as the increase in the amount of sediments that seems to have occurred in this period would suggest.[7] In the case of Central Greece, although beyond doubt the Black Death also brought about a population collapse, the crisis started already in the 13th century, with an increase in beech pollen occurring even prior to AD 1200 (but within some 150 years forest again started to be cut down). In the case of Central Greece, the late medieval crisis of agricultural production must have had to do not only with the pandemic, but also with the general insecurity that followed the events of AD 1204.[8]

Notes

1 Izdebski *et al.* 2015.
2 Eastwood 2006; Izdebski 2013; Izdebski 2019.
3 For a full description see Izdebski *et al.* 2016.
4 Dunn 2003; Sanders, 2004.
5 Whittow 2008.
6 Dols 1979.
7 Geyer 1986.
8 Jacoby 2009.

References

Athanasiadis, N. (1975), 'Zur postglazialen Vegetationsentwicklung von Litochoro Katerinis und Pertouli Trikalon (Griechenland)', *Flora* 164, 99–132.

214 *Adam Izdebski*

Bottema, S. (1974), *Late quaternary vegetation history of North-Western Greece*, Unpublished PhD thesis, University of Groningen.

Dols, M. (1979), 'The second plague pandemic and its recurrences in the Middle East: 1347–1894', *Journal of Economic and Social History of the Orient* 22: 162–189.

Dunn, A. (2003), 'Continuity and change in the Macedonian countryside from Gallienus to Justinian', in W. Bowden and L. Lavan, eds., *Recent Research on the Late Antique Countryside*, Late Antique Archaeology 2, Leiden: 535–585.

Eastwood, W. (2006), 'Palaeoecology and eastern Mediterranean landscapes: theoretical and practical approaches', in J. Haldon, ed., *General Issues in the Study of Medieval Logistics: Sources, Problems, and Methodologies*, History of Warfare 36, Leiden: 119–158.

Gerasimidis, A., and Athanasiadis, N. (1995), 'Woodland history of northern Greece from the mid Holocene to recent time based on evidence from peat pollen profiles', *Vegetation History and Archaeobotany* 4, 109–116.

Geyer, B. (1986), 'Esquisse pour une histoire du paysage depuis l'An Mil', in J. Lefort, ed., *Paysages de Macédoine: leurs caractères, leur évolution à travers les documents et les récits des voyageurs*, Paris: 99–116.

Izdebski, A. (2013), *A Rural Economy in Transition: Asia Minor from Late Antiquity into the Early Middle Ages*, Journal of Juristic Papyrology Supplement Series 18, Warsaw.

Izdebski, A. (2019), 'Palynology and historical research', in A. Izdebski and J. Preiser-Kapeller, eds., *Companion to the Environmental History of Byzantium*, Brill Companions to Byzantium, Leiden.

Izdebski, A., Koloch, G., and Słoczyński, T. (2015), 'Exploring Byzantine and Ottoman economic history with the use of palynological data: a quantitative approach', *Jahrbuch der österreichischen Byzantinistik* 65: 67–110.

Izdebski, A., Koloch, G., Słoczyński, T., and Tycner-Wolicka, M. (2016), 'On the use of palynological data in economic history: new methods and an application to agricultural output in Central Europe, 0--2000 AD', *Explorations in Economic History* 59: 17–39.

Jacoby, D. (2009), 'Peasant mobility across the Venetian, Frankish and Byzantine Borders in Latin Romania, thirteenth-fifteenth centuries', in D. Vlassi, Ch. Maltezou, and A. Tzavara, eds., *I Greci Durante La Venetocrazia: Uomini, Spazio, Idee (13.-18. Sec.): Atti Del Convegno Internazionale Di Studi, Venezia, 3–7 Dicembre 2007*, Venezia: 525–539.

Jahns, S. (1993), 'On the Holocene vegetation history of the Argive Plain (Peloponnese, southern Greece)', *Vegetation History and Archaeobotany* 2, 187–203.

Jahns, S. (2005), 'The Holocene history of vegetation and settlement at the coastal site of Lake Voulkaria in Acarnania, western Greece', *Vegetation History and Archaeobotany* 14, 55–66.

Kouli, K., and Dermitzakis, M. (2010), 'Contributions to the European Pollen Database. 11. Lake Orestiás (Kastoria, northern Greece)', *Grana* 49, 154–6.

Kouli, K. (2012), 'Vegetation development and human activities in Attiki (SE Greece) during the last 5,000 years', *Vegetation History and Archaeobotany* 21, 267–278.

Sanders, G.D.R. (2004), 'Problems in interpreting rural and urban settlement in southern Greece, AD 365–700', in N. Christie, ed., *Landscapes of Change: Rural Evolutions in Late Antiquity and Middle Ages*, Aldershot: 163–193.

Whittow, M. (2008), 'The Middle Byzantine economy (600–1204)', in J. Shepard, ed., *The Cambridge History of the Byzantine Empire c. 500—1492*, Cambridge: 465–492.

13 Middle Byzantine Hierissos

Archaeological Research at the Entrance to Mount Athos

Aikaterini Tsanana

Byzantine Hierissos is located on the eastern coast of the peninsula of Chalkidike, 15 km northwest of the modern border of Mount Athos. At the same place, on the hills close to the sea, was founded the ancient city of Acanthos. The settlement was inhabited continuously until 1932, when a catastrophic earthquake destroyed it, and the inhabitants were resettled by the shore.

The ancient city of Acanthos, which was founded in the 7th century BC, and was inhabited up to the Late Roman period, has yet to be researched. By contrast, its cemetery, which is found along the shore, has been excavated for the last 40 years. Around 13,000 tombs have been researched and are dated from the Archaic period to the 4th century AD.[1] Information on Early Christian Acanthos (or Hierissos) is scarce however. In 2000, a three-aisled Early Christian basilica with atrium and adjacent structures was revealed at the south-eastern part of the ancient cemetery, in a region with post-Hellenistic ceramic workshops (Figure 13.1.1). It was erected in the 4th century and was in use throughout the 5th century. A Middle Byzantine cemetery was organised on its ruins, destroying several parts of it.[2] Parts of the foundations of another large Early Christian building of the 5th century of unknown use (Figure 13.1.2) were revealed close to the port. According to the present archaeological data, the Early Christian settlements of Chalkidike were abandoned or largely destroyed by the barbarian raids and natural disasters in the 6th century.[3]

Although we share scarce information on Early Christian Hierissos, we do have abundant information on medieval Hierissos, thanks to the documents kept in the monasteries of Mt Athos.[4] For instance, the important imperial monastery of St John Prodromos was founded by the Constantinopolitan monk John Kolovos some years before 883, but its ruins have not yet been discovered. It dominated the region until the foundation of the Great Lavra in 963. By the late 10th century the Prodromos monastery declined and became a dependency of Iviron.[5] The name of Byzantine Hierissos (τοῦ Ερισου ἡ ἐνορία, the parish of Hierissos) is attested for the very first time in 883, in a *sigillion* of the emperor Basil I (867–886). The document was issued in order to recognise and secure the Athonite monastic society.[6] From the second quarter of the 10th century Hierissos seems to have been a well-organised community fighting for the rights on the fields over its territory.

DOI: 10.4324/9781003429470-16

Figure 13.1 Topographic plan of Byzantine and modern Hierissos; excavated sites.

The bishopric of Hierissos was founded after 972 and came under the metropolis of Thessalonike, a fact that proves the importance of the medieval city.[7] The seat of the bishopric was kept there until the 16th century. The 'God-saved *kastron* of Hierissos' (θεωσόστου [sic] κάστρου Ἱερισσοῦ)[8] flourished, according to the historical sources, up to the early 12th century.

The archaeological data for medieval Hierissos are, more or less, the following.[9] The ruins of the church of Panagia, which was demolished by the earthquake of 1932, were excavated in the 1990s. It is located within the walls of ancient Acanthos, where the medieval *kastron* is to be found. The church, which must have been founded in the late 14th century over a settlement of the Iron Age, was probably burnt and rebuilt in the late 15th century and had been in use up to 1932. Remnants of the medieval fortification survive under the foundations of its Southern and Western walls. Archaeological evidence dated in the Early Christian and Byzantine periods was not revealed in that location. On the contrary, finds from the Ottoman era are abundant there. Therefore, an archaeological *desideratum* remains the identification of the place where the Middle Byzantine settlement flourished within the fortifications of ancient Acanthos.

On the shore of modern Hierissos, 282 Middle Byzantine tombs have already been researched in the ruins of the Early Christian basilica (Figure 13.1.1). As far as their construction is concerned, they belong in three categories. The earlier seem to be, on the one hand, 43 isolated graves and, on the other hand, a rare type of pit-grave covered by arrangements of fragments of tiles creating a kind of decoration. The third group consists of elaborated pit-graves, covered or not. Personal items of the dead were found in 55 graves, mainly either isolated or belonging to children. We are talking about jewellery: necklaces, beads, rings, copper or silver earrings, and crosses. Almost half of the graves show removals of remains. Moreover, an interesting funerary custom is attested in 27 cases: setting fragments of tiles with incised crosses, either on the covering or into the grave. It is hard to determine for how long the cemetery had been in use.[10] The jewellery found in the cemetery can be dated between the 9th and the 12th centuries.

Middle Byzantine ruins have been revealed from 2006 onwards at the eastern outskirts of modern Hierissos, quite close to the port and on the fringe of ancient Acanthos. A long building divided into three succeeding rooms was excavated in a small plot by the shore of Hierissos (Figure 13.1.3). Another building, to the southwest of the latter, was also revealed. Between them there was found a narrow street. The masonry of the buildings, which had openings to the street and to the sea, is typical Middle Byzantine (Figure 13.2.1). The ceramic finds include many sherds of storage jars as far as the southern building is concerned. In the northern building, the sherds belonged to cooking pots and tableware,

Figure 13.2 (1–3) Ruins of houses dated to the 10th–11th centuries, (4) Middle-Byzantine tombs.

Figure 13.3 (1) Polychrome White Ware sherds, (2) zoomorphic padlock, late 12th century, (3) buckle with a representation of Pegasus, second half of the 11th century.

objects of everyday life (e.g., a padlock: Figure 13.3.2),[11] and around 500 isolated fragments of glass bracelets.[12] The coin finds date the buildings to the second half of the 11th century.[13]

Under the northern building, there was revealed a larger one and to the east of it a small room, which was probably a workshop that had to do with metals. Much fewer ceramic finds of everyday life were collected there, some copper coins, needles, tiny implements, a buckle representing a Pegasus (Figure 13.3.4)[14]; and a part of a scale and of a nib. Numismatic evidence dates this construction phase, which was finally burned, at the end of the 10th century.

A hoard of around 700 corroded copper coins of the 5th century – alongside other copper and lead waste, a weight of one ounce, and two *folleis* of Constantine VII – were interestingly found under the floor of this building. The Early Christian coin hoard had apparently only a metallic and no monetary value in a layer of the 10th century. Additionally, the tiny implements found there, and the fact that the place was used in the 11th century as a workshop (e.g., fragments of glass bracelets), may indicate that the owners of the building had something to do with gold or silver smithing and the recycling and reusing of metal waste.

Another indication of the importance of the building is the lead seal of Samonas, the imperial *protospatharios* and judge of Thessalonike (Figure 13.4).[15]

Figure 13.4 Lead seal of the judge Samonas of Thessaloniki (927 AD).

The same *boulloterion* produced another seal,[16] now kept in Iviron Monastery, which sealed a document of 927, concerning an economic dispute between the Monastery of Kolovou and the community of Hierissos about some fields in the region.[17] We argue that this very seal, which was found in Hierissos, sealed the second copy of the document that was kept by the community of the *kastron*. The fact may be a further indication of the social status of the owner of the building.

According to the historical sources, the *kastron* of Hierissos was inhabited by strong and less strong owners of land, of houses, and of workshops, who signed in several documents as *oikitores* or *oikodespotai*.[18] The archaeological evidence of those buildings of the 10th and 11th centuries implies that we are concerned with urban and not rural houses, inhabited by wealthy owners who were entrepreneurs. The case of the ceramic finds is eloquent: we must not underestimate the fact that 700 sherds of glazed white ware were gathered in such a restricted area located far away from great urban centres and in a period when the glazed pottery was not produced on a massive scale.[19]

220   *Aikaterini Tsanana*

Additionally, the fact that we found 33 sherds of polychrome glazed white ware (Figure 13.3.1), a type of ware which is very scarce even in Constantinople, is rather important.[20] Finally, the port of Hierissos was serving significant activities connecting commercial centres, namely the emerging Mount Athos, Thessalonike, and the rest of the Northern Aegean. All the above mentioned explain in a way the presence of those finds and the buildings in the *extra muros* region of the *kastron* of Hierissos, in a period of insecurity due to constant hostile raids. Indeed, after the destruction of those buildings in the late 12th century, a pottery workshop must have been settled there, as is indicated by the glazed sherds, the clay fire-bars, and the tripods from kilns, which were collected in the upper layer of the southern building.

Some 50 m to the southeast of those buildings, three more buildings were researched.[21] The northern one had two long rooms separated by a yard, while to the east of it there was an open-air space, something like a square. To the south of this building there is another one, similar to the previous and separated from it by a street (Figure 13.1.4). The numismatic evidence indicates that the buildings were in use from the late 10th century to the second half of the 11th century. During their last construction phase they were modified, and a kiln functioned also in this place (Figure 13.2.2).

From the whole excavated area 370 fragments of glass bracelets were collected that had nothing to do with each other, and 65 fragments of clay fire-bars, from a kiln with drops of glaze.[22] The ceramic kiln can be dated in the late 11th century.

Another building with successive construction phases was revealed on the same axis to the south (Figure 13.1.5). In the first phase (of the 10th century) the building had two rooms in a row and a main exit to the south. Two granite steps led to a semi-underground room. Standing slabs defined a small yard to the south and to the east side of it.

The ruins of another building of a different plan were excavated to the south of this building. It was founded on an Early Christian wall. In the 11th century the building was extended to the east and the interior openings, except for the main door, were closed. In its last construction phase it was partly modified with the addition of some new walls extending it to the south (Figure 13.2.3). In this area we could identify the earlier *extra muros* construction activity of the 12th century according to the ceramic and numismatic finds. The destruction of this building is dated in the late 12th century.

The third building was excavated some meters to the south. It had three construction phases, namely of the 10th century, of the 11th century and of the post-Byzantine era. It is founded on an Early Christian building (4th–6th century), where we found stored amphorae and the detritus of glass manufacture (Figure 13.1.6).

The research of the three aforementioned buildings yielded several objects of everyday use, agricultural and building implements, sherds of cooking and tableware, and some storage vessels in the large rooms of the first building.

On the fringe of the ancient city of Acanthos, and of the *kastron* of Hierissos, there has been excavated another complex of buildings, which is differentiated from the rest because of the densely arranged construction phases, which are difficult to identify but are dated between the Early Christian period and the late 12th century (Figure 13.1.7). A building of the 5th–6th centuries, of unknown use, and some remnants of earlier buildings, of the 4th century, are revealed in the deeper layers. Over these structures there are walls probably of the 9th century or even earlier. The first clear construction phase is dated to the 10th century. To the south of the whole complex there is a well-arranged cemetery with cist and pit-graves with no burial objects and some removals of contents (Figure 13.2.4). The funerary use of the area is further identified by isolated graves over the ruins of the 11th and 12th centuries. At a distance of some 300 m to the west of this place there was revealed the main Middle Byzantine cemetery of Hierissos. The fact that there was a second smaller cemetery leads us to deduce that it must belong to a church or a monastery. The hypothesis is based, firstly, on a tradition that there was a church of St Nicholas near the port, and, secondly, on the architectural sculptures found there. The most important finds of the excavation were some ridged plain wares, objects of everyday life, a solidus of Theodosius II (430–440), three lead seals (of the 10th–12th centuries) and a brick on which there were inscribed eight male names and numbers, concerning probably an economic transaction.[23]

Although the rescue excavations carried out up to now were restricted, the archaeological evidence sheds light on the flourishing community of Hierissos between the second half of the 10th century and the late 11th century, a fact that is also attested by the Athonite documents. New buildings are erected in this period, due to the commercial activity of the port. The inhabitants, apart from agriculture, have also other professions. The cemetery indicates demographic increase and wealth. It is the period of the foundation of a new bishopric, which means that Hierissos was the most important and populated centre in the region and was therefore well-protected. The few finds of the Komnenian period in the *extra muros* district imply that Hierissos gradually declined during the 12th century and from a *kastron* was transformed into a *chorion* (i.e., village). Such a decline could not otherwise be explained than by the evolution of the neighbouring powerful landowner, namely Mount Athos. The gradual dependence of Hierissos upon it commenced by the late 12th century and kept on going until the 14th century.[24]

Notes

1 Trakasopoulou-Salakidou 1987; Trakasopoulou-Salakidou 1996.
2 Papaggelos 1988.
3 Papaggelos 2000: 26–27.
4 In the Middle Byzantine period Hierissos is mentioned in several documents dating from 883 to c.1200. They can be found in the archives of the monasteries of Protaton (Protaton: nos. 1–6), of Iviron (Iviron I: nos. 1–2, 4–5, 7–8, 12–13,

222 *Aikaterini Tsanana*

15–16, 27, 29; Iviron II: nos. 31–32, 39, 41, 50, 52), of Lavra (Lavra I: nos. 6–8, 18, 24, 35, 39–40, 60), of Zographou (Zographou: no. 5), and of Xeropotamou (Xeropotamou: nos. 1, 4, 7–8). For a full list and discussion of the relevant mentions see Poutouroglou 1993.
5 Protaton: 36–38.
6 Protaton: 45–48 and no. 1.
7 Papachryssanthou 1981: 374.
8 Lavra I: no. 18, line 26.
9 The archaeological material on which the following pages are based has been revealed during rescue excavations in the castle area and within the modern town of Hierissos undertaken by the 10th Ephorate of Byzantine Antiquities between 1993–1995 and 2009–2012. Preliminary reports of the latter can be found in Tsanana, Mpitzikopoulos, and Eugenikos 2010: 411–415; Tsanana and Eugenikos 2012; Tsanana and Eugenikos 2013.
10 Papaggelos 1988; Papaggelos and Tsanana forthcoming.
11 Cf. Yashayeva 2010.
12 Cf. Antonaras 2002; Doukata-Demertzi 2002.
13 Numismatic finds from the aforementioned excavations in Hierissos are listed in Maladaki 2013: Index I, nos. 186–279.
14 Cf. Tsilipakou 2002; Koutsikou 2002a; Koutsikou 2002b; Gkini-Tsofopoulou 2002; Davidson 1952: 273, Pl. 115, nos. 2213–2215.
15 Tavlakis and Maladakis 2005–2006.
16 Oikonomides 1986: 67–68, no. 61.
17 Iviron I: no 1.
18 See for example Iviron I: no 4; Poutouroglou 1993: 56–70 for a full list and discussion.
19 Papanikola-Mpakirtzi 2003: 46–50.
20 Tsanana and Amprazogoula forthcoming. Morgan 1942: 64–80, Figs. 47–50, Pl. XIII-XIV. Hayes 1992: 35–37, Pl. 8–9. Sanders 2001.
21 Tsanana, Mpitzikopoulos, and Eugenikos 2010.
22 Konstantinou and Raptis 2015.
23 Tsanana and Eugenikos 2012, 510. Papaggelos and Tsanana forthcoming.
24 Poutouroglou 1993: 18–31, 71–77.

References

Primary sources

Iviron I: Lefort, J., Oikonomidès, N., Papachryssanthou, D., in collaboration with Métrévéli, H., (1985) *Actes d'Iviron I. Des origines au milieu du XIe siècle*, Archives de l'Athos XIV, Paris.
Iviron II: Lefort, J., Oikonomidès, N., Papachryssanthou, D., in collaboration with Kravari, V., and Métrévéli, H., eds. (1990), *Actes d'Iviron II. Du milieu du XIe siècle à 1204*, Archives de l'Athos XVI, Paris.
Lavra I: Lemerle, P., Guillou, A., Svoronos, N., in collaboration with Papachryssanthou, D., ed. (1970), *Actes de Lavra I. Des origines à 1204*, Archives de l'Athos V, Paris.
Prôtaton: Papachryssanthou, D., ed. (1975), *Actes du Prôtaton*, Archives de l'Athos VII, Paris.
Xéropotamou: Bompaire, J., ed. (1964), *Actes de* Xéropotamou, Archives de l'Athos III, Paris.

Middle Byzantine Hierissos 223

Zographou: Regel, W., Kurtz, E., and Korablev, B., eds. (1907), *Actes de l'Athos IV. Actes de Zographou, VV* 13, Priloženie 1. Amsterdam (reprinted, 1975).

Secondary sources

Antonaras, A. (2002), 'Γυάλινο βραχιόλι', in D. Papanikola-Mpakirtzi, ed., *Καθημερινή ζωή στο Βυζάντιο,* exhibition catalogue, October 2001-January 2002, Thessaloniki, White Tower. Athens: 418, no. 531.

Davidson, G. (1952), *Corinth XII. The Minor Objects*. Princeton, NJ.

Doukata-Demertzi, S. (2002), 'Γυάλινα βραχιόλια', in D. Papanikola-Mpakirtzi, ed., *Καθημερινή ζωή στο Βυζάντιο,* exhibition catalogue, October 2001-January 2002, Thessaloniki, White Tower. Athens: 418, no. 533.

Gkini-Tsofopoulou, E. (2002), 'Χάλκινη πόρπη ζώνης', in D. Papanikola-Mpakirtzi, ed., *Καθημερινή ζωή στο Βυζάντιο,* exhibition catalogue, October 2001-January 2002, Thessaloniki, White Tower. Athens: 394–395, no. 485.

Hayes, J.W. (1992), *Excavations at Saraçhane in Istanbul II*. Princeton, NJ.

Konstantidou, K., and Raptis, K. (2015), 'Archaeological evidence of an eleventh-century kiln with rods in Thessaloniki', in M. Gonçalves and S. Gónzalez-Martínez, eds., *X Congresso International a Cerâmica Medieval no Mediterraneo. Silves-Mértola, 22–27 outubro '12*, Silves: 589–595.

Koutsikou, Ch. (2002a), 'Χάλκινη πόρπη ζώνης', in D. Papanikola-Mpakirtzi, ed., *Καθημερινή ζωή στο Βυζάντιο,* exhibition catalogue, October 2001-January 2002, Thessaloniki, White Tower. Athens: 394, no. 483.

Koutsikou, Ch. (2002b), 'Χάλκινη πόρπη ζώνης', in D. Papanikola-Mpakirtzi, ed., *Καθημερινή ζωή στο Βυζάντιο,* exhibition catalogue, October 2001-January 2002, Thessaloniki, White Tower. Athens: 394, no. 484.

Maladakis, V. (2013), *Νομισματική κυκλοφορία και χρηματική οικονομία στη μεσαιωνική Χαλκιδική (10ος-14ος αι.),* Unpublished PhD thesis, Aristotle University of Thessaloniki.

Morgan, C. (1942), *Corinth XI. The Byzantine Pottery*. Princeton, NJ.

Oikonomides, N. (1986), *A Collection of Dated Byzantine Lead Seals*. Washington, DC.

Papachryssanthou, D. (1981), 'Histoire d'un évêché byzantin. Hiérissos en Chalcidique', *Travaux et Mémoires* 8 *(Hommage à M. Paul Lemerle)*: 373–396.

Papaggelos, I. (1988), 'Το μεσαιωνικόν νεκροταφείον της Ιερισσού', *8th Annual Symposium of the Christian Archaeological Society. Programme and Abstracts*, Athens: 78–79.

Papaggelos, I. (2000), *Η Σιθωνία κατά τους Βυζαντινούς χρόνους. Ιστορία – Μνημεία – Τοπογραφία*, Unpublished PhD thesis, Aristotle University of Thessaloniki.

Papaggelos, I., and Tsanana, A. (forthcoming), 'Περί της μεσοβυζαντινής Ιερισσού', in Fl. Karagianni and G. Fousteris, eds., *Πρακτικά Διεθνούς Επιστημονικού Συμποσίου προς τιμήν του ομότιμου καθηγητή Γεωργίου Βελένη, Θεσσαλονίκη, Οκτώβριος 2017*. Athens.

Papanikola-Mpakirtzi, D. (2003), 'Εργαστήρια εφυαλωμένης κεραμικής στο βυζαντινό κόσμο', in Ch. Bakirtzis, ed., *VIIe Congrès International sur la Céramique Médiévale en Méditerranée, Thessaloniki, 11–16 Octobre 1999. Actes*, Athens: 45–66.

Poutouroglou, K. (1993), *Η παρουσία της κοινότητας Ιερισσού στα έγγραφα των μονών του Αγίου Όρους (10ος-14ος αι.),* Unpublished M.A. thesis, Aristotle University of Thessaloniki.

Sanders, G. (2001), 'Byzantine polychrome pottery', in J. Herrin, M. Mullet, and C. Otten-Froux, eds., *MOSAIC. Festschrift for A.H.S. Megaw*, London: 89–103.

Tavlakis, I., and Maladakis, V. (2005-2006), 'Ο κριτής Θεσσαλονίκης Σαμωνάς, η μονή

224   *Aikaterini Tsanana*

Κολοβού και το *κάστρον* Ιερισσού: *απείθεια και σκληρότης* στον 10ο αιώνα', *Dekati* 2: 88–93.

Trakosopoulou-Salakidou, E. (1987), 'Αρχαία Άκανθος: πόλη και νεκροταφείο', *To Archaiologiko Ergo ste Makedonia kai Thrake* 1: 295–304.

Trakosopoulou-Salakidou, E. (1996), 'Αρχαία Άκανθος: 1986–1996', *To Archaiologiko Ergo ste Makedonia kai Thrake* 10A: 297–312.

Tsanana, A., and Amprazogoula, A. (forthcoming), 'Céramique à pâte blanche du type Polychrome Ware provenant de Chalcidique (Grèce du Nord)', in *Proceedings of the 12th International Congress on Medieval and Modern Period Mediterranean Ceramics (AIECM3)*, Athens, 21–27 October 2018.

Tsanana, A., and Eugenikos, P. (2012), 'Στα ίχνη της βυζαντινής Ιερισσού', *To Archaiologiko Ergo ste Makedonia kai Thrake* 26: 501–511 [published in 2017].

Tsanana, A., and Eugenikos, P. (2013), 'Νέα στοιχεία από την μεσαιωνική Ιερισσό. Η ανασκαφική έρευνα κατά το 2013', *To Archaiologiko Ergo ste Makedonia kai Thrake* 27 [forthcoming].

Tsanana, A., Mpitzikopoulos, D., and Eugenikos, P. (2010), 'Σωστικές ανασκαφικές έρευνες στη Χαλκιδική κατά το 2010', *To Archaiologiko Ergo ste Makedonia kai Thrake* 24: 411–420.

Tsilipakou, A. (2002), 'Χάλκινη πόρπη ζώνης', in D. Papanikola-Mpakirtzi, ed., *Καθημερινή ζωή στο Βυζάντιο*, exhibition catalogue, October 2001-January 2002, Thessaloniki, White Tower. Athens: 393, no. 482.

Yashayeva, T. (2010), 'Klappe eines Schlosses in Form eines Pferdes', in J. Frings and H. Willinghöfer, eds., *Byzanz. Pracht und Alltag. Kunst- und Ausstellungshalle der Bundesrepublik Deutschland, Bonn, bis 13. Juni 2010*, München: 307, no. 389.

Part 4

Patronage and Sacred Space

14 Patronage of Religious Foundations in Middle Byzantine Greece (867–1204)

The Evidence of Inscriptions and Donor Portraits

Sophia Kalopissi-Verti

The evidence of church inscriptions and donor portraits regarding patronage of religious foundations in Greece points to two distinctive periods within the Middle Byzantine era, which reflect the historical circumstances of the time. I will first examine the evidence in the period of the reign of the Macedonian and the Doukas dynasties and then the testimony in the period of the Komnenoi and Angeloi, attempting to point out similarities and differences in patronage patterns. In the last part of the chapter I will focus on a regional example, the Mani in the southern Peloponnese, which offers rich inscriptional evidence regarding local patronage.

From the late 9th to approximately the third quarter of the 11th century, i.e., roughly during the reign of the Macedonians and the Doukai (867–1081), the intervention of the central authorities and the imposition and diffusion of the new religious policy that developed in the capital after the end of the iconoclastic controversy are evident. Ecclesiastical, administrative and military officials representing the emperor and/or the patriarch were the patrons who supported the imperial ideology and policy of re-establishing Orthodoxy in cities, smaller towns, and in the countryside of the Greek mainland and the Aegean islands.[1]

In Hagia Sophia, the metropolitan church of Thessalonike, the dome mosaic, representing the Ascension of Christ, was completed in the year 885 by Archbishop Paul,[2] if dome composition and dedicatory inscription, placed under the scene and interrupting a garland decorative band, belong together.[3] The iconography of the dome has been interpreted as a variant of the figure of the Pantokrator, namely the new iconographic scheme introduced after the end of Iconoclasm because of the identical theological content of both images regarding the dogma of Incarnation and eschatological notions.[4] Nonetheless, it has also been regarded as a reflection of the iconography of the central dome of the church of the Holy Apostles in Constantinople.[5] Despite the fact that for technical reasons many scholars have disconnected the Ascension scene from the inscription, which has been dated earlier, it is generally accepted that the dome mosaic was sponsored by an archbishop of

DOI: 10.4324/9781003429470-18

the city of Thessalonike in the 880s.[6] The outstanding quality and stylistic features directly connect the dome composition of Hagia Sophia in Thessalonike with the contemporary mosaics of the Great Church in Constantinople.[7] It can thus be argued that the mosaic decoration in the two churches dedicated to Hagia Sophia, in the capital and in the second most important city of the empire, were part of the same programme initiated by the central authorities.

One of the earliest episcopal churches in the Greek provinces bearing epigraphic documentation is the Episkope of Skyros, a cross-in-square church of the transitional type.[8] Besides the date of 895, the foundation inscription carved on a marble architrave mentions, in hierarchical order, the names of the Emperors Leo and Alexander first, then that of the metropolitan of Athens Sabas (879–913),[9] and lastly that of the Bishop of Skyros Sabas (Figure 14.1a, 14.1b): +Ἔτους ˏϚυγ΄ ἐπὶ βασιλεί(ας) Λέοντ(ος) κ(αὶ) Ἀλεξάν(δρου) ἐπὶ Σάβα μητροπο(λίτου) Ἀθηνῶ(ν) κ(αὶ) Σάβα ἐπ(ισ)κόπου τὸν ὧδε ('+In the year 6403 [=895] in the reign of Leo and Alexander and the time of the metropolitan of Athens Sabas and of Sabas, the bishop here').[10]

It is evident that the last-mentioned bishop of Skyros, a suffragan of the metropolitan of Athens, is the actual patron of the church; however, his initiative seems to be in accordance with, or rather part of, the policy of the emperors, who are recorded first in the inscription. The solemn character and the hierarchical listing of the authorities – emperors, metropolitan, bishop – named in the inscription seem to point to the ways central policy was promoted in the provinces.

Epigraphic evidence in the Peloponnese going back to the early period of the reign of the Macedonian dynasty is scarce. An inscription of the year 903 testifies to the foundation of a church that is no longer extant, dedicated to St Christophoros, at Pallantion of Arcadia, by Nikolaos Bishop of Lakedaimon,

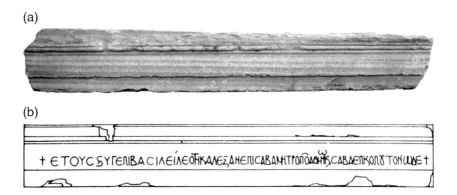

Figure 14.1 (a) Episkope, Skyros. Foundation inscription of the bishop of Skyros, Savas (895 AD) (Photo: Michalis Karambinis). (b) Drawing of the inscription after Bouras 1960–1961: pl. 29B.

Patronage of Religious Foundations in Middle Byzantine Greece 229

a suffragan of the metropolis of Corinth, bearing further testimony to the role of ecclesiastical authorities in patronage and in implementing imperial policy at that time.[11] The inscription, which has been recently connected with the efforts of the central authorities to Christianise the Slav settlers and to consolidate Byzantine rule in the region,[12] runs as follows: +Ἐνεκενήσθη ὁ ναὸς τοῦ ἁγίου Χριστωφό/ρου ὑπὸ Νικολάου τοῦ ἁγιοτάτου ἐπησκό/που Λακεδαιμονίας μηνὴ Μαΐῳ ιε΄ ἰνδ(ικτιῶνος) ϛ΄/ ἔτους, ϛυια΄ ('The church of St Christopher was renovated by Nikolaos the most holy bishop of Lakedaimonia in the month of May 14, sixth indiction, of the year 6411[=903]').[13]

Imperial dignitaries, often local *archontes,* undertook the task of erecting churches in provincial towns and in the countryside as well. In Thebes, *Basilikos Kandidatos* Basileios, an imperial dignitary, built on the Kadmeia the church of St Gregory the Theologian in the year 871/2.[14] An inscription in prose immured in the eastern part inside the now ruined church records: Ἐθεμελιώθη ὁ πάνσεπτος ναὸς τοῦ ἁγίου Γρηγ<ο>ρίου τοῦ Θεολόγου ἐπὶ τῆς βασιλείας Βασιλείου, Κωνσταντ(ίνου) κ(αὶ) Λέοντος, παρὰ Βασιλείου βασιλικοῦ Κανδ(ιδά)τ(ου), ἔτους ἀπὸ κτίσεως κόσμου ϛτπ΄ ἰ(ν)δ(ικτιῶνος) ε΄. Ἀμήν ('The most venerable church of Saint Gregory the Theologian was founded in the reign of Basil, Constantine and Leo by Basileios the Basilikos Kandidatos, in the year 6380 [=871/2] from the creation of the world, fifth indiction. Amen').[15]

In the vicinity of Thebes, Leon, a local landowner bearing the titles of *basilikos protospatharios* and *epi ton oikiakon,* was the donor of the imposing church of the Virgin at Skripou (873/74).[16] Four inscriptions immured in the outer walls, three in prose and one metrical, include implications of the patron's stand in favour of the imperial and patriarchal religious policy,[17] which he introduced and propagated through a stately church in the environs of Thebes, where his local property obviously lay. The impressive building of the transitional cross-in-square type, which dominated in the Greek provinces at the time, comprised a rich relief decoration executed by a local workshop probably based in Thebes, where it executed the sculpted decoration of St Gregorios Theologos as well.[18] Moreover, the church at Skripou systematically incorporated in its walls *spolia* from the nearby ruins of ancient Orchomenos. The wealthy local *archon* underlines his relation to Constantinople through the inscriptions and at the same time is proud of the local traditions and the glorious ancient past of his region, which he embodies as *spolia* in his church.

Of interest is an inscribed marble slab in the Byzantine Museum at Athens recording the foundation of the church of St John the Baptist, known as Hagios Ioannes tou Magkoute and preserved up to the 19th century, by a lay couple and their son, *Droungarios* Ioannes, in the year 871:[19] +Ἔτ(ου)ς ϛτοθ΄ ἀπὸ κτ(ίσεως) κόσμ(ου) μ(ηνὶ) Φεβρ(ουαρίῳ) δ΄ ἰν(δικτιῶνος) δ΄, Κον(σταντῖνος)/ κ(αὶ) Ἀναστασὼ κ(αὶ) Ἰω(άννης) δρογγάριος τὸ φίλ/τατο(ν) ἡμ(ῶν) τέκν(ον) ἐκ/ συνφόνου ἐκτίσαμ[εν]/ τὸ{χ} πάνσεπτον να[ὸν]/ τοῦ Ἁγίου Ἰω(άννου) τοῦ Βαπ[τιστοῦ]/ ὁρίσαντ(ες) κ(αὶ) προστάζ(οντες)/ πάντα τὰ ὑπάρχον[τα]/ ἡμῶν

230 *Sophia Kalopissi-Verti*

αὐτον τε τ … /..τῶν ἀδελφῶν … / [εἰς μ]νημόσι. + ('In the year 6371 [=871] from the creation of the world, on the fourth of February, fourth indiction, Konstantinos and Anastaso and the Droungarios Ioannes our dearest child, by common consent erected the holy church of St John the Baptist defining and commanding all our resources and … that of the brothers … in commemoration … '). Thus the church of St. John in Athens was a private, lay-family benefaction to which the founders left all their property in order to be commemorated. The couple's son had the military rank of a *droungarios,* not very highly valued by this time.[20]

The recapture of Crete in 961 and the expulsion of the Arabs from the Aegean had a great impact on Greek lands. The role of the church of the Virgin at Hosios Loukas monastery, built immediately after this significant victory, on Constantinopolitan models combined with features of the so-called Helladic School, was crucial for the development of church architecture in southern Greece.[21]

In Corfu, two inscriptions incised on the west facade on both sides of the entrance door of the church of SS. Iason and Sosipatros, close to Palaiopolis, mention the founder, the priest/bishop Stephanos (*thyepolos*), who erected the church in memory of Bishop (*proedros*) of Corfu Theophanes: Μνημοσύνης τόδ᾽ ἔτευξεν ὑπ[οδεεστ]έρης σοφὸν ἔργον/ Στέφανος θυηπόλος ἀμπλ[ακημάτων … …ψυχῆς]/ ποικιλόμορφον τῶν ἁγίων καινὸν[᾽αποστόλων … …/ Θεοφάνους προέδρου εἰς εὐρέα ἥμα[τα]μνήμης ('This wise work was constructed by the priest/bishop Stephanos in inadequate remembrance of the sins of his soul, a many faceted new [church dedicated] to the apostles, in order to remember Bishop Theophanes for a long time to come').[22]

The two-columned cross-in-square church, dated to about the year 1000, introduces to the island the new architectural type, as well as the new structural and morphological characteristics of the so-called Helladic School of architecture.[23] The founder's policy was twofold: to introduce the most updated developments in architecture only a few decades after their first implementation in the church of the Virgin at Hosios Loukas, on the one hand, and to promote local traditions related to the evangelisation of the island, on the other. In fact, Iason and Sosipatros, to whom the church is dedicated, were the disciples of Paul who first taught the Gospel in Corfu. The status of the founder, a learned priest, probably also abbot, of high aspirations, as testified by the use of versed inscriptions and of very 'modern' features in architecture, and obviously close to the deceased bishop mentioned in the inscription, points to the role of ecclesiastics in diffusing the new trends and re-enforcing Orthodoxy after a period of crisis.

This is evident particularly if we compare this church with a slightly later private foundation in Corfu, St Merkourios, close to the village of Hagios Markos,[24] founded, according to the painted dedicatory inscription, by Nikolaos Droungarios, Eugenios and their brothers and wives, in the year 1074/75: … παρὰ Νικολάου Δρωνγγαρίου/ καὶ Εὐγενίου καὶ τῶν δὲ λοιπ[ῶ]/ν ἀδελφῶν ἄ[μ]α δὲ [κα]ὶ τῶν συ/νεύνων αὐτῶν ἔτ(ους) ͵ϛφπγ᾽ ἰνδ(ικτιῶνος) ιγ᾽ …

Patronage of Religious Foundations in Middle Byzantine Greece 231

('by Nikolaos Droungarios and Eugenios and the rest of (their) brothers together with their wives, in the year 6583 [=1074/75] 13th indiction').[25]

Even if here the term *droungarios* does not refer to a family name, as has been proposed, but rather to the military rank, it should be noted that this rank was very low in the military hierarchy by the 11th century.[26] The architectural type of the church of St Merkourios, a timber-roofed single-nave church, is simple and the fresco decoration is characterised by archaisms in iconography and a provincialism in style. In these two 11th-century monuments of Corfu it becomes apparent that the status, capacity, erudition, and aspirations of the patrons play a crucial role in the implementation of the new political and ecclesiastical ideals and the new trends in architecture and decoration.

Patronage throughout the 11th century continues, overwhelmingly, to lie in the hands either of bishops or of state officials. It is reasonable to postulate the predominant role of bishops in the foundation of episcopal churches,[27] mostly basilicas, erected or rather renovated in great numbers towards the end of the 10th and during the 11th century in the Greek provinces, especially after the victorious wars of Basil II and the crushing of the Bulgarians (1014), such as the basilica of Servia (beginning of 11th century), the basilica at Stagoi (Kalampaka) (c. 1100), etc.[28] Epigraphic evidence documenting the role of bishops as patrons of episcopal churches is found in the Old Metropolis (SS Theodoroi) in Serres,[29] a three-aisled basilica first built at the end of the 10th/beginning of the 11th century. An inscription, previously dated to the year 1430 recording the founder, Metropolitan Philippos, was recently re-dated to about the year 1000 and connected with the upgrading of the archbishopric of Serres to a metropolis.[30] A renovation phase including the mosaic decoration and sculptures goes back to the last quarter of the 11th century.[31]

Moreover, an inscription on a marble lintel in second use in the Old Metropolis at Berroia records Bishop Niketas, who is also known from a document of the year 1078 in the monastery of Esphigmenou on Mt Athos.[32] Niketas is thus probably related to the Middle Byzantine phase of the metropolitan church of Berroia.

Further epigraphic evidence on the role of bishops as patrons is found on the island of Skopelos. An inscription in the church of the bishopric testifies that the three-aisled vaulted basilica was erected by Bishop Anastasios in the year 1078 during the reign of Nikephoros III Botaneiates: ... ἐπὶ Ἀναστασίου ἐπισκόπου τῆς πα/ρούσης νήσου Σκοπέλλων ἐκ πόθου ὑπὲρ μνήμης καὶ ἀφέσεως ἑκουσίων τε καὶ [ἀ]κουσίων ἁ[μαρ]τημάτων. Μη(νὶ)Ἀπριλ(ίῳ) ἰνδ(ικτιῶνος) Αʹ τοῦ ͵ϛΦΠϚʹ ἔτους ἐπὶ βασιλείας Νικηφόρου/ τοῦ Βοτανειάτου † (' ... [erected] in the time of Anastasios bishop of this island of Skopelos with devotion in order to be remembered and for remission of (his) intentional and unintentional sins, in the month of April, first indiction, of the year 6586 [=1078] in the reign of Nikephoros Botaneiates').[33]

Of special interest is an inscription engraved on a marble screen-epistyle immured in the western façade of the church of the Virgin Protothronos in

232   *Sophia Kalopissi-Verti*

Chalki on the island of Naxos, which bears evidence of the collaboration of Bishop Leon with the *tourmarches* of Naxos, *Protospatharios* Niketas, and the *komes* Stephanos Kamelares: Θ(εοτό)κε Δέσποινα καὶ Μ(ήτη)ρ τοῦ Κ(υρίο)υ/ σκέπε, φρούρει, φύλατ<τε> τοὺ(ς) σοὺ(ς) οἰ/κέτας τοὺς ἀνακαινίσα[ν]τ(ας) τ(ὸν) ἔνδο/ξον ναὸ<ν> σ(ου)/ Λέοντα θεοφιλέστατον ἐπίσκοπον καὶ/ Νικήτ (αν) πρωτοσπαθάριον καὶ τουρμάρχην/ Ναξίας καὶ Στέφανον κ(ό)μ(ητα) τ(ὸν) Καμηλάρην καὶ/ τοὺς ἐν πίστει ἐν φόβῳ εἰσιόντας ἀ[μ]ήν/ [σῶσο]ν αὐτοῖς κ(αὶ) τούτους ῥῦσον ἰνδ(ικτιῶνος) Ε΄ ἔτους/ ͵ϛφξ‘ ('Theotokos, Our Lady and Mother of our Lord / cover, guard, and protect your se/rvants, who renovated your glo/ rious church / Bishop Leon most dear to God and / Niketas *protospatharios* and *tourmarches* / of Naxos, and *Komes* Stephanos Kamelares, and / bless all those who in faith and reverence enter here, amen./ Save them and deliver them, fifth indiction, in the year 6560 [=1052]').[34] Dated to the year 1052 the inscription has been related to a renovation of the episcopal church at Chalki.[35] The second layer of the dome paintings belongs to this mid- 11th century renovation of the church initiated by, and based on the cooperation of, the ecclesiastical, military and administrative authorities of the island.[36] A bishop by the name of Leon, probably the same person mentioned in the inscription of Protothronos, is recorded moreover in another inscription referring to a church dedicated to the Virgin. It is carved on a marble door lintel found in second use in the church of St Mamas at Potamia,[37] a transitional cross-in-square type which has been re-dated to the first half/middle of the 11th century.[38]

In parallel, the benefactory role of office-holders ranking high in the state's civil hierarchy or dignitaries is attested in several 11th-century churches in the Greek provinces. The church of the Panagia ton Chalkeon in Thessalonike,[39] for example, was donated by a high official, *basilikos protospatharios* and *katepano* of *Longobardia, i.e.,* governor of southern Italy, Christophoros, in 1028. The inscription carved on the lintel of the western entrance door runs as follows: Ἀφιερώθη ὁ πρὶν βέβηλος τόπος/ εἰς ναὸν περίβλεπτον τῆς Θ(εοτό)κου/ παρὰ Χριστοφό(ρου) τοῦ ἐνδοξοτά(του) βασιλικοῦ/ (πρωτο)σπαθαρίου κ(αὶ) κατ(ε)πάνω Λαγουβαρδίας κ(αὶ) τῆς συμβίου αὐτοῦ Μαρίας κ(αὶ) τῶν τέκνων αὐτῶν Νικηφό(ρου), Ἄννης κ(αὶ) Κατακαλῆς· μηνί Σεπτεμβρίῳ ἰνδ(ικτιῶνος) ιβ‘ ἔτ(ους) ͵ϛφλζ‘ ('This once profane place was dedicated as a celebrated church of the Virgin by Christophoros, the illustrious imperial *protospathatios* and *katepano* of Longobardia and his spouse Maria and their children, Nikephoros, Anna and Katakale, in the month of September, 12th indiction, of the year 6537[=1028]').[40] A fully developed four-columned cross-in-square type, the church of the Panagia ton Chalkeon was built to house the founder's grave. Iconography and style of the painted decoration follow the latest developments in monumental art.

Protospatharios Eustathios renovated, according to the dedicatory inscription the episcopal church of Besaina (today Aetolophos) in Thessaly, a three-aisled timber-roofed basilica with piers dedicated to the Dormition of the Virgin, erected on the ruins of an Early Christian basilica at the beginning of the 11th century.[41]

Spatharokandidatos Nikolaos Kalomalos renovated the church of Hagioi Theodoroi in Athens according to the dedicatory inscription, walled in the west façade of the church: Τὸν πρὶν παλαι[ὸν ὄν]τα σου ναόν, μάρτ[υς,/ καὶ μικρ]ὸν καὶ πήλινον καὶ σαθρὸν λίαν/ ἀνήγειρε Νικόλαος σὸς οἰκέτης/ ὁ Καλό[μαλος σ]παθαροκανδιδάτος/… … … … . μη(νὶ) Σεπτεμβρίῳ ἰνδ(ικτιῶνος) γʹ, ἔτους ‚ϛφνηʹ ('Your church, o martyr, which was formerly small and built of mud and very decayed, your servant Nikolaos Kalomalos, *spatharokandidatos*,… . … … restored it in the month of September, third indiction, of the year 6558 [=1049]').[42] The date mentioned in the inscription was the object of controversy between scholars in the 1930s.[43] In a recent study Charalambos Bouras proposed the date of 1049 or even earlier on the basis of the architectural type of the church (a cross-in-square transitional type), its morphological features, the chronology of the immured bowls and the reliefs of the screen epistyle that were re-used in the belfry.[44]

In addition, the decisive support offered abundantly by emperors in the foundation and luxurious decoration of monastic ensembles during the first half of the 11th century[45] illustrates the direct imperial interest and involvement in church matters in the Greek provinces and the collaboration with local influential individuals and/or monks.

Of special interest and unique content are two early 11th-century inscriptions referring to patronage of religious foundations. The first inscription is immured in a later church at Aliveri on Euboea and refers to a dependency of the monastery of Hosios Loukas. + Ἀνεκ(αι)νίσθη ὁ [πάνσεπτος ναὸς τῶν Ἁγίων Κοσμᾶ] κ(αὶ) Δαμηανοῦ μετὰ θʹ ἔτ(η) τῆς Κοιμ(ήσ)εως τοῦ Ὁσ(ίου) Λουκᾶ κ(αὶ) πν(ευμα)τικ(οῦ) ἡμῶν π(ατ)ρ(ὸ)ς ὑπὸ τῶ(ν) αὐτοῦ/ φυτητῶν κ(αὶ) δ(εύτερον) [… . … …] ἅμα τῇ ἐν Χ(ριστ)ῷ συνοδίᾳ βασιλέ[ων] Βασιλείου κ(αὶ) Κωνσταν(τίνου). Ἔ(τους) ‚ϛφκβʹ ἰνδ(ικτιῶνος) ιβʹ ('The venerable church of Saints Kosmas and Damian was renovated nine years after the death of Hosios Lukas, our spiritual father, by his disciples and for a second time … .together with his followers in Christ, [in the reign] of Emperors Basil and Constantine. In the year 6522 [=1014] 12th indiction').[46] According to the inscription, the disciples (*phoitetai*) of Hosios Loukas renovated the church of SS Kosmas and Damian nine years after the death of their spiritual father (+953) while approximately 50 years later, in 1014, the church was renovated again by the monks. A *unicum* among the Middle Byzantine inscriptions in the Greek provinces, the inscription at Aliveri deviates in content from the norm and introduces an emotional tone and a sense of collectiveness and belonging together complying with monastic life.

The second example is found in a now lost, long inscription of the year 1027 which renders, in fact, a monastic *typikon* written in stone. The monk Nikodemos donated a bridge over the Iris (=Eurotas) River in the vicinity of Sparta (*kastron Lakedaimonos*) and founded a small monastic church on its left side to protect it. In the testament-like inscription the founder defines that his monastery will be supervised in the future by the civil authorities, the *strategos* and the *krites* of the *thema*, and not by the bishop and clergy of the town, revealing a local controversy between civil and ecclesiastical authorities.[47]

234 *Sophia Kalopissi-Verti*

I will now turn to the time of the reign of the Komnenoi and the Angeloi (1081–1204). Alexios I Komnenos' (1081–1118) building policy can be traced along the Egnatia, as a result of the Norman invasions, as well as on the islands of the Aegean and the Eastern Mediterranean in the aftermath of the Seljuk advance in Asia Minor and the installation of the Crusaders in the Levant. Monasteries, often fortified, were founded by monks or by civil or military officials with imperial support.[48] A conspicuous example is the monastery of St. John the Theologian on Patmos founded in 1088 by the monk Christodoulos.[49]

Another example, epigraphically related to Alexios, occurs in the church of the Episkope at Mesa Gonia on the island of Santorini.[50] A now lost inscription, transcribed by Antonio Giustiniani in 1701, mentioned Emperor Alexios Komnenos.[51] A controversial discussion has considered whether the inscription refers to Alexios I (1081–1118)[52] or Alexios II (1180–1183).[53] The fresco decoration, which does not surpass the provincial level, should be ascribed, in my opinion, to the end of the 11th or beginning of the 12th rather than to the end of the 12th century.[54] Of exceptional quality however is the sanctuary marble screen decorated in the champlevé technique with coloured inlay. Introduced to Greece, evidently from Constantinople, in the late 10th century in the church of the Virgin at Hosios Loukas monastery,[55] this technique has its most conspicuous 11th-century parallels in the church of San Marco in Venice (the renovation after 1063).[56] In a recent study of the architecture of the church it has been convincingly argued that both the initial phase of the construction of the church, and the second phase which includes the addition of the side chapels and the mural paintings, go back to the reign of Alexios I Komnenos.[57] The exceptional quality of the screen points to an important patron (an official?), who had contacts with Constantinople and possibly the support of Alexios I Komnenos.

While in the last decades of the 11th century, according to the epigraphic evidence, there still occur instances of high-ranking officers as patrons of churches,[58] during the 12th century, particularly towards its end, there is a shift in patronage from officials representing central authority to the regional aristocratic class.[59] This development is in accord with the decline of the central government in the Greek provinces at this time.[60] As deduced from the inscriptional evidence and donors' images, now it is the local aristocracy, great and small, that plays a predominant role as patron of religious foundations, both in towns and in the country. Sporadically these obviously wealthy and influential persons bear the title of *magistros*, a low-ranking dignity and close to disappearing by this time.[61] In two cases the patron's name is accompanied by the title of *sebastos*.[62] Evidence is found in churches of mainland Greece and on the islands as shown in the following examples.

Two noble couples representing the local lay aristocracy are depicted as patrons in two churches of Kastoria in the final decades of the 12th century.[63] The *Magistros* Nikephoros Kasnitzes[64] and his wife Anna are represented standing on both sides of St Nicholas on the east wall of the narthex in the

Patronage of Religious Foundations in Middle Byzantine Greece 235

church of Hagios Nikolaos tou Kasnitze (ca. 1170), while an epigram refer-ring to the founder is painted on the west wall of the naos.[65] Theodoros Lemniotes, holding a church model, and his wife Anna Radene are depicted flanking the Virgin with the Infant Christ in the north aisle of the church of the Holy Anargyroi, which he renovated in about 1180–1190.[66] Their son Ioannes follows the father. Anna Radene, a descendant of a noble family, dressed in luxurious garments and a lavish hat and bearing exaggerated jewellery (earrings and two rings on each finger), takes the place of honour to the right of the Virgin and is depicted in a slightly larger scale than her husband. The ostentatiously extravagant garments and hair-style, the noble lineage of the Radenoi, the donors' wish to stress their devotion, the scholarly language, the impeccable meter of the epigrams,[67] and the quality of the fresco decoration all bear testimony to the wealth, ideology, cultural level and taste of these local aristocrats in a provincial town at the end of the 12th century.

There are several less conspicuous examples of donations by lay people, documented by inscriptions that confirm this trend of lay patronage by in-dividuals ranking high or in the middle of the social hierarchy of the Greek provinces in the second half of the 12th century. Two now lost inscriptions, one metrical, one in prose, once painted in the katholikon of the Virgin in the monastery of Betoumas, SW of Stagoi, a copy of which has been preserved in codex no. 141 of the Monastery of the Transfiguration in Meteora, men-tioned two private persons as founders of the church of the Virgin Betoumas, namely Konstantinos Tarchaneiotes with his wife Zoe, and *Sebastos* Andronikos, in the year 1161, at the time of Manuel I Komnenos (1143–1180) and Patriarch Loukas Chrysoberges (1157–1170).[68]

Furthermore, a lay person, Germanos Sporgites, with his children reno-vated the church of Hagios Ioannes the Baptist, so-called tou Magkoute in Athens in the second half of the 12th century according to an inscription now in the Byzantine Museum at Athens.[69]

Similar phenomena are documented on financially well-to-do islands. The dedicatory inscription of the church of the Taxiarches in Messaria on the island of Andros mentions the patrons, Konstantinos Monasteriotes and Eirene Prasine, Emperor Manuel Komnenos, Patriarch Loukas (Chrysoberges) and the date 1158. +Ὁ πάνσεπτος ναὸς οὗτος ὁ τοῦ/ μεγάλου ταξιάρχου Μυχαὴλ ἀνηκοδομή(θη) ἐπὶ β/ασιλέως κυροῦ Μανουὴλ τοῦ Κομνηνοῦ, πα/τριάρχου κυροῦ Λουκᾶ, κτητόρων δὲ/ συνεύνων Κωνσταντοίνου/ κὲ Ἡρίνης οὗ κλῆσις ἐστὴν ἐπονήμω/ς Μοναστηριώτου κὲ τῆς Πρασήν(η)ς/ μηνή Μαρτ(ίω) ἰν(δικτιῶνος) ς‘ ἔτ(ους) ‚ϛχξϛ.’ ('+This most venerable church of the great archangel Michael was erected in the time of Emperor Lord Manuel Komnenos (and) Patriarch Lord Loukas, by the founders, the married couple Konstantinos and Eirene whose surnames are Monasteriotes and Prasine, in the month of March, sixth indiction of the year 6666 [=1158]').[70] The extended representation of the Second Coming in the narthex of the two-columned cross-in-square church indicates that it was probably meant to be the donors' funerary chapel. The pretentious church, the high quality of the relief and painted decoration, as well as the reference to the emperor and the patriarch of Constantinople in the inscription, indeed before the names of the donor couple, indicate that the patrons were well-to-do aristocrats, may be involved in the process of silk production on the island;[71] they obviously had good relations with Constantinople, a fact which they wished to stress in the dedicatory inscription.

Panagia Krena on the island of Chios offers a further example of an aristocratic foundation, dated to 1197.[72] On the east wall of the inner narthex the founder, *Sebastos* Eustathios Kodratos, is depicted offering a model of the church to the enthroned Virgin. The accompanying painted epigraph runs: Δέ(ησις) τοῦ δούλ(ου) τοῦ Θ[εοῦ]/ Εὐσταθίου σεβ[α]/στοῦ τοῦ Κοδρά[του]/ καὶ κτίτορος ('Prayer of the servant of God Eustathios Kodratos sebastos and founder').[73] His wife bearing the family name Pagomene, of noble lineage, was a niece of a metropolitan of Hypaipa in Asia Minor, Stephanos Pepagomenos, who is depicted in the *prothesis* accompanied by the inscription Ὁ εὐτελὴς/ Μητροπολίτ(ης)/ Ὑπέπων/ κ(αὶ) ὑπέρτιμος/ Στέφανος/ Πεπαγο/μένος καὶ θεῖος/ τοῦ κτίτορος ('The humble Metropolitan of Hypaipa and *hypertimos* Stephanos Pepagomenos, uncle of the founder').[74] The aristocratic founders of Krena had thus close links to Asia Minor as well as to Constantinople.

Ecclesiastics of high rank are also attested as founders in the 12th century. The most conspicuous example is that of Hagia Mone at Areia in the Argolid, a donation by Bishop Leon of Argos,[75] in 1149, according to the inscription walled in the west façade of the church (Figure 14.2): +Ἔπηξε βάθρα τῷ ναῷ σου, Παρθένε,/ Λέων Ἀργείων ἀλιτρὸς θυηπόλος·/ ὧπερ παράσχοις λύτρον ἀμπλακημάτων/ εἰς ἀντάμειψιν, εὐλογημένη κόρη·/ ἔτους ͵ϛχνζʹ, μηνὶ Ἀπριλλίῳ

Figure 14.2 Areia near Nauplion, Monastery of Hagia Monê (Zôodochos Pêgê), west façade. Foundation inscription of the bishop of Argos Leon (1149 AD). (Photo: Dr Anastasia Vasileiou).

ἰνδ(ικτιῶνο)ς ιβ'.+ ('+Leon, the sinful priest of the Argives, laid the foundations of your church, O Virgin. May you, blessed Maiden, grant him in repayment the remission of his sins, in the year 6657 [=1149], in the month of April, 12th indiction+').[76] The building, a four-columned cross-in-square type, is one of the most prominent examples of the Helladic School of architecture, on a par with the fine sculpted decoration, reflecting the preferences of the high-ranking erudite patron.[77]

Well documented in the inscriptions of the late 11th and 12th centuries are also monks as founders or renovators of monastic churches, for example at the monastery of Barnakova, northeast of Naupaktos (1076 and 1147/48),[78] at Therma in Phokis (1092)[79] and in Hagia Mone Doridos (1198).[80] One of the most conspicuous examples however is the mosaic of the Deesis in the lunette of the exonarthex in the monastery of Vatopedi (c. 1100) donated by an abbot and a monk, who was probably his successor.[81] One could possibly assume that in some cases these monks were local aristocrats and landowners who took monastic vows.

I will now turn to a case study, the Mani, a 'waterless and inaccessible' region in southern Peloponnese, according to Constantine VII,[82] which preserves a large number of inscriptional materials. One of the earliest epigraphic records regarding patronage was found in the excavation of the basilica on the peninsula of Tigani, which has been identified with the castle of Maïna. Carved on a marble cornice, the inscription mentions *Komes* Dakios as founder. Anna Avramea dated the inscription to the 9th/10th century and related Dakios to an officer of the imperial fleet whose presence in the castle of Maïna may be connected with the *thema* of the Peloponnese based in Corinth and with the struggles against the Arabs.[83] Recently Angeliki Mexia redated the foundation of the basilica at Tigani, initially thought by the excavators to have been erected in the late 7th century, to the second half of the 10th or early 11th century.[84] Thus *Komes* Dakios could possibly be related to the erection of this building. Mexia considered furthermore the ambitious edifice, which introduced a new architectural style in the area, to be the seat of the Bishopric of Maïna, first mentioned in episcopal lists between 901 and 907 under the metropolis of Corinth. The creation of the Bishopric of Maïna and the erection of the episcopal church may be thus related to the efforts of the central authority to reorganise the Orthodox church in this remote area, as testified also by the missionary campaigns undertaken by Nikon Metanoeite at about the same time (see below).

The next oldest known dedicatory inscription is preserved in the church of St Panteleemon at Boularioi and mentions a priest-monk as donor and the date 991/2.[85] The stylistic similarities with a group of churches in the Mani, which show frescoes of a very provincial character but in accord with the new iconographic developments, have been pointed out.[86] This particular group of painted churches and, in general, the flourishing of wall painting in the Mani at the end of the 10th century and the emergence of new architectural types at approximately the same time or the beginning of the 11th century

238 *Sophia Kalopissi-Verti*

have been connected with the missionary and building activities of Hosios Nikon Metanoeite (+998) in Laconia. In fact, they seem to point to a policy of directed religious propagation, probably initiated by Nikon himself, within the frame of the efforts of the central government to reorganise the Greek provinces after the withdrawal of the Arabs from the Aegean.

There is rich epigraphic evidence from Maniot churches, dated to the 11th century, especially its second half, providing precious information not only on patrons but also on craftsmen, namely marble workers.[87] A key monument is the church of St. Theodore at Bambaka, where the collaboration of a priest, the *ktetor* of the church, with a lay family who offered the carved tie-beams, is testified. There is also mention of the date 1075 and of the marble worker, *marmaras* Niketas. +Μνήσθητη Κ(ύρι)ε τὸν σὸ(ν)/ δοῦλο(ν) Θεοδόρου πρ(εσβυτέρου)/ κ(αὶ) Καλῆς τοῦ κτησαμ/ένου τὴν ἁγήαν μονὴν τ[αύ]τη(ν) ('Remember, o Lord, thy servant the priest Theodore and Kale, the *ktetor* of this holy monastery'). And +Μν(ήσ)θη(τι) Κ(ύρι)ε τοῦ δουλου σου Λέοντος ἅμα σηνβήου κ(αὶ) τὸν τέκνον αὐτοῦ τοῦ πόθου πολοῦ κτησαμένου τοὺς κοσμῆτες/ {σ} τούτους ἡ ψάλοντες εὔχεσθε ἡπὲρ αὐτοῦ ἀμὴ γένητο Κ(ύρι)ε ἐτελυόθησα δέ χηρὺ Νηκήτ(α) μαρμαρᾶ μην(ὸς) Αὐγούστου ἰνδ(ικτιῶνος) ιγ᾿ ἔτο(ς) ϛφπγ᾿ ('+Remember, o Lord, thy servant Leon with his wife and children who, with great devotion, commissioned these tie-beams; chanters, pray for him. Amen, so be it, Lord. They were finished by the hand of the marble-carver Niketas in the month of August, 13th indiction, of the year 6583 [=1075]').[88] Approximately twenty further inscriptions allow us to draw conclusions concerning patronage in 11th-century Mani. Patrons include priests and lay people, in fact, private individuals, probably landowners. Counter to other provinces of mainland and insular Greece in the 11th century, there is not a single civil or military official belonging to the state hierarchy recorded in the extant inscriptions. On the contrary, local individuals with their nuclear families, cooperating relatives or small collaborating groups of three or four laymen, having no title or office, as well as clerics and monks, constitute the usual scheme of patrons, who assume the costs for the erection and for the relief carving and painted decoration of a church. Therefore, a patronage scheme based on local society with no representatives of the state is testified.[89]

A final note should be made of an inscription carved on a late 11th-century marble architrave from the village of Pangeia, which mentions the collaboration of two clerics, a layman, and a group of anonymous faithful who contributed to the foundation of a church.[90] It constitutes the earliest evidence of collective sponsorship, which is implemented more systematically in the 13th century.[91]

In accord with the evidence in other regions of the Greek mainland, as mentioned above, in 12th-century Mani the prevailing patronage scheme indicates the participation mainly of laymen, probably well-to-do landowners.[92] Such an example is the church of Saints Sergios, Bacchos, and Georgios in Kitta (Figure 14.3a, 14.3b): +Κ(ύρι)ε βωήθ(ει) σὼν δοῦλ(ον)

(a)

(b)

Figure 14.3 (a) Kitta, Mani. Church of Saints Sergios, Bacchos, and Georgios, lintel of west façade. Foundation inscription of a lay donor, Georgios Marasiatis, and his family, third quarter of 12th century (Photo: Author). (b) Drawing of the inscription after Bouras and Boura 2002: fig. 208 (M. Korres, K. Tzanaki).

Γαιώργη/ων τὸν μαρασηάτην ἅμα συν/βήου καὶ τῶν τέκνων αὐτοῦ/ τῶν κτήσαντα τὸν πάσεπτων ναὸν τὸν ἁ/γήων μαρτύρων Σεργήου καὶ Βάχου/ καὶ τοῦ ἁγήου Γεωργήου μετὰ πω/λοῦ πώθο(υ) καὶ μώκτου+ ('+Lord, help thy servant Georgios Marasiatis with his wife and children who has erected this most venerable church of the saints martyrs Sergios and Bacchos and of Saint George with much devotion and labour+').[93] According to the inscriptional evidence there is no reference to state officials involved in patronage with one exception mentioning a *tourmarches*,[94] which seems to refer here rather to a family name than to the military officer, nor is there any single mention of Byzantine emperors. This shows the rather loose relation of the Mani to the capital, a phenomenon that is in accord with the decline of the imperial administration, which has been noted in the Greek provinces in the late 12th century.[95] If the evidence of inscriptions in the 10th century shows the implementation of the policy of the central authority, this is not the case in

240 *Sophia Kalopissi-Verti*

the 11th and 12th centuries. However, the great number of churches erected in this period, some of which are pretentious cross-in-square buildings, and the painted decoration preserved in several of them, show that the region participated in the developments of architecture and painting of the empire, while maintaining its local particularities.

To sum up, from the late 9th to the late 11th century, the new imperial policy of evangelising and re-establishing Orthodoxy, after the end of the iconoclastic controversy (843), and of reorganising the provinces, particularly after the expulsion of the Arabs from Crete (961) and the Aegean, and the victory over the Bulgarians (1014), is introduced in the Greek provinces. Vehicles for the implementation of imperial policy are, according to epigraphic evidence, clerics ranking high in the ecclesiastical hierarchy and state administrative or military officials. Private foundations by laypeople are rarely attested. The imperial political and ecclesiastical ideology penetrates in both towns and the countryside. The 11th century is an epoch of great flourishing; the bulk of episcopal churches and the most luxurious and prestigious monasteries are founded then. In the aftermath of the Seljuk invasions in Asia Minor (1071), Alexios I Komnenos (1081–1118) seems to follow a distinctive building policy by supporting the foundation of monasteries especially on the islands of the Aegean. Many churches are still founded in all Greek provinces by laymen and clerics during the reign of Manuel I Komnenos (1143–1180). In the second half of the 12th century and particularly towards its end, a shift to local aristocratic patronage is observed. A parallel development has been observed in book production. While lay commissioners of books in the 9th–11th centuries are persons close to the emperor, who rank high in the civil and military hierarchy, contrariwise, in the 12th century lay commissioners of extant manuscripts bear no title or rank.[96] The region of the Mani in the Peloponnese, which was examined as a case study, follows to a certain extent the mainstream developments in art and architecture under a predominant local patronage scheme.

Sophia Kalopissi-Verti, January 2019.

Notes

1 On the provincial administration in Byzantium, see Glykatzi-Ahrweiler 1971: VIII, 1–101; Neville 2004.
2 On the archbishop Paul, *PmbZ II* (2013): vol. 5, 303, no. 26314.
3 The inscription runs as follows: [+Ἐ]πὶ Παύλου τοῦ ἁγιωτάτο[υ ἡμ/ῶ]ν ἀρχιεπισκόπου ἐγέ[νετο]/ [σ]ὺν Θ(ε)ῷ τὸ ἔργον τοῦ[το]/ +μηνὶ νοεμβρίῳ ἰνδικ /κτιόνι τετάρτῃ/ ἔτους/ ἀπὸ κτίσεως κόσμου ͵ϛ[...] ('+In the time of Paul our most saintly archbishop this work was done with God; + in the month of November, fourth indiction of the year 6 ... from the creation of the world'). Text after Spieser 1973: 160. On the inscription and its date, Spieser 1973: 160-1, no. 10 (885); Panayotidi 1974: 70–71, n. 2 (885); Theocharidou 1976: 265–273 (540, 570, or 690); Cormack (1980-81): 123–126 (885); Bakirtzis (1982): 167–180 (*ca.* 690); Velenis 1997: 70–77, (840). See also Moulet 2011: 401.

Patronage of Religious Foundations in Middle Byzantine Greece 241

4 Panayotidi 1974: 69–89.
5 Xyngopoulos 1938: 39–46.
6 See above, n. 3.
7 Mango and Hawkins 1972: 1–41; Cormack and Hawkins 1977: 212–251; Panayotidi 1986: 75–76. The imperial interest in the church of Hagia Sophia in Thessalonike and the role of the archbishop are also attested in the aniconic mosaic decoration of the sanctuary according to the monograms of Eirene, Konstantinos and Archbishop Theophilos (784): Spieser 1973: 159, no. 9.
8 Bouras 1960–1961: 57–75; Karambinis 2015: 249–250, 398–401.
9 Sabas is known from lead seals and a graffito on the Parthenon which mentions his death in 913: see Orlandos and Vranousis 1973: 67–68, no. 75; *PmbZ* II (2013): vol. 5, 650, no. 26915.
10 Text after Bouras 1960–1961: 66, pl. 29B; on the inscription, moreover, Koder 1998: 190–191; Karambinis 2015: 401, fig. C.7. The metropolitan of Athens Sabas (second half of the 9th c.) is also attested on seals, *PmbZ* I (2001): vol. 4, 65–66, no. 6453 and *PmbZ* II (2013): vol. 5, 109, no. 25939, as well as in a *graffito* on the Parthenon recording his death in the year 6422=913/4: Orlandos and Vranousis 1973: 67–68, no. 75. On bishops of the Middle Byzantine period, their role in society and their relation to central authority, see Moulet 2011.
11 On Bishop Nikolaos, Kislinger 2007: 27–34; Moulet 2011: 401; *PmbZ*, II (2013), vol. 5, 109, no. 25939.
12 Athanasoulis *et al.* (forthcoming). On recent finds of the Slav settlers in Arcadia found mainly in cemeteries, see Athanasoulis and Vasileiou 2016: 228-37; Metaxas 2018: 689–700.
13 Text after Feissel, Philippidis-Braat 1985: 300, no. 42.
14 On the church, Soteriou 1924: 1–26; Symeonoglou 1985: 164–165; Koilakou 2013: 183; Koilakou 2018: 569-80. On the dignity mentioned, Guilland 1966: 210–225; Oikonomidès 1972: 298 and *passim*.
15 Text after Soteriou 1924: 1–2, figs 3–4. An epigram from the same church, now exhibited in the Archaeological Museum of Thebes, records once more the founder's name: Τέρεμνον ὅνπερ ὡραϊσμένον βλέπεις/ Βασίλειος τέτευχεν ἐκ βάθρων πόθῳ/ δέχοιο τόνδ᾽ ἐμοῦ πονήματος δόμον/ τὸ γρήγορον φῶς τῶν Θεοῦ αὐγασμάτων/ ἀντεισάγων μοι ἁ[μπλα]κημάτων λύσιν ('The house you see embellished was erected from (its) foundations by Basileios with devotion; accept this building of my toil, the swift light of God's radiance, granting me in return remission of (my) sins'). Text after Rhoby 2014: 366–368, no. GR117. I wish to warmly thank Dr Rhoby for sending me the relevant chapter of his then-forthcoming book.
16 On the church and its inscriptions, Soteriou 1931: 119–157; Oikonomidès 1994: 479–493; Papalexandrou 1998: 111–155; Papalexandrou 2001: 259–283; Papalexandrou 2007: 171–176; Bevilacqua 2011: 411–420; Prieto-Domínguez 2013: 166–191. On the metrical inscription of the west façade, Rhoby 2014: 319–324, no. GR98; Drpić 2016: 77–79. On Leon, *PmbZ* II (2013): vol. 4, 75, no. 24350.
17 Oikonomidès, 1994: 479–493. The inscriptions in the eastern part of the church are as follows: On the apse, +Παναγία Θεοτόκε σὺν τῷ μονογενεῖ σου υἱῷ βοήθει τοῦ σοῦ δούλου Λέοντος βασιλικοῦ πρωτοσπαθαρίου καὶ ἐπὶ τῶν οἰκειακῶν σὺν τῇ συνεύνῳ καὶ τοῖς φιλτάτοις τέκνοις αὐτοῦ ἐκ πόθου καὶ πίστεως μεγίστης ἀναστήσαντος τὸν σὸν ἅγιον ναόν. Ἀμήν.+ Ἐπὶ Βασιλείου καὶ Κωνσταντίνου καὶ Λέοντος τῶν θειοτάτων βασιλέων τῶν Ῥωμαίων ('God Bearer, with your only Son, help your servant Leon, imperial *protospatharios* and *epi ton oikeiakon* who, out of devotion and great faith, erected your holy church together with his wife and his most beloved children. Amen. In the time of the most holy emperors of the Romans, Basil and Constantine and Leon'). On the south wall, +Ἐκαλλιέργησεν τὸν ναὸν τοῦ ἁγίου Πέτρου τοῦ

242   *Sophia Kalopissi-Verti*

κορυφαίου τῶν ἀποστόλων Λέων ὁ πανεύφημος βασιλικὸς πρωτοσπαθάριος καὶ ἐπὶ τῶν οἰκειακῶν ὑπὲρ λύτρου καὶ ἀφέσεως τῶν πολλῶν αὐτοῦ ἁμαρτιῶν ἐπὶ Ἰγνατίου τοῦ οἰκουμενικοῦ πατριάρχου. Ἀμήν ('Leon the celebrated imperial *protospatharios* and *epi ton oikeiakon* embellished the church of St Peter the chief apostle for the forgiveness and remission of his numerous sins, in the time of Ignatios the Ecumenical Patriarch. Amen'). On the north wall, +Ἐκαλλιέργησεν τὸν ναὸν τοῦ ἁγίου Παύλου τοῦ ἀποστόλου Λέων ὁ πανεύφημος βασιλικὸς πρωτοσπαθάριος καὶ ἐπὶ τῶν οἰκειακῶν ὑπὲρ λύτρου καὶ ἀφέσεως τῶν πολλῶν αὐτοῦ ἁμαρτιῶν ἔτους ἀπὸ κτίσεως κόσμου ἑξακισχιλιοστῷ τριακοσιοστῷ ὀγδοηκοστῷ β΄ ('Leon the celebrated imperial *protospatharios* and *epi ton oikeiakon* embellished the church of St Paul the Apostle for the forgiveness and remission of his many sins, in the year 6382 [=873/4] from the creation of the world'). Text after Oikonomidès, 1994: 481–483.

18 Grabar 1963: 90–99.
19 Sklavou-Mavroidi 1999: 87, no. 120.
20 On the *droungarios*, Oikonomidès, 1972: 341; McGeer 1991: 663.
21 Boura 1980. See also below n. 45.
22 Text after Rhoby 2014: 254–256, no. GR68; this is the epigram on the left side. For the epigram on the right, *ibid.*, 252–254, no. GR67. The word *thyepolos* means priest but can also refer to a bishop, see below n. 32 and p. 12 (inscription of Mone Areias).
23 Vocotopoulos 1966–1969: 149–174; Vocotopoulos 1971: 177–178; Vocotopoulos 2018: 62–73.
24 Vocotopoulos 1971: 131–172; Vocotopoulos 2018: 74–85.
25 Text after Vocotopoulos 1971: 153.
26 Vocotopoulos 1971: 153. On the *droungarioi* who by 949 were only 'slightly higher than the common soldiers in rank and pay', see McGeer 1991: 663.
27 On the Middle Byzantine episcopal churches in Macedonia, see Karagianni 2006.
28 Xyngopoulos 1957; Sythiakakis-Kritsimallis and Voyadjis 2011: 195–227. On the 11th-century episcopal basilicas, Korać 1987: 57–67; Karagianni, 2006; Ćurčić 2010: 395–398.
29 Penna, ed. 2013.
30 Ἱερὸς ὁ Φίλιππος Μητρ(οπολίτης)/ τὸν σηκὸν ἐδόμησ(ε) της ἐκκλησί(ας)/ Θεοδ(ώρου) μ(άρτυρος) τοῦ Καλλινίκου ('The venerable Metropolitan Philip erected the central part [?] of the church of the triumphal martyr Theodore'). Text after Dadaki 2013: 186–189 and 216, fig. 43; Penna 2013: 115.
31 On the architectural phases of the basilica, see Tsouris 2015: 97–106 (with previous bibliography); on the mosaic decoration of the late 11th or beginning of the 12th century, Papatheophanous-Tsouri 2016: 122–134. On the mosaic of St Andrew, the only figure preserved from the Communion scene, which was almost devastated by the disastrous fire of 1913, see Kalavrezou 2013: 219-26.
32 The inscription runs Καὶ τοῦτο ἔργον Νικήτα θυηπόλου ('And this is the work of bishop Niketas'). Text after Rhoby 2014: 202–203, no. GR41; see also Papazotos 1994: 90, no. 1; Skiadaresis 2016: 118–121, 186–187. On bishop Niketas, *PBW* (2016) Niketas 161, http://pbw2016.kdl.kcl.ac.uk/person/Niketas/161/.
33 Text after Pallis 2013: 797–798, no. 57. On the church, see Xyngopoulos 1956: 181–198.
34 Text and translation after Panayotidi and Konstantellou 2018: 259, n. 15.
35 In the previous phase of the church, dated to *ca.* 970–980, the original Early Christian basilica was turned into a cross-in-square church of the transitional type. The iconographic programme of this phase (dome, south aisle) has been related to the historical circumstances as developed after the re-conquest of Crete in 961 and to the efforts to strengthen imperial power and Orthodox identity, see Panayotidi and Konstantellou, 2018, 260–268; Aslanidis, 2018a, 316-7 and *passim*.

Patronage of Religious Foundations in Middle Byzantine Greece 243

36 Panayotidi 1986: 99–100, n. 128; Zias 1989: 30–34; Mitsani 2004–2006: 415, no 18a; Pallis 2013: 798–799, no. 59; Rhoby 2014: 313–315, no. GR9; Zarras 2016: 54–58; Panayotidi and Konstantellou 2018: 268–272. Furthermore, a *proto-spatharios* is documented in an inscription of the 12th century in the narthex of the church of St George Diasorites near Chalki. See Acheimastou-Potamianou 2016: 28–29; Zarras 2016: 59–62.

37 Τὸν πρὶν βραχὺν τε καὶ κατηυτε[λισμ]ένον/ εὑρὼν δόμον σοῦ τῆς πανάγνου Παρθένου/ θυηπό[λος σὸς εὐτελὴς Λέων πόθῳ/ τοῦτον] νεουργ<εῖ> κ(αὶ) πρὸς [... ...] κρεί [τ]τ[ονα/ νῦν] εὐπρεπῆ τε καὶ <κε>καλλωπι[σμένον]/ ὅνπερ προσηνῶς προσδέχου, <σὺ> [Παρθένε],/ οἴκησιν ταύτη<ν> τοῦ τὸν ἐρασ[... ....../ ... ...] τοῦ νεουργητοῦ δόμου ('Your worthless priest Leon, having found your house, most chaste Virgin, formerly small and neglected, has renovated it and [made it ...] better, which, now [that it is] acceptable and embellished, may you kindly accept as your dwelling place, the..... ... ... of the house made new'). Text after Rhoby 2014: 315–318, no. GR96. See also Mastoropoulos 2005: 114–115; Mitsani, 2004–2006: 414–415, no. 17; Zarras 2016: 55–56.

38 Aslanidis 2018a: 316; Aslanidis 2018b: 168–171.

39 Papadopoulos 1966; Tsitouridou 1982: 435–441; Païssidou 2015: 121–133.

40 Text after Rhoby 2014: 384–388, no. GR126. A second inscription painted on the front of the apse mentions again the founder's name, Spieser 1973: 164, no. 14.

41 ... ...[E]ὐστάθιος τεῦξε [τ]έγεον ὅς λάχεν ἄγ[ε]ιν/ γαῖαν τήνδε Βεσαίνης κυδάλιμος πρωτοσπαθ(άριος)... . ... ('Eustathios, the renowned *protospatharios*, who happened to lead this land of Besaina, constucted the roof ... '). Nikonanos 1979: 16–27; Avraméa and Feissel 1987: 368–369, no. 12; Rhoby 2014 230–233, no. GR58.

42 Text after Rhoby 2014: 168–171, no. GR15.

43 Laurent 1934: 72–82; Megaw 1931–1932: 96, 129; Megaw 1932–1933: 163–169.

44 Bouras 2010: 173–179, no. 19.

45 For example the *katholikon* of Hosios Lukas (Chatzidakis 1969: 127–150; Chatzidakis 1972: 87–88; Stikas 1970; Stikas 1974; Pallas 1985: 94–107; Mylonas 1992: 115–122; Oikonomides 1992: 245–255; Schminck 2003: 349–380; Chatzidaki 1997; Chatzidaki 2011: 17–32; on the epigrams of monk Gregorios who offered the marble revetment, Rhoby 2014: 354–361, nos. GR110–112) and Nea Mone on Chios (Bouras 1981; Mouriki 1985). On monastic founders in the Middle Byzantine period, see Morris 1995: 64–89.

46 Text after Velenis 1990–1991: 353–361, esp. 358. See also Orlandos 1951a: 139–145; Chatzidakis 1969: 129, n. 16; Koder 1973: 150–152. The term *phoitetai* in the sense of disciples of a monk is also attested in a 16th-century inscription of the Philanthropenon monastery at Ioannina (1542/43), Acheimastou-Potamianou 1983: 21–22.

47 Feissel and Philippidis-Braat 1985: 300–303, no. 43. For comments, see Gerolymatou 2004: 42–44.

48 On monasticism in the period of the Komnenoi and the role of the ruling family as patrons and promoters of monastic piety, see Angold 1995: 265–384. On the changes in Byzantine society in this period, see Kazhdan and Wharton Epstein 1985.

49 Orlandos 1970; Kollias 1986; Vranousi 1980; Angold 1995: 275–276, 360–362 and *passim*.

50 Orlandos 1951b: 178–214; Tsitouridou 1987: II, 917–921; Bouras and Boura 2002: 156–158.

51 Ἀλέξιος ἐν Χ(ριστ)ῷ τῷ Θε)ῷ αὐτοκράτωρ Ῥωμαίων ὁ Κομνινὸς καὶ πιστὸς βασιλεὺς ('Alexios Komnenos in Christ our God emperor of the Romans, and devout king'). Text after Orlandos 1951b: 181.

244 *Sophia Kalopissi-Verti*

52 Orlandos 1951b: 180-81, 214; Barsanti and Pedone 2005: 415–425.
53 Tsitouridou 1987: 917–921; Bouras and Boura 2002: 157.
54 See Mouriki 1982: 125–126 (first decades of the 12th century) and Skawran 1982: 161–162 (probably in the time of Alexios I).
55 Boura 1980: 22–56.
56 Barsanti and Pedone 2005: 407–425.
57 Aslanidis 2015: 107–114; Aslanidis 2018b: 173–175.
58 Avraméa, in Avraméa and Feissel 1987: 370–372, no. 14, identified Demetrios, *proedros* and *ktetor* (founder) of a church, mentioned in an inscription on a marble lintel in Hypati/Neai Patrai (second half of the 11th century), with an important officer in the civil administration, well known from seals.
59 On issues of aristocratic patronage, Cormack 1984: 158–172; Bevilacqua 2013.
60 Herrin 1975: 255–284.
61 Guilland 1972–1973: 25; for examples see below n. 65.
62 Stiernon 1965: 226–232; for examples see below (monastery of Betouma and Panagia Krena on Chios).
63 Tomeković-Reggiani 1981: 823–836.
64 Drakopoulou 1997: 31–32, 37–38, 41–44; Panayotidi 2006: 157–159. Another *magistros* is documented in connection with the founder of a church, in an inscription in the church of St. Barnabas close to the village Louros, in the region of Preveza, Epiros in the year 1148/49: Mamaloukos 1995: 195–200.
65 ... τανῦν ἀνιστῶ τὸν νεὼν Νικηφόρος/ τύχη μάγιστρος καὶ τοὐπίκλην Κασνίτζης ... (' ... now I Nikephoros, surnamed Kasnitzes, who happen to be *magistros*, am erecting this church ... ') Text after Rhoby 2009: 175–179, no. 94.
66 Drakopoulou 1997: 32–34, 36–37, 44–53; Kyriakoudis 1981: 1–23; Panayotidi 2004: 158–165; Panayotidi 2006: 160–161; Mamangakis 2012: 71–100.
67 Rhoby 2009: 161–168, nos. 83–85.
68 ... ταύτη προσδείμ(ας) τόνδε τὸν δόμον πόθῳ/ αἰτῶ θελήμων ὡς ἐνόν λύσιν ὅπ(ως) ἐν ἡμέρᾳ φεῦ κρίσε(ως) χρε(ῶν) λάβω/ Ταρχανειώτης Κωνσταντῖνος ὁ λάτρης/ σὺν τῇ συζύγῳ Ζωῆ δὲ τῇ κυρίᾳ/ κλεινῷ σεβαστῷ λαμπρῷ τῷ Ἀνδρονίκῳ/ εὐεργέτι<ν> τείνοντι χεῖρα μοι πάλαι ... . (' ... .having built this house for her [the Virgin] with devotion, I ask willingly that I receive, as far as possible, remission of my sins on the fateful Day of Judgement, Konstantinos Tarchaneiotes your devotee together with his spouse the lady Zoe (and) the famous *sebastos*, brilliant Andronikos, who has stretched out a benevolent hand to me in the past ... '). Text after Rhoby 2009: 258–260, no. 175. The date and the names of the emperor and the patriarch are mentioned in the inscription in prose, Avraméa and Feissel 1987: 372–374, no. 16. The first founder maybe identified with Konstantinos Tarchaneiotes testified by lead seals, *PBW* 2016: Konstantinos 20448, http://pbw2016.kdl.kcl.ac.uk/person/ Konstantinos/20448/. On the Tarchaneiotes family, see Leontiades 1998; on the church, Voyatzis 1998: 37–52.
69 Sklavou-Mavroidi 1999: 128–130, no. 175–176; Pallis 2013: 787–788, no. 31a–b; Rhoby 2014: 154–158, no. GR9. On the church, Bouras 2010: 191–192, no. 26. On the inscription of the first phase of the church see above n. 19.
70 Text after Orlandos 1955–1956: 28–30; on the church, see 8–34; Acheimastou-Potamianou 2009: 117–132.
71 On silk production on Andros, Jacoby 1991–1992: 460–461.
72 Pennas 1991: 61–66; Mamangakis 2012: 83–85; Pennas 2017: 6–15, 121–128.
73 Text and translation after Pennas 2017: 13, fig. 282.
74 Text and translation after Pennas 2017: 14, figs 8, 115, 116.
75 *PBW* 2016: Leon 159, http://pbw2016.kdl.kcl.ac.uk/person/Leon/159/.
76 Text after Rhoby 2014: 310–312, no. GR93; translation after Drpić 2014: 899–901, and Drpić, 2016: 80.

Patronage of Religious Foundations in Middle Byzantine Greece 245

77 Bouras and Boura 2002: 81–85; Pinatsi 2018: 179–194. Less ambitious is the dedicatory inscription of Niketas, bishop of Argos and Nauplion (1173/4) found in Larisa, the citadel of Argos, now in the Byzantine Museum of the Argolid: Athanasoulis and Vasileiou, 2016: 103, no. 104.
78 The inscription in the narthex mentions the first founder, monk Arsenios, and the year 1076. The monk Ioannes erected the second church in the year 1147/48, Rhoby 2014: 189–190.
79 Katsaros 2013: 33–40.
80 The inscription mentions the founder, monk Myron; see Mastrokostas 1953: 355–357; Bouras and Boura 2002: 25-6.
81 Tsigaridas 1996: vol. I, 224–230; Rhoby 2009: 381–385, no. M1.
82 Constantine VII Porphyrogenitus (ed. Moravcsik) 1967: 236–237 (ch. 50, 76–78).
83 Δακήου κόμητος τῷ κτησαμένῳ τοῦτ(ον?) … ('Komes Dakios, founder of … ') Avraméa 1998: 56, n. 29; Mexia 2005: 121, no. 46. The inscription had been assigned a mid-12th-century date by the excavators. See Drandakis, Gioles, and Konstantinidi 1978: 190; cf. Feissel and Philippidis-Braat 1985: 308, no. 50.
84 Mexia 2015: 57–66.
85 Drandakis 1969–1970: 446; Drandakis 1995: 365.
86 Panayotidi 1989: 316–322; Panayotidi 1999: 178; Panayotidi 2005: 196–197.
87 For an overall survey and relevant bibliography, see Kalopissi-Verti 2003: 339–354.
88 Text after Drandakis 2002: 3–12; Feissel and Philippidis-Braat 1985: 305–306, no. 46; Kalopissi-Verti 2003: 339–340. On the marble-worker Niketas, Drandakis 1972; Drandakis 1975-76; Vanderheyde 1998: 767–769; Pallis 2013: 768, 793–794, nos. 45–47.
89 Kalopissi-Verti 2003: 339–346.
90 … κ(αὶ) πάντον το(ν) σηδραμόντο(ν) … (' … and all those who assisted … '): Drandakis 2002: 42–45; Pallis 2013: 794–795, no. 50.
91 Kalopissi-Verti 2012: 126–130.
92 Kalopissi-Verti 2003: 346–349.
93 Text after Drandakis 2002: 171; Bouras and Boura 2002: 187–190.
94 The inscription is carved on an epistyle re-employed in the belfry of the post-Byzantine church of the Taxiarches at Dryalo (1103), Feissel and Philippidis-Braat 1985: 307–308, no. 49; Drandakis 2002, 143–148; Pallis 2013: 793, no. 44.
95 See above, n. 60.
96 Evangelatou-Notara 2003: 483–496, esp. 486.

References

Acheimastou-Potamianou, M. (2009), 'Τοιχογραφίες του Μεγάλου Ταξιάρχη Μιχαήλ στη Μεσαριά της Άνδρου', in O. Gratziou and Ch. Loukos (eds), *Ψηφίδες. Μελέτες Ιστορίας, Αρχαιολογίας και Τέχνης στη Μνήμη της Στέλλας Παπαδάκη-Oekland*, Herakleio: 117–132.
Acheimastou-Potamianou, M. (1983), *Η Μονή Φιλανθρωπηνών και η πρώτη φάση της μεταβυζαντινής ζωγραφικής*. Athens.
Acheimastou-Potamianou, M. (2016), *Άγιος Γεώργιος ο Διασορίτης της Νάξου. Οι τοιχογραφίες του 11ου αιώνα*. Athens.
Angold, M. (1995), *Church and Society in Byzantium under the Comneni, 1081–1261*. Cambridge/New York.
Aslanidis, K. (2015), 'Επανεξέταση της αρχιτεκτονικής του ναού της Επισκοπής Σαντορίνης', in Katsaros and Tourta, eds., *Αφιέρωμα στον ακαδημαϊκό Παναγιώτη Λ. Βοκοτόπουλο*, Athens: 107–113.

246 *Sophia Kalopissi-Verti*

Aslanidis, K. (2018a), 'The evolution from early Christian to middle Byzantine church architecture on the island of Naxos', in J. Crow and D. Hill, eds., *Naxos and the Byzantine Aegean: Insular Responses to Regional Change*, Papers and Monographs from the Norwegian Institute at Athens 7, Athens: 311–337.

Aslanidis, K. (2018b), 'Early Christian architecture as a source of inspiration for eleventh century churches on the Aegean islands', *DChAE* 39: 167–178.

Athanasoulis, D., and Vasileiou, A. (2016), *Βυζαντινό Μουσείο Αργολίδας. Κατάλογος μόνιμης έκθεσης*. Athens.

Athanasoulis, D. *et al.* (forthcoming), 'Οι Σλάβοι στην Πελοπόννησο. Τα νέα στοιχεία από την ανασκαφή δύο νεκροταφείων στην Αρκαδία', Lecture at the National Research Foundation, Athens, 14-2-2014.

Avraméa, A. (1998), 'Le Magne byzantin: problèmes d'histoire et de topographie', in M. Balard (ed.), *Ευψυχία. Mélanges offerts à Hélène Ahrweiler*, Byzantina Sorbonensia, 16, Paris: vol. 1, 49–62.

Avraméa A., and Feissel, D. (1987), 'Inscriptions de Thessalie (à l'exception des Météores). Inventaire en vue d'un recueil des inscriptions historiques de Byzance', *TM* 10: 357–398.

Bakirtzis, C. (1982), 'Νεώτερες παρατηρήσεις στὴν κτιτορικὴ ἐπιγραφὴ τοῦ τρούλλου τῆς Ἁγίας Σοφίας Θεσσαλονίκης', *Byzantina* 11: 165–180.

Barsanti, C., and Pedone, S. (2005), 'Una nota sulla scultura ad incrostazione e il templon della Panaghia Episcopi di Santorini', in F. Baratte *et al.* (eds), *Travaux et Mémoires 15, Mélanges Jean-Pierre Sodini*: 407–425.

Bevilacqua, L. (2011), 'Committenza aristocratica a Bisanzio in età macedone: Leone protospatario e la Panagia di Skripou (873–874)', in A.C. Quintavalle (ed.), *Medioevo: i committenti. Atti del Convegno internazionale di studi, Parma, 21–26 settembre 2010*. Associazione Italiana Storici dell'Arte Medievale, Milan: 411–420.

Bevilacqua, L. (2013), *Arte e aristocrazia a Bisanzio nell' età dei Macedoni. Constantinopoli, la Grecia e l'Asia Minore*, Million 9, Rome.

Boura, L. (1980), *Ὁ γλυπτὸς διάκοσμος τῆς Παναγίας στὸ μοναστήρι τοῦ Ὁσίου Λουκᾶ.* Athens.

Bouras, Ch. (1960–1961), 'Ἡ ἀρχιτεκτονικὴ τοῦ ναοῦ τῆς Ἐπισκοπῆς Σκύρου', *DChAE* 2: 57–75.

Bouras, Ch. (1981), *Ἡ Νέα Μονὴ τῆς Χίου. Ἱστορία καὶ Ἀρχιτεκτονική*. Athens.

Bouras, Ch. (2010), *Βυζαντινή Ἀθήνα, 10ος–12ος αι.* Athens.

Bouras, Ch., and Boura, L. (2002), *Ἡ ἑλλαδικὴ ναοδομία κατά τόν 12ο αιῶνα.* Athens.

Chatzidaki, N. (1997), 'Hosios Loukas' in M. Chatzidakis (ed.), *Byzantine Art in Greece. Mosaics, Wall Paintings.* Athens.

Chatzidaki, N. (2011), 'La présence de l'higoumène Philotheos dans le catholicon de Saint-Luc en Phocide (Hosios Loukas). Nouvelles remarques', *CahArch* 54: 17–32.

Chatzidakis, M. (1969), 'A propos de la date et du fondateur de Saint-Luc', *CahArch* 19: 127–150.

Chatzidakis, M. (1972), 'Précisions sur le fondateur de Saint-Luc', *CahArch* 22: 87–88.

Constantine VII Porphyrogenitus (1967), *De administrando imperio*, in G. Moravcsik (ed.), R.J.H. Jenkins (tr.), Corpus Fontium Historiae Byzantinae 1, Dumbarton Oaks Center for Byzantine Studies, Washington, D.C.

Cormack, R. (1980–1981), 'The apse mosaics of S. Sophia at Thessaloniki', *DChAE* 10: 111–135.

Cormack R., and Hawkins, E.J.W. (1977), 'The Mosaics of St. Sophia at Istanbul: The Rooms above the Southwest Vestibule and Ramp', *DOP* 31: 212–251.

Cormack, R. (1984), 'Aristocratic Patronage of the Arts in 11th- and 12th-Century Byzantium', in M. Angold (ed.), *The Byzantine Aristocracy IX to XIII Centuries*, B.A.R. International Series 221, Oxford: 158–172.

Ćurčić, S. (2010), *Architecture in the Balkans. From Diocletian to Süleyman the Magnificent*. New Haven.

Dadaki, S. (2013), 'Συμβολή στην οικοδομική ιστορία του ναού των Αγίων Θεοδώρων Σερρών', in V. Penna (ed.), *Ναός περικαλλής. Ψηφίδες ιστορίας και ταυτότητας του ιερού ναού των Αγίων Θεοδώρων Σερρών*, Serres: 167–218.

Drakopoulou, E. (1997), *Ή πόλη της Καστοριάς τη βυζαντινή και μεταβυζαντινή εποχή (12ος–16ος αι.) Ιστορία - Τέχνη – Επιγραφές*. Athens.

Drandakis, N. (1969–1970), 'Ἅγιος Παντελεήμων Μπουλαριῶν', *EEBS* 37: 437–458.

Drandakis, N. (1972), 'Νικήτας Μαρμαρᾶς (1075)', *Dodone* 1: 21–44.

Drandakis, N. (1975–1976), 'Ἄγνωστα γλυπτὰ ἀποδιδόμενα στὸ μαρμαρᾶ Νικήτα καὶ στὸ ἐργαστήρι του', *DChAE* 8: 19–28.

Drandakis, N. (1995), *Βυζαντινὲς τοιχογραφίες τῆς Μέσα Μάνης*. Athens.

Drandakis, N. (2002), *Βυζαντινὰ γλυπτὰ τῆς Μάνης*. Athens.

Drandakis, N., Gioles, N., and Konstantinidi, Ch. (1978), 'Ἀνασκαφὴ στὸ Τηγάνι τῆς Μάνης', *PraktArchEt*: 183–191.

Drpić, I. (2014), 'The Patron's 'I'. Art, selfhood, and the Later Byzantine Dedicatory Epigram', *Speculum* 89/4: 895–935.

Drpić, I. (2016), *Epigram, Art and Devotion in Later Byzantium*. Cambridge.

Evangelatou-Notara, F. (2003), 'Χορηγοί και δωρητές χειρογράφων τον 11ο αιώνα', in V. Vlyssidou (ed.), *The Empire in Crisis (?). Byzantium in the 11th Century (1025–1081)*. International Symposium 11, National Hellenic Research Foundation, Institute for Byzantine Research, Athens: 483–496.

Feissel D., and Philippidis-Braat, A. (1985), 'Inscriptions de Peloponnèse (à l'exception de Mistra). Inventaires en vue d'un recueil des inscriptions historiques de Byzance', *TM*: 267–395.

Gerolymatou, M. (2004), 'Πελοποννησιακὲς μονὲς καὶ ἐξουσία (10ος–11ος αἰ.)', in V. Konti (ed.), *Monasticism in the Peloponnese 4th–15th c.*, International Symposium 14, National Hellenic Research Foundation, Institute for Byzantine Research, Athens: 37–53.

Glykatzi-Ahrweiler, H. (1971), 'Recherches sur l'administration de l'empire byzantin aux IXe-XIe siècles', in *Études sur les structures administratives et sociales de Byzance*, London: no. VIII, 1–101.

Grabar, A. (1963), *Sculptures byzantines de Constantinople (IVe-Xe siècle)*. Paris.

Guilland, R. (1966), 'Le titre de candidat, candidatus, ο κανδιδᾶτος', in P. Wirth (ed.), *Polychronion. Festschrift Franz Dölger zum 75. Geburtstag*, Heidelberg: 210–225.

Guilland, R. (1972–1973), 'Études sur l'histoire administrative de l'empire byzantin. L'ordre (τάξις) des Maîtres (τῶν Μαγίστρων)', *EEBS* 39–40: 14–28.

Herrin, J. (1975), 'Realities of Byzantine Provincial Government: Hellas and Peloponnesos, 1180–1205', *DOP* 29: 255–284.

Jacoby D. (1991/1992), 'Silk in Western Byzantium before the Fourth Crusade', *BZ* 84–85: 452–500.

Kalavrezou, I. (2013), "Approach to receive'. The apostle Andrew from the Communion Scene of the Old Metropolis of Serres', in V. Penna (ed.), *Ναός*

248 *Sophia Kalopissi-Verti*

περικαλλής. *Ψηφίδες ιστορίας και ταυτότητας του ιερού ναού των Αγίων Θεοδώρων Σερρών*, Serres: 219–225.

Kalopissi-Verti, S. (2003), 'Epigraphic evidence in Middle Byzantine Churches of the Mani. Patronage and art production', in M. Aspra-Vardavaki (ed.), *Λαμπηδών. Αφιέρωμα στη μνήμη της Ντούλας Μουρίκη*, Athens: vol. I, 339–354.

Kalopissi-Verti, S. (2012), 'Collective patterns of patronage in the Late Byzantine Village: The evidence of Church Inscriptions', in J.-M. Spieser and É. Yota, eds., *Donation et donateurs dans le monde byzantine*, Réalités Byzantines 14, Paris: 125–140.

Karagianni, F. (2006), *Επισκοπικοί ναοί της μέσης βυζαντινής περιόδου. Το παράδειγμα της Μακεδονίας*, Unpublished PhD thesis, Aristotle University of Thessaloniki.

Karambinis, M. (2015), *The Island of Skyros from Late Roman to Early Modern times. An archaeological survey*, Archaeological Studies, Leiden University 28. Leiden.

Katsaros, B. (2013), 'Άγνωστη βυζαντινή κτητορική επιγραφή (1092) από τη δυτική Φωκίδα', *DChAE* 34: 33–40.

Katsaros, B., and Tourta, A. (eds), (2015), *Αφιέρωμα στον ακαδημαϊκό Παναγιώτη Λ. Βοκοτόπουλο*. Athens.

Kazhdan A., and Wharton Epstein, A. (1985), *Change in Byzantine Culture in the Eleventh and Twelfth Centuries*. Berkeley/Los Angeles/London.

Kislinger, E. (2007), 'Nikolaos Episkopos Lakedaimonias. Chronologische Präzisierungen zur Bischofsliste im Bodleianus Holkham gr. 6', *JÖB* 57: 27–34.

Koder, J. (1973), *Negroponte. Untersuchungen zur Topographie und Siedlungsgeschichte der Insel Euboia während der Zeit der Venezianerherrschaft*, Veröffentlichungen der Kommission für die Tabula Imperii Byzantini 1. Vienna.

Koder, J. (1998), *Aigaion Pelagos (Die nördliche Ägäis)*, Tabula Imperii Byzantini 10. Vienna.

Koilakou, Ch. (2013), 'Byzantine Thebes', in J. Albani and E. Chalkia, eds., *Heaven and Earth. Cities and Countryside in Byzantine Greece*. Athens: 180–191.

Koilakou, Ch. (2018), 'Ο ναός του Αγίου Γρηγορίου Θεολόγου στη Θήβα. νεότερα στοιχεία', in M. Korres, S. Mamaloukos, K. Zampas and Ph. Mallouchou-Tufano, eds., *Ήρως Κτίστης. Μνήμη Χαράλαμπου Μπούρα*, Athens: vol. I, 569–580.

Kollias, E. (1986), *Patmos*, in series: M. Chatzidakis (ed.), Βυζαντινή Τέχνη στην Ελλάδα. Ψηφιδωτά, Τοιχογραφίες. Athens.

Korać, V. (1987), 'O arhitekturi katedralnih crkva XI veka na vizantijskom kuturnom području' (Architecture of 11-c. cathedral churches within the Byzantine cultural sphere), in *Izmedju Vizantije i zapada: Odobrane studije o arhitekturi*, Belgrade: 57–67.

Kyriakoudis, E. (1981), 'Ο κτίτορας τοῦ ναοῦ τῶν Ἁγ. Ἀναργύρων Καστοριᾶς Θεόδωρος (Θεόφιλος) Λημνιώτης', *Balkanika Symmeikta* 1: 1–23.

Laurent, V. (1934), 'Nicholas Kalomalos et l'église des Saints Théodores à Athènes', *Hellenika* 7: 72–82.

Leontiades, I. (1998), *Die Tarchaneiotai. Eine prosopographisch-sigillographische Studie*, Byzantina Keimena kai Meletai 29. Thessalonike.

Mamaloukos, S. (1995), 'Παρατηρήσεις σε μία βυζαντινή κτιτορική επιγραφή από την Ήπειρο', *DChAE* 18: 195–200.

Mamangakis, D. (2012), 'Άννα Ραδηνή: η γυναίκα της επαρχιακής αριστοκρατίας στο Βυζάντιο του 12ου αι. μέσα από κτητορικές παραστάσεις', *Byzantina Symmeikta* 22: 71–100.

Patronage of Religious Foundations in Middle Byzantine Greece 249

Mango, C., and Hawkins, E.J.W. (1972), 'The Mosaics of St. Sophia at Istanbul. The Church Fathers in the North Tympanum', *DOP* 26: 1–41.

Mastoropoulos, G., (2005(?)), *Νάξος το άλλο κάλλος: περιηγήσεις σε βυζαντινά μνημεία / Naxos: Byzantine monuments*. Athens.

Mastrokostas, E. (1953), 'Κτιτορικὴ ἐπιγραφὴ Ἁγίας Μονῆς Δωρίδος', *EEBS* 23: 355–357.

Megaw, H. (1931–1932), 'The Chronology of Some Middle Byzantine Churches', *BSA*: 90–130.

Megaw, H. (1932–1933), 'The Date of H. Theodoroi at Athens', *BSA* 33: 163–169.

Metaxas, S. (2018), 'Νέα αρχαιολογικά στοιχεία για την οικιστική δραστηριότητα στο Παλλάντιον στην πρωτοβυζαντινή εποχή', in E. Zymi, A.-V. Karapanayotou and M. Xanthopoulou, eds., *Το Αρχαιολογικό Έργο στην Πελοπόννησο (ΑΕΠΕΛ 1). Πρακτικά του Διεθνούς Συνεδρίου Τρίπολη, 7–11 Νοεμβρίου 2012*, Kalamata: 689–700.

McGeer, E. (1991), 'Droungarios', in A. Kazhdan, A.-M. Talbot *et al.*, eds., *Oxford Dictionary of Byzantium*, New York/Oxford: vol. 1, 663.

Mexia, A. (2005), 'Inscribed cornice', in *Tales of Religious Faith*. Network of Mani Museums, Athens: 121, no. 46.

Mexia, A. (2015), 'Ἡ βασιλική στο Τηγάνι της Μέσα Μάνης. Συμβολή στην οικοδομική ιστορία του ναού', in Katsaros and Tourta, eds.: 57–66.

Mitsani, A. (2004-2006), 'Ἡ χορηγία στὶς Κυκλάδες ἀπὸ τὸν 6ο μέχρι τὸν 14ο αἰ. Ἡ μαρτυρία τῶν ἐπιγραφῶν', *EEBS* 52: 391–446.

Morris, R. (1995), *Monks and Laymen in Byzantium 843–1118*. Cambridge/New York.

Moulet, B. (2011), *Évêques, pouvoir et société à Byzance (VIIIe-XIe siècle). Territoires, communautés et individus dans la société provinciale byzantine*, Byzantina Sorbonensia 25. Paris.

Mouriki, D. (1982), 'Stylistic trends in monumental painting in Greece during the eleventh and twelfth centuries', *DOP* 34–35: 77–124.

Mouriki, D. (1985), *The Mosaics of Nea Moni on Chios*, vols. 1–2. Athens.

Mylonas, P. (1992), 'Nouvelles remarques sur le complexe de Saint-Luc en Phocide', *CahArch* 40: 115–122.

Neville, L. (2004), *Authority in Byzantine provincial society, 950–1100*. Cambridge/New York.

Nikonanos, N. (1979), *Βυζαντινοι ναοι τῆς Θεσσαλίας ἀπό τὸ 10ο αιῶνα ὡς τὴν κατάκτηση τῆς περιοχῆς ἀπὸ τοὺς Τούρκους τὸ 1393. Συμβολή στὴ βυζαντινὴ ἀρχιτεκτονικὴ*, Δημοσιεύματα του Αρχαιολογικού Δελτίου, 26. Athens.

Oikonomidès, N. (1972), *Les listes de préséance byzantines des IXe et Xe siècles*. Paris.

Oikonomides, N. (1992), 'The first century of the Monastery of Hosios Loukas', *DOP* 46: 245–255.

Oikonomidès, N. (1994), 'Pour une nouvelle lecture des inscriptions de Skripou en Béotie', *TM* 12: 479–493.

Orlandos, A. (1951a), 'Τὸ περὶ τὸ Ἀλιβέρι Μετόχιον τοῦ Ὁσίου Λουκᾶ Φωκίδος', *ABME* 7: 139–145.

Orlandos, A. (1951b), 'Ἡ Ἐπισκοπὴ τῆς Σαντορίνης (Παναγία τῆς Γωνιάς)', *ABME* 7: 178–214.

Orlandos, A. (1955–1956), 'Βυζαντινὰ μνημεῖα τῆς Ἄνδρου', *ABME* 8: 3–67.

Orlandos, A. (1970) *Ἡ ἀρχιτεκτονικὴ και αι βυζαντιναι τοιχογραφίαι τῆς Μονῆς τοῦ θεολόγου Πάτμου*. Πραγματεῖαι τῆς Ἀκαδημίας Ἀθηνῶν 28. Athens.

Orlandos, A., and Vranousis, L. (1973), *Les graffiti du Parthénon: inscriptions gravées sur les colonnes du Parthénon à l'époque paléochrétienne et byzantine* [in Greek]. Athens.

250 Sophia Kalopissi-Verti

Païssidou, M. (2015), 'The Church "Panagia ton Chalkeon in Thessaloniki": A different approach of a monastic institution and its founder', *Siris* 15: 121–133.

Pallas, D. (1985), 'Zur Topographie und Chronologie von Hosios Lukas: eine kritische Übersicht', *BZ* 78: 94–107.

Pallis, G. (2013), 'Inscriptions on middle Byzantine marble templon screens', *BZ* 106: 761–810.

Panayotidi, M. (1974), Ἡ παράσταση τῆς Ἀνάληψης στον τρούλο τῆς Ἁγίας Σοφίας Θεσσαλονίκης. Εικονογραφικά προβλήματα', *Epistemonike Epeteris tes Polytechnikes Scholes Panepistemiou Thessalonikes, Tmema Architektonon* 6: Part 2, 69–89.

Panayotidi, M. (1986), 'La peinture monumentale en Grèce de la fin de l'Iconoclasme jusqu'à l'avènement des Comnènes (843–1081)', *CahArch* 34: 75–108.

Panayotidi, M. (1989), 'The Character of Monumental Painting in the Tenth Century. The Question of Patronage', in A. Markopoulos (ed.), *Constantine VII Porphyrogenitus and His Age, Second International Byzantine Conference, Delphi 1987*, Athens: 285–331.

Panayotidi, M. (1999), 'Un aspect de l'art provincial, témoignage des ateliers locaux dans la peinture monumentale', in *Drevnerusskoe iskusstvo Vizanija i drevnjaja Rus' K 100-letnju Andreja Nikolaeviča Grabara (1896–1990)*, St Petersburg: 178–192.

Panayotidi, M. (2004), 'Donor personality traits in 12th century painting. Some examples', in Ch. Angelidi (ed.), *Byzantium matures. Choices, sensitivities and modes of expression (eleventh to fifteenth centuries*. International Symposium 13, The National Hellenic Research Foundation, Institute for Byzantine Research, Athens: 145–166.

Panayotidi, M. (2005), 'Village Painting and the Question of Local "Workshops"', in J. Lefort, C. Morrisson and J.-P. Sodini (eds), *Les Villages dans l'Empire byzantin (IVe-XVe siècle)*, Réalités Byzantines 11, Paris: 193–212.

Panayotidi, M. (2006), Ἡ προσωπικότητα δύο αρχόντων της Καστοριάς και ο χαρακτήρας της πόλης στο δεύτερο μισό του 12ου αιώνα', in G. Karadedos (ed.), *Doron. Timetikos tomos ston kathegete Niko Nikonano*, Thessalonike: 157–167.

Panayotidi, M., and Konstantellou, D. (2018), 'The byzantine wall paintings of Panagia Protothronos at Chalki, Naxos (10th–11th century phases). Meanings, function and historical context', in J. Crow and D. Hill (eds), *Naxos and the Byzantine Aegean: Insular Responses to Regional Change,* Papers and Monographs from the Norwegian Institute at Athens, 7, Athens: 257–282.

Papadopoulos, K. (1966), *Die Wandmalereien des XI. Jahrhunderts in der Kirche Παναγία τῶν Χαλκέων in Thessalonikii*. Byzantina Vindobonensia II. Graz/Köln.

Papalexandrou, A. (1998), *The Church of the Virgin of Skripou: Architecture, Sculpture and Inscriptions in Ninth-Century Byzantium*, Unpublished PhD thesis. Princeton University.

Papalexandrou, A. (2001), 'Text in context: Eloquent monuments and the Byzantine beholder', *Word and Image* 17/3: 259–283.

Papalexandrou, A. (2007), 'Echoes of orality in the monumental inscriptions of Byzantium', in L. James (ed.), *Art and Text in Byzantine Culture*, Cambridge/New York: 171–176.

Papatheophanous-Tsouri, E. (2016), *Macédoine orientale, Thrace occidentale*, in P. Vocotopoulos (ed.), *Corpus de la Peinture Monumentale Byzantine de la Grèce*. Athens.

Papazotos, Th. (1994), Ἡ Βέροια καί οι ναοί της (11ος–18ος αι.). Δημοσιεύματα του Αρχαιολογικού Δελτίου 54. Athens.

Patronage of Religious Foundations in Middle Byzantine Greece 251

Penna, V. (ed.) (2013), *Ναός περικαλλής. Ψηφίδες ιστορίας και ταυτότητας του ιερού ναού των Αγίων Θεοδώρων Σερρών*. Serres.

Penna, V. (2013), 'Οι Σέρρες και ο ναός των Αγίων Θεοδώρων: ιστορικά και αρχαιολογικά τεκμήρια (4ος–12ος αι.)', in V. Penna (ed.), 2013: 107–124.

Pennas, C. (1991), 'Some aristocratic founders: The foundation of Panaghia Krena on Chios', in J. Perreault (ed.), *Les femmes et le monachisme byzantin. Actes du Symposium d'Athènes 1988*, Athens: 61–66.

Pennas, C. (2017), *The Byzantine church of Panagia Krena in Chios: history, architecture, sculpture, painting (late 12th century)*. Leiden.

Pinatsi, C. (2018), 'Some remarks on the sculpted decoration and the templon of the katholikon of Hagia Moni in Areia, Nauplion', *DChAE* 39: 179–194.

Prieto-Domínguez, O. (2013), 'On the founder of the Skripou Church: Literary trends in the milieu of Photius', *GRBS* 53: 166–191.

Rhoby, A. (2009), *Byzantinische Epigramme auf Fresken und Mosaiken*. Byzantinische Epigramme in in inschriflticher Überlieferung 1. Vienna.

Rhoby, A. (2014), *Byzantinische Epigramme auf Stein. Nebst Addenda zu den Bänden 1 und 2*. Byzantinische Epigramme in inschriflticher Überlieferung 3, 2 vols. Vienna.

Schminck, A. (2003), 'Hosios Lukas: eine kaiserliche Stiftung?', in V. Vlyssidou (ed.), *The Empire in Crisis (?). Byzantium in the 11th Century (1025–1081)*. International Symposium 11, National Hellenic Research Foundation, Institute for Byzantine Research, Athens: 349–380.

Skawran, K. (1982), *The Development of Middle Byzantine Fresco Painting in Greece*. Pretoria.

Skiadaresis, G. (2016), *Η Παλαιά Μητρόπολη της Βέροιας στο πλαίσιο της βυζαντινής αρχιτεκτονικής*, Unpublished PhD thesis. Aristotle University of Thessaloniki.

Sklavou-Mavroidi, M. (1999), *Γλυπτά του Βυζαντινού Μουσείου Αθηνών*. Athens.

Soteriou, G. (1924), 'Ὁ ἐν Θήβαις ναὸς Γρηγορίου τοῦ Θεολόγου', *ArchEph*: 1–26.

Soteriou, M. (1931), 'Ὁ ναὸς τῆς Σκριποῦς τῆς Βοιωτίας', *ArchEph*: 119–157.

Spieser, J.-M. (1973), 'Les inscriptions de Thessalonique. Inventaires en vue d'un recueil des inscriptions historiques de Byzance', *TM* 5: 145–180.

Stiernon, L. (1965), 'Notes de titulature et de prosopographie byzantines. Sébaste et gambros', *REB* 23: 226–232.

Stikas, E. (1970), *Τὸ οἰκοδομικὸν χρονικὸν τῆς Μονῆς Ὁσίου Λουκᾶ Φωκίδος*. Athens.

Stikas, E. (1974), *Ὁ κτίτωρ τοῦ καθολικοῦ τῆς Μονῆς Ὁσίου Λουκᾶ*. Athens.

Symeonoglou, S. (1985), *The Topography of Thebes from the Bronze Age to Modern Times*. Princeton, N.J.

Sythiakakis-Kritsimallis V., and Voyadjis, S. (2011), 'Redating the basilica of Dormition, Kalampaka, Thessaly', *JÖB* 61: 195–227.

Theocharidou, K. (1976), 'Τὰ ψηφιδωτὰ τοῦ τρούλλου στὴν Ἁγία Σοφία Θεσσαλονίκης. Φάσεις καὶ προβλήματα χρονολόγησης', *ArchDelt* 31 A: 265–273.

Tomeković-Reggiani, S. (1981), 'Portraits et structures sociales au XIIe siècle. Un aspect du problème: Le portrait laïque', in *Actes du XVe Congrès International d'Études byzantines, II B, Art et Archéologie*, Athens: 823–836.

Tsigaridas, E. (1996), 'Τά ψηφιδωτά καί οι βυζαντινές τοιχογραφίες', in *Hiera Megiste Mone Batopaidiou*, Agion Oros: Holy Monastery of Vatopaidi: vol. I, 220–284.

Tsitouridou, A. (1982), 'Die Grabkonzeption des ikonographischen Programms der Kirche Panagia ton Chalkeon in Thessalonike', *JÖB* 32/5: 435–441.

252 *Sophia Kalopissi-Verti*

Tsitouridou, A. (1987), '"Επισκοπή Σαντορίνης" ίδρυμα του Αλεξίου Α΄ Κομνηνού ή του Β΄;', in *Ametos. Timetikos tomos gia ton kathegete Manole Androniko*, Thessalonike: vol. 2, 917–921.

Tsouris, K. (2015), 'Η χρονολόγηση της Παλαιάς Μητροπόλεως Σερρών', in Katsaros and Tourta (eds): 97–106.

Vanderheyde, C. (1998), 'Deux exemples de sculpteurs locaux et itinérants en Grèce au XIe siècle', *Topoi* 8/2: 765–775.

Velenis, G. (1990–1991), 'Επιλεγόμενα σε επιγραφές του μετοχίου του Οσίου Λουκά Εύβοιας', in *Armos. Timetikos tomos ston kathegete N.K. Moutsopoulo*, Thessalonike: vol. 1, 353–361.

Velenis, G. (1997), 'Η χρονολόγηση της Αγίας Σοφίας Θεσσαλονίκης μέσα από τα επιγραφικά δεδομένα', in *Thessalonikeon polis: graphes kai peges 6000 chronon* 3, Thessalonike: 70–77.

Vocotopoulos, P. (1966–1969), 'Περὶ τὴν χρονολόγησιν τοῦ ἐν Κερκύρᾳ ναοῦ τῶν Ἁγίων Ἰάσωνος καὶ Σωσιπάτρου', *DChAE* 5: 149–174.

Vocotopoulos, P. (1971), 'Fresques du XIe siècle à Corfou', *CahArch* 21: 131–172.

Vocotopoulos, P., Dimitrakopoulou P., Rigakou D., Triantaphyllopoulos, D., and Chouliaras, I. (2018), *Îles Ioniennes*, in P. Vocotopoulos (ed.), *Corpus de la Peinture Monumentale Byzantine de la Grèce*. Athens.

Voyatzis, S. (1998), 'Η Μονή Βητουμά στα Τρίκαλα, Θεσσαλίας', in *Ekklesies meta ten Alose* 5, Athens: 37–52.

Vranousi, E. (ed.) (1980), *Βυζαντινὰ Ἔγγραφα τῆς Μονῆς Πάτμου. Ι. Αὐτοκρατορικά*, 2 vols. Athens.

Xyngopoulos, A. (1938), 'Η τοιχογραφία τῆς Ἀναλήψεως ἐν τῇ ἁψῖδι τοῦ Ἁγίου Γεωργίου τῆς Θεσσαλονίκης', *ArchEph*: 39–46.

Xyngopoulos, A. (1956), 'Ὁ ναὸς τῆς Ἐπισκοπῆς Σκοπέλου', *Archaiologike Ephemeris*: 181–198.

Xyngopoulos, A. (1957), *Τα μνημεια τῶν Σερβίων, Ἑταιρεία Μακεδονικῶνν Σπουδῶν. Ἵδρυμα Μελετῶν Χερσονήσου τοῦ Αἵμου* 18. Athens.

Zarras, N. (2016), 'Identity and Patronage in Byzantium: Epigraphic Evidence and Donor Portraits of Naxos', in C. Stavrakos (ed.), *Inscriptions in the Byzantine and Post-Byzantine History and History of Art, Proceedings of the International Symposium "Inscriptions: their Contribution to the Byzantine and post-Byzantine History and History of Art" (Ioannina, June 26–27, 2015)*, Wiesbaden: 53–78.

Zias, N. (1989), 'Πρωτόθρονη στό Χαλκί', in M. Chatzidakis *et al.*, Βυζαντινή Τέχνη στην Ελλάδα: Νάξος, Athens: 30–49.

15 Church-Building in the Peloponnese
Reflections of Social and Economic Trends in the Countryside in the Middle Byzantine Period

Maria Papadaki

One of the most meaningful challenges archaeology faces today is to work more constructively to take up the task of contextualising all ranges of archaeological evidence, and to offer interpretations from alternative perspectives and inter-connecting angles. New avenues pertaining to regional studies have already been opened by examining topography in conjunction with physical remains, and by incorporating studies of churches into the reconstruction of their social fabric and economic context.[1] Churches, as hubs of social attention and economic activity, can provide evidence of stability, continuity, and economic growth, which is amongst the desiderata of the study of the Middle Byzantine countryside. Their study contributes substantially to the discussion of settlement patterns and the determination of socio-economic activities whatever the region under examination.[2] In particular, for the Peloponnesian countryside during the 11th and 12th centuries, where historical records are lacking, ecclesiastical buildings can be considered an essential tool to test the implications of economic growth indicated by documentary and archaeological evidence from other regions of the Byzantine Empire.[3] The purpose of the chapter is to illustrate the potent role of ecclesiastical buildings when viewed from a different perspective and in particular when used for the study of settlements with reference to two key aspects, the extent of building activity and topography of churches.

The contextualised study of the archaeological data has shown that an unprecedented number of churches survive today in the Peloponnesian countryside that were built or renovated in this period.[4] Having looked at the issues of the state of preservation of the examined Peloponnesian churches and their dating as important factors of reliability, it can be noted: first, in terms of preservation, that the majority of churches remain in good condition and they offer dating evidence (see Figure 15.1). Second, in terms of dating, the overall picture suggests that the majority – two-thirds of all the churches examined – are now well-studied buildings whose proposed dating has been accepted by all scholars. Even the chronological variations that were observed are slight, and all have been placed within the 11th and 12th century period. Although scholarly consensus does not ensure that the churches are

DOI: 10.4324/9781003429470-19

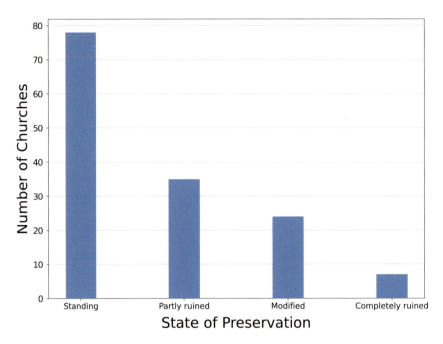

Figure 15.1 State of preservation of the Peloponnesian churches examined (© M. Papadaki).

correctly dated, it is nevertheless a strong indication that the buildings belong to the period to which they have been ascribed based on our current knowledge. Only a small proportion of the churches have not been revisited since their first publications from the 1940s to the 1960s or are of uncertain dating.[5] Establishing this is all the more important, since the churches – the largest body of local evidence for the period – can thus be used as a reliable indicator of human activity and a marker for the existence of a settlement.[6]

The study of church construction provides a useful indication of developments in the Byzantine Peloponnese, proving significant change in the region from the Early to the Middle Byzantine period.[7] By putting churches into a comparative framework and charting fluctuations across the centuries,[8] we could map the following changes (see Figure 15.2): in the Early Byzantine period (4th to 7th centuries) the total number of ecclesiastical monuments is 127, indicating significant building activity. Although the chronology of the majority of the Early Christian buildings is not refined (almost half the total number of churches from the Early Byzantine period – that is 61 out of 127 – have been vaguely assigned to the period from the late 4th to the late 7th century), it is nevertheless observable that the construction of churches and their density all over the peninsula point to a level of socio-economic activity and continuity, the extent of which needs to be further addressed elsewhere, being beyond the scope of this chapter.[9] This picture is in keeping with the regional surface surveys' results from

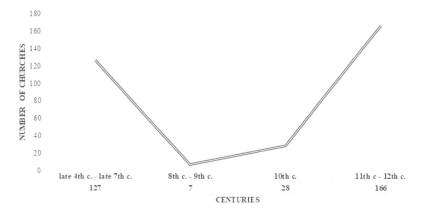

Figure 15.2 Chronology of church construction in the Peloponnese (© M. Papadaki).

several other areas in the Peloponnese: there is an increase in the number of sites in the period from the 4th to the late 6th centuries, corresponding to population growth and land exploitation.[10] In the following period, in the 8th and 9th centuries, there was a sharp drop in the number of churches built or re-used: only seven churches have been recorded in the whole Peloponnese. A similar trend in church-building activity can be seen in other parts of Greece in this period.[11] Also, field survey demonstrates that the archaeological evidence in the Peloponnese is very scanty for the 8th and 9th centuries.[12] This change has been associated with severe plagues, the threat of invasions, and the arrival of the Slavs in the Peloponnese. It has been further interpreted as resulting from economic collapse, instability, the departure of populations, and the abandonment of sites.[13] Beyond these reflections, the paucity of archaeological material relating to the 7th- to 9th-century period, not only in the Peloponnese but around the Aegean as well, has prompted the question of whether sufficient knowledge of the typologies and chronology of pottery and architectural materials of this period exists, and over the use of materials which might not be archaeologically visible today.[14] In such a case, the scenario of depopulation or land abandonment may have been less dramatic. Future research and new evidence will refine the historical perspective. As things now stand, it is essential to be aware of these trends. Moving into the following period, from the 10th century there is an increase in the number of churches, which follows an upward curve, starting slowly and reaching a peak in the 11th and 12th centuries with a total number of 166 recorded churches. The political and economic stabilisation that followed the recovery of the islands of Crete in 961 and Cyprus in 965 by Nikephoros Phokas may have created security for populations in the Peloponnese, which in turn favoured new settlement and church-building activity. The creation of new bishoprics as well as the promotion of some bishoprics to archbishoprics in the Peloponnese during the 10th- to 12th-century period may have also resulted from an increasing population.[15] Evidence for building activity is furnished by hagiographical accounts of the Middle Byzantine period. Holy men, above all Saint Nikon,[16] are greatly involved in the organisation of ecclesiastical life in various localities: they established a network of priests, built churches, and created religious hubs for the strengthening of social cohesion and religious ties within local communities.[17] The intense activity is also ascertained by field survey archaeology which has identified an increasing number of sites in the countryside in the 11th and mostly in the 12th century, providing strong indications of the change and the revival that occurred during the Middle Byzantine period in the Peloponnese.[18]

Not only the intensified church construction serves as evidence of relative growth in population and productivity, but the study of location and geographical distribution of churches indicates a preference for sites with agricultural potential, conducive to rural exploitation and production. The study of topography of the church sites has shown that the overwhelming majority of rural churches in the Peloponnese, which is a mostly mountainous country, are located in plains and valleys in low altitude with gentle terrain (see Figure 15.3).[19]

A similar site pattern is further attested through survey data produced by field archaeological projects in recent years in various Peloponnesian localities. The study of the location of 164 surveyed sites with activity in the 11th and 12th centuries has shown a consistent pattern of site selection for land

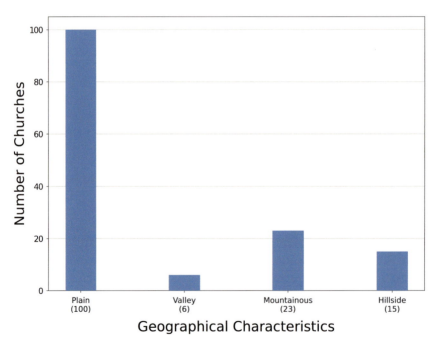

Figure 15.3 Distribution of churches based on geographical characteristics (© M. Papadaki).

Church-Building in the Peloponnese 257

which offers better potential for agricultural activities. Almost all the sites have grown up around abundant water resources and good agricultural lands and, most importantly, in the most fertile zones of the whole area surveyed.[20] The overall patterning of church and surveyed sites illustrates that there is a clear locational preference for areas that offer good quality arable land and which can be conducive to self-sufficiency; the assumed fertile soil of plains and valley floors must have formed the background for a flourishing agricultural economy. The agricultural intensification may have led to population increase and consequently, in many cases, to the occupation of new sites and the development of a denser settlement pattern.

Another key aspect that stands out, regarding the geographical distribution of church sites, is their concentration in specific locations of the Peloponnese (see Figure 15.4). The chart shows that there is a limited distribution of churches in the northern and south-eastern parts of the Peloponnese. To be more specific, the regions of Achaia and Elis have a very small number of monuments: four and six respectively. The regions of Argolid and Corinthia, which in terms of administration and connections is the most important centre of the Peloponnese, have only 18 churches altogether.[21] Of course, there are certainly survival factors that may account for this picture. It is possible that Elis may not be suitable for occupation mainly due to the combination of high percentage of rainfall and occurrence of alluvial deposits, while the whole region of the Gulf of Corinth in the northern Peloponnese is prone to seismic activity and, therefore, several churches would have been destroyed along the northern coasts.[22] Also, the central part of the Peloponnese, which is mainly mountainous and prone to flooding, does not offer many possibilities for agriculture, which seems to be a vital feature for site preference in the 11th- and 12th-century period.[23] A

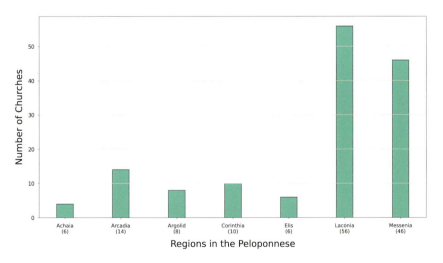

Figure 15.4 Distribution of churches per region in the Peloponnese (© M. Papadaki).

258   *Maria Papadaki*

larger concentration of churches can be observed in specific districts in the south-western Peloponnese, namely Messenia and Laconia; these districts have the largest numbers of churches, 56 and 46 respectively.[24] From this survey it emerges that there is apparently a disparity between the other areas and the southern Peloponnese, which features a dense concentration of ecclesiastical monuments. This difference can be understood by considering the following: (i) in terms of research, Nikolaos Drandakes and his associates carried out a project aiming exclusively at the systematic documentation and study of the Byzantine and post-Byzantine churches in the southern Peloponnese, and in particular in Mani peninsula, which is the southernmost part of the Peloponnese, for a long period of time (approximately from the 1960s to 1980s), having produced plentiful archaeological information and having composed a rich and meticulous record of monuments. Similar projects in terms of duration and aims have not been conducted in other regions of the Peloponnese and, therefore, a picture of the number of the Middle Byzantine churches elsewhere is not yet complete.[25] (ii) In terms of preservation, following the capture of Constantinople by the Ottomans in 1453, Mani retained a self-governing status. The relatively secure environment would have helped in the preservation of Byzantine monuments over time. The subjugation of the other regions of the Peloponnese to the Ottomans had implications for the built environment, with constant warfare causing damage to standing monuments and resulting in the survival of fewer churches.[26] Also, the seismic activity in Mani, a region mainly consisting of rock formations, is not as intense as in other regions of the Peloponnese, such as the western and northern coasts, where the operation of plate-tectonic forces caused strong earthquakes. This suggests that the Maniot landscape and its built environment could have remained almost intact up to modern times.[27] (iii) In terms of economic development, the proliferation of churches in the southern Peloponnese and expansion of the episcopacy, as mentioned above, reflects rural development and population increase in the region.

The study of distribution of church sites in Messenia and Laconia demonstrates a site preference associated with good-quality farmland and potential for productivity.[28] Both regions have extensive mountainous zones and plains; however, very few churches are found in the mountains, with the overwhelming majority of churches located in the Messenian plain, on plains along the Messenian and Laconian coasts, in smaller valleys lying among the low mountains in the hinterland of Messenia, on the plain of Embros in Mani and in valleys in the hinterland of Laconia. Messenia and Laconia are attested in contemporary textual sources as fertile lands and rich in olive cultivation. In the 10th century, the emperor Constantine VII Porphyrogennetos in the *De Administrando Imperio* referring to the inhabitants of the city of Mani states that 'the place where they live is waterless and inaccessible, but bears the olive, whence the comfort is'.[29] A 13th-century dedicatory inscription of the church of the Archangel Michael in Polemitas in Mani also records the donations of over thirty villagers, listing among other items olive trees.[30] According to the

Testament of Saint Nikon, olive trees are to be found among the properties of churches at the villages of Slavochori and Parori in the vicinity of Sparta.[31] The *Life* of Saint Nikon mentions that the Saint built a church in the city of Sparta which included an olive press.[32] Importantly, this olive workshop constituted a source of conflict over rights of access, indicating the significance of olives within local communities.[33] Also four Middle Byzantine presses, which were found at Sparta by the Ephorate of Antiquities of Laconia, further suggest that the city and its wider area indeed constituted an important oil-producing area.[34] Towards the end of the 12th century, the significance of olive groves was highlighted by an English pilgrim, Benedict of Peterborough, who reported that Korone in Messenia produced more olives than any other region in the world.[35] Analysis of pollen samples in the region of Messenia, undertaken by the Pylos Regional Archaeological Project, provides extremely significant results for olive cultivation in the southern Peloponnese, showing an increase in olive cultivation, possibly between 1000 and 1200.[36] It becomes clear from the evidence furnished above that the southern Peloponnese is intensively cultivated. Socio-economic conditions and political events of the late 11th century favoured the exploitation of the region; in particular, the double loss of Asia Minor to the Seljuks and of Byzantine Italy to the Normans by the 1070s resulted in the shrinkage of the Byzantine empire and contributed to intensive exploitation of the still-available land in rural areas. Messenia and Laconia greatly benefited from their geographical position, having rich land resources, and emerged as new economic zones.

But the commercial privileges and fiscal exceptions granted to Italians also increased commercial activities in the Peloponnesian towns, while the growing need for agricultural products, such as olive oil, stimulated, in turn, the increase of agriculture-related activities in the countryside.[37] In trade contracts of the 12th century, Venetian merchants are attested in Sparta purchasing olive oil from local landowners and selling it in Alexandria and Constantinople.[38] Also, Methone constituted a significant port of call on the way from Venice to Constantinople, and obviously vice versa, as well as from Egypt to Venice. The dispatch of oil from the port of Methone is suggestive of the existence of olive cultivation in Messenia.[39] Sparta and Methone in the south were agricultural outlets for the Peloponnesian hinterland and meeting points for trade between Byzantine and Italian merchants. Products would have regularly been conveyed to permanent markets or those organised for special occasions, such as fairs associated with the feast day of a saint or with a commercial character.[40] The *Life* of Saint Nikon reveals that a fair was held at Sparta on the Saint's nameday.[41] Apart from urban markets, local markets and rural fairs may have also been held, offering peasants the opportunity to sell their produce to itinerant merchants.[42] During the 11th- and 12th-century period, there is a growth in trade for agricultural products which favoured demographic and settlement growth.[43] It seems, therefore, that availability of natural resources coupled with the need for olive cultivation both for local consumption and trade in the southern Peloponnese may have appealed to

260 *Maria Papadaki*

settlers, and resulted in intensified cultivation and the formation of nearby settlements, whose remains are the ecclesiastical buildings.

The Peloponnese, having acquired a central role in the military stabilisation and the political upturn of the 10th century within the Byzantine Empire, played an instrumental role in the following centuries in economic developments. Key factors are the geographical location and land resources: the Peloponnese enjoyed a particularly favourable location along the land route and the waterways linking west to east and it possesses a rich rural hinterland. The commercial activities of Venetians in the Peloponnesian towns contributed the increase of agricultural-related activities in the countryside.[44] The intensified building activity in the Peloponnese not only left a Christian imprint, as mentioned above, but offers further confirmation of the population increase in the region and rising productivity in the countryside. This pattern agrees with the regional surface survey data in the Peloponnese, namely an increasing number of sites providing strong indications that the Peloponnese participated in the general trend of revival in this period.[45]

In conclusion, the research I reported here has demonstrated that the contextualised study of churches, with reference to their historical, social, and economic contexts, and in juxtaposition with other types of archaeological and textual materials, offers us the potential to understand changes in the Byzantine countryside.

Notes

1 Significant works on Byzantine churches include the studies of Wharton-Epstein 1980 (Kastoria), Ousterhout 2005 (western Cappadocia).
2 See also Dunn 1995: 755.
3 For the economic expansion during the middle Byzantine period, see Harvey 1989, and Laiou and Morrisson 2007: 90–165.
4 A detailed gazetteer of the Middle Byzantine churches in the Peloponnese can be found in the Appendix of Papadaki 2014 (Table 5: 24–37). It provides the generally accepted date for each monument (including alternative dates proposed), bibliographic references and the condition of each monument.
5 Papadaki 2014: 111–112.
6 See Laiou 2005: 48; Gerstel 2005: 165–166.
7 The Early Byzantine ecclesiastical buildings in the Peloponnese have been studied by Anna Avramea, William Caraher, and Rebecca Sweetman. See Avramea 1997, esp. 164–203, Caraher 2003, esp. 342–521 and Sweetman 2010, esp. 248–261.
8 The data gathered for charting chronological fluctuations in church-building activity is based on compiled catalogues of the ecclesiastical monuments – presented for a first time in Papadaki 2014 – including those that have been excavated/identified on the ground, and also those mentioned in texts. The catalogues contain information on proposed dating, location, and bibliographies for each monument. See Papadaki 2014: Appendix, Table 5, 24–37; Table 7, 39–48 and Table 8, 49–50. Figure 15.2 includes churches both in urban and rural sites, since the majority of ecclesiastical buildings in the Early Byzantine period were built in urban or suburban spaces and there is little evidence for the construction of churches in truly rural settings. See Sweetman 2010, esp. 222, 226–227, 243 and 245 and Papadaki 2014: 113–114.

9 See also Sweetman, 2010: 247.

10 For survey archaeology in the Peloponnese, see Papadaki 2014: 41–84.

11 See Bintliff 2012: 391.

12 See Papadaki, 2014, 70.

13 See Hahn 1996: 439 (with bibliographic references).

14 See Sanders 2004: 186–187; Gregory 2009: 80–81; Bintliff 2012: 384–385.

15 For the ecclesiastical history of the Byzantine Peloponnese, see Vasilikopoulou 1987–1988 and Yannopoulos 1993.

16 Primary sources of information for Nikon's actions are provided by three texts: his Testament and two overlapping texts of his Life. Nikon's Testament is presumably dated from shortly before Nikon's death, which is estimated to have taken place towards the end of the 10th century (c.1000?). The Greek text of Nikon's Testament and commentary can be found in Lampsides 1982: 251–256, 452–465 (respectively). For an English translation (and comments), see Bandy 2000: 317–320. His Life was composed in the 11th or 12th century by an anonymous hagiographer, an abbot of Nikon's monastery in Sparta. The Life can be found in Lampsides 1982 and Sullivan 1987.

17 For the activity of Saints in the Peloponnese during the Middle Byzantine period, see Papadaki 2013.

18 For an analysis of relevant findings of the survey projects in the Peloponnese, see Papadaki 2014: 70–84.

19 For a statistical analysis of the church sites and discussion on their topography, see Papadaki, 2014, 213–225.

20 For an analysis of location and distribution of surveyed sites in the Peloponnese, see Papadaki 2014: 70–84.

21 From the beginning of the 9th century the city of Corinth became the centre of the new administrative unit (theme) of the Peloponnese, see Gregory 2005: 221–223.

22 For the geography and physical setting of the Peloponnese, see Higgins and Higgins 1996; for an overview, see Bintliff 2012: 11–15; Papadaki 2014: 14–25 (with bibliography).

23 See Papadaki 2014: 222.

24 The increased number of bishoprics and archbishoprics in the south-western Peloponnese during the 10th- to 12th-century period suggests greater development and denser population of the region. The same sense of expansion of the church hierarchy and structures during the period can also be gleaned from the study of the circulation of Byzantine lead seals struck by ecclesiastics. This reveals that the *concentration* of seal finds in the Middle Byzantine period is highest in the southern Peloponnese and in particular Messenia and Laconia. See Papadaki 2014: 226–229.

25 For the work of Nikolaos Drandakes in Messenia and Laconia, see Papadaki 2014: 103–104.

26 For the history of Mani during the Ottoman period, see Mexes 1977; Adanir 2006: 159–160.

27 See Higgins and Higgins 1996; Bintliff 2012: 11–15; Papadaki 2014: 14–24.

28 Messenia and Laconia have the highest concentration of churches, and offer more reliable material for statistical analysis.

29 Moravcsik and Jenkins 1967: ch. 50, 236–237, l. 76–78.

30 For the inscription, see Drandakes 1982: 46–47 and 55; Feissel and Philippidis-Braat 1985: 314–317, no. 57; Kalopissi-Verti 1992: 71–74, no. 21.

31 Bandy 2000: 319.

32 Sullivan 1987: ch. 67, 228–229.

33 See also Sullivan 1987: ch. 67, 228–231; Armstrong 2009: 318.

34 See also Mexia 2006: 208–211; Bakourou 2009: 307–310.

262　*Maria Papadaki*

35　Stubbs 1867: vol. II, 199; see also Davis 1998: 215–216.
36　Zangger, et al. 1997: 594–595.
37　See Angold 1984: 19–33; Laiou 2002, esp. 736–756; Armstrong 2009: 319–320; Athanassopoulos 1993, esp. 112–114; Athanassopoulos 2010: 261–262.
38　Harvey 1989: 217, 223; Armstrong 2009. The shipping of Peloponnesian oil by Venetians had presumably been started in the 11th century, see Jacoby 2009: 379.
39　See Jacoby 2013: 234–235.
40　See Lambropoulou 1989; Bouras 2002: 514; Laiou 2002: 730–732 and 754–756.
41　Lampsides 1982: 138, l.6 and 212, l.13–14.
42　Harvey 2008: 330.
43　Other agricultural products include silk and cereals. See Papadaki 2014, esp. 84–89 with all bibliographic references. For the trade systems functioned in the Middle Byzantine Peloponnese, see Gerolymatou 2008: 61–170 and Laiou 2012, esp. 138–146.
44　See also Athanassopoulos 1993, esp. 112–114; Armstrong 2009, esp. 319; Athanassopoulos 2010: 261.
45　For an overview of the developments in the Middle Byzantine Greek countryside, see Bintliff 2012: 391–394. For the economic expansion in the period, see Harvey 1989.

References

Adanir, F. (2006), 'Semi-autonomous provincial forces in the Balkans and Anatolia', in S. Faroqhi, ed., *The Cambridge History of Turkey*, Cambridge: vol. 3, 157–185.

Angold, M. (1984), *The Byzantine Empire 1025–1204. A Political History*. London.

Armstrong, P. (2009), 'Merchants of Venice at Sparta in the 12th century', in W. Cavanagh, C. Gallou, and M. Georgiadis, eds., *Sparta and Laconia: From Prehistory to Pre-modern*, London: 313–321.

Athanassopoulos, E.-F. (1993), *Intensive Survey and Medieval Rural Settlement: the Case of Nemea*, Unpublished PhD dissertation. University of Pennsylvania.

Athanassopoulos, E.-F. (2010), 'Landscape archaeology and the medieval countryside: Settlement and abandonment in the Nemea Region', *International Journal of Historical Archaeology* 14/2: 255–270.

Avramea, A. (1997), *Le Péloponnèse du IVe au VIIIe siècle. Changements et persistances*. Paris.

Bakourou, A. (2009), 'Topographikes paratereseis gia te Mesovyzantine Lakedaemonia' [Topographical observations on the Middle Byzantine Lakedaimon], in W. Cavanagh, C. Gallou, and M. Georgiadis, eds., *Sparta and Laconia: From Prehistory to Pre-modern*, London: 301–311.

Bandy, A. (2000), '*Nikon Metanoeite*: *Testament* of Nikon the Metanoeite for the Church and Monastery of the Savior, the Mother of God, and St. Kyriake in Lakedaimon', in J. Thomas and A. Constantinides-Hero eds., *Byzantine Monastic Foundation Documents: A Complete Translation of the Surviving Founders' Typika and Testaments*. Washington, D.C.: vol. 1, 313–322.

Bintliff, J.L. (2012), *The Complete Archaeology of Greece. From Hunter-Gatherers to the 20th Century A.D.* Chichester.

Bouras, Ch. (2002), 'Aspects of the Byzantine city, eighth-fifteenth centuries', in A. Laiou, ed., *The Economic History of Byzantium from the Seventh through the Fifteenth Century*, Washington, D.C.: vol. 2, 497–554.

Caraher, W.R. (2003), *Church, Society and the Sacred in Early Christian Greece*, Unpublished PhD thesis. Ohio State University.

Davis, J., ed. (1998), *Sandy Pylos: An Archaeological History from Nestor to Navarino*. Austin, TX.

Drandakes, N. (1982), 'Dyo epigraphes naon tes Laconias· tou Michael Archaggelou (1278) ston Polemita tes Manes kai tes Chysaphitissas (1290)' [Two inscriptions of churches in Laconia; of Michael Archaggelos (1278) in Polemitas in Mani and of Chyssafitissa (1290)], *Lakonikai Spoudai* 6: 44–61.

Dunn, A. (1995), 'Historical and archaeological indicators of economic change in Middle Byzantine Boeotia and their problems', *Epeteris Hetaireias Boiotikon Meleton* [Annual of the Society of Boeotian Studies] 2/2: 755–774.

Feissel, D., and Philippidis-Braat, A. (1985), 'Inventaires en vue d'un recueil des inscriptions historiques de Byzance. III. Inscriptions du Péloponnèse (à l'exception de Mistra)', *TM* 9: 267–395.

Gerolymatou, M. (2008), *Agores, emporoi kai emporio sto Vyzantio (9os–12os αι.)* [Markets, merchants and trade in Byzantium (9th–12th c.)]. Athens.

Gerstel, E. (2005), 'The Byzantine village church: Observations on its location and on agricultural aspects of its program', in J. Lefort, C. Morrisson and J.-P. Sodini, eds., *Les villages dans l'Empire byzantine (IVe-XVe siècle)*. Paris: 165–178.

Gregory, T. (2005), *A history of Byzantium*. Malden, MA/Oxford.

Gregory, T. (2009), 'Ceramics, metadata, and expectations: The problems of synthetic interpretation of survey data for medieval Greece', in J. Bintliff and H. Stöger, eds., *Medieval and Post-Medieval Greece: The Corfu Papers*, Oxford: 79–88.

Hahn, M. (1996), '"The Berbati-Limnes Project, the Early Byzantine to Modern Periods", in B. Wells and C. Runnels', *The Berbati-Limnes Archaeological Survey 1988–1990*, Stockholm: 345–451.

Harvey, A. (1989), *Economic Expansion in the Byzantine Empire 900–1200*. Cambridge.

Harvey, A. (2008), 'The village', in E. Jeffreys, J. Haldon and R. Cormack, eds., *The Oxford Handbook of Byzantine Studies*, Oxford: 328–333.

Higgins, M.D., and Higgins, R. (1996), *A Geological Companion to Greece and the Aegean*. New York.

Jacoby, D. (2009), 'Venetian commercial expansion in the eastern Mediterranean, 8th–11th centuries', in M. Mango, ed., *Byzantine Trade, 4th–12th Centuries: the Archaeology of Local, Regional and International Exchange*, Aldershot: 371–392.

Jacoby, D. (2013), 'Rural exploitation and market economy in the Late Medieval Peloponnese', in S. Gerstel, ed., *Viewing the Morea: Land and People in the Late Medieval Peloponnese*, Washington, D. C.: 213–275.

Kalopissi-Verti, S. (1992), *Dedicatory Inscriptions and Donor Portraits in Thirteenth Century Churches of Greece*. Vienna.

Laiou, A. (2002), 'Exchange and trade, seventh to twelfth centuries', in A. Laiou, ed., *The Economic History of Byzantium from the Seventh through the Fifteenth Century*, Washington, D.C.: vol. 2, 697–759.

Laiou, A. (2005), 'The Byzantine village (5th–14th century)', in J. Lefort, C. Morrisson and J.-P. Sodini, eds., *Les villages dans l'Empire byzantine (IVe-XVe siècle)*, Paris: 31–54.

Laiou A. (2012), 'Regional networks in the Balkans in the Middle and Late Byzantine Periods', in C. Morrisson, ed., *Trade and Markets in Byzantium*, Washington, D.C.: 125–146.

Laiou, A., and Morrisson, C. (2007), *The Byzantine Economy*. Cambridge.

264 *Maria Papadaki*

Lambropoulou, A. (1989), 'Oi panegyreis sten Peloponneso kata te mesaionike epoche' [Fairs in the Peloponnese in medieval times] in Ch. Angelidi, ed., *He kathemerine zoe sto Vyzantio*, [Everyday life in Byzantium], Athens: 291–310.

Lampsides, O. (1982), *Ho ek Pontou Hosios Nikon ho Metanoeite* [Hosios Nikon *You Should Repent* from Pontus]. Athens.

Mexes, D. (1977), *He Mane kai hoi Maniates: themata gia ten istoria toys, te laographia kai ten techne* [Mani and the Maniots: themes in history, folklore and art]. Athens.

Mexia, A. (2006), 'Elaiokomia ste Vyzantine Lakedaimona: peges kai archaiologika tekmeria' [Olive culture in Byzantine Lacedaemon: sources and archaeological evidence], *Lakonikai Spoudai* 18: 205–223.

Moravcsik, G., ed., and Jenkins, R.J.H., tr. (1967), *Constantine Porphyrogenitus De administrando imperio*. Washington, D.C.

Ousterhout, R. (2005), *A Byzantine Settlement in Cappadocia*. Washington D.C.

Papadaki, M. (2013), 'Exploring ecclesiastical landscapes: Holy men in the Peloponnese during the Middle Byzantine period and their role in the formation of religious landscapes in the region', in M. Lau, C. Franchi and M. Di Rodi, eds., *Landscapes of Power: Selected Papers from the XV Oxford University Byzantine Society International Graduate Conference*, Oxford: 143–158.

Papadaki, M. (2014), *The Peloponnese in Middle Byzantine Times: Archaeology and Topography of Rural Landscapes*, unpublished PhD thesis. King's College London.

Sanders, G.D.R. (2004), 'Problems in interpreting rural and urban settlement in Southern Greece, AD 365–700', in N. Christie, ed., *Landscapes of Change, Rural Evolutions in Late Antiquity and the Early Middle Ages*, Aldershot: 163–193.

Sullivan, D. (1987), *The Life of Saint Nikon, Text, Translation and Commentary*. Brookline, Mass.

Sweetman, R. (2010), 'The Christianization of the Peloponnese: The topography and function of Late Antique Churches', *Journal of Late Antiquity* 3: 203–261.

Stubbs, W. (1867), *Gesta Regis Henrici Secundi Benedicti Abbatis. The Chronicle of the Reigns of Henry II and Richard I, AD 1169–1192. Known Commonly under the Name of Benedict of Peterborough*, 2 vols. London.

Vasilikopoulou, A. (1987–1988), 'He ekklesiastike organose tes Peloponnesou ste Vyzantine epoche' ['The ecclesiastical organisation in the Peloponnese during the Byzantine period'], *Peloponnesiaka, Parartema* 13/2: 193–207.

Yannopoulos, P. (1993), 'Métropoles du Péloponnèse mésobyzantin: un souvenir des invasions avaro-slaves', *Byzantion* 63: 388–400.

Wharton-Epstein, A. (1980), 'Middle Byzantine Churches of Kastoria: Dates and implications', *The Art Bulletin* 62/2: 190–207.

Zangger, E., Timpson, M.E., Yazvenko, S.B., Kuhnke, F., and Kanuss, J. (1997), 'The Pylos regional archaeological project: Part II: Landscape evolution and site preservation', *Hesperia* 66/4: 549–641.

16 Hermits, Monks, and Nuns on Chalke, a Small Island of the Dodecanese from Early Christian to Middle Byzantine Times

Maria Z. Sigala

Chalke belongs to the Dodecanese group of islands, which spreads north to south along the coast of Asia Minor, and more specifically along ancient Caria and Lycia. It is small, barren, and mountainous, with rugged coasts and lots of caves, an environment suitable for asceticism.

There are no monks or nuns on the island today. There is an area though called *Kellia* (Cells), recalling, mainly, Kellia in the western borders of Nile Delta in Egypt, where monasticism flourished between the 4th and 8th centuries.[1] There is a cave known as *Ascetario sta Kellia* (*ascetarion*, hermitage);[2] there is a ravine called *Dyrokelli* or *Dyokelli* (Two Cells), which 'took its name from two cells in the district' and a cave known as *t' Ascete e trypa* (the Ascetic's Hole or Cave) in the same area.[3] More importantly, there is a dedicatory inscription in a painted chapel, dated 1367, mentioning two nuns amongst its donors (*Agnese* and *Magdalene*).[4] There are also churches and chapels known as *monasteria* (monasteries), some of which, like *Palarniotis stou Ai Nofri to Vouno* or *Taxiarchis Michael o Panormitis,* have their own property, as monasteries usually do; and there are laymen, who take care of them, still called *kalogeroi* (monks). In the 19th century, there were at times and at some *monasteries rassophoroi kalogeroi*, that is, real monks, dressed in monastic habits.[5] I gathered and confirmed all this scattered and indirect information about monasticism on Chalke a few years ago in my doctoral thesis, in which all the monuments of the Christian era on the island are studied: castles, churches, hermitages, cells, and even medieval huts, locally called *kyphes*.[6]

First I proved that Kellia (Figure 16.1), a little bay on the barren inaccessible north-eastern coast of Chalke, like the place Kellia in Egypt and others elsewhere, such as Cyprus and Greece,[7] was used as a place for seclusion by hermits at least from the mid-6th till the 8th century AD.[8] The place is approachable mainly by boat, when the sea is entirely calm (Figure 16.2). In the innermost recess of the bay, just above sea level, there is a shallow cave which was used as a hermitage (the *Ascetario sta Kellia*). In a cavity at the back of this cave are some quite well-preserved wall paintings (Figure 16.3) depicting the young Christ Emmanuel among the Archangels

DOI: 10.4324/9781003429470-20

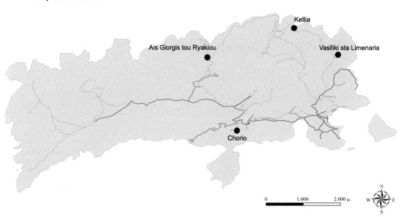

Figure 16.1 Map of Chalke.

Michael and Gabriel and martyrs, two at each side of him, one of whom, the young St Kerykos, is offering a wreath.[9] The presentation is enclosed by a garland of flowers and leaves. Meticulous analysis of all the iconographic and stylistic details of the scene, in a detailed publication on Kellia, led me to date the wall paintings from as early as the mid-6th to the early 7th century AD.[10] The subject, young Christ between angels and martyrs who very often offer him their gifts, mainly wreaths and gospels, as here, is popular in Early Christian apses, like St Vitale's in Ravenna (540–547) and Euphrasian Basilica in Porec, Croatia (c. 550),[11] but altogether absent after the 7th century.[12] The iconographic and the stylistic details, such as the depiction of Christ as young and beardless with the epithet Emmanuel, the offering of wreaths, the depiction of St Faust or Faustinus, unknown later amongst the Orthodox Byzantine saints, the type of sandal Faustinus is wearing, the depiction of a garland framing the scene (Figure 16.4)[13] and Christ's monogram, that is, the cross with a Greek R (P) at the top of its vertical branch, at the beginning of each hagionym, plus many more details, supported the above date. This date, consequently, provides *a terminus ante quem* for the use of the cave as a hermitage.

At the entrance to this cave rises another hermitage 'cell' (Figure 16.5). It is a box-like building, bipartite, with a trapezoid ground plan and a flat roof at the same level as the floor of the cave.[14] Its northern very dark part has been arranged as a chapel. It has a small conch with a built altar and wall paintings in two layers. From the second layer, a fine head of St Andrew survives (Figure 16.6), which recalls the depiction of St Andrew in Santa Maria Antiqua in Rome and can be dated to the early 8th century.[15] Its southern part, which looks like a corridor, gave access to a now collapsed space excavated in the cliff, which most probably housed another cell or cells. High on

Figure 16.2 Kellia: the cave and the box-like cell in front of it.

the rock, before the entrance to the cave, there is a painted head of a saint, probably belonging to a cell that has collapsed.

Even if there was an isolated hermitage, the cave, the *Ascetario*, at the very beginning, in the 6th century or even earlier, there developed a small community of hermits later on, with at least three cells, which gave the place its

268 *Maria Z. Sigala*

Figure 16.3 Kellia: the Early Christian wall paintings in a cavity of the cave.

Figure 16.4 Kellia: detail of the garland which frames the scene.

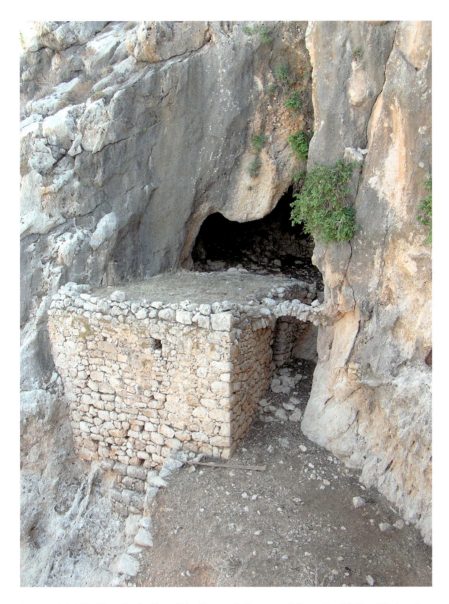

Figure 16.5 Kellia: the built cell in front of the cave (photo by Neilos Pitsinos).

name: *Kellia*. The cave and the surviving cell can provide room for more than one monk or nun. Foundations of two walls inside the cave prove that it was divided into at least three sections, probably the one with the wall paintings serving as a prayer chapel, the other as a refectory and the third, maybe, as a dwelling, at a certain period. The complex is completed by a cistern, a steep

Figure 16.6 Kellia: the head of Saint Andrew in the second layer of wall paintings in the built cell.

path leading up the rock in which the cave opens and a tomb on the right of the cave, near its entrance, which shows that at least some of the monks, or perhaps the first ascetic who occupied the cave, were buried there. There are many known cases of hermitages which eventually became the focus of a monastic community, like Great Laura of St Sabas in Palestine[16] and the Enkleistra of St Neophytos on Cyprus.[17] In the Aegean, there are a few caves around which monastic settlements developed, and which, to my opinion,

Hermits, Monks, and Nuns on Chalke   271

must have served as hermitages at first, like Panagia i Kaloritsa on Naxos and Panagia i Chozoviotissa on Amorgos.[18]

But how were the hermits at Kellia of Chalke organised? Was it a group of independent cells in spite of the fact that they were close to each other? Did they create a kind of *koinobion*[19] at some stage? Where did the hermits attend service? Were the painted cells suitable for attending services or were they used only as prayer chapels (*proseukterioi oikoi*)? Their orientation is to the south for the cave and north for the cell. Thus, was a proper church needed for services?

There is a small possibility, though, that the function of this community was connected with an early Christian basilica, the *Vasilike sta Limenaria* or *ston Peukia*, the ruins of which are visible not very far away from Kellia, to its southeast (Figure 16.1).[20] The place, a flat space surrounded by hills and rocks, closer to Kellia than Emporeios, the main town and port at the time and also nowadays, seems suitable for a monastery. If that was the case,[21] then the hermits living in Kellia could be dependent from it. Or else, the basilica could have served as a *Kyriakos naos* (Sunday church) of a *lavra*,[22] that is for hermits living in nearby Kellia and perhaps in hermitage caves not yet spotted all around. South of the basilica there is a cistern.

The role played by another Early Christian basilica, west of Kellia, on the same rugged northern coast of Chalki, is more certain. Ruins and remnants of it can be discerned around and inside *Aghios Georgios tou Ryakiou* (St George of the Rivulet), an 18th-century chapel built on top of the Early Christian basilica.[23] This cannot have been anything other than a monastic church. Tradition has it that a real monk, a *rassophoros kalogeros*, lived there in the 19th century. The sanctity of the place, the devotion the locals feel for it up till today, the fact that it is a sort of pilgrimage for them, is, for us, among the criteria – used for Chalke at least – to classify a chapel as monastic.[24] But the best criterion of all is its location. It is in a most inaccessible spot, in a gorge, far away from every inhabited area on the island, not too far away from the sea but not too close to it either. It seems like the ideal place for isolation and spiritual occupation. Quite near, there is the cave known as *t' Askiti i Tripa*, the 'Hermit's Hole', and the ravine known as *Dyokelli* or *Dyrokelli*, that is, 'Two Cells', which makes one wonder if this was the Sunday church for hermits living in caves around about and attending services there, thus being organised in a kind of *lavra*. The only other visible facility the place could provide to hermits is a cistern in the yard of the church.

So Chalke opens up the question about hermits on the Greek islands and especially on the Dodecanese Islands in the Early Christian Period, perhaps even before the establishment of monks on the neighbouring Latros or Latmos Mountain in Asia Minor (7th century).[25] There is almost nothing known apart from the archaeological data derived from the study of the monuments of Chalke about hermits in the Dodecanese. We know only that in 401 AD, in Rhodes, a monk called Prokopios had his hermitage by the sea, which recalls the case of the *Ascetario sta Kellia* on Chalke.[26] However, the archaeological evidence is there waiting for interpretation. Apart from the evidence Chalke provides, there are plenty of small basilicas, for example on the tiny islets of Aghia Kyriake, Aghios Andreas, Nera, and Sari around the island of Kalymnos, which should be seen rather as being monastic churches than having any other use. Islets have often and in various places been preferred for reclusion by hermits and monks.[27] There is a place on Telos island, facing Chalke, named *Ascetario*, which could very well have been an *ascetarion* of the Early Christian Period, like the homonym *Ascetario sta Kellia* on Chalke. There are a few cave monasteries and chapels on various islands of the Dodecanese (Patmos, Nisyros) which likewise could have been initially cave hermitages of the Early Christian Era. The case of Chalke has turned it into a very strong possibility.

It is not certain when these 'communities of hermits' on Chalke declined or were abandoned. All that is certain is that later monuments dating between the 8th and 12th centuries, whether they belong to rural settlements or monastic establishments, are not near the coasts anymore. As a rule, they appear in the interior of the island, invisible from the coasts and even from the nearby islands and the open sea.[28] In fact it seems that from the Middle Byzantine period onwards hermits and monks preferred the mountainous area around the now abandoned late medieval, post-Byzantine village of Chorio as a place for their retreat (Figure 16.1, 16.7). Mountains and grounds

Figure 16.7 The mountainous area of Chorio in the interior of Chalke (aerial photograph by P. Matsouka).

difficult of access were, in fact, as a rule, preferred by Byzantines for their monasteries.[29]

On the hill crest east of the medieval castle of Chalke, in a very rocky spot, there is a little anonymous cross-shaped chapel, discovered a few years ago, with traces of wall paintings. Its dimensions, its location – almost completely inaccessible – and its plan (cross-shaped chapels were especially favoured by monks) make it appropriate for monastic use. It could either be a cross-shaped prayer chapel (a hermitage, a *proseukterios oikos*), used both for living and praying, as, for example, on Athos, where ascetics in the 9th century built, amongst others, chapels in which they stayed on their own or in groups,[30] or a church for services used by hermits dispersed round about.[31]

The other Middle Byzantine chapel which we think is monastic is that of *Ais Andrias* (St Andrew) *stou Ai Andria to Vouno* (Figure 16.8), on the peak of the low hill just opposite the castle and Chorio. The spot is again rocky and inaccessible, inappropriate for any other use. The chapel is decorated with wall paintings in two layers, the second of which has been dated to the 11th century, giving thus a *terminus ante quem* for the building and the first layer of wall paintings.[32] Two arcosolia were added on its southern external side. Very near the chapel, to its south and southwest, there are two *kyphes*, huts built of rocks, which are dated to the same period. Thus, it seems that here we have a small monastic habitation, a kind of *kathisma*,[33] consisting of a chapel and two *kyphes* (cells). Another church which seems to belong to a monastic

Figure 16.8 Ais Adrias stou Ai Adria to Vouno.

274   *Maria Z. Sigala*

establishment is *Ais Elias* (mid-7th to mid-9th century) on Prophet Elijah's Mountain with four little *kyphes* dispersed around which could also have served as cells.[34]

This kind of asceticism, that is chapel-hermitages, and monasticism organised in small monastic establishments, consisting of a chapel, a few *kyphes*[35] and cisterns, was continued in the Late Byzantine period and never developed into more organised monasteries with walls all around, towers, refectories, and libraries, the typical Byzantine monastery.

Thus, the archaeological and art-historical data have proved that asceticism and monasticism were an important part of the social and spiritual life of Chalke, as they were everywhere else in the Byzantine Empire in the Early Christian[36] and Middle Byzantine Periods, when 'the monk as a living being was a vital element of the Byzantine Society and the monastery a characteristic feature of the Byzantine landscape'.[37]

But monks and nuns adjusted to the poor conditions they found on the island, living in caves and later in huts (*kyphes*), the typical housing for the locals, even when elsewhere, including the neighbouring islands (Rhodos,[38] Kos, Telos, Nisyros, Patmos[39]), monasteries were rich and influential, and at least better housed than the average people. The example of Skellig Michael in Ireland, where also huts, similar to *kyphes*, served as cells proves that Chalke is not the only exception.[40]

Notes

1 Kasser 1967: 7.
2 Sigala 2009.
3 Skandalidis 1982: 43, 51.
4 Sigala 2000: 333.
5 Iliadis 1950: 313, 318–319.
6 Sigala 2011: 351–371; Sigala 2018: 359–360.
7 Stylianou and Stylianou 1997: 433; Gouloulis 1992: 473–498.
8 Sigala 2009: 157. For the various uses of the term *kellion*, see *ODB* 2, 1120. In the Early Christian Period *kellion* referred to hermitages, whilst later on to cells in a monastery (Sigala 2009: 150–151).
9 On Christ's right hand-side, there survive the archangel Michael, saint Faustus or Faustinus and the young saint Kerykos. On Christ's left-hand side, only the name of the archangel Gabriel and part of his wings, together with the haloes of two more saints survive.
10 Sigala 2009: 152–156.
11 Volbach 1958: fig. 158; Ihm 1960: 167–168, pl. XV.2.
12 Sigala 2009: 152.
13 Garlands are very common from the 4th to the 7th century AD, as frames of scenes, portraits, and crosses, and as decorative motifs in intrados. In fact, they are so common that it has even been argued that their disappearance after the 7th century signals the passage from the Early Christian to the Middle Byzantine Era (Sigala 2009: 155; Marki 2005).
14 Sigala 2009: 153, plan 4.
15 Nordhagen 1968: 5, 15, 18, 107, 108, pl. VI, pl. IX.
16 Patrich 1995: 84.

Hermits, Monks, and Nuns on Chalke 275

17 Mango and Hawkins 1966: 123–129.
18 Kaloritsa with many layers of wall paintings, the first of which dates either to the 7th or 9th century (Panayiotidi 1974; Chatzidakis 1989: 11; Panayotidi 1994) is a large cave with quite a few chapels in it, a refectory at the entrance to the cave and post-Byzantine buildings outside the cave which belonged to a 17th c. monastery. It is in an inaccessible place, on a mountain, and since we know there were quite a few basilicas on the island at the time of its first decoration, it seems natural to me that it would have served as a reclusion place for hermits rather than as a church when it was first decorated. Chozoviotissa is literally hanging on a cliff (Marangou 2005: 18–26). Tradition has it that it was built by Alexius I Comnenus in 1088. It would be absurd, though, to build a monastery there, unless there were already hermits around, in the caves of the mountain, some of which have been included in the monastic complex.
19 *ODB*: 2, 1136.
20 Sigala 2011: part 2, 77–78; part 3, map 4, X14.
21 The reasons that made me consider this basilica as a monastic church are (a) its position far away from any known, or identified from any archaeological remains, 'village'; (b) the need of the hermits at Kellia of a church for the Sunday service and the vicinity of this church with Kellia; (c) the fact that overall the northern part of the island seems to have housed hermits and monks in the Early Christian period.
22 *Lavra* is a group of dispersed monastic cells associated with a central complex, whereas a *koinobion* is a monastery housing a community of monks or nuns (*ODB* 2: 1190, 1136).
23 Sigala 2011: part 2, 89–90; part 3, map 4, X43.
24 There are more than 50 medieval chapels on the small island of Chalke (32 square kilometres), the majority of them still standing and a few in ruins. The locals know the names of most of them, but still venerate very few, having services there on the day the saints, to which the chapels are dedicated, are celebrated, or visiting them as a 'pilgrimage', to light the candles and the lamps and burn incense. During my long-term study of the island, I noticed that the venerated chapels are never related to any agricultural hamlets or shepherds' settlements. Moreover, they have property of their own, which the 'parish' chapels haven't. In the 19th century, in some of these cases, a new chapel was built next to the medieval one, as if to renovate the veneration, and, according to written tradition, monks lived in them. The above I have considered amongst the criteria I used to attribute to a chapel on Chalke monastic use (Sigala 2011: part 1, 251–271).
25 Vocotopoulos 1966/67: 75.
26 Evangelides 1929: 148.
27 See Bourke, Hayden and Lynch 2011, and St Nicholas islet off the west coast of Rhodes (Papavassiliou 2014).
28 Sigala 2011: 225, 229.
29 Charanis 1971: 64; Vocotopoulos 1966/7: 14.
30 Ktenas 1929: 235.
31 One cannot tell at the moment if the chapel had a screen or not because of the debris inside. If there was a screen, then it was most likely a church, a kind of *kyriakos* naos. If there was no screen, then it was probably a chapel-shaped cell. The fact that it is anonymous today and the locals did not even know it existed, leads me to accept the latter possibility, since, as it was mentioned above, the locals still remember the names of the chapels. So, most probably, this mustn't have been a chapel at all.
32 Katsioti 2002: 115.
33 Kathisma is a small monastic habitation, dependent on a larger monastery (*ODB* 2: 1116).

276   *Maria Z. Sigala*

34 Sigala 2011: part 1, 356–357; part 2, 27.
35 Monastic establishments housing only a few monks were commonplace in Byzantium (Thomas, Constantinides Hero 1998: xvi).
36 In the 7th century, monasticism had already existed for over three hundred years in the Eastern Mediterranean (Thomas, Hero 1998: 21).
37 Charanis 1971: 63, 84.
38 Acheimastou-Potamianou 2006.
39 Kominis 1988.
40 Bourke, Hayden and Lynch 2011.

References

Acheimastou-Potamianou, M. (2006), *At Thari on Rhodes. The Church and the Wall-paintings in the Monastery of the Archangel Michael* [in Greek with an extended English Summary]. Athens.

Bourke, E., Hayden, A.R., and Lynch, A. (2011), *Skellig Michael, Co. Kerry: The Monastery and South Peak Archaeological Stratigraphic Report: Excavations 1986–2010.* Ireland.

Charanis, P. (1971), 'The monk as an element of Byzantine society', *DOP* 25: 61–84.

Chatzidakis, M. (1989), *Naxos. Bizantini texni stin Ellada. Psiphidota-tixografies* [Naxos. Byzantine Art in Greece. Mosaics-wall paintings]. Athens: 9–16.

Evangelides, Tr.E. (1929), 'Ekklesia Rodou' ['Church of Rhodes'], *EEBS* 6: 145–179.

Gouloulis, St. (1992), 'Oros ton Kellion'. Symvoli topografiki gia tin arhaia Thessalia. *Diethnes Synedrio gia tin arhaia Thessalia sti mnimi tou D. R. Theochari* ['Mountain of Cells']. Topographic and historical contribution, *International Congress about ancient Thessaly in the memory of D. R. Theocharis*. Athens: 473–498.

Iliadis, K. (1950), *I Halki tis Dodekanisou (istoria-laographia-ithi kai ethima), tomos protos* [Chalke in Dodecanese (history-folklore-morals and customs)], vol. 1. Athens.

Ihm, Ch. (1960), *Die Programme der christlichen Apsismalerei von vierten Jahrhundert bis zur Mitte des achten Jahrhunderts.* Wiesbaden.

Kasser, R. (1967), *KELLIA 1965*, v. I. Geneva.

Katsioti, A. (2002), 'I paleoteres toihografies tou Agiou Georgiou tou Plakotou sti Malona tis Rodou. Paratirisis stin texni tou 11ou eona sta Dodekanesa' ['The earlier wall-paintings in the church of St. George at Plakoto, Malona on Rhodes. Remarks on 11th c. art in the Dodecanese'] [in Greek with a brief English Summary], *DChAE* 23: 105–120.

Ktenas, Chr. (1929), 'O Protos tou Agiou Orous Atho kai i "Megali Mesi" i "Synaxis"' ['The first of the Holy Mountain Athos and the "Grand Mesi" or "Synaxis"'], *EEBS* 6: 233–281.

Kominis, A. D. (1988), *I thisavri tis Monis Patmou* [*The Treasures of the Monastery of Patmos*]. Athens.

Mango, C., and Hawkins, E.J.W. (1966), 'The Hermitage of St. Neophytos and its Wall Paintings', *DOP* 20: 119–206.

Marangou, L. (2005), *The Monastery of Panayia Khozoviotissa, Amorgos.* Athens.

Marki, E. (2005), 'I apikonisi ton oporon stin paleochristianiki tehni. I periptosi tis Thessalonikis' ['Presentations of fruits in Early Christian art. The case of Thessaloniki'], *DChAE* 26: 85–92.

Nordhagen, J. (1968), The Frescoes of John VII (A.D. 705–707) in S. Maria Antiqua in Rome, *Acta ad Archaeologiam et Artium Historiam pertinentia* 3. Rome.

Panayotidi, M. (1974), 'L'église rupestre de la Nativité dans l'île de Naxos', *Cahiers Archéologiques* 23: 107–120.

Panayotidi, M. (1994), 'I ekklesia tis Gennesis sto Monastiri tis Panagias Kaloritissas sti Naxo. Phasis toihografisis', *Antifonon. Afieroma ston kathiyiti N. B. Drandaki* [The church of the Nativity in the Monastery of Panagia Kaloritissa on Naxos. Decoration phases', Antiphonon. Volume dedicated to professor N.B. Drandakis], Thessaloniki: 540–559.

Papavassiliou, E. (2014), 'I ekklessia-pyrgos tou Agiou Nikolaou sto omonymo nissaki tou horiou Arhagelos sti Rodo' ['The church-tower of St Nicholas on the homonym islet of the village Archagelos on Rhodes'], in P. Triantaphyllides, ed., *Sofia adolos, Timetikos tomos gia ton Ioanni Papahristodoulou*, [Sofia adolos. Volume dedicated to Ioannis Papachistodoulou], Rhodes: 369–390.

Patrich, J. (1995), *Sabas, Leader of Palestinian Monasticism. A comparative Study in Eastern Monasticism, Fourth to Seventh Centuries*, Dumbarton Oaks Studies XXXII, Washington, D.C.

Sigala, M. Z. (2000), 'I Panaghia i Odegetria i Enniameritissa sti Halki tis Dodecanesou (1367)' ['Virgin Mary Hodegetria or Enniameritissa on Chalke in the Dodecanese'], *ArchDelt* 55: 333–334.

Sigala, M. Z. (2009), 'Ta Kellia tis Halkis Dodecanesou. I hronologese ton toihografion kai i semasia tous' ['Kellia on Ckalke in the Dodecanese. The Date of their Wall-Paintings and their Significance'] [In Greek with a brief English summary], *DChAE* 30: 149–158.

Sigala, M. Z. (2011), *I Halki apo tin palaiohriastianiki epohi mehri kai to telos tis periodou tis Ippotokratias (5os ai.-1523): mnemia, arhitectoniki, topografia, koinonia* [*Chalke from the Early Christian Period till the end of the Period of the Knights (5th c.-1523): Monuments, Architecture, Topography, Society*], unpublished doctoral thesis, Athens.

Sigala, M. Z. (2018), 'The use of the corbelling technique in the Aegean islands during the middle ages. Examples from the Cyclades and the Dodecanese' in J. Crow, and D. Hill eds., *Naxos and the Byzantine Aegean: Insular Responses to Regional Change*, Athens: 355–370.

Skandalidis, M.E. (1982), *To Tomonymiko tis Halkis Dodecanesou* [*The List of Place Names on Chalke in the Dodecanese*]. Rhodes.

Stylianou, A., and Stylianou, J. (1997), *The Painted Churches of Cyprus* (2nd ed.). Cyprus.

Thomas, J., and Hero, A.C. (1998), *Byzantine Monastic Foundation Documents*, vol. I. Washington, D.C.

Vocotopoulos, P. (1966/67), 'Latros' [in Greek], *EEBS*: 69–106.

Volbach, W. Fr. (1958), *Fruchristliche Kunst*. Munchen.

Part 5

The Bureaucrat, the Bishop, the Farmer, and the Merchant

17 Loving the Poor
Charity and Justice in Middle Byzantine Greece

Teresa Shawcross

In 1218, John Apokaukos, the metropolitan of Naupaktos, wrote to his suffragan George, the bishop of Vonitsa, lambasting him for his reluctance to distribute the produce of his see to those who needed sustenance. Apokaukos invoked the biblical example of the widow, who, in a time of drought and famine, had just enough for one last meal for herself and her child – yet, when asked, shared what she had. The bishop, by contrast, had hoarded substantial quantities of food. Of this, he relinquished to those in need only a storage jar that was practically empty. Apokaukos claimed that its remarkably light heft was immediately noticeable to him when he picked it up, while not even a thin trickle of oil came forth when he tipped it over to pour out its contents. Pressing his eye to its mouth, he could discern only the faintest hint of oil at the bottom. He recalled a popular ditty describing a mouse's ingenuity in extracting oil from a narrow-necked jar: 'There is no room for its snout-o / Nor any room for its paw-o, / But room there is to let down its tail-o, / Which, turning around, it then licks!' He commented bitterly that, had the mouse sought to let its tail down into this particular jar, there would not have been enough oil inside to grease even the tip – even had the tail been of prodigious length and flexibility! The conduct of another George, the suffragan of Chimara, had not proven any better, for that bishop reluctantly provided a crust or two of bread, but no oil – let alone any meats.[1] Such sequestering of resources had grave consequences: when inclement weather and a bad local harvest were compounded by crushing imperial taxation, food stocks dwindled and the parishioners of the archdiocese of Naupaktos were condemned to starvation.[2]

Incensed though he was with his fellow prelates for withholding aid, Apokaukos reserved his full ire for the future emperor, Theodore Komnenos, whose policies he blamed for the predicament in which Naupaktos found itself. He explained that the inhabitants could at most collect together 180 gold coins, a sum far short of the 1000 that the fisc demanded. To try to make up the shortfall, Apokaukos had been compelled to lay hands on church plate, silk vestments, and clerical mounts. He reminded Komnenos that the holy church had a mission to alleviate poverty, and that for this reason its land and revenue were referred to as 'of the poor' (*ptochika*). A secular lord

DOI: 10.4324/9781003429470-22

who forced a bishop to use ecclesiastical property for other purposes was guilty of sacrilege. 'My indignation knows no bounds when I see the poor who are entrusted to the church being tormented, plundered, and forced to flee for the sake of gold', Apokaukos continued, warning that, if his words were not heeded, 'the Lord of vengeance, Who does not forget the poor, shall give His verdict', smiting those 'who wrong the poor'.[3] He underscored his point by sending a 'poor man' to demand of Komnenos' treasurer that the ruler stump up the requisite aid since the needs of the destitute could no longer be met using the church's resources.[4]

By the 11th century, the economy of the Byzantine Empire had begun to be radically transformed as a result of the integration of the Mediterranean within expanding global networks of trade. Shifts in production, distribution, and finance – together with increased urbanisation and the migration of rural populations – created unprecedented opportunity for the accumulation of private wealth.[5] But these shifts also destabilised the traditional structures of society, resulting in a rise in the numbers of those who were unable to earn a living wage as craftsmen or day labourers – and the creation of new categories of the needy, destitute, and disenfranchised.[6] To this problem were added imperial policies intended to increase fiscal revenue from the provinces. Supplementary taxes, introduced to pay for the defence of the state and its institutions from the armies of Frankish and Turkic expansion, were directed against the lay fortunes recently built on manufacturing and trade. But provincials acquiring and managing these fortunes had no desire to fund conflicts that did more to disrupt that to protect mercantile initiatives. They found ways to hide their money. This meant that the fiscal burden fell disproportionately on those – such as agricultural workers – whose less innovative endeavours remained visible to tax collectors.[7]

Into this crisis stepped the figure of the bishop stretching out his hands to unite rich and poor within a system of philanthropic patronage. The idea that relieving the suffering of the indigent, weak, and defenceless was among bishops' paramount duties was not, of course, new. Indeed, its lineage could be traced back to the early church.[8] Nonetheless, the second half of the 12th and early 13th centuries saw a dramatic surge of references, in churchmen's writings and speeches, to the distribution of charity. Such references were increasingly accompanied by an emphasis on the role of the bishop's court in hearing disputes and providing justice. The promotion of the episcopate as the main source not only of almsgiving but also of law was a feature primarily of the Balkans. The interior of Asia Minor had been largely lost to invasion, while even the situation on the coast was precarious. Consequently, Anatolian bishops were often titular, residing in the capital. In contrast to their colleagues from the eastern imperial provinces, the ecclesiastical hierarchy of the western imperial provinces underwent substantial reorganisation, resulting in greater dynamism and adaptability.[9] A young friend of Apokaukos', Euthymios Tornikios – whose family had established a base for itself in the province of Hellas and the Peloponnese, settling in Thebes, Evripos, Athens, and Corinth – in many ways represented the ultimate ecclesiastical product of this process.

Tornikios' great-great-grandfather was Theophylact Hephaistos, who had held the position of autocephalous archbishop to the Bulgarian church of Ochrid; his paternal and maternal uncles and brother had been appointed metropolitans of Ephesos, Neopatras (Ypati), and Palaiopatras (Patras) respectively. Trained for an episcopal career at the patriarchate and in the entourage of a prominent bishop, Tornikios allowed himself c. 1219 to be put forward for election. Many of the key works expressing the development of the episcopate's views of itself and its function in society owe their survival to this candidate's industriousness, as editor and copyist, in gathering together texts that might guide a newly minted bishop.[10]

Crucially, although bishops were educated in the imperial capital and were meant to be appointed by the emperor, episcopal interests did not coincide with those of the secular imperial administration. The emperor not only claimed for himself the role of *epistemonarches,* or expert theologian and disciplinarian of the church, but also encouraged the faithful to bypass ecclesiastics and address their concerns directly to him. For their part, bishops opposed restrictions to the authority of the ecclesiastical arm of the empire.[11] They were aware their status depended less on the dictates of the central regime than on their own ability to present themselves as the primary protectors of the local population. Over time, however, these populations too began to assert their own fierce sense of agency. As we shall see, the power of bishops in the provinces would end up being undermined by the emergence of modalities of giving and legal frameworks that fed a form of beneficence focused on civic ideals.[12]

Imperial claims

Let us trace these momentous changes in greater detail. In the late 11th and early 12th centuries, the ecclesiastical establishment had been wont to declare itself incapable of fighting the provincial poverty caused by the state's predatory activities.[13] The routine oppression of dioceses by tax collectors in the first half of the 12th century discouraged clerics from taking up or keeping episcopal appointments. The bishop of Amyklion in the Peloponnese resigned on account of 'the violence of the *praitor*'. Likewise, the autocephalous archbishop of the island of Cyprus 'was forced by a *praktor* to become a monk'.[14] Yet another cleric, when offered the see of Corinth, was so disconcerted by reports of the archdiocese's limited resources that he simply turned down the appointment. He was then offered the see of Ephesus instead, which he did take up, only to regret the decision almost immediately, writing to his friends back at the patriarchate to complain about the dilapidated state of his archdiocese and elicit their sympathy regarding the squalid conditions he encountered on a daily basis when trying to discharge his pastoral duties.[15]

One of the abdicating prelates, Nicholas Mouzalon, who had abandoned his sea in 1111, had written a highly dramatic poem about the circumstances that had led him to take such a desperate course of action. In the poem, Mouzalon had set out the anguished debate which he had had with himself before

284   *Teresa Shawcross*

reaching the decision to hand in his notice. He had explained that, although he had tried his best to look after his flock and be a 'shepherd' and 'good father' to it, conditions on the ground had rendered it impossible for him to do so. The 'tyranny' of heavy imperial taxation had ravaged Cyprus. Most local inhabitants had been deprived of their livelihood. The land was by its nature fertile and capable of producing an abundant harvest, but fiscal officials had seized all the products of the farmers' labour and were employing violence in order to try and extract still more. The state had not only flogged and hanged those who had been in arrears, but also forced their compatriots to stand surety for them and either contribute to the shortfall or face punishment in turn:

> – Are they all poor and destitute?
> – Many are in dire straits. – And why is that? Explain now!
> – Because of oppressive dues and levies.
> – What does the soil produce? – Every kind of produce!
> – Here, at least, is something good! – No, their woes are all the greater!
> – How can this be? – The fruits of the farmers' labour are all seized.
> – What a calamity! – And then further demands are made.
> – Alas! – Those who do not have the means to pay are tortured.
> – Woe! – They bind them by the hands and feet.
> – Woe is me! – And then they string them up and tear their flesh into ribbons [...]

> Many are killed through these acts of violence.
> – And if the money is still not forthcoming? – Then another man

> Has to make up the shortfall or suffer in turn [...]
> – Suffer what? – Hanging like the others.
> – Without being at fault? – It is what the administrators call 'providing securities'.

Cypriots had been able to find respite only 'under their tombstones'. Although the archbishop had told himself he ought to continue the fight on their behalf, he could bear it no longer. He had tried desperately to give 'money' to those who could not 'pay their taxes', but had come to the realisation he simply did not have sufficient funds available to make a perceptible difference. He had felt guilty for giving up, but had believed he had had no choice: a solution could not be found to his flock's predicament unless his archdiocese was provided with suitable support for its ministry.[16]

When tending his personal resignation, Mouzalon had proposed a remedy to the situation he and his peers had encountered. This was for the emperor to surrender to the church of a larger proportion than hitherto of provincial revenues, and to allow bishops to decide how these revenues should be used to benefit the population. Mouzalon's ideas appear to have gained traction, for they appeared with greater regularity in ecclesiastical correspondence and dominated the legal commentaries of the canonists, while he himself was eventually raised to the patriarchate.[17] Indeed, the early Komnenian emperors, Isaac I and Alexios I, had taken steps to regularise the income of the church by demanding compulsory payment to bishops of an annual tithe, known as the *kanonikon*. They had also determined the sums that bishops could collect in fees for ordinations, marriages, baptisms, and funerals, as well as in fines assessed for moral transgressions.[18] John II similarly had been keen to put the provincial ecclesiastical hierarchy of his empire on a sound financial footing, declaring his intention to ensure that the possessions of the holy church be spared 'all vexations and offences, and not suffer any harm'. John had sought to protect the episcopate during crises such as the death of a bishop by decreeing that it was forbidden to seize any wealth from the buildings and lands belonging to a metropolis, archbishopric or bishopric within a city. Any imperial officials or other lords (or their subordinates) who attempted to disobey these orders were to be required to pay heavy compensation.[19]

This liberality appears within decades to have increased the power of the provincial church to a degree that alarmed the imperial administration. Consequently, policy underwent another shift under John's youngest son, Manuel I. Although Manuel had begun by confirming and extending his predecessors' measures, he later proceeded to suspend the 'flow of munificence', indeed to force the 'flow backwards' so that it returned to him.[20]

Seeking to acquire ecclesiastical support for his reign, in 1143–1146 the newly crowned Manuel had made large donations in gold to the patriarchate and raised the income of its officers, as well as granted privileges to monasteries in the greater region of the capital and its hinterland, and to priests throughout the empire. In 1148, he had issued a chrysobull in which he had declared that the immovable property of all provincial churches would be maintained and indeed strengthened, with titles being confirmed and restitutions being made of land, installations, and labourers, even in cases where documentary proof of ownership was imprecise or faulty.[21] A flurry of benefactions had followed to episcopal sees in the western provinces that included Athens, Corfu, Croia (Krujë), Thebes, and Thessalonike. The imperial administration had drawn up inventories of current possessions and privileges, made further donations and granted tax exemptions, and issued up-to-date deeds and titles.[22] In 1153 and 1158, these earlier concessions had been extended, with emphasis being put on the renunciation by the fisc of all claims on land in ecclesiastical possession. Property was to remain in the hands of the church even when titles failed to fulfil the criteria of imperial laws and ordinances, or were absent altogether.[23] In a memorandum to an official, the emperor had gone so far as to declare that he permitted possession by bishops and abbots of otherwise unclaimed lands even where chrysobulls existed demonstrating that the land belonged to 'other notables or ... peasants, or ... imperial ministries and foundations'.[24] Moreover, in order to get around the disapproval of his chief minister of finance, Manuel had chosen not to work through the fiscal bureau, instead assigning to his private secretary, the *mystikos*, direct responsibility for dispensing payments to the church from the treasury.[25]

286   Teresa Shawcross

From the end of 1158, however, Manuel changed tack, issuing another chrysobull that revoked all earlier benefactions to the church. He insisted that the illegal possession of land by 'any church whatsoever' would no longer be sanctioned.[26] A number of test cases followed, such as that of the bishopric of Stagoi (Kalambaka), which had profited from a large grant by the emperor of land and peasants in 1148, but which was then forced to relinquish a portion of its possessions in 1163.[27] Moreover, through a later ordinance, dated to 1176, the emperor published his intention to revive 10th-century laws in favour of the 'poor' that explicitly restricted clerical and monastic fortunes, and set strict limits on the tax exemptions and other privileges of the church.[28]

The ecclesiastical establishment was targeted further through a series of imperial edicts that came close to accusing it – and especially its bishops – of obstructing justice. The legislation insisted on the need to abolish 'all human suffering'. To this end, it reorganised the tribunals at which victims could seek redress, making them more accessible and efficient: courts were to remain open on all but a limited number of holy days; deferrals of hearings were to be eschewed; and judgements were to be given in a timely fashion 'so that the provincials are not forced, because of the protracted length of proceedings and the lack of resources, to consider the avoidance of the courts more profitable than recourse to them'. Care was taken to dispatch copies of this legislation to provincial churches.[29]

Manuel presented himself as instituting social justice not only by ensuring that the rights of all full imperial subjects were equal in the eyes of the law, but also by insisting that respect for 'God's Law' had motivated him to annul all previous imperial acts contrary to its principles. Manuel and his administration sought to redefine charity, eliding it with a manifestation of imperial justice that was itself portrayed as a reflection of divine justice. An edict from the 1160s acknowledged that 'God is served by mercy and pity', but it then quibbled that what had recently passed for these had in fact allowed some subjects to take advantage of legal loopholes to the injury of other subjects. The emperor claimed to implement a different and truer kind of compassion, making injuries 'good by right judgement'. Manuel insisted that he acted as the main champion of the poor against oppression and suffering through the establishment and implementation of just legislation and a robust judicial process.[30] Many of these late Komnenian policies were extended in the reign of the next imperial dynasty of the Angeloi. In a decree of 1192, for example, Isaac II Angelos paid lip service to the privileges of the 'most holy churches of God', but then sought to siphon off to the imperial treasury two-thirds of the fines collectable by the churches for offences against them.[31]

Episcopal responses

These measures could not curb the rise of bishops as figures of authority. One of the most successful prelates of the second half of the 12th century was Michael Choniates, a skilled administrator and noted intellectual who was elevated in the 1180s to the metropolis of Athens.[32] Invoking the language of pastoral duty that clerics habitually favoured, Choniates drew attention to the plight of the downtrodden soon after taking up his post. There were, he stated, 'so many poor' and 'destitute' in his archdiocese.[33]

However, instead of playing up the powerlessness of the church and insisting he was overwhelmed, as bishops had done earlier in the 12th century in order to appeal to the emperor's generosity, Choniates adopted a more self-assured tone. Projecting an image of himself as a highly competent and influential community leader, a spokesman for the 'commonality of us Athenians', the metropolitan insisted that the 'church of Athens' was a force with which to be reckoned.[34] Pushed to the limits of endurance, the Athenians, he argued, felt that the empire had all but forfeited its legitimacy. There was a real possibility this disaffection with the regime would lead to outright rebellion – perhaps even to a bid for regional independence. Only the church could resolve the crisis because it alone knew how to succour the indigent 'as much as possible' and avoid being 'unjust' to them without 'doing damage' to the state.[35] The emperor should not expect to achieve anything locally, Choniates intimated, without the bishop's collaboration and support.[36]

Choniates repeatedly named and shamed those within the imperial administration whom he accused of being 'destroyers of the poor'.[37] Blaming Constantinople for bleeding the provinces dry, he gave the 'delicate residents of the capital' a dressing-down for being wilfully oblivious to the suffering of others. 'What do you lack?' he asked them:

> The fertile fields of corn in Thrace and Macedonia and Thessaly feed you; Euboea, Cos, Chios and Rhodes provide you with wine. In Thebes and Corinth, fingers weave garments for you. All the rivers of riches flow to the city of Constantine as real rivers to the sea.[38]

Was this how the 'deep channels of imperial philanthropy' were supposed to irrigate Athens 'with charity'? He listed the depredations the Athenians had suffered at the hands of various tax collectors who 'came collecting not simply the tax for the navy, but the hearth tax, the land tax', and so on – often multiple times in one year.[39] Attica had become a 'vale of tears'. Ravaged by 'hunger and thirst' as a result of the confiscation of their produce and destruction of their fields, its inhabitants were left with only 'wails and lamentations' to sustain them.[40] Had imperial officials behaved benevolently, God would have given them material rewards in the form of 'money, lands, followers, friends, advancement in office and proximity to the emperor' as well as spiritual awards 'of greater value than gold, precious stones and pearls'.[41] But the Athenians had not, Choniates declared, received fair treatment, let alone aid, from these officials.[42]

Choniates reminded officials that – while they claimed to govern in accordance with vaunted Roman laws that would bring peace and justified the high levels of tax collection by asserting that the funds went toward local

288   *Teresa Shawcross*

security – they did not in reality maintain an effective military defence, but instead allowed imperial citizens to suffer from repeated raids.[43] The population of his archdiocese had been 'brought low by the attacks of robbers, bandits, pirates and wild beasts'.[44] This behaviour, the bishop argued, made assertions on the part of the regime to protect 'all the lands under Roman authority' increasingly unconvincing. He was forced to question whether Attica – suffering from an unslaked thirst to be treated 'in accordance with the laws of justice and legitimate authority' – should be considered 'a Roman possession'. It is up to you, Choniates admonished the first minister of the empire, 'to decide through the actions you take whether this region should be numbered any longer among the lands under Roman authority'.[45]

Such warnings were not meant idly. They strongly hinted that notions were being entertained in southern Greece similar to those that had already cost the empire portions of coastal Asia Minor and the western Balkans.[46] Constantinople took the threat seriously and placated the bishop and his flock. The immunity from taxation enjoyed by the cathedral and its estates in the mid-11th century appears to have been extended to the entire 'Athenian fiscal district', which included the walled city and probably also the burg and wider surroundings. As a result of concessions made by the central administration, Athens possessed a significant measure of independence by the end of the 12th century, with its privileges and exemptions being recorded in a chrysobull signed in the emperor's own hand. Within the limits of that district, neither the imperial governor of Hellas and the Peloponnese nor any of his representatives could collect taxes or impose corvées. Moreover, the governor did not possess legal jurisdiction over the district, and his very entry into the city on any pretext whatsoever was expressly forbidden.[47]

By the end of the 12th century, only the word of the metropolitan bishop held sway in Athens. But to what extent did that word come to be considered also to be law? Choniates' surviving letters contain no reference to the operation in his see of an episcopal court, although it is likely such a court did convene and that the metropolitan did render judgement. From the early 13th century onwards, certainly, bishops' papers preserve detailed records of the workings of their courts, reflecting an attempt to present the episcopate as the most efficacious source of justice to which people could have access. While the impact of foreign invasion and occupation after 1204 cannot be ignored here, records suggest that episcopal courts' annexation of much of the business of civil courts had begun significantly earlier.[48]

Indicative are the 29 surviving court decisions and other legal documents associated with the court convened by John Apokaukos of Naupaktos, who was in post from c. 1199 to c. 1232. Complaining about the unjust pronouncements of the secular courts, Apokaukos advertised his own knowledge of the law, as well as his will to uphold order by defending the rights of the weak and delivering just verdicts.[49] Most of the cases coming before him involved lay persons: he took measures to protect girls from being married off below the legal age or in contravention of the permitted degrees of affinity; he punished rape; gave annulments where the marriage had been contracted as a result of compulsion or deceit; and he approved divorces not only on the grounds of adultery or impotence, but also because of 'hatred' between the two parties.[50] Other cases dealt with property disputes and issues of inheritance and, finally, homicide.[51] The activities of Apokaukos' younger colleague, Demetrios Chomatenos, archbishop of Ochrid from 1216 to 1236, are preserved in a more extensive dossier, consisting of 152 expert opinions, judgements, and 'penitential rulings'. In these, the prelate displayed his training in law not only by specifying the exact statutory bases of his legal advice and judgements, but in most cases by quoting them verbatim – a tactic that surely helped boost people's confidence in him.[52] Litigants represented a broad cross-section of society: from the emperor, members of the military aristocracy, and lay landowners; to bishops, monks, and members of the clergy; to townsmen, farmers, and peasants.[53]

Irrespective of their actual age and social background, the parties that appealed to Chomatenos' justice frequently underscored both their vulnerability and their reliance on ecclesiastical protection. One petitioner introduced himself by emphasising that his surname was *Chamelos,* or 'the lowly one'.[54] Another referred to the 'great prelates' whom God had placed in office so that they could protect the vulnerable and right wrongs. 'I […] take refuge', the suppliant asserted, addressing Chomatenos, 'in the mercy of your great holiness and beg to receive help against the injustices that I suffer'.[55] That these remarks tallied with the episcopal court's own understanding of its role is apparent from the order in which Chomatenos organised his records during his lifetime: his dossier was designed to culminate with an account of those cases explicitly concerned with the 'weak', 'humble', and 'poor'.[56]

While the episcopal court of Ochrid could have refused to accept the requests of petitioners from territories outside its episcopal jurisdiction, it appears that Chomatenos was judicially proactive, and over time became one of the leading legal arbiters in the southern Balkans.[57] Petitioners declared that 'everyone' had heard of the 'righteous dispensation of justice' of the court and synod over which he presided.[58] Although on one occasion he asked for the emperor Theodore Komnenos Angelos of Thessalonike to have the secular court check his judgement and, if it found it correct, to provide support for its enforcement, his court mostly served as a court of final recourse for a wronged person. Indeed, in one 13-year legal dispute concerning the ownership of a vineyard, the case travelled all the way through the secular courts to the imperial high court without resolution, only finally to be decided at Chomatenos' regional ecclesiastical court.[59] This suggests that the archbishop had at his disposal powers of enforcement unavailable even to the emperor.

The new order

If the secular officials of the empire had ceded ground to the ecclesiastical establishment, the latter imposing its authority on judicial matters, the

290   *Teresa Shawcross*

inhabitants of the provinces did not always take kindly to the heavy guiding hand of the bishop. Reactionaries at heart, bishops such as Eustathios of Thessalonike corresponded in the 1180s–1190s with their fellow clerics about the need for a rigid social order.[60] Those communities that did 'not have guides assigned to them' – but permitted their members' 'self-government' on the pretext that anything else was incompatible with free will – fell prey to that 'destructive evil' that was 'leaderless anarchy'.[61] At the dawn of history, according to Eustathios, there may have been 'no law or rule', but civilisation had emerged with stratification as its distinguishing feature. In any civilised society, there would always be a minority who were numbered among the 'great', while the majority belonged to the 'little' folk.[62]

Furthermore, Eustathios asserted, toil through which man aims to live off his own capabilities without being a burden to others was pleasing to God.[63] Given this, the poor should be hardworking and meekly accept their suffering; they should not complain about hunger, cold, and lack of raiment, but be thankful that physical effort mortifies their bodies, allowing them to fix their minds more easily on the constant hope of the life thereafter.[64] Conversely, the rich and notable should be comforted by the thought they had been raised above the humble not by accident, but by Divine Providence. They would not be damned by the accumulation of excessive wealth as long as they undertook, by giving of that wealth, to reverse the exploitation that, arising out of 'laziness, unproductivity, and luxuriousness', uses others' labour in such a way as to degrade them either by hiring them on a daily wage or, worse still, by imposing on them slavery 'without payment'.[65] Through donations from their hoarded treasure, the wealthy are able to expunge their sins and save their own souls. Acting in imitation of the ultimate benefactor, God, they would have God's mercy reflected back on them.[66] The distribution of this treasure, moreover, was to be entrusted to the church, which alone could identify the most deserving recipients.[67] If such a system of charitable giving – spurred by mankind's greatest good, love – were practised throughout the world, Eustathios argued, it would not merely lead to rewards in the hereafter, but would eliminate all the world's current problems 'Contention, the mother of war, would have no say, but instead of the multitude of weapons we would have a glut of ploughshares', and 'councils, laws, [and] schools', would flourish, along with 'marriages', 'commerce', and 'every art and science'.[68]

Such views did not sit well, Eustathios acknowledged, with contemporary reality. In a rapidly growing city such as Thessalonike, society had become disrupted. He explained:

> Hardly is there time to proclaim one of our citizens "honourable" today, before he is tomorrow proscribed as dishonourable and condemned to oblivion. At this instant in time he is revered as a rich man, but then soon afterwards he is a pauper [...] One moment he is considered noble, while the next he is accused of descending from a family to be reviled and is

rejected as if he were a slave – which indeed is what he is now called instead of a free man.[69]

Life was like an 'ever-revolving whirligig' that spun one hither and thither.[70] Those who found themselves prospering at a specific moment argued that social relations should be deregulated, reckoning that it was such deregulation that provided the opportunity for limitless self-advancement. They considered all to be well as long as their business interests were not harmed and they could persevere unhindered in their commercial transactions, increasing their fortune 'by a few coins'. Instead of taking pride in the quality of their merchandise, they conducted transactions in a manner unchecked by moral concerns, habitually cheating and deceiving 'their brother' in order to maximise profit.[71]

According to Eustathios, the merchants of Thessalonike were so wholly devoid of scruples that they had the temerity to ask why it was necessary to provide sustenance for the poor, asserting that 'we too were once poor, and yet have succeeded in prospering without receiving aid from others'.[72] To such free-thinkers, the church's ministry to the poor constituted at best a nuisance, at worst a danger.[73] The call to give alms, Eustathios wrote, 'is a heavy sound that grates with the audience, scattering them'.[74] The citizens stayed away from religious ceremonies and turned a deaf ear to sermons, refusing to dig into their pockets. They displayed an outright lack of reverence for the ecclesiastical establishment, comporting themselves as 'cheap philosophers' who claimed on the one hand 'to respect and revere the church, and to be her supporters – even to be ready to die for her' – and on the other hand set churchmen and church property at naught, reasoning that 'everything on earth is incompatible with the divine, and both churchmen and their affairs are earthly'. They maintained that God has no need to possess either 'persons or things'. 'Among us the great saying is', Eustathios reported despairingly of the Thessalonians, 'What need have God and his saints of such things, who neither sow nor reap nor eat nor drink?'.[75]

Bishops could be regarded with extreme suspicion by citizens and become the subject of slanderous campaigns. A defamatory caricature that bore the legend *A Malicious Man in the Guise of the Present Bishop of Thessalonike* was doing the rounds in the city, and, though he initially tried to laugh it off as a prank, he trembled at the permanent damage it could do his reputation.[76] The mutterings of his detractors grew so loud that, after his death, charges of his having loved wealth and hoarded money had to be rebutted during his funeral elegy.[77]

Other prelates faced similar attacks. Even in Athens, Choniates – although generally more respected by his flock than Eustathios had been – had to respond to charges c. 1210 that, during his tenure of office, his church had accumulated a vast treasure, which he had then embezzled and was using for his private gratification. In Naupaktos, too, John Apokaukos was accused in 1217 of misusing church funds.[78] A little later, churchmen in western Greece were perturbed by news of a brash youth in the archdiocese of Corfu who claimed he had seen a vision of his metropolitan, George Vardanes, being punished in hell for having abused God's trust on earth. The youth also alleged he had heard a heavenly voice promising that before the metropolitan died he would be forced to distribute to the poor the possessions he had amassed.[79] Vardanes tried to counter such slander by having the fiscal concessions and other privileges he and his predecessors had secured for the archdiocese from the imperial administration inscribed in stone and erected in public view. This had little effect upon the Corfiots.[80] Some episcopal flocks, indeed, went further than mere words: a colleague of Vardanes', the bishop George of Chimara, who fell into a coma and after five days was given up for dead, discovered, when he unexpectedly regained consciousness, that a good portion of his church's property had been seized and duly dispersed to the 'common and unruly people' and to the 'paupers' for whose assistance it had always been meant to be dedicated.[81]

Indicative of this trend was also the fate of Euthymios Tornikios. Despite appearing on paper to be the perfect candidate for appointment to the metropolis of Neopatras, he was passed over in 1222, after three years of earnest deliberations, by the synod entrusted with the election. Though other reasons for the failure of his candidature cannot be excluded, such as the stain of an old family scandal, or suspicions that he would be too often absent from his see, it is hard to shake off the feeling that what was decisive was something less precisely definable.[82] As the client of Choniates and Apokaukos, and the peer of Vardanes, Tornikios was too closely associated with the circle that was increasingly coming under attack for its attitudes to ecclesiastical wealth.[83] Moreover, because he was known as an avid reader and collector of that circle's writings, there may have been a feeling that there was an air about his person and an inflection in his discourse that, quite simply, seemed to be out of date. Advanced in years, he seemed too old-school.[84] Although there remained a few bastions among the cities – such as Ochrid – of the southern Balkans, generally the state of affairs had been transformed beyond recognition. The close association of their office with the regulation of charity and justice that ecclesiastics had been pushing seems, as the second quarter of the 13th century approached, to have exhausted its usefulness as a strategy.

Conclusions

We have sketched the outline of a debate in the Byzantine Empire during the long 12th century about the nature of the impact of wealth, the stratification of imperial society, and the limits of legitimate state action. The period was one of notable economic growth and social mobility for the western provinces as a result of their greater integration within long-distance commercial networks. The increasingly complex fiscal apparatus through which emperors sought to secure control of the new wealth being produced within their territories – by collecting it in the public treasury and employing it to defend

Loving the Poor 293

the secular fabric of the state – was considered overly intrusive and burdensome. In this context, bishops, long entrusted with the moral guardianship of local communities, also advocated for the preservation of capital within the locality in order to achieve a philanthropic purpose that brought households and neighbourhoods closer to the Heavenly Kingdom.

These bishops were able to take advantage of the difficulties the Komnenian dynasty faced when attempting to render their usurping regime legitimate. Although the second half of the 12th century saw emperors responding with a flurry of legislation championing an incandescent ideal of social justice whose implementation was to be achieved through paternalistic oversight by imperial law and imperial tribunals, they were unable to prevent the expansion of the institutional jurisdiction of ecclesiastical courts. By the end of the century, indeed, bishops such as Michael Choniates, the prelate of Athens, could claim considerable autonomy of action as the main administrators and arbiters of provincial life.

Yet, as these same bishops realised, the people over whom they asserted their authority could not be counted upon to continue to share unquestioningly in the ecclesiastical establishment's understanding of its mission. The uncooperative behaviour not only of the citizens of Thessalonike, but also of Athens, Naupaktos, Corfu, and Chimara, led these citizens to be damned from the pulpit more than once as irredeemably wicked. But the economic forces in operation – which were beyond any individual's control – could not be halted by means of sermons. The position of bishops as the primary stewards of wealth and organisers of charitable giving began to erode. The brutal binary model in which the rich faced the poor across a chasm with no group in between – and only the splendidly isolated figure of the bishop acting as a bridge – no longer applied with the rise of a middle class: the so-called *mesoi*.[85]

With time, alternative safety nets and forms of solidarity dominated in cities – and new public displays of religious piety would emerge – as provincial society continued to settle into the new patterns of land use, manufacturing, and trade. These expressions of civic cohesion and regional patriotism would be focused on the religious confraternity, the professional guild, and, above all, the political assembly (the *boule* and the *ekklesia tou demou*).[86]

Unless otherwise noted, all translations and paraphrases are by the author of the present chapter.

Notes

1 1 Kings 17; see also the folk verses, which preserve the octosyllabic metre: 'Μουσουδέντι δὲν χωρέντει / ποδαρέντι δὲν χωρέντει / Βάζει οὐρέντι καὶ χωρέντει / καὶ γυρίζει καὶ γλυφέντει'; Pétrides (ed.) 1909a: 76–77. For similar critiques of bishops' lack of generosity, but also justification for the small quantities of food Apokaukos sent colleagues, see 73–74, and Bees and Bees-Seferli (eds.) 1976: 84–85.

2 Pétrides (ed.) 1909a: 78–81.

294 *Teresa Shawcross*

3 Pétrides (ed.) 1909a: 78–85; Bees and Bees-Seferli (eds.) 1976: 102–132; Papadopoulos-Kerameus (ed.) 1913: 259–260, 272–278; translation adapted from Angold 1995: 219–221; see also Lampropoulos 1988: 73–75, 138–142.

4 Bees and Bees-Seferli (eds.) 1976: 92–94.

5 Harvey 1989; Harvey 1995: 243–261; Laiou and Morrison 2007: 90–165; Shawcross 2013: 57–94.

6 Shawcross 2013: 72–79; Browning 1995b: 91–104; Barker 2003: 5–28.

7 Ahrweiler 1966: 211–25; Maniatis 2017.

8 For the role of the church in the development of ideals of charity, see Constantelos 1968; Herrin 1990: 151–164; Brown 2002; Brown 2012; Brown 2015; Harper 2013; Horden 2005: 137–146; Stathakopoulos 2007.

9 Angold 1995: 240–243; Mullett 1997a: 237–252.

10 For the family's association with the province of Hellas and the Peloponnese, its members, and its writings and intellectual interests, see Gautier (ed.) 1980–6; Darrouzès (ed.) 1970; Darrouzès (ed.) 1968: 49–121; Mpones (ed.) 1937; Jeffreys *et al.* 2011: *Tornikios 102*; Gautier 1963: 159–178; Mullett 1997b.

11 Angold 1995: 77–108; Magdalino 1993: 276–315.

12 Shawcross 2021.

13 For the possibility that the tax burden of many of the provinces, especially those in the west, increased substantially as a result of administrative reorganisation under the Komnenoi, see Zakythenos 1955: 204–274; Glykatzi-Ahrweiler 1960–61: 1–111; Oikonomides 1973; Rouillard 1935: 81–89; Harvey 1993: 139–154; Papagianne 1960–61: 391–407.

14 Rhalles and Potles (eds.) 1852–59: III 27, 427; Saradi 1991b: 375–404; 52–59, 3: hens, 1991, 375–404 vs. Juridical Practice'; Angold 1995: 257–260.

15 Darrouzès (ed.) 1970: 25–32; 52–59, 3: hens, 1991, 375–404 vs. Juridical Practice; Angold 1995: 146.

16 Doanidou (ed.) 1934: 109–150; Maas and Dölger 1935: 2–14; Zeses 1978: 240–246.

17 Kormpete (ed.) 1934: 301–322; Zeses 1978: 247–257; Magdalino 1993: 278–279; Darrouzès (ed.) 1970: 152–155; Mpones (ed.) 1937: 49–50, 70; PG 137 372–380, 1072–1076; PG 138 496–501; Demetrakopoulos (ed.) 1866: 266–292; Zeses 1978: 258–280; Merianos 2011: 273–291.

18 Zepos and Zepos (eds.) 1931: I 275–277, 311–312; Rhalles and Potles (eds.) 1852–9: V 60–62; Gautier (ed.) 1973: 169–201; Angold 1995: 144–145; Magdalino 1993: 267–274; Magdalino 1996b: 199–218.

19 Darrouzès 1982: 143.

20 van Dieten (ed.) 1975: I 60.

21 Zepos and Zepos (eds.) 1931: I 275–277, 366–367, 376–378; Pétrides (ed.) 1909b: 203–208; Lampros 1916: 321–328; Lampros (ed.) 1879: I 308–309; Svoronos (ed.) 1965: 328–379; Magdalino 1993: 285.

22 Miklosich and Müller (eds.) 1860–90: V 14–16; Regel (ed.) 1892–1917: I 139; Thalloczy *et al.* (eds.) 1913–18: I 30, 254; Lampros (ed.) 1879: I 308–309; Svoronos (ed.) 1965: 360–363.

23 Zepos and Zepos (eds.) 1931: II 378–385; Angold 1995: 145; Magdalino 1993: 285.

24 Svoronos (ed.) 1965: 326.

25 Magdalino 1984: 229–240.

26 Zepos and Zepos (eds.) 1931: I 385–387; Magdalino 1993: 286–287. See Svoronos (ed.) 1965: 370, for a different interpretation.

27 Astruc (ed.) 1959: 206–246; Branousse (ed.) 1987: 19–32; Svoronos (ed.) 1965: 364, 374.

28 Macrides (ed.) 1984: 118–120; Svoronos (ed.) 1965: 372, 381–382; also legislation concerning imperial jurisdiction over ecclesiastical provinces, discussed in

Saradi 1991a: 149–163; for the earlier legislation, see especially Morris 1976: 19–27.

29 Translation adapted from Macrides (ed.) 1984: 99–204; see also Magdalino 1993: 286–288; Angold 1995: 103–108; Svoronos (ed.) 1965: 345–381.

30 Translation adapted from Macrides (ed.) 1984: 140.

31 Darrouzès 1982: 136–155; in this decree, Isaac imitated and expanded on Manuel's earlier revisions of John I's measures.

32 Angold 1995: 197–262; Stadtmüller 1934; Setton 1946: 234–236; Herrin 1980: 131–137; Kolovou 1999; Shawcross 2010: 9–46; Shawcross 2014: 65–96.

33 Kolovou (ed.) 2001: 44, 69, 82.

34 Kolovou (ed.) 2001: 44, 60.

35 Kolovou (ed.) 2001: 60.

36 Kolovou (ed.) 2001: 44, 60, 68.

37 Kolovou (ed.) 2001: 44, 60, 68. ampros (ed.) 1879: I 146, 307.

38 Kolovou (ed.) 2001: 69–70.

39 Kolovou (ed.) 2001: 36–37 and 88–89.

40 Kolovou (ed.) 2001: 19, 36–37 and 88–89; for an assessment of the accuracy of this image, see Herrin 1975: 253–284.

41 Kolovou (ed.) 2001: 69, 82.

42 Kolovou (ed.) 2001: 44, 86, 89.

43 Kolovou (ed.) 2001: 58.

44 Kolovou (ed.) 2001: 19.

45 Kolovou (ed.) 2001: 59, 68, 89.

46 Angold 1995: 139–179; Magdalino 1991: 179–198; Cheynet 1990: 116–131, 454–458; Cheynet 1984: 39–54; Brand 1968: 55, 124, 172; Vlachopoulou 2002.

47 Lampros (ed.) 1879: I 307–311; Dendrinos 1991–92: 189–207; Angold 1995: 204–205.

48 Saradi 1991b: 398–402.

49 Bees and Bees-Seferli (eds.) 1976: 91–92; the records are discussed in Angold 1995: 223–235, and Lampropoulos 1988: 62, 104–107, 254–299.

50 Bees and Bees-Seferli (eds.) 1976: 57–81; Pétrides (ed.) 1909a: 85–98; Papadopoulos-Kerameus (ed.) 1909a: 27–28.

51 Bees and Bees-Seferli (eds.) 1976: 58–83, 241–242; Pétrides (ed.) 1909a: 75–88; Papadopoulos-Kerameus (ed.) 1891–98: IV 124–125; Papadopoulos-Kerameus (ed.) 1909a: 29–30; Papadopoulos-Kerameus (ed.) 1909b: 79–82.

52 Prinzing 2013: 144.

53 Prinzing (ed.) 2002: 274–304 (81–88); Angold 1995: 246.

54 Prinzing (ed.) 2002: 227.

55 Prinzing (ed.) 2002: 287.

56 Prinzing (ed.) 2002: 274; Angold 1995: 241.

57 Prinzing 2004: 165–182.

58 Prinzing (ed.) 2002: 227.

59 Prinzing (ed.) 2002: 249–252.

60 On Eustathios' life and career, see Angold 1995: 179–196; Wirth 1960a: 83–85; Wirth 1961: 86–87; Wirth 1960b: ssen', 293–4 293–294; Kazhdan and Franklin 1984: 115–119; Magdalino 1996a: 225–238; Browning 1995a: 83–90.

61 Tafel (ed.) 1832: 24.

62 Tafel (ed.) 1832: 13, 28, 135–138; Kyriakides et al. (eds.) 1961: 32.

63 Tafel (ed.) 1832: 7–13, 143–149, 219.

64 Tafel (ed.) 1832: 13–29, 70, 219.

65 Tafel (ed.) 1832: 14, 22, 28, 72, 78, 80, 128, 133–138, 163, 230, 334; Wirth (ed.) 2000: 152–169, 192.

66 Wirth (ed.) 2000: 61–77.
67 Tafel (ed.) 1832: 61.
68 Tafel (ed.) 1832: 62–63; Magdalino 1996a: 234.
69 Tafel (ed.) 1832: 109–110; translation adapted from Magdalino 1996a: 235; see also Magdalino 1993; 158–159.
70 Tafel, (ed.) 1832: 109–110; Magdalino 1996a: 235; Magdalino 1993: 158–159; on Eustathios' economic thought, see Merianos 2008.
71 Partial edition in Magdalino 1996a: 235; Tafel (ed.) 1832: 70–73: 140, 156, 163, 229, 307.
72 Tafel (ed.) 1832: 72.
73 Magdalino 1993: 158–159.
74 Translation adapted from the partial edition and translation in Magdalino 1996a: 230–231.
75 Translation adapted from the partial edition and translation in Magdalino 1996a: 230–231. See also Tafel (ed.) 1832: 64–65; Magdalino 1996a: 233.
76 Tafel (ed.) 1832: 98.
77 Mpones (ed.) 1937: 82.
78 Kolovou (ed.) 2001: 251; Pétrides 1909a: 72, 81–84; Papadopoulos-Kerameus (ed.) 1906: 335–351; Vasiljevskij (ed.) 1896: 260–263.
79 Papadopoulos-Kerameus (ed.) 1896: 348–349; Angold 1995: 237.
80 Martin (ed.) 1882: 379–389.
81 Bees and Bees-Seferli (eds.) 1976: 242–243; Angold 1995: 238.
82 Both Euthymios Malakes and George Tornikios were more concerned with the imperial court than with their Sees. The synod may have feared that Euthymios Tornikios would behave in the same way; for the family scandal, see Darrouzès (ed.) 1970: 26–27, 115–116.
83 For Choniates, Apokaukos, Tornikios, Vardanes and Chomatenos as part of a network, see Kolovou (ed.) 2001: 153–288; Bees and Bees-Seferli (eds.) 1976: 84–135; Papadopoulos-Kerameus (ed.) 1901: 285–288; Papadopoulos-Kerameus (ed.) 1905: 573–574; Papadopoulos-Kerameus (ed.) 1907: I 232–48; Papadopoulos-Kerameus (ed.) 1906: 338–351; Papadopoulos-Kerameus (ed.) 1909a: 8–9; Lampropoulos 1988: 174–175; Vasiljevskij (ed.) 1896: 250–279, 355–356. Also, on friendship between ecclesiastics, Mullett 1995: 41; Mullett 1988: 3–24.
84 Apokaukos describes both Michael Choniates and Euthymios Tornikios as his contemporaries: Bees and Bees-Seferli (eds.) 1976: 111; Papadopoulos-Kerameus (ed.) 1905: 285.
85 Matschke and Tinnefeld 2001: 99–157.
86 Horden 1986; Shawcross 2021.

References

Primary Sources

Astruc, C. (1959), 'Un document inédit de 1163 sur l'éveché théssalien de Stagi. Paris Suppl. gr. 1371', *BCH* 8: 206–246.
Bees, N.A., and Bees-Seferli, E., eds. (1976), 'Unedierte Schriftstücke aus der Kanzlei des Johannes Apokaukos des Metropoliten von Naupakten (in Aetolien)̀, *BNJ* 21: 57–160.
Branousse, E. (1987), 'Το αρχαιότερο σωζόμενο έγγραφο για τη Θεσσαλική επισκοπή Σταγών (του έτους 1163), ανέκδοτα τεμάχια του εγγράφου και μερικές πρώτες παρατηρήσεις', *Σύμμεικτα* 7: 19–32.
Darrouzès, J., ed. (1970), *Georges et Dèmètrios Tornikès. Lettres et discours.* Paris.

Demetrakopoulos, A., ed. (1866), Ἐκκλησιαστικὴ βιβλιοθήκη. Leipzig.

Doanidou, S., ed. (1934), 'Ἡ παραίτησις Νικολάου τοῦ Μουζάλωνος ἀπὸ τῆς Ἀρχιεπισκοπῆς Κύπρου. Ἀνέκδοτον ἀπολογητικὸν ποίημα', Ἑλληνικά 7: 109–150.

Gautier, P., ed. (1973), 'L'édit d'Alexis Ier Comnène sur la réforme du clergé', REB 31: 165–201.

Gautier, P., ed. (1980-86), Théophylacte d'Achrida. 2 vols. Thessalonike.

Kolovou, F., ed. (2001), Michaelis Choniatae epistulae. Berlin.

Kormpete, H., ed. (1934), 'γκώμιον εἰς τὸν πατριάρχην Νικόλαον δ' τὸν Μουζάλωνα', Ἑλληνικὰ 7: 301–322.

Kyriakides, S. et al., eds. (1961), La espugnazione di Tessalonica: [di] Eustazio di Tessalonica. Palermo.

Lampros, S., ed. (1879), Μιχαὴλ Ἀκομινάτου τοῦ Χωνιάτου τὰ σωζόμενα, 2 vols. Athens.

Macrides, R. (1984), 'Justice under Manuel I Komnenos: four novels on court business and murder', Fontes minores 6: 99–204.

Martin, A., ed. (1882), 'Inscription grecque de Corcyre de 1228', Mélanges d'archéologie et d'histoire 2: 379–389.

Miklosich, F., and Müller, J., eds. (1860–1890), Acta et diplomata graeca medii aevi, 6 vols. Vienna.

Mpones, K., ed. (1937), Εὐθυμίου τοῦ Μαλάκη μητροπολίτου Νέων Πατρῶν (Ὑπάτης) τὰ σωζόμενα. Athens.

Papadopoulos-Kerameus, A., ed. (1891–1898), Ἀνάλεκτα Ἱεροσολυμιτικῆς σταχυολογίας, 5 vols. St Petersburg.

Papadopoulos-Kerameus, A., ed. (1901), 'Ἀθηναϊκὰ ἐκ τοῦ ιβ καὶ ιγ αἰῶνος', Ἁρμονία 3: 285–288.

Papadopoulos-Kerameus, A., ed. (1905), 'Δυρραχηνά', BZ 14: 568–574.

Papadopoulos-Kerameus, A., ed. (1906), 'Κερκυραϊκά', Visantiiski Vremennik 12: 334–351.

Papadopoulos-Kerameus, A., ed. (1907), 'Συμβολὴ εἰς τὴν ἱστορίαν τῆς ἀρχιεπισκοπῆς Ἀχρίδος', in Сборник статей, посвященных почитателями академику и заслуженному профессору В.И. Ламанскому по случаю пятидесятилетия его ученой деятельности, 2 vols., St Petersburg: I 227–250.

Papadopoulos-Kerameus, A., ed. (1909a), 'Συνοδικὰ γράμματα Ἀποκαύκου', Βυζαντίς 1: 3–30.

Papadopoulos-Kerameus, A., ed. (1909b), 'Ἰωάννης Ἀπόκαυκος καὶ Νικήτας Χωνιάτης', in Τεσσαρακονταετηρὶς τῆς καθηγεσίας Κ. Σ. Κόντου, Athens: 373–382.

Papadopoulos-Kerameus, A., ed. (1913), Noctes Petropolitanae. St Petersburg.

Pétrides, S., ed. (1909a), 'Jean Apokaukos, lettres et autres documents inédits', Bulletin de l'institut archéologique russe à Constantinople 14: 69–100.

Pétrides, S., ed. (1909b), 'Le chrysobulle de Manuel Comnène sur les biens de l'église', ROC 4: 203–208.

Prinzing, G., ed. (2002), Demetrii Chomateni Ponemata Diaphora. Berlin.

Regel, W., ed. (1892–1917), Fontes rerum Byzantinarum sumptibus Academiae caesareae scientiarum, 2 vols. St Petersburg.

Rhalles, G., and Potles, M., eds. (1852–1859), Σύνταγμα τῶν θείων καὶ ἱερῶν κανόνων τῶν τε ἁγίων καὶ πανευφήμων Ἀποστόλων, καὶ τῶν ἱερῶν Οἰκουμενικῶν Συνόδων καὶ τῶν κατὰ μέρος ἁγίων Πατέρων, 6 vols. Athens.

Svoronos, N., ed. (1965), 'Les privilèges de l'église de l'époque des Comnènes: un rescrit inédit de Manuel Ier Comnène', TM 1: 325–391.

298   *Teresa Shawcross*

Tafel, T., ed. (1832), *Eustathii metropolitae Thessalonicensis opscula*. Frankfurt.
Thalloczy, L. *et al.*, eds. (1913–1918), *Acta et diplomata res Albaniae mediae aetatis illustrantia*, 2 vols. Vienna.
Vasiljevskij, V., ed. (1896), 'Epirotica saeculi XIII', *Visantiiski Vremennik* 3: 233–299.
van Dieten, J.-L., ed. (1975), *Nicetae Choniatae historia*, 2 vols. Berlin.
Wirth, P., ed. (2000), *Eustathii Thessalonicensis opera minora*. Berlin.
Zepos, I., and Zepos P., eds. (1931), *Ius graecoromanum*, 6 vols. Athens.

Studies

Ahrweiler, H. (1966), *Byzance et la mer: la marine de guerre, la politique et les institutions maritimes de Byzance aux VII-XV siècles*. Paris.
Angold, M. (1995), *Church and Society in Byzantium under the Comneni, 1081–1261*. Cambridge.
Barker, J. (2003), 'Late Byzantine Thessalonike: a second city's challenges and responses', *DOP* 57: 5–28.
Brand, C. (1968), *Byzantium Confronts the West, 1180–1204*. Cambridge, Mass.
Brown, P. (2002), *Poverty and Leadership in the Later Roman Empire*. Hanover, NH.
Brown, P. (2012), *Through the Eye of a Needle: Wealth, the Fall of Rome, and the Making of Christianity in the West, 350–550 AD*. Princeton.
Brown, P. (2015), *The Ransom of the Soul: Afterlife and Wealth in Early Western Christianity*. Cambridge, Mass.
Browning, R. (1995a), 'Eustathios of Thessalonike revisited', *Bulletin of the Institute of Classical Studies* 40: 83–90.
Browning, R. (1995b), 'Byzantine Thessalonike: unique city?', *Dialogos* 2: 91–104.
Cheynet, J.-C. (1984), 'Philadelphie: un quart de siècle de dissidence, 1182–1206', in *Philadelphie et autres études*, Paris: 39–54.
Cheynet, J.-C. (1990), *Pouvoir et contestations à Byzance (963–1210)*. Paris.
Constantelos, D. (1968), *Byzantine Philanthropy and Social Welfare*. New Brunswick.
Darrouzès, J. (1968), 'Les discours d'Euthyme Tornikès (1200–1205)', *REB* 26: 49–121.
Darrouzès, J. (1982), 'Un décret d'Isaac II Angélos', *REB* 40: 135–155.
Dendrinos, G. (1991–1992), 'Το Ὑπομνηστικὸν του Μιχαὴλ Χωνιάτη: εισαγωγή, νεοελληνική απόδοση, σχόλια', *Βυζαντινός Δόμος* 5–6: 189–207.
Gautier, P. (1963), 'L'épiscopat de Théophylacte Héphaistos, archevêque de Bulgarie', *REB* 21: 159–178.
Glykatzi-Ahrweiler, H. (1960–1961), 'Recherches sur l'administration de l'empire byzantin aux IX-XIe siècles', *BCH* 84: 1–111.
Harper, K. (2013), 'Review of Peter Brown', *Through the Eye of a Needle: Wealth, the Fall of Rome, and the Making of Christianity in the West, 350–550 AD*. Princeton University Press, Princeton; Oxford, 2012. xxx, 759. ISBN 9780691152905 $39.95', *Bryn Mawr Classical Review* 2013.02.35 [Accessed 21/12/2015].
Harvey, A. (1989), *Economic Expansion in the Byzantine Empire, 900–1200*. Cambridge.
Harvey, A. (1993), 'The land and taxation in the reign of Alexios I Komnenos: the evidence of Theophylakt of Ochrid', *REB* 51: 139–154.
Harvey, A. (1995), 'The middle Byzantine economy, growth or stagnation?', *BMGS* 19: 243–261.
Herrin, J. (1975), 'Realities of Byzantine Provincial Government: Hellas and Peloponnesos', *DOP* 29: 253–284.

Herrin, J. (1980), 'The ecclesiastical organisation of central Greece at the time of Michael Choniates: new evidence from the Codex Atheniensis 1371', in *Actes du XVe congrès international d'études byzantines*, 4 vols. Athens: 4, 131–137.

Herrin, J. (1990), 'Ideals of charity, realities of welfare: the philanthropic activity of the Byzantine church', in R. Morris, ed., *Church and People in Byzantium*, Birmingham: 151–164.

Horden, P. (1986), 'The confraternities of Byzantium', *Studies in Church History* 23: 25–45.

Horden, P. (2005), 'Memoria, salvation, and other motives of Byzantine philanthropy', in M. Borgolte, (ed.), *Stiftungen in Christentum, Judentum und Islam vor der Moderne*. Akademie Verlag, Berlin, 137–146.

Jeffreys, M. *et al.* (2011), *Prosopography of the Byzantine World* (http://db.pbw.kcl.ac.uk/pbw2011/entity/person/108491): *Tornikios 102*. [Accessed 21/12/2015]

Kazhdan, A. and Franklin, S. (1984), *Studies on Byzantine Literature of the Eleventh and Twelfth Centuries*. Cambridge.

Kolovou, F. (1999), *Μιχαὴλ Χωνιάτης (Συμβολὴ στὴ μελέτη τοῦ βίου καὶ τοῦ ἔργου του: τὸ Corpus τῶν ἐπιστολῶν)*. Athens.

Laiou, A. and Morrison, C. (2007), *The Byzantine Economy*. Cambridge.

Lampropoulos, K. (1988), *Ἰωάννης Ἀπόκαυκος: συμβολὴ στην έρευνα του βίου και του συγγραφικού έργου του*. Athens.

Lampros, S. (1916), 'Ὁ ἰατὴρ τοῦ Μανουὴλ Κομνηνοῦ διορθούμενος καὶ συμπληρούμενος', *NE* 13: 321–328.

Maas, P. and Dölger, F. (1935), 'Zu dem Abdankungsgedicht des Nikolaos Muzaloṅ, *BZ* 35: 2–14.

Magdalino, P. (1984), 'The Not-So-Secret Functions of the Mystikos', *REB* 42: 229–240.

Magdalino, P. (1991), 'Constantinople and the ἔξω χῶραι in the time of Balsamon', in N. Oikonomides, ed., *Byzantium in the 12th Century: Canon Law, State, and Society*, Athens: 179–198.

Magdalino, P. (1993), *The Empire of Manuel I Komnenos, 1143–1180*. Cambridge.

Magdalino, P. (1996a), 'Eustathios and Thessalonica', in C. Constantinides, N. Panagiotakes, E. Jeffreys and A. Angelou, eds., *PHILELLEN. Studies in Honour of Robert Browning*, Venice: 225–238.

Magdalino, P. (1996b), 'The reform edict of 1107', in M. Mullett and D. Smythe, eds., *Alexios I Komnenos*, Belfast: 199–218.

Maniatis, G.D. (2017), 'The organic structure and effectiveness of the Byzantine fiscal system: a critical evaluation', *Зборник радова Византолошког института (Zbornik radova Vizantološkog instituta)*, 54: 87–115.

Matschke, K.-P. and F.H. Tinnefeld (2001), *Die Gesellschaft im späten Byzanz: Gruppen, Strukturen und Lebensformen*. Köln; Weimar; Wien.

Merianos, G. (2008), *Οικονομικές ιδέες στο Βυζάντιο τον 12ο αιώνα: οι περί οικονομίας απόψεις του Ευσταθίου Θεσσαλονίκης*. Athens.

Merianos, G. (2011), 'Προστατεύοντας τα συμφέροντα ποιμνίου και μητρόπολης. Κατάδειξη δημοσιονομικών ατασθαλιών με αφορμή επιστολές του Ευθυμίου Μαλάκη', in D. Gonis, ed., *Η Υπάτη στην εκκλησιαστική ιστορία, την εκκλησιαστική τέχνη και τον ελλαδικόν μοναχισμό*, Athens: 273–291.

Morris, R. (1976), 'The powerful and the poor in tenth-century Byzantium: law and reality', *Past and Present* 73: 19–27.

300 *Teresa Shawcross*

Mullett, M. (1988), 'Byzantium: a friendly society?', *Past and Present* 118: 3–24.
Mullett, M. (1995), 'Originality in the Byzantine letter: the case of exile', in A. Littlewood, ed., *Originality in Byzantine Literature, Art and Music*, Oxford: 39–58.
Mullett, M. (1997a), '1098 and all that: Theophylact, the Bishop of Semnea and the Alexian reconquest of Anatolia', *Peritia* 10: 237–252.
Mullett, M., (1997b), *Theophylact of Ochrid. Reading the Letters of a Byzantine Archbishop*. Aldershot.
Oikonomides, N. (1973), 'L'évolution de l'organisation administrative de l'empire byzantin au XIe siècle (1025–1118)', *TM* 6: 126–152.
Papagianne, E. (1960–1961), 'Φορολογικές πληροφορίες από επιστολές του Μεγάλου Βασιλείου (329/31-379) και του Θεοφυλάκτου Αχρίδας (1050/55-1125/26)', *BCH* 84: 391–407.
Prinzing, G. (2004), 'A quasi patriarch in the state of Epiros: the Autocephalous Archbishop of 'Boulgaria' (Ohrid) Demetrios Chomatenos', *ZRVI* 41: 165–182.
Prinzing, G. (2013), 'The authority of the church in uneasy times: the example of Demetrios Chomatenos, Archbishop of Ohrid, in the state of Epirus, 1216–1236', in P. Armstrong, ed., *Authority in Byzantium*, Farnham: 137–150.
Rouillard, G. (1935), 'L'épibolè au temps d'Alexis I Comnène', *Byzantion* 10: 81–89.
Saradi, H. (1991a), 'Imperial jurisdiction over ecclesiastical provinces: the ranking of new cities as seats of bishops or metropolitans', in N. Oikonomides, ed., *Byzantium in the 12th Century: Canon Law, State, and Society*, Athens: 149–163.
Saradi, H. (1991b), 'The twelfth century canon law commentaries on the ἀρχοντικὴ δυναστεία: ecclesiastical theory vs. juridical practice', in N. Oikonomides, ed., *Byzantium in the 12th Century: Canon Law, State, and Society*, Athens: 375–404.
Setton, K. (1946), 'A note on Michael Choniates, Archbishop of Athens (1182–1204)', *Speculum* 21: 234–236.
Shawcross, T. (2010), 'The lost generation (c.1204–c.1222): political allegiance and local interests under the impact of the Fourth Crusade', in J. Herrin and G. Saint-Guillain, eds., *Identities and Allegiances in the Eastern Mediterranean after 1204*, Aldershot: 9–46.
Shawcross, T. (2013), 'Mediterranean encounters before the Renaissance: Byzantine and Italian political thought concerning the rise of cities', in M. Brownlee and D. Gondicas, eds., *Renaissance Encounters: Greek East and Latin West*, Leiden: 57–94.
Shawcross, T. (2014), 'Golden Athens: episcopal wealth and power in Greece at the time of the Crusades', in N. Chrissis and M. Carr, eds., *Contact and Conflict in Frankish Greece and the Aegean, 1204–1453: Crusade, Religion and Trade between Latins, Greeks and Turks*, Aldershot: 65–96.
Shawcross, T. (2021), 'Cities and imperial authority in the western provinces of the Byzantine Empire, 12th–14th centuries', *Medieval Worlds* 14: 57–94.
Stadtmüller, G. (1934), *Michael Choniates, Metropolit von Athen (ca.1138-ca.1222)*. Rome.
Stathakopoulos, D. (2007), *The Kindness of Strangers: Charity in the Pre-Modern Mediterranean*. London.
Vlachopoulou, F. (2002), *Λέων Σγουρός: Ο βίος και η πολιτεία του βυζαντινού άρχοντα της βορειοανατολικής Πελοποννήσου στις αρχές του 13ου αιώνα*. Thessalonike.
Wirth, P. (1960a), 'Die Flucht des Erzbischofs Eustathios aus Thessalonike', *BZ* 53: 83–85.

Wirth, P. (1960b), 'Das religiöse Leben in Thessalonike under dem Episkopat des Eustathios im Urteil von Zeitgenossen', *Ostkirchliche Studien* 9: 293–294.

Wirth, P. (1961), 'Ein neuer Terminus ante quem non für das Ableben des Erzbischofs Eustathios von Thessalonike', *BZ* 54: 86–87.

Zakythenos, D. (1955), 'Μελέται περὶ τῆς διοικητικῆς διαιρέσεως καὶ τῆς ἐπαρχιακῆς διοικήσεως ἐν τῷ Βυζαντινῷ κράτει', *EEBS* 21: 204–274.

Zeses, T. (1978), 'Ὁ Πατριάρχης Νικόλαος δʹ Μουζάλων', *Epistemonike Epeteris Theologikes Scholes Aristoteleiou Panepistemiou Thessalonikes* 23: 240–246.

18 Economic Strategies of Landowners and Peasant Farmers during the 11th and 12th Centuries in Greece

Alan Harvey

The history of the rural economy during this period was marked by an intensification of agricultural production, in part facilitated by an increase in population, and also by the greater possibilities for specialisation due to an increase in the quantity of money in circulation and the growing commercialisation of the economy.[1] Although this general pattern has been clearly established, its impact on the economic strategies of landowners and peasants requires further investigation. The emphasis in this chapter will be on longer-term strategies, because our understanding of responses to short-term economic fluctuations is restricted by a lack of detailed evidence. The study is based largely on archival documents from Mt Athos and the results of archaeological surveys in southern Greece. The documents provide significant information about the rural economy of eastern Macedonia and, in particular, very detailed information about the village of Radolivos in the early 12th century, shortly after it came into the possession of the monastery of Iviron. In 1103 the monastery received a *praktikon*, a document drawn up by fiscal officials setting out the obligations of the estate's *paroikoi*, peasants who owed rent and a range of other obligations in cash and kind to the landowner. For other parts of Greece, where such a wealth of evidence is not available, we must rely on archaeological evidence. Surveys have added to our knowledge of settlement patterns and land use and have improved our understanding of the rural economy of Byzantine Greece.

A crucial pre-condition for economic expansion in Byzantine Greece was the increased security which limited the impact of warfare on the rural economy, enabling agriculture to prosper. The Byzantine conquest of Crete in 961 reduced the threat of raids from the sea and the incorporation of Bulgaria into the empire improved security in northern Greece.[2] Evidence from the archives of the monasteries of Mount Athos shows that agricultural production in the Chalkidiki peninsula had been seriously affected by Bulgarian campaigns in the 10th century and extensive areas were underexploited.[3] Of course, there were raids on Greece during the 11th and 12th centuries, but the Norman attacks were intermittent and, although disruptive in the short term, did not have damaging effects in the longer term.[4] Thebes and Corinth continued to prosper in the second half of the 12th century, despite their

DOI: 10.4324/9781003429470-23

Economic Strategies of Landowners and Peasant Farmers   303

sacking by the Normans in 1147. Both cities remained centres for international and regional trade and provided markets for landowners and farmers to sell their produce.[5] Attacks were launched on islands of the empire by the Venetians in the 1120s and again in 1172 and piracy became a problem towards the end of the 12th century, but there was never the chronic instability that would have seriously undermined the economy of the Greek provinces.[6] There was a striking contrast between the provinces of Greece and Asia Minor from the later 11th century. Economic activity in Asia Minor was disrupted by Turkish advances from the 1070s and for a short time the emir Çaka ("Tzachas") established his rule at Smyrna.[7] It has recently been argued convincingly that the Byzantine position in Asia Minor was still extremely precarious on the eve of the First Crusade.[8] Instability continued well into the 12th century, even in north-western parts. Manuel Komnenos was praised for his rebuilding of the fortifications of Adramyttion, Chliara, and Pergamon which, according to Niketas Choniates, greatly enhanced the security of the region.[9] Consequently, from the 1070s onwards there was a shift in economic importance from the eastern part of the empire towards Europe and the Greek provinces became increasingly important 'core' regions of the empire. Improved security was one of the most significant factors that made economic expansion possible there.

Any assessment of economic strategies has to consider the consequences of social change. The period was marked by a concentration of land in the hands of powerful landowners. Members of the imperial family had rights to properties and fiscal revenues in Greece. Adrian Komnenos, the brother of Alexios I, was granted fiscal revenues from the peninsula of Kassandra and another brother, Isaac, also had rights in the region of Thessalonike.[10] In 1198 relatives of the emperor Alexios III and the great religious houses of Constantinople had extensive lands in Greece and there is no reason to think that this represented a recent development.[11] In 1136 the monastery of the Pantokrator was endowed with properties in Thrace, Macedonia, and some islands.[12] The spread of estates belonging to Athonite monasteries is well known due to the survival of documents in their archives. As the monasteries' lands became more extensive in the Chalkidiki during the 10th and 11th centuries, they imposed serious restrictions on the ability of peasant communities to bring new land into cultivation and gradually undermined the viability and independence of these communities. The community of Adrameri came into dispute with Lavra over encroachments on its land by the monastery's *paroikoi* and succeeded in obtaining financial compensation for the land in question, but its landed wealth was eroded as a result of the actions of the monks and their *paroikoi*.[13] But the impact of the social and economic changes of the 11th and 12th centuries on peasants and landowners varied according to environmental conditions and location (ready access to markets). At the same time, peasant priorities were always household consumption and the payment of rent and tax. Their options for engaging with markets were restricted by location and the size of their landholdings. In contrast, wealthy landowners had greater flexibility in their decision-making.

The economic calculations of peasants involved a number of objectives, notably profit maximisation and risk aversion.[14] These were not always incompatible and, depending on the environmental constraints within which a peasant household worked, could complement each other. The profit maximisation approach implies rational calculation and efficiency in production.[15] The resources of the peasant household have to be deployed in a way that maximises the income (in kind or cash) of the household. An alternative approach places emphasis on the importance of risk reduction in peasant calculations.[16] Peasant agriculture was, of course, vulnerable to adverse weather conditions and coping with lower yields in poorer years had to be a factor in peasant planning, especially in the case of smaller landholdings where the subsistence of the household was more precarious. Two strategies that were important in minimising risk were diversity in the farming of crops and holding a range of smaller plots in different fields. The former is not incompatible with economic efficiency. It permitted a more even use of household labour throughout the agricultural year. Diversity in production could also have been a rational response to local variations in the quality of soils and topographical features.[17] The division of peasant holdings into a number of small plots in different parts of the territory of a peasant community represented a clearer trade-off between security and the efficient use of household resources. Such arrangements involved a greater allocation of time cultivating fields that were scattered, but in compensation peasants received some protection from the threats of crop disease and localised storms. The dispersal of peasant holdings is best shown by a survey of the village of Radolivos in eastern Macedonia dating from the first decade of the 12th century, soon after the village came into the possession of the monastery of Iviron. The text lists the fields held by the *paroikoi* who had come into the possession of the monastery. Every peasant holding consisted of a large number of small fields.[18] It is possible that such fragmentation of landholdings was the result of divisions through inheritance, but had the peasants wanted to consolidate their lands, it would have been possible through exchange or possibly an informal land market. It is likely therefore that they were seeking security through the dispersal of their lands which offered a greater variety of options for cultivation. The surviving source material does not permit an analysis of the allocation of peasant labour, but it is possible that the fields closer to the village were the most intensively cultivated.[19]

Work on the rural economy has often underestimated the resilience of the peasant economy. One of its greatest strengths was the diversity of its activities. Calculations of the viability of the peasant household have concentrated on grain production to a very large extent and have understated the significance of other agricultural and non-agricultural resources – wine, oil, pasture, fishing, woodland, and scrubland. The latter two were important resources which greatly diversified the peasant economy, providing pasture for pigs and scope for hunting. Nuts and berries gave valuable additional nutrients to a diet which was heavily dependent on grain production. Other important resources included raw materials for building, tanning, and dyeing cloth, charcoal-making, and arboreal resins which enabled artisans to supplement the income that they derived from agricultural production.[20] Woodland was especially significant in the 11th and 12th centuries, because rural settlements were not as densely inhabited as in the early 14th century, when the medieval population reached its peak in most places and the extension of arable cultivation reduced the area of woodland.[21] Fishing also offered opportunities for greater economic diversification in villages located close to rivers, lakes, and the sea. The most detailed evidence concerns the village of Doxompous in 1317, where a large proportion of the revenues owed by the peasants to Lavra were derived from fishing.[22] For earlier centuries the evidence is less precise, but it is clear that fishing rights were important to peasants and landowners. They were a factor in a dispute between the monastery of Kolovou and the villagers of Siderokausia in the Chalkidiki in the late 10th century.[23]

The archives of Mt Athos provide good evidence about the properties of large landowners and also peasant agriculture in Macedonia, but for most of Byzantine Greece, the farming regime can be assessed only through evidence from archaeological surveys. In the southern Argolid, when population began to increase from about 1000, settlements were based around good arable land. There was predominantly a mixed regime of wheat, barley, olives, vines, and animal grazing. As settlements became denser, improvements were made through terracing, drainage and the interplanting of different crops. Olive production offered the main possibility for specialisation.[24] This was even more the case in Lakonia, where there was large-scale olive cultivation and archaeological surveying has revealed evidence of peasant prosperity in the 11th and 12th centuries.[25] Demand from the urban centres of the Peloponnese was, no doubt, a factor, but this is difficult to assess with any precision. The produce of the Lakonia region had an outlet to the sea through the port of Skala and from the late 11th century the presence of Venetian merchants significantly increased demand for olive oil. In the 12th century, they were actively purchasing oil in Sparta for resale in more lucrative markets such as Constantinople and Alexandria, contributing to the prosperity of landowners and peasants in Lakonia.[26] Elsewhere in Greece wine production offered the greater scope for producing for markets. The cultivation of the vine involves a substantial input of labour, which became increasingly available during this period.[27] Lefort has estimated that a peasant with a vineyard of more than two *modioi* would have produced more than was needed for subsistence.[28] Wine production was very lucrative for larger landowners with greater capacity for specialisation, and expenditure on the improvement of estates belonging to the monasteries of Athos most often involved the development of vineyards.[29]

For peasant farmers and smaller landowners, decisions relating to pastoral farming were restricted by local environmental conditions, whereas more

306   Alan Harvey

powerful landowners had a greater range of options. In most villages, pastoral farming was part of a mixed regime where the animals provided much-needed fertiliser. Pasture was more accessible to peasant communities in the 10th century than in following centuries, when it became more restricted because of denser settlement, an extension of the land under cultivation and also the increase in property held by powerful landowners. During the 10th century, when the Chalkidiki peninsula was not so densely populated, pasture was abundant. There were sales of 'klasmatic' land – abandoned land that had come into the possession of the fiscal administration – in the Kassandra peninsula and elsewhere in the Chalkidiki. The purchasers, who included peasants and inhabitants of the small town of Hierissos as well as monastic landowners, received the right to pasture their animals on uncultivated parts of these lands and outsiders were permitted to take their animals there in the event of invasion.[30] In some places environmental conditions necessitated a greater specialisation. Many islands in the Aegean had a rugged terrain, best suited to animal grazing. This was the case with lands that came into the possession of Christodoulos and his monastery on Patmos. Its properties on Leros included little arable land, but extensive pasture which became the object of a dispute with neighbouring peasants who claimed the right to use this pasture.[31] Powerful landowners had great scope for specialisation in agricultural production due to the resources available to them for spending on cash crops and building up herds and flocks. Crucially they also had control over extensive grazing land. In 1089 the monastery of Xenophon owned 100 horses and donkeys, 130 buffaloes, 150 cows, and 2,000 sheep and goats. Its lands in the Kassandra peninsula and the theme of Kalamaria provided the pasture and a good location for produce to be marketed in Thessalonike.[32]

The decision-making of landowners and peasants was determined by location and accessibility of markets. Their marketing of produce cannot be assessed without taking into account the quality of the road network. The *Via Egnatia* was the main route from Constantinople to Thessalonike and Dyrrachion. It was kept in reasonable condition throughout the period under consideration.[33] Routes leading south through Thessaly and central Greece to the Peloponnese were important given the commercial significance of Almyros, Thebes, and Corinth.[34] We know much less about the network of smaller roads that were essential to support commerce. The main exception to this is the region covered by documents from the archives of the monasteries of Mt Athos, which reveal an elaborate network of local roads that would have enabled produce to be transported to local markets.[35]

The greatest market for agricultural produce was, of course, Constantinople. From the 10th to the 12th century the population of the capital increased. Of course, there are no reliable figures, but the general trend of denser settlement is clear.[36] The evidence of seals of *horreiarioi* indicates that imperial granaries were numerous in northern Asia Minor in particular and it is likely that grain produced on imperial estates in that region played an important role in the supply to Constantinople, at least until the later 11th century.[37] Otherwise throughout the 11th and 12th centuries the capital was largely supplied through commercial exchange unimpeded by state intervention.[38] Interestingly, in the late 12th century Michael Choniates claimed that the supply of wheat to Constantinople came from the productive regions of Thrace, Macedonia, and Thessaly and its wine from islands such as Crete, Lesbos, and Euboia.[39] Even allowing for rhetorical bias it should reflect the growing importance of the Greek provinces to the Byzantine economy and imperial finances during the late 11th and 12th centuries. The commercial options open to landowners and peasant farmers in Byzantine Greece also increased due to the greater involvement of Italian merchants in the trade of the empire from the late 11th century. The Venetians were especially active in southern and central Greece. But the survival of archival material relating to the Venetians, Genoese, and Pisans can distort our understanding of trade in the empire in this period. Little is known about Byzantine merchants, although there are hints of the activity of traders from Monemvasia and also Jewish merchants from Strobilos in Asia Minor.[40]

There was a strong concentration of imperial and aristocratic properties along the coastal region of Thrace and Macedonia during the 11th and 12th centuries. The best example is the monastery of the Pantokrator, an imperial foundation established in 1136. Its foundation document includes a list of properties with a strong concentration in Thrace and Macedonia, but also some of the Aegean islands and other parts of the empire. In addition to its villages and estates, it held urban properties including harbour facilities. The distribution of properties, which were located close to ports and the major land routes, was clearly intended to facilitate trade and the transport of food supplies to Constantinople.[41]

The interests of wealthy landowners were reflected in the content of agricultural treatises. The best-known of these was the *Geoponika*. It was a 10th-century reworking of a 6th-century text, largely derived from the writings of Roman agronomists, and it circulated widely. Arable farming was treated very briefly and there was much greater concentration on wine production and arboriculture two sectors of farming that offered scope for specialisation and production for sale at markets. Its influence on farming practice is open to question. Observation of best practice by farmers with knowledge of local conditions must have been far more important, but the circulation of the *Geoponika* was indicative of the growing possibilities for commercial production as a result of the growth of towns and increase in trade during this period.[42]

Peasant farmers and most landowners were restricted to marketing produce in their region, but a small number of powerful landowners had a greater range of access to markets and a strong competitive advantage due to their commercial privileges. The shipping of agricultural produce was vulnerable to disruption by imperial officials, who could impound boats to serve the purposes of the state, most often when supplies were needed to support military campaigns. But the most privileged landowners obtained some protection

308 *Alan Harvey*

against the actions of officials by securing exemptions through chrysobulls granted by the emperor and they gained a competitive advantage in cases where the chrysobull also included an exemption from the taxes on commercial transactions (*kommerkion, dekateia*).[43] This is best documented for the Athos monasteries which operated boats with exemptions from state obligations. Intermittent attempts were made by imperial officials to restrict the range of the monks' commercial activities. The emperor John Tzimiskes (969–976) attempted to limit their trade in wine, but it is clear that their vessels were sailing to Thessalonike and Constantinople. Basil II (976–1025) then attempted to confine the sale of their produce to Thessalonike and ports on the route there. Constantine IX (1042–1055) later allowed the monks to sail their vessels to Thessalonike to the west, and Ainos to the east.[44] The regularity of these imperial efforts to impose limitations on the activities of the monks suggests that their commerce continued largely unabated. As their estates became more extensive in the 10th and 11th centuries, their disposable agricultural produce and other non-agricultural resources would have increased in volume. It is also likely that the monks or their agents exploited their strong commercial position to buy produce from other landowners and peasant farmers to sell in larger markets where demand was stronger, but there is no direct evidence to confirm this. There might have been a distinction between their trade over shorter distances, where the cargoes could have been more varied, and the longer and less frequent voyages to Constantinople, when wine was the most significant commodity.

Lavra received an exemption from taxes on its commerce in 1102. These privileges were granted more frequently in the 12th century. The monastery of Patmos had received a limited exemption from Alexios Komnenos, but this was extended by Isaac II (1185–1195) to include commercial taxes.[45] Early in the reign of Alexios III (1195–1203) previous grants of maritime privileges were rescinded, but the monasteries of Lavra and Patmos were both able to maintain their exempted status. References to the tax on wine suggest that this was the major commodity shipped to Constantinople by monastic landowners. The trade was targeted by officials in Constantinople at the end of the 12th century, but a court case ended with the confirmation that the commercial privileges of Lavra included the right to trade wine free of tax.[46] Our understanding of the commercial activity of landowners is skewed towards powerful monasteries because of the surviving source material, but it is extremely likely that aristocratic landowners also benefitted from such commercial privileges, although the evidence is scarce. Isaac Komnenos, the brother of the emperor John II, did transfer a similar grant to his monastery of Kosmosoteira in southern Thrace.[47]

A general pattern of economic strategies can be drawn from the archival documents and archaeological evidence, but the heavy reliance on official documents is a major problem when investigating the rural economy. The standardised format of these texts can create an artificially uniform perspective that underestimates the flexibility of economic decision-making and

Economic Strategies of Landowners and Peasant Farmers 309

the impact of regional variations. A unique piece of evidence does, however, give a different perspective on local decision-making in the village of Radolivos in eastern Macedonia and suggests that there was much greater variation in economic conditions than the official documentation reveals. Records by estate managers do not survive except for some accounts written by a monk of Iviron, most probably the *oikonomos* (bursar), on the reverse of an official document dating from the early 12th century. These offer a glimpse of a more complicated situation. The accounts provide a list of *paroikoi* in the village with the payments in kind that they owed to the monastery. It is written in Georgian letters and a mixture of Greek and Georgian words are used. Sixty-seven of these *paroikoi* can be identified from those listed in the *praktikon* of 1103 and from a survey of the first decade of the 12th century. So this record clearly dates from that time. Payments in wheat and barley were specified for the *pakton* (rent) and the *zeugologion* and were linked to peasant wealth expressed in terms of the number of their oxen. Some payments were given in cash, but most were in kind. It is possible that this arrangement originated in the period before the village came into the possession of Iviron and it is not known whether it was imposed by the landowner or, more likely, the result of negotiations with the peasants. There are problems in interpreting this text because not all the peasants of Radolivos were listed – the *praktikon* of 1103 named 122 *paroikoi* – but the accounts do show that payments in kind were more significant than a superficial assessment of the *praktikon* would suggest.[48] The official documentation places the emphasis on money payments, reflecting the usual priorities of tax collectors, but in practice landowners had the option of using them as terms of account and exacting payments in kind. Their ability to transport produce greater distances to larger markets gave them much greater flexibility than peasants in their decision-making. The social and economic changes of the 11th and 12th centuries – the growing number of *paroikoi* in the rural population and the increasing volume of commerce – might have led, paradoxically, to parts of the rural population becoming less engaged with markets as their produce, exacted through obligations in kind, was marketed by their landowners.

To conclude, the economic strategies of peasant farmers were constrained by a range of factors – environmental constraints, location, the size of their holding, the labour available to the household, and relations with their landowner. Nevertheless, the resources at the disposal of peasant communities varied enough to permit economic strategies that served the dual purpose of sustaining the peasant household and providing the income in cash or kind that was needed to pay rent. They reduced the risk to their livelihood through a range of agricultural and non-agricultural activities without compromising the efficiency of their farming to any large extent. Growing urban demand for agricultural produce increased the scope for specialisation for both peasant farmers and landowners. The options of the latter were also constrained by the location of their estates. Properties near to major cities or coastal ports had greater potential for profit maximisation, especially during the 12th

310   *Alan Harvey*

century. Most landowners would have been limited to selling produce at markets near their estates, but those wealthy enough to operate or lease vessels had greater choice in disposing of their produce, especially the privileged landowners who benefitted from exemptions from commercial taxes. Nevertheless, the economic expansion of the 11th and 12th centuries had an impact on the strategies of both peasants and landowners and, at least in the locations best suited to commercial exchange, permitted greater flexibility in decision-making.

Notes

1 Laiou and Morrisson 2007: 90–165. Lefort 2002: 231–310. Harvey 1989; Harvey 1995: 243–261.
2 Curta 2011.
3 In 941 large tracts of 'klasmatic' land (abandoned land that had reverted to the treasury) were sold by the state, Lemerle *et al.* 1970: nos. 2, 3; Papachryssanthou 1975: nos. 4–6; Kaplan 1992: 533–536. For a legal dispute between the monastery of Kovolou and the inhabitants of Hierissos that arose from these sales, see Morris 1986: 125–147. In the late 10th century farmers from villages that were destroyed by Bulgarian raids took refuge in the village of Polygyros, belonging to the monastery of Iviron, Lefort *et al.* 1985: no. 10.
4 Magdalino 1993: 137; Harvey 1989: 219.
5 Magdalino 1993: 145; Harvey 1989: 215, 219; Gerolymatou 2008: 158–167.
6 Magdalino 1993: 137–140.
7 Vryonis 1971: 115–117, 150.
8 Frankopan 2012.
9 van Dieten 1975: I 140; Magdalino 1993: 126.
10 Lemerle *et al.* 1970: nos. 46, 51.
11 Pozza and Ravegnani 1993: 130–131.
12 Gautier 1974: 121–125.
13 Lemerle *et al.* 1970: no. 37. For the most comprehensive assessment of the charges imposed on the peasantry, Oikonomides 1996.
14 For a discussion of these and other approaches, see Ellis 1993.
15 'By our very definition of peasants – their partial engagement in usually imperfect markets – strict economic efficiency is ruled out'. Ellis 1993: 65.
16 Harvey 1998: 73–82, where the contrast between profit maximisation and risk aversion is overstated. The current paper presents a more balanced interpretation of peasant economic strategies.
17 Ellis 1993: 98.
18 Lefort *et al.* 1990: no.53. The survey lists seventy-seven peasant holdings and 979 fields. For a detailed analysis of this document see Lefort 1981: 269–313.
19 For a discussion of these problems in another medieval society, Dodds 2007: 147–161.
20 Dunn 1992: 255–257.
21 Lefort 1986: 11–21; Lefort 1985: 195–234.
22 Lemerle *et al.* 1977: no. 104; Harvey 1989: 254.
23 Lefort *et al.* 1985: no. 9; Lefort, 2002: 263; Harvey 1989: 158–159.
24 Jameson, Runnels and van Andel 1994.
25 Armstrong 2002: 353–365.
26 Gerolymatou 2008: 168–169.
27 Harvey 1989: 143–144.

Economic Strategies of Landowners and Peasant Farmers 311

28 Lefort 2002: 256.
29 Harvey 1989: 145–146.
30 See the references above, n. 3.
31 Nystazapoulou-Pelekidou 1980: no. 52. For an overview of the economy of the monastery, Oikonomides 2004: 10–17.
32 Papachryssanthou 1986: no. 1, lines 153–155.
33 Belke 2002: 85.
34 Avramea 2002: 72–74.
35 Belke 2002: 86.
36 Magdalino 2007: 61–67. Evidence of prices of wheat and other agricultural produce is woefully inadequate, but it is inconceivable that the growth of the city's population did not lead to higher prices. The main concern of the administration in Constantinople was to control profit margins, not to fix prices; Maniatis 2003: 401–444.
37 Lefort 2002: 250–251.
38 Magdalino 1995: 35–47.
39 Kolovou 2001: 69–70.
40 Magdalino 1995: 45–46. There are differing assessments of the importance of commerce in the Byzantine economy. Hendy 1985, stresses the role of the state, which put money into circulation and reclaimed it through taxation, creating a cycle of redistribution. According to Laiou and Morrisson 2007: 136, 'From the 11th century on, commerce was the dynamic sector, ... which became the motor of the Byzantine economy'. In my view, the opposition between these interpretations is overdrawn, but it is beyond the scope of this chapter to develop the argument.
41 Gautier 1974: 114–124; Dunn 1990: 307–314.
42 Grélois and Lefort 2012; White 1970: 15, 32; Lefort 2002: 297–298.
43 Harvey 1989: 238–241.
44 Papachryssanthou 1975: nos. 7, 8.
45 Vranousi 1980: nos. 7, 9.
46 Lemerle *et al.* 1970: nos. 67, 68; Vranousi, 1980: no 9.
47 Petit 1908: 53.
48 Lefort *et al.* 1990: Appendix 2.

References

Armstrong, P. (2002), 'The survey area in the Byzantine and Ottoman periods', in W. Cavanagh, J. Crouwel, R.W.V. Catling, and G. Shipley, eds., *Continuity and change in a Greek rural landscape: The Laconia survey*, I, *Methodology and interpretation*. London: 353–365.

Avramea, A. (2002), 'Land and sea communications, fourth-fifteenth centuries', in Laiou 2002: I 57–90.

Belke, K. (2002), 'Roads and travel in Macedonia and Thrace in the middle and late Byzantine period', in R. Macrides, ed., *Travel in the Byzantine world*, Aldershot: 73–90.

Curta, S. (2011), *The Edinburgh History of the Greeks, c.500 to 1050*. Edinburgh.

Dodds, B. (2007), *Peasants and Production in the Medieval North-east: The Evidence from Tithes, 1270–1536*. Woodbridge.

Dunn, A. (1990), 'A contribution to the Byzantine topography of southeastern Macedonia', in *Mneme D.Lazaride. Polis kai chora sten archaia Makedonia kai Thrake*, Athens: 307–332.

Dunn, A. (1992), 'The exploitation and control of woodland and scrubland in the Byzantine world', *Byzantine and Modern Greek Studies* 16: 255–257.

312   Alan Harvey

Ellis, F. (1993), *Peasant Economics: Farm Households and Agrarian Development*, 2nd ed. Cambridge.

Frankopan, P. (2012), *The First Crusade: The Call from the East*. London.

Gautier, P. (1974), 'Le typikon du Christ Sauveur Pantocrator', *Revue des Études Byzantines* 32: 1–145.

Gerolymatou, M. (2008), *Agores, emporoi kai emporio sto Byzantio (9os–12os ai.)*. Athens.

Grélois, J-P., and Lefort, J., eds. (2012), *Géoponiques*. Paris.

Harvey, A. (1989), *Economic Expansion in the Byzantine Empire 900–1200*. Cambridge.

Harvey, A. (1995), 'The middle Byzantine economy: Growth or stagnation?', *Byzantine and Modern Greek Studies* 19: 243–261.

Harvey, A. (1998), 'Risk aversion in the eleventh-century peasant economy', in S. Lampakis, ed., *E Byzantine Mikra Asia (6os–120s ai.)*, Athens: 73–82.

Hendy, M.F. (1985), *Studies in the Byzantine Monetary Economy, c. 300–1450*. Cambridge.

Jameson, M.H., Runnels, C.N., and van Andel, T. (1994), *A Greek Countryside: The Southern Argolid from Prehistory to the Present Day*. Stanford, California.

Kaplan, M. (1992), *Les homes et la terre à Byzance du VIe au XIe siècle: propriété et exploitation du sol*. Paris.

Kolovou, F., ed. (2001), *Michaelis Choniatae epistulae*. Berlin.

Laiou, A.E., ed. (2002), *The Economic History of Byzantium from the Seventh through the Fifteenth Centuries*, 3 vols. Washington D.C.

Laiou, A., and Morrisson, C. (2007), *The Byzantine Economy*. Cambridge.

Lefort, J. (1981), 'Le cadastre de Radolibos [**début XIIe siècle], les géomètres et leurs mathématiques', *Travaux et mémoires* 8: 269–313.

Lefort, J. (1985), 'Radolibos: population et paysage', *Travaux et mémoires* 9: 195–234.

Lefort, J. (1986), 'Population and landscape in eastern Macedonia during the middle ages: the example of Radolivos', in A. Bryer, and H. Lowry, eds., *Continuity and Change in late Byzantine and Early Ottoman Society*, Birmingham/ Washington D.C.: 11–21.

Lefort, J. (2002), 'The rural economy, seventh–twelfth centuries', in Laiou 2002: 231–310.

Lefort, J. *et al.*, eds. (1985), *Actes d'Iviron*, I, *Des origines au milieu du XIe siècle*. Paris.

Lefort, J. *et al.*, eds. (1990), *Actes d'Iviron*, II, *Du milieu du XIe siècle à 1204*. Paris.

Lemerle, P. *et al.*, eds. (1970), *Actes de Lavra*, I, *Des origines à 1204*. Paris.

Lemerle, P. *et al.*, eds. (1977), *Actes de Lavra*, II, *De 1204 à 1328*. Paris.

Magdalino, P. (1993), *The empire of Manuel I Komnenos 1143–1180*. Cambridge.

Magdalino, P. (1995), 'The grain supply of Constantinople, ninth–twelfth centuries', in C. Mango, and G. Dagron, eds., *Constantinople and Its Hinterland*, Aldershot: 35–47.

Magdalino, P. (2007), 'Medieval Constantinopl', in P. Magdalino ed, *Studies on the History and Topography of Byzantine Constantinople*, Aldershot.

Maniatis, G.C. (2003), 'Price formation in the Byzantine economy tenth to fifteenth centuries', *Byzantion* 73: 401–444.

Morris, R. (1986), 'Dispute settlement in the Byzantine provinces in the tenth century', in W. Davies, and P. Fouracre, eds., *The Settlement of Disputes in Early Medieval Europe*, Cambridge: 125–147.

Economic Strategies of Landowners and Peasant Farmers 313

Nystazapoulou-Pelekidou, M., ed. (1980), *Byzantina engrapha tes mones Patmou*, II, *Demosion leitourgon*. Athens.

Oikonomides, N. (1996), *Fiscalité et exemption fiscale à Byzance (IXe-XIe s.)*. Athens.

Oikonomides, N. (2004), 'The monastery of Patmos and its economic functions (11th–12th centuries)', in N. Oikonomides ed, *Social and Economic Life in Byzantium*, Study VII, Aldershot: 10–17.

Papachryssanthou, D., ed. (1975), *Actes du Prôtaton*. Paris.

Papachryssanthou, D., ed. (1986), *Actes de Xénophon*, Paris.

Petit, L. (1908), 'Typikon du monastère de la Kosmosotira près d'Aenos (1152)', *Izvestija Russkogo Arheologičeskogo Instituta v Konstantinopole* 13: 17–77.

Pozza, M., and Ravegnani, G. (1993), *I trattati con Bisanzio 992–1198*, Pacta Veneta, 4. Venice.

Van Dieten, J., ed. (1975), *Nicetae Choniatae Historia*, 2 vols. Berlin.

Vranousi, E. (1980), *Byzantina engrapha tes mones tou Patmou*, I, *Autokratorika*. Athens.

Vryonis, S. (1971), *The Decline of Medieval Hellenism in Asia Minor and the Process of Islamization from the Eleventh through the Fifteenth Century*. Los Angeles/London.

White, K. (1970), *Roman Farming*. London.

19 The Merchant in Middle Byzantine Greece

Maria Gerolymatou

The first attempt to approach the question of the identity, the characteristics and the activities of the provincial merchant during the Middle Byzantine period was made by N. Oikonomides more than two decades ago.[1] In the introduction of this remarkable article the author stated that by the term merchant he meant the man who bought some merchandise in order to resell it and make a profit. He explained that he was interested neither in the artisans who fabricated an object and then sold it nor in the mass of small farmers who sold their own agricultural surplus.[2] Neither did he take account of the great landowners whose role in the provisioning of markets was much more important. Despite the fact that this kind of classification seems quite practical, one should actually take account of the artisans, given that the distinction between artisan and merchant is not always clear. Only in the 11th century did a distinction between the artisan and the merchant, in the narrow sense, make its appearance.[3]

Very little is known about trade and even less about merchants during the so-called Dark Ages (7th to early 9th centuries). It has been argued that commercial activity was mainly handled by the state during this period. A pivotal institution would have been the *kommerkiarioi*. From the end of the 8th century the *kommerkion* was a tax imposed on trade. Its exact nature is open to guesswork. It is probable that initially it was a forfeit tax on luxury trade as well as on merchandise imported into Constantinople either from the rest of the Empire or from abroad.[4] A tax of 10%, the so-called *dekate,* is attested only from the end of the 10th century and mainly in the 11th and 12th centuries.[5] But according to N. Oikonomides, during the last quarter of the 7th and the beginning of the 8th century the *kommerkiarioi* would have the monopoly of buying and selling the silk produced in a province. They usually held the post for one or two years and often acted in cooperation with other *kommerkiarioi*. In addition to silk, they seem to have traded in other commodities. Their activities would have been carried out in warehouses called, in Greek, ἀποθῆκαι. By the end of the 7th century the term ἀποθήκη would designate a whole administrative circumscription including one or more provinces. According to this theory the *kommerkiarioi* were authorised to buy all the silk produced within the boundaries of one or more

DOI: 10.4324/9781003429470-24

The Merchant in Middle Byzantine Greece 315

circumscription(s) and resell it.[6] To whom? No answer is suggested. In the 30s of the 8th century both the ἀποθῆκαι and the *kommerkiarioi* disappeared and were replaced by the impersonal institution of the βασιλικὰ κομμέρκια. This would represent a major modification of state policy and mentality. Instead of farming out the office to wealthy individuals, the state would have assumed direct control of trade in different provinces.[7]

However, it is not at all certain that the *kommerkiarioi* carried trade in the name of the state or that they were dealing primarily in silk. Reservations consist mainly in two points: first, it is quite doubtful if in a period of recession there were so many wealthy individuals who could invest in farming out such a post. They would have to promote the culture of mulberries and consequently of silkworms and to buy the silk of whole provinces.[8] Second, and far more important, it is difficult to admit that in this early period sericulture was so important from the point of view of quantities and that it was widespread almost everywhere in Byzantium. It seems that until the beginning of the 10th century silk production in the Byzantine province was rather small. The restrictions and prohibitions imposed by the Book of the Eparch on exportation of raw silk from Constantinople to the provinces suggest the limited production.[9] It is beyond the scope of this chapter to debate further the nature of the ἀποθῆκαι: warehouses for merchandise, a sort of *entrepôt*, or warehouses where military material and equipment or even food provisions destined for the army were concentrated.[10] It has also been suggested that the *apothekai* were associated with the provisioning of urban centres such as Constantinople and that they were called to act *ad hoc* rather than assume regular duties such as tax collection.[11] As far as the *basilika kommerkia* are concerned, they have recently been interpreted as an institution having to do with the provisioning of the capital as well as with taxation (regular or trade taxation) in regions recently incorporated in the Empire or in which trade in coined money was still limited.[12] This second point would also be valid for the *kommerkiarioi* of specific ports or regions such as the Peloponnese who timidly appear in the first years of the 9th century.[13]

What does Greece have to do with all this? If one admits this point of view, it would mean that the *kommerkiarioi* of the ἀποθήκη Ἑλλάδος were entitled to buy all the silk produced in the south of the Greek peninsula. Until the last decades of the 8th century the theme of Hellas included the south of Greece, actually the Peloponnese, or more accurately the parts of it which were under Byzantine control, and continental Greece until Thessaly.[14] The Peloponnese was organised as a separate theme only in the last decades of the 8th century, most probably between 784 and 788.[15]

The *basilika kommerkia* of Hellas (which appear for the first time in 738/739)[16] as well as the *kommerkiarioi* who appear for the first time in the 9th century[17] were probably associated with the control of trade that transited from these regions and with collecting taxes on this trade.[18] There is plenty of evidence about trade between Constantinople and both the north and south coasts of the Mediterranean in the first half of the 7th century.[19] The

316   Maria Gerolymatou

collection of miracles of saint Artemios dated between 658 and 668 reveals that trade between Constantinople and Gaul was quite active in the first half of the 7th century.[20] It possibly transited from the ports of the Peloponnese. The 8th-century *Vita Willibaldi*, which narrates the pilgrimage of the saint in the Holy Land, informs us that he sailed from Syracuse to Monemvasia *in the country of Slavs* (Manamfasiam in Slaweniae terra).[21] The story about the contamination of the plague arriving from Calabria and Sicily in the Byzantine Empire on an Italian ship which had entered the port of Monemvasia is quite suggestive.[22] From Monemvasia Willibaldus sailed to the island of Cos, where some Corinthians disembarked. Then, the ship continued its journey to Samos and Ephesos. Were the Corinthians merchants? They could have been, but this is not certain. They might have started their journey in Sicily, but it seems more probable that they had embarked in Monemvasia. If that is true, it means that it was easier for them to find a ship in Monemvasia in order to cross to the other side of the Aegean, than in Corinth. In any case, two observations can be made: first, Monemvasia was frequently visited by foreign ships and second, and more important, a number of individuals, probably merchants, did not hesitate to cross the Aegean Sea having as destination the south of Asia Minor or the coast of Syria.

Not only Monemvasia but also the whole of the southern Peloponnese were frequented by merchants during the next two centuries.[23] It is noteworthy that from the 9th century we have a great number of seals of *kommerkiarioi* of the Peloponnese.[24] Some of them associate Peloponnese, Hellas and the island of Cephalonia,[25] while others do the same with Thessalonike, the 'West' and Hellas.[26] The above information suggests that the most important part of trade transited from the ports of the Peloponnese and/or the western coast of Greece and the Ionian Islands. The so-called Chronicle of Monemvasia, despite the fact that its author (Arethas of Caesaria?) is committed to sustain the claims of the metropolis of Patras, illustrates the density of communication between the western Peloponnese and Sicily as well as southern Italy.[27] Merchants had to face the difficulties of communication in the northern part of Greece which were due to the insecurity of the Via Egnatia. Consequently, the sea-route was the only solution for those who desired to travel from Constantinople to Italy and vice versa. Merchants, pilgrims, and ambassadors who wished to continue their journey to the north had to travel along the axis Corinth, Thebes, Larissa, and thus reach Thessalonike.[28] Even that option was not absolutely safe. The Life of Saint Blasius of Amorion, dated to the end of the 9th century, narrates that the ship owner, on whose ship the saint had sailed from Italy to Modon, continued his journey to Demetrias in Thessaly in order to trade (δι᾽ ἐμπορίαν τινὰ), probably in cereals.[29] Demetrias was able to survive the major changes of the late 6th and 7th centuries, while, on the contrary, the nearby Thessalian Thebes proved unable to do so.[30] Unfortunately, the ship owner (ναύκληρος) fell victim to an attack – on the part of the Bulgars who had invaded Greece[31] or of the Slavs who had been long established in Thessaly and traded with

Thessalonike.[32] Meanwhile, Corinth imported White Ware ceramics from Constantinople for a short period at the end of the 8th century.[33] In the 9th and 10th centuries Sparta seems to have entertained sustained commercial relations with Constantinople, as is suggested by the imported White Ware ceramics dating from the 9th and 10th centuries, a further indication of the full reintegration of the peninsula into the Byzantine Empire.[34] There are also examples of White Ware pottery imported in Thebes and dated from the 10th century.[35]

Unfortunately, very little is known about merchants themselves. The Monastery of Saint Nikon offered for hire installations to individuals who exercised a commercial activity, for instance a woman who sold bread.[36] In the surroundings of the same town there was an industry specialised in the production of textiles in which Jewish people were engaged.[37] It seems that the textile trade was an important economic activity in a lot of towns of the Greek peninsula. A considerable number of individuals, both artisans and merchants, profited from it, but very little is known about them. Corinth, Thebes, and Patras were the most prominent among the production centres. The famous narration about the rich widow Danielis on whose estates raw materials were produced as well as manufactured goods, such as textiles, is quite suggestive.[38]

John Kaminiates reports that in the early 10th century Thessalonike one could buy copper, lead, iron, glass, objects made of gold and silver as well as textiles of silk and wool.[39] It seems therefore that the town had an important artisanal activity which probably met not only its own needs, but also those of a broader region. Thebes became in the 11th–12th centuries the most conspicuous production centre for silk clothes.[40] However, there is evidence that textile production was developed in other urban sites of minor importance. The so-called *praktikon* of Athens mentions the quarter of the κογχυλάριοι, the purple-dyers, on the south side of the Acropolis.[41] Although writers of the late 12th century like Michael Choniates deplore the fact that Athens, in contrast to Corinth or Thebes, did not produce anything – and of course no textiles either[42] – the reality was probably not so bad.[43] It is probable that textiles were transported to Athens from other production centres in order to be dyed. We know for instance that part, at least, of the textile production of Thebes was being dyed in Kastorion on the Gulf of Krissa.[44] It seems that Athens profited from active maritime trade. The city was probably a link in a larger network of exchange. Michael Choniates reminds the *megas doukas* Michael Stryphnos that when the latter visited Athens – in 1201–1202 – he was impressed by the number of trade ships that sailed to Athens. Unfortunately, sometime later, this prosperity would have been a thing of the past. Certainly Choniates' objective is to provoke Stryphnos' sympathy for the misfortunes of the local population and to ask, as usual, for tax remissions. Nevertheless, his assertion about wealth originating from maritime trade (ὡς καὶ τὴν θάλασσαν αὐτήν, ἐξ ἧς εὐετηρίαν τινὰ πρότερον εἶχον αἱ Ἀθῆναι ... οὐ γὰρ ἕτερον εὐτυχοῦσιν ... ἀγαθόν, ὅτι μὴ τὸ ἐπὶ θαλάττῃ κεῖσθαι καὶ πρὸς τὸν ἐκ θαλάττης πλοῦτον εὖ ἔχειν τῆς κατὰ φύσιν θέσεως) is sufficiently fluent.[45] We do not know if Pireus was the port of Athens during the Middle Byzantine period. It has recently been argued that it was nothing more than an insignificant settlement (πολίχνη).[46] However, the fact that rescue excavations have not brought to light port installations as well as that the *praktikon* of Athens mentions a group of land holdings in Pireus[47] do not provide decisive evidence that medieval Athens did not profit from commercial and maritime activity. Actually, Athens had some kind of artisanal activity (ceramic production[48] and textile dying), which was probably not only destined for local consumption.

There were also markets for agricultural products. Demetrias in the 9th and 10th centuries,[49] Halmyros and possibly Kitros in the 11th and 12th centuries,[50] were cereal markets. Thessalonike was an outlet for the agricultural production of its hinterland, where both Slavs and Greeks were established, and was at the same time a centre for regional and interregional trade between the local populations, the Slavs of the countryside and the Bulgars.[51] It is not a coincidence that in 12th-century Thessalonike there was a market bearing the meaningful name of Σθλαβομέση,[52] serving probably the transactions of the Slavs.

Apart from permanent markets, we may safely presume the periodical organisation of open-air markets on certain days of the week in most parts of Greece. That was the also the case in Constantinople[53] and in Asia Minor.[54] We have evidence that such a market operated in Sparta in the early 11th century.[55] These markets gave the opportunity to itinerant merchants and to small local producers who were not merchants in the narrow sense to dispose of their surplus. The co-existence of permanent and occasional markets is also revealed in other sources from this period. Kekaumenos reports in his *Strategikon* of the 11th century a story about pirate ships which sailed to Demetrias and proposed to the locals to organise a market (ποιῆσαι φόρον) and sell the captives as well as the merchandise they carried on board. The imprudence of the population and the avidity of the local *dynastes* (δυνάστης), a man of Constantinopolitan origin called Noah, who would have tried to control the transactions and, presumably, to levy taxes, led to the plundering of the town.[56] A *dynastes* was someone who exercised authority he held from the state.[57] We probably have a case of a corrupt public servant whose task was to control transactions and who abused his authority. Anyway, it is obvious that the type of trade described by Kekaumenos was carried on within a rather lax framework where the indigenous, not necessarily merchants, had the possibility to buy and sell variable articles.

Fairs organised on the occasion of religious festivals provided another major occasion for merchants.[58] One of the most important was the fair of Saint Demetrius in Thessalonike. Its famous description in the *Timarion* reveals that the city got crowded with numbers of foreign merchants during this event. The Slavs held probably the first place.[59] However, they were not the only ones. Italians as well as Muslims from Spain, Syria and Egypt were present.[60] The fair was also frequented by merchants coming from the south of the Greek peninsula, like textile merchants from Thebes, as well as from the coasts of the Black Sea.

In the 8th–10th century sources merchants are quite often confused or identified with sailors and ship-owners who, at the same time, transported people and merchandise and got involved in trade, like the one mentioned in the Life of Saint Blasios of Amorion. Merchants were mainly itinerant merchants not specialised in specific merchandise. But there must have also been merchants established in their home towns who were sought-after intermediaries. The economic condition of the merchants is unknown. It is significant, however, that until the end of the 10th century, we have no evidence regarding the accumulation of wealth based on trade. It is likely that there were no such cases. One of the malicious anecdotes concerning the emperor Nicephorus I (802–811) and his notorious stinginess is that when the emperor was informed that a *keroularios*[61] (wax producer) of the capital had a personal property of 100 pounds of gold, he confiscated the greater part leaving him only ten pounds.[62] Beyond the usual clichés defaming Nicephorus I, one can discern a certain reservation towards wealth created through commercial activities. But this attitude was modified with time as the economy expanded.[63]

To my knowledge, the first nominal mention of individuals involved in trade in Greece is to be found in Theophanes Continuatus. In his narration of the events of the first Bulgarian war between Tsar Symeon and Byzantium in 894, the author assigns the responsibility for the outbreak of the war upon the *kommerkiarioi* Stavrakios and Mousikos, two favourites of the *basileopator* Stylianos Zaoutzes. Thanks to their personal connections, they apparently managed to transfer the centre of trade between the two states from Constantinople to Thessalonike. Additionally, they apparently started to tax heavily (or arbitrarily?) the transactions (κακῶς κουμερκεύοντες τοὺς Βουλγάρους).[64] It is beyond the scope of this chapter to assess the reasons that led to this war. It has been argued that the Byzantine state wished to establish an alternative centre of trade with the Bulgarian state, which would function at the same time as Constantinople.[65] However, it rather seems that there was actually no shift of trade centre. Both Constantinople and Thessalonike served as exportation-importation centres before and after 894.[66] The reason for the violent Bulgarian reaction lay probably in the decision of the Byzantine state to oblige both the Bulgarians and the merchants from the neighbouring area of Thessalonike to carry out their transactions in specific places, something like the *mitata* which were in place in Constantinople during the same period.[67] It also seems that the Byzantine state tried to impose taxation on transactions that until that moment had not been taxed. It is quite doubtful if the attempt succeeded. The decision provoked the reaction of the Bulgarian side and possibly of those of the Byzantines whose interests were at stake. It is not clear if Stavrakios and Mousikos were only tax collectors, or if they also acted as merchants. It is likely that they were both. They may have bought out the monopoly of acting as intermediaries between the Byzantines and the Bulgars, who were not allowed to conclude transactions directly.[68] In the 7th decade of the 11th century, the Byzantine state made an attempt to impose taxation on the cereal trade carried out between the harbours of the Thracian peninsula and the capital. The decision was imputed to Nikephoritzes, *paradynasteuon* of Michael VII Ducas. It provoked an artificial cereal shortage and consequently an increase in prices.[69] According to the historian Michael Attaleiates, Nikephoritzes forbade the free sale of cereals and ordered that crops had to be concentrated in a specific building, the *phoundax*, where they were bought by cereal traders, under the supervision of the *phoundakarios*, at prices fixed by him.[70] In the case of the *phoundax* of Rhaidestos, the state tried to impose the taxation on a type of trade that until then had remained out of its scope.[71] It is difficult not to notice the common points between the story about Stavrakios and Mousikos on the one side and that concerning Nikephoritzes, on the other.

In the 11th century, the unification of the Balkan peninsula under Byzantine control and the ensuing relative security had as a result the intensification of trade between the northern and the southern parts of the Greek peninsula. The western section of the Via Egnatia, between Thessalonike and Dyrrachion also became relatively safe after the middle of the 11th century. From this time until the end of the 12th century merchants could travel there safely by land.[72] At the same time merchants from the Italian peninsula started to visit Greece more regularly. The first archival testimony dates from the year 1072 and it concerns a commercial journey to Thebes.[73] Commercial relations between Italy and Thebes are indirectly attested already from the 9th century.[74] Corinth knew a period of great prosperity in the 12th century. Excavations have shown that the place of the Roman forum was gradually occupied by shops and *ergasteria* which expanded dynamically.[75] Nicetas Choniates, while narrating the Norman incursion against Corinth in 1147, refers to the ἐμπορεῖον, that is to say a place outside the walls, not far from sea, where commercial transactions took place.[76]

On the other hand, economic expansion accompanied by demographic growth had a favourable effect on trade. The demand for everyday products as well as luxury items increased. People desired and had the means to acquire expensive articles. We observe an increase in the demand for silk textiles mixed with wool and linen.[77] This was probably the result of the desire of middle classes to have access to fine products at a reasonable cost.[78] There is plenty of evidence of this tendency in Constantinople and it may have also been the case in Greece and elsewhere in the Empire. The findings of fine pottery made of white clay in Corinth, Argos, and Sparta[79] testify to the new refined tastes and habits and suggest, naturally, prosperity.[80] It seems therefore that merchants in Greece were quite in touch with what was going on in the capital and contributed to diffusing these trends in Greece. Even Athens, a town of rather minor importance, had ceramic industries where *sgraffito* ware was produced, destined partially to exportation.[81]

Economic expansion had certainly some impact on the financial situation and the social profile of the merchants. In the 11th century the inhabitants of

The urban revolt in Constantinople in favour of the empress Zoe is the best known example.[82] Nevertheless, similar cases are also known in the provinces. The historian Nikephoros Bryennios, writing about those inhabitants of Antioch who pushed the population to revolt against the authorities, uses the following term: οἱ νεωστὶ προκόπτειν ἀρξάμενοι.[83] In other words, those who had recently become rich, apparently through commercial or artisanal activity. The same might have been true in the case of the urban revolt of the inhabitants of Naupaktos, the capital of the theme of Nikopolis, in western Greece, against the *strategos* in 1025–1028. According to the historian John Skylitzes, the reason was the heavy taxation imposed by the *strategos*.[84] It is reasonable to assume that the inhabitants of urban centres were mainly active in artisanal production and trade. The exact nature of the taxes is not known. We may presume, however, that they were taxes on commercial and artisanal activities.

The involvement of the Venetians and later of Pisans and Genoese in the domestic and foreign trade of the Byzantine Empire had certainly an impact on the merchants active in Greece. Venetians visited the Greek peninsula from the first decades of the 11th century for reasons of trade. We find them occasionally in Laconia, where they most probably traded in oil,[85] in Corinth and in Thebes. They became more numerous as years went by. They also started to visit Thessalonike, Halmyros, Kitros[86] and other towns of the north Aegean coast.[87] Silk and silk clothes,[88] ceramics and agricultural products, such as oil,[89] were being exported from Greece to Constantinople and other markets of the eastern Mediterranean. The privileges accorded to the Venetians and the Pisans first by Alexios I Komnenos and then by his successors greatly favoured their activity.[90] Some of them resided permanently in Greece. Whole quarters in Byzantine cities were inhabited by foreigners. Venetians were established in Halmyros before 1155,[91] while Genoese were sometime between 1159 and 1171.[92] Eustathios of Thessalonike, writing about the plunder of Thessalonike by the Normans in 1185, mentions the quarter of the βουργέσιοι, the foreigners who dwelled in Thessalonike, probably in proximity of the sea and the city wall.[93] The βουργέσιοι were foreigners established more or less permanently in Byzantium. Their position seemed scandalous to Byzantine eyes, since they profited from the advantages of a permanent dweller while having none of the disadvantages; they actually profited from the privileges bestowed by Byzantium on the cities of their origin.[94]

At the same time Byzantium suffered serious drawbacks in Asia Minor and, as a result, Greece became a very dynamic pole of commercial activity. Local producers and tradesmen started to do business with foreigners. It is difficult to ascertain whether or not they formed partnerships. In any case, in 1126 the Byzantines who traded with Venetians were exempted from the *kommerkion*, a development which offered them a considerable advantage.[95] Foreign merchants encouraged the investments in such cultures as olive trees and mulberries, which presented major economic interest.[96] However, one

322 *Maria Gerolymatou*

has also to take account of the intermediate role played by the local, Greek, merchants who intervened between the producers and the exporters.[97] We know from the sources of major transactions between western exporters and the local aristocracy. A famous case is that of a Venetian merchant who, in 1201, bought a large quantity of olive oil from Pisan merchants.[98] In this type of transaction Greek merchants acted probably as middlemen, who assured the necessary supplies thanks to their connections with the local producers. At the same time Greek ship-owners active between the south of the Peloponnese and the eastern coast of Greece[99] may have also ventured further to the north.

An important question that rises is that of the organisation of merchants in the provinces. In other words, to decide whether there was in Middle Byzantine Greece a structure with features similar to those of the professional corporation system which was in place in Constantinople. First of all, one has to remark that in Byzantium the aim of the organisation of professionals in *corps de metiers* was not to defend the interests of the members, but rather those of the state. Their *raison d'être* was to assure the provisioning of the capital in basic foodstuffs such as bread, wine, fish and meat; to control the trade of valuable raw materials and luxury items such as silk and silk clothes; and to prohibit the exportation of precious metals. The whole mechanism was controlled by the state, which provided the necessary money and the officials who assured its function.[100]

It is quite doubtful if a similar mechanism exercising strict control was ever established in the Byzantine provinces however.[101] There were not any big cities like Constantinople either in Asia Minor or in the Balkans, and their supply with everyday necessities did not face the same difficulties. The capital constituted a separate economic zone from the rest of the Empire.[102] There was probably no reason for the state to spend money on the maintenance of such a mechanism in the provinces. The duties of the *eparchoi* (ἔπαρχοι) of Nicaea and Thessalonike, who are known from seals dated in the 8th–9th centuries,[103] are not defined, so it is risky to associate them with those of the *eparchos* of Constantinople. In any case the *eparchos* of Thessalonike may have been a late reminiscence of the *Praefectus praetorio per Illyricum*. Even in Constantinople the organisation of professionals on the initiative of the state was to loosen in the 11th and 12th centuries.[104] However, that does not mean that there was absolutely no form of organisation of different categories of professionals in Middle Byzantine Greece. It is inconceivable for medieval artisans and tradesmen to act outside a certain frame. According to Constantine Porphyrogenitus the κογχυλευταὶ (purple-dyers) and the sailors of the Peloponnese were exempted from the obligation to contribute collectively to the preparation of a military expedition.[105] That presupposes the existence of some form of organisation which would make possible the collective taxation. In the 12th century some, at least, of the merchants in Thessalonike formed separate *corps de métiers* under their own chiefs. The mention of a πρῶτος τῶν καμελαυκάδων in a document of Mount Athos[106] suggests a kind of hierarchy which was not in place, however, for safe-guarding the interests of the state. At the end of the 12th century metro-politan bishop Michael Choniates, while pleading with Demetrios Tornikes for fiscal mitigations for his people, notices that βραχεῖα ἡ τῶν συστημάτων ποσότης καὶ οὐδ᾿αὐτὴ κοινωφελής.[107] Is it an allusion to the limited contri-bution of the συστήματα to the economics of the small metropolis of Athens?[108] It may be so. In any case, the combination of available evidence suggests some organisation of provincial tradesmen and craftsmen destined mainly for the collective coverage of taxation.

To sum up, there was not only one type of merchant in Greece. Next to the local artisan-merchant who held a shop or a workshop and commercialised either his own production, or goods bought from other merchants, there was the merchant who was on the move travelling to other parts of Greece or to the capital and who, from the 11th century onwards, was often a foreigner. On the other hand, it is not certain if these merchants who were on the move undertook commercial journeys to Asia Minor. It seems that contacts between the two great entities of the Empire were rather indirect, through Constantinople. Greek merchants succeeded in adapting quite satisfactorily to the situations each time present. Did some of them have the opportunity to become something like Kalomodios, the notorious businessman and banker who at the end of the 12th century launched large-scale commercial en-terprises from Constantinople?[109] The answer is probably no. The markets of Greece were after all provincial markets and the volume of the transactions which were taking place there could not be compared with the sums engaged in business by certain Constantinopolitan merchants. Nevertheless, mer-chants active in Byzantine Greece had some advantages which their col-leagues from Asia Minor probably lacked, because of the different political context. That is to say they had better opportunities to commercialise local production and a better motivation to invest in trade. Despite the fact that their position was not an enviable one in comparison with that of some of their foreign colleagues they seem to have functioned quite satisfactorily.

Notes

  1 Oikonomides 1993.
  2 Oikonomides 1993: 639–641.
  3 JGR IV, § 51.7.
  4 Gerolymatou 2008: 204–205.
  5 Gerolymatou 2008: 206–211.
  6 Oikonomides 1986: 36–41.
  7 Oikonomides 1986: 41.
  8 Oikonomides 1986: 43.
  9 Gerolymatou 2008: 86–87.
10 Hendy 1985: 640, note 13. For Oikonomides' arguments against this point of view, see Oikonomides 1993. Brandes 1999: 55 argues that the *kommerkiarioi* were responsible for levying taxes in kind which were concentrated in ἀποθῆκαι and distributed to the army.

324 *Maria Gerolymatou*

11 Brubaker and Haldon 2011: 685–693.
12 Brubaker and Haldon 2011: 704–705.
13 Brubaker and Haldon 2011: 702–703.
14 See the introductory note in Nesbitt and Oikonomides 1994: 22.
15 Živković 1999: 141–154.
16 For references, see Brubaker and Haldon 2011: 698, note 110.
17 See Winkelmann 1985: 124 for a list of *kommerkiarioi* of Hellas; Nesbitt and Oikonomides 1994: no. 8.29.
18 It has been argued that the *kommerkiarioi* of the early 9th century, numerous in southern and western Greece, were primarily involved in areas which had recently passed under the control of the Byzantine state (Brubaker and Haldon 2011: 702–703).
19 Gerolymatou 2001: 353–355.
20 *The Miracles of St Artemius*: 7.
21 *Vita Willibaldi*: 93.
22 *Theophanis Chronographia*: 422–423.
23 For references, see Gagtzis, Leontsini, and Panopoulou 1993.
24 For references, see Nesbitt and Oikonomides 1994: nos. 22.10–22.14.
25 Zacos – Veglery, vol. 1.2, no 1865 (=Nesbitt and Oikonomides, 1994, no. 1.5). The same seems to be true for a seal from Corinth attributed by the editor to a *kommerkiarios* of Hellas, who seemingly associated the posts of *kommerkiarioi* of Hellas, Peloponnesos and Cephalonia (oral communication of A. Dunn to Nesbitt and Oikonomides 1994: no. 1.5).
26 Nesbitt and Oikonomides 1994: no. 8.30. On the 'West', see Dunn 1993: 3–24.
27 Lampropoulou and Moutzale 2011.
28 Oikonomides 1996.
29 *Vita S. Blasii*: 666. On the grain supply of the Byzantine Empire, see Teall 1959: 117–123. It still remains a basic study. The author emphasises the role of Thrace and Macedonia as grain supply regions of the south Balkans.
30 Karagiorgou 2013: 166.
31 Bazaiou-Barabas 1989: 383–387.
32 Lemerle 1979: § 254.
33 Sanders 2003: 390; Poulou-Papademetriou 2001: 239.
34 Armstrong 2001: 57–67, especially 63–64.
35 Koilakou 2013: 187, Fig. 164.
36 *Life of Saint Nikon*: § 71.6–8.
37 *Life of Saint Nikon*: § 35.68–75.
38 *Vita Basilii*: § 73.8–9, 74.30–36; Gerolymatou 2008: 169–170.
39 *Ioannis Caminiatae De expugnatione*: 11.74–85.
40 For references, see Gerolymatou 2008: 159; more recently, see Koilakou 2013: 185–186.
41 Granstrem, Medvedev, and Papachryssanthou 1976: 35 (A2.25).
42 *Michaelis Choniatae Epistulae*: nos. 60.11–12. Athens' 'poverty' is indirectly compared with Constantinople's opulence (*Michaelis Choniatae Epistulae*: no. 50.60–65).
43 Bouras 2010: 113–114.
44 Dunn 2006: 53–58.
45 *Michaelis Choniatae Epistulae*: no. 60.10–21.
46 Pallis 2013: 145–146.
47 Granstrem, Medvedev and Papachryssanthou 1976: 30 (A1.7-11).
48 Bouras 2017: 117–119.
49 Gerolymatou 2008, 154–155.
50 Gerolymatou 2008: 156–158.

The Merchant in Middle Byzantine Greece 325

51 *Ioannis Caminiatae De expugnatione*: 8.80–86.
52 *Actes de Docheiariou*: no 4.27–28 and comments on page 79.
53 *Das Eparchenbuch*: § 9.7.
54 *Life of Constantine the Jew*: § 5.
55 *Life of Saint Nikon*: § 75.16–17.
56 *Kekaumenos*: 125–127.
57 Ragia 2016: 331–341.
58 Vryonis 1981.
59 *Pseudo-Luciano, Timarione*: 53.116–120.
60 *Pseudo-Luciano, Timarione*: 54–55.150–158.
61 On the *keroularioi*, see *Das Eparchenbuch*: § 11.
62 *Theophanis Chronographia*: 487.29–488.6.
63 Gerolymatou 2008: 236.
64 *Theophanis Continuatus*: 357.12–19.
65 Oikonomides 1991: 241–248.
66 Gerolymatou, 2008: 144–146.
67 *Das Eparchenbuch*: § 5.2, 5.5, 9.1, 9.6.
68 Gerolymatou 2008: 94–95.
69 Cheynet and Morrisson: 2002, 822–823, 830.
70 *Michaelis Attaliatae Historia*: 155.23–157.26.
71 Gerolymatou 2008: 209–211.
72 Oikonomides 1996: 12–13.
73 Morozzo della Rocca and Lombardo 1940: no. 12.
74 Koilakou 2013: 183.
75 Athanasoulis 2013: 201–203.
76 *Nicetae Choniatae Historia*: 75. On the term ἐμπόριον, ἐμπορεῖον, see Gerolymatou 2009, especially 105.
77 For the term *αιγειομέταξαγα*, see *Ptochoprodromos*: 202.87.
78 Gerolymatou 2004: 264; Gerolymatou 2018.
79 On the importation of white clay pottery from Constantinople to Argos and Sparta in the late 10th–11th centuries, see Bakourou, Katsara, and Kalamara 2003: 234.
80 Gerolymatou 2008: 166, 168, 169, with relevant references; Gerolymatou 2018.
81 Bouras 2010: 113.
82 Vryonis 1963: 287–314.
83 *Nicephorus Bryennius*: 205.20–1.
84 *Ioannis Skylitzae Synopsis Historiarum*: 372.73–8.
85 *Life of Saint Nikon*: § 74.1–3.
86 On ceramics from Kitros, see Marki, Aggelkou, and Cheimonopoulou 2007: 271–281.
87 For references, see Gerolymatou 2008: nos. 155–158.
88 On the exportation of silk clothes and textiles from Corinth and Thebes to Constantinople, see *Nicetae Choniatae Historia*; cf. Jacoby 1991–1992.
89 Morozzo della Rocca and Lombardo 1940: I, nos. 65, 112, 117, 135.
90 For the diplomatic edition of the chrysobulls in favour of Venice, see *I Trattati*: nos. 2–11. For those in favour of Pisa, see *MM*: vol. III, no. III (chrysobull of Isaakios II Angelos, into which the chrysobull of Alexios I Komnenos is inserted).
91 Morozzo della Rocca and Lombardo 1940: I, no. 115.
92 Lilie 1984.
93 *Eustazio di Tessalonica*: 92.7–9; Jacoby 2003: 90–91.
94 *Ioannis Cinnami Epitome*: 281–282.
95 *I Trattati* 1993: no. 3, p. 55.

326 *Maria Gerolymatou*

96 Jacoby 1991–1992; Gerolymatou 2008: 168; Jacoby 2013: 234–238.
97 Jacoby 2013: 236–237.
98 Morozzo della Rocca and Lombardo 1940: I, no. 456.
99 *Michaelis Choniatae Epistulae*: nos. 84.14–19.
100 Maniatis 2001: 366.
101 Gerolymatou 2008: 115–116.
102 Oikonomides 1997: 222–224; Gerolymatou 2008: 55–59.
103 Konstantakopoulou 1985: 157–162.
104 Gerolymatou 2008: 55.
105 *Constantine Porphyrogenitus De administrando imperio*: § 52.11
106 *Actes de Lavra*: I, no. 53.39–40.
107 *Michaelis Choniatae Epistulae*: no. 32.56–57.
108 The term ποσότης means the amount of a fiscal assessment (Dölger 1960: 126).
109 *Nicetae Choniatae Historia*: 523–524; see also Gerolymatou 2015: 210–212.

References

Actes de Docheiariou, Oikonomides, N., ed. (1984), 'Archives de l'Athos XIII'. Paris.
Actes de Lavra, Lemerle, P., Guillou, A. and Svoronos, N., eds. (1970), 'Archives de l'Athos V'. Paris.
Armstrong, P. (2001), 'From Constantinople to Lakedaimon: impressed white wares', in C. Otten-Froux, J. Herrin, and M. Mullett, eds., *Mosaic. Festschrift for A.H.S Megaw*, British School at Athens Studies 8, London: 57–68.
Athanasoulis, D. (2013), 'Corinth', in J. Albani and E. Chalkia, eds., *Heaven and Earth: Cities and Countryside in Byzantine Greece*, Athens: 192–210.
Bakourou, A., Katsara, E., and Kalamara, P. (2003), 'Argos and Sparta: pottery of the 12th and 13th centuries', in Ch. Bakirtzes, ed., *7o Diethnes Synedrio Mesaionikes Kerameikes tes Mesogeiou*, Athens: 233–236.
Bazaiou-Barabas, T. (1989), 'Semeioma gia ten epidrome tou Symeon kata tes kyrios Hellados (arches 10ou aiona)', *Byzantina Symmeikta* 8: 383–387.
Bouras, Ch. (2010), *Vyzantine Athena, 10os–12os ai.*, Benaki Museum, Supplement 6, Athens.
Bouras, Ch. (2017), *Byzantine Athens 10th–12th centuries*. London/New York.
Brandes, W. (1999), 'Byzantine sources in the seventh and eighth centuries – different sources, different histories?', in G. Brogiolo and B. Ward-Perkins, eds., *The Idea and Ideal of the Town between Late Antiquity and the Early Middle Ages*. Leiden/Boston/Köln.
Brubaker, L., and Haldon, J. (2011), *Byzantium in the Iconoclastic Era, c. 680–850*. Cambridge.
Cheynet, J.-C., and Morrisson, C. (2002), 'Prices and wages in the Byzantine world', in A. Laiou, ed., *The Economic History of Byzantium*, 3 vols. Dumbarton Oaks Studies XXIX, Washington, DC: vol. 2, 815–878.
Constantine Porphyrogenitus De administrando imperio, Moravcik, G., Jenkins, R. (ed., trad.), 1967, CFHB I, Washington, DC: Dumbarton Oaks.
Das Eparchenbuch Leons des Weisen, Koder, J., ed. (1991), *CFHB* XXXIII, Vienna.
Dölger, F. (1960), *Beiträge zur Geschichte der byzantinischen Finanzverwaltung besonders des 10. und 11. Jahrhunderts*. Darmstadt.
Dunn, A. (1993), 'The kommerkiarios, the Apotheke, the Dromos, the Vardarios and the West', *Byzantine and Modern Greek Studies* 17: 3–24.

Dunn, A. (2006), 'The rise and fall of towns, loci of maritime traffic, and silk production: the problem of Thisvi Kastorion', in E. Jeffreys, ed., *Byzantine Style, Religion and Civilization: In Honour of Sir Steven Runciman*, Cambridge: 38–71.

Eustazio di Tessalonica, L'espugnazione di Tessalonica [di], Kyriakides, S., ed., and Rotolo, V., tr. (1961), Testi e monumenti 5. Palermo.

Gagtzis, D., Leontsini, M., and Panopoulou, A. (1993), 'Peloponnesos kai notia Italia. Stathmoi epikoinonias ste mese vyzantine periodo', in N. Moschonas, ed., *H epikoinonia sto Vyzantio*, Athens: 469–486.

Gerolymatou, M. (2001), 'Emporike drasterioteta kata tous skoteinous aiones', in E. Kountoura-Galake, ed., *Oi skoteinoi aiones tou Vyzantiou (7os–9os ai)*, National Hellenic Research Foundation. Institute for Byzantine Research. International Symposium 9, Athens: 347–364.

Gerolymatou, M. (2004), 'Emporio, koinonia kai aisthiseis', in Ch. Angelidi, ed., *Byzantium Matures. Choices, Sensitivities and Modes of Expression (Eleventh to Fifteenth Centuries)*, National Hellenic Research Foundation. Institute for Byzantine Research, Athens: 257–268.

Gerolymatou, M. (2008), *Agores, emporoi kai emporio sto Vyzantio (9os–12. ai.)*, National Hellenic Research Foundation. Institute for Byzantine Research. Monographies 9. Athens.

Gerolymatou, M. (2009), 'Note sur l'*emporion* byzantin', in *Kapetanios kai logios. Meletes sti mnimi tou Dimitri I. Polemi*, Andros: 103–113.

Gerolymatou, M. (2015), 'Private investment in trade in the final years of the twelfth century', in A. Simpson, ed., *Byzantium 1180–1204: "The Sad Quarter of a century"*, Institute of Historical Research. International Symposium 22, Athens: 205–220.

Gerolymatou, M. (2018), 'Mikra antikeimena, megales prosdokies. E diamorfosi ton epithymion ton «meson» kata ton 11o–12o aiona', in A. Giagkaki and A. Panopoulou, eds., *To Vyzantio choris lampsi. Ta tapeina antikeimena kai i chrisi tous ston kathimerion vio ton Vyzantinon*, Institute for Historical Research, Athens: 283–305.

Granstrem, E., Medvedev, I., and Papachryssanthou, D. (1976), 'Fragment d'un praktikon de la région d'Athènes (avant 1204)', *REB* 34: 5–44.

Hendy, M. (1985), *Studies on the Byzantine Monetary Economy, c. 300–1450.* Cambridge.

Ioannis Caminiatae De expugnatione Thessalonicae, Böhlig, G., ed. (1974), CFHB IV. Berlin/New York.

Ioannis Cinnami Epitome rerum ab Ioanne et Alexio Comnenis gestarum, Meineke, A., ed. (1836). Bonn.

Ioannis Skylitzae Synopsis Historiarum, Thurn, I., ed. (1973), CFHB V. Berlin/New York.

Jacoby, D. (1991–1992), 'Silk in western Byzantium', *BZ* 84/85: 452–500.

Jacoby, D. (2003), 'Foreigners and the urban economy in Thessalonike, c. 1150–c. 1430', *DOP* 57: 85–132.

Jacoby, D. (2013), 'Rural exploitation and market economy in the Late Medieval Peloponnese', in S. Gerstel, ed., *Viewing the Morea: Land and People in the Late Medieval Peloponnese*, Dumbarton Oaks Byzantina Symposia and Colloquia, Washington, DC: 213–275.

JGR: *Jus Graecoromanum*, Zepos, I., and Zepos, P., eds. (1931), vols. 1–6, phot. repr., 1962. Athens.

328 *Maria Gerolymatou*

Karagiorgou, O. (2013), '"Christian" or "Thessalian Thebes": the port city of Late Antique Thessaly', in J. Albani and E. Chalkia, eds., *Heaven and Earth: Cities and Countryside in Byzantine Greece*, Athens: 156–167.

Kekaumenos Strategikon, Litavrin, G., ed., and Tsoungarakis, D. (1996). Athens.

Koilakou, Ch. (2013), 'Byzantine Thebes', in J. Albani and E. Chalkia, eds., *Heaven and Earth: Cities and Countryside in Byzantine Greece*, Athens: 181–191.

Konstantakopoulou, A. (1985), 'L'éparque de Thessalonique: les origines d'une institution administrative (VIIIe-IXe siècles)', *Ellinikes anakoinoseis sto Pempto Diethnes Synedrio Spoudon Notioanatolikis Europis, Veligradi, 11–17 Septemvriou 1984*, Athens: 157–162.

Lampropoulou, A., and Moutzale, A. (2011), 'H metoikia ton katoikon tes Patras sto Region tes Kalavrias (tele 6ou - arches 9ou aiona). E anairese mias martyrias', in L. Droulia and A. Rizakis, eds., *Achaia kai notios Italia. Epikoinonia, antallages kai scheseis apo tin Archaiotita os simera*, Athens: 239–271.

Lemerle, P. (1979–1981), *Les plus anciens recueils des Miracles de Saint Démétrius et la pénétration des Slaves dans les Balkans*, 2 vols. Paris.

*Life of Saint Constantine: Βίος τοῦ ὁσίου πατρὸς ἡμῶν Κωνσταντίνου τοῦ ἐξ Ἰουδαίων, Acta Sanctorum, Novembris*t. IV: 628–656.

The Life of Saint Nikon, Sullivan, D., tr. (1987), Brookline, MA.

Lilie, R.-J. (1984), *Handel und Politik zwischen dem byzantinischen Reich und den italienischen Kommunen Venedig, Pisa und Genua in der Epoche der Komnenen und der Angeloi, 1081–1204*. Amsterdam.

Maniatis, G. (2001), 'The domain of private guilds in the Byzantine economy, tenth to fifteenth centuries', *DOP* 55: 339–369.

Marki, E., Aggelkou, E., and Cheimonopoulou, M. (2007), 'H keramiki enos meso-vyzantinou limaniou tes Makedonias. H periptose tou Kitrous', *Deltion tes Christianikes Archaiologikes Hetaireias* 28: 271–282.

Michaelis Attaliatae Historia, Tsolakis, E., ed. (2011), CFHB L, Athens.

Michaelis Choniatae Epistulae, Kolovou, F., ed. (2001), CFHB XLI. Berlin/New York.

MM Miklosich, F., and Müller, I. (1860–1890), *Acta et diplomata graeca medii aevi*, I–VI. Vienna.

The Miracles of St. Artemius: A Collection of Miracle Stories by an Anonymous Author of Seventh Century Byzantium, Crisafulli, V., and Nesbitt, J. (1997). Leiden.

Morozzo della Rocca, R., and Lombardo, A., eds. (1940), *Documenti del commercio veneziano nei secoli XIe–XIIIe*, vols. I-II. Turin.

Nesbitt, J., and Oikonomides, N., eds. (1994), *Catalogue of Byzantine Seals at Dumbarton Oaks and in the Fogg Museum of Art*, vol. 2. Washington, DC.

Nicephori Bryennii Historiarum libri quattuor, Gautier, P., ed. (1975), CFHB IX. Brussels.

Nicetae Choniatae Historia, van Dieten, I.-A., ed. (1975), CFHB XI. Berlin/New York.

Oikonomides, N. (1986), 'Silk trade and production in Byzantium from the sixth to ninth century: the seals of kommerkiarioi', *DOP* 40: 33–53.

Oikonomides, N. (1991), 'Le kommerkion d'Abydos, Thessalonique et le commerce bulgare au IXe siècle', in V. Kravari, J. Lefort, and C. Morrisson, eds., *Hommes et richesses dans l'Empire byzantin*, t.2, *VIIIe-XVe siècle*, Réalités byzantines 3. Paris.

Oikonomides, N. (1993), 'Le marchand byzantin des provinces (IXe-XIe s.)', in *Mercati e mercanti nell'alto Medioevo: l'area euroasiatica e l'area mediterranea*, Spoleto: 633–665 (= N. Oikonomides, 2004, *Social and Economic Life in Byzantium*, Aldershot: no. VIII).

Oikonomides, N. (1996), 'The medieval Via Egnatia', in E. Zachariadou, ed., *The Via Egnatia under Ottoman Rule (1380–1669)*, Rethymno (= N. Oikonomides (2004), *Social and Economic Life in Byzantium*, Aldershot: no. XXIII).

Oikonomides, N. (1997), 'The economic region of Constantinople: from directed economy to free economy, and the role of the Italians', in G. Arnaldi and G. Cavallo, eds., *Europa medievale e mondo bizantino*, Rome: 221–238.

Pallis, G. (2013), 'Topografika tou athenaikou pediou kata te mese vyzantine periodo (9os–12os ai.)', *Byzantina Symmeikta* 23: 105–182.

Poulou-Papademetriou, N. (2001), 'Byzantine keramike apo ton elleniko nesiotiko choro kai apo ten Peloponneso', in E. Kountoura-Galake, ed., *Oi skoteinoi aiones tou Vyzantiou (7os–9os ai.)*, Institute for Byzantine Research. International Symposium 9, Athens: 231–248.

Pseudo-Luciano, Timarione, Romano, R., ed. (1974). Naples.

Ptochoprodromos, Eideneier, H., ed. (2012). Herakleion.

Ragia, E. (2016), 'Social group profiles in Byzantium', *Byzantina Symmeikta* 26: 309–372.

Sanders, G. (2003), 'Recent developments in the chronology of Byzantine Corinth', in C.K. Williams II and N. Bookidis, eds., *Corinth: The Centenary, 1896–1996*, Results of Excavations XX, The American School of Classical Studies at Athens, Corinth: 385–399.

Teall, J. (1959), 'The grain supply of the Byzantine Empire, 330–1025', *DOP* 13: 87–139.

Theophanis Chronographia, de Boor, C., ed. (1883), vol. 1. Leipzig.

Theophanis Continuatus, Bekker, I., ed. (1828). Bonn.

I trattati con Bizanzio. 992–1198, Pozza, M., and Ravegnani, G., eds. (1993), Pacta veneta 4. Venice.

Vita Basilii: Chronographiae quae Theophanis Continuatui nomine fertur liber quo Vita Basilii Imperatoris amplectitur, Ševčenko, I., ed. (2011), CFHB XLII. Berlin/Boston.

Vita Blasii Amoriensis: Βίος τοῦ ὁσίου πατρὸς ἡμῶν Βλασίου, *Acta Sanctorum Novembris* t. IV: 656–669.

Vita Willibaldi episcopi Eichstetensis, in *Monumenta Germaniae Historica. Scriptores in folio*, vol. 15.1 (1887). Hanover.

Vryonis, S. (1963), 'Byzantine Δημοκρατία and the guilds in the eleventh century', *DOP* 17: 287–314.

Vryonis, S. (1981), 'The Panegyris of the Byzantine Saint: a study in the nature of a medieval institution, its origins and fate', in S. Hackel, ed., *The Byzantine Saint*, Fourteenth Spring Symposium of Byzantine Studies. University of Birmingham, London: 196–226.

Winkelmann, F. (1985), *Byzantinische Rang-und Ämterstruktur im 8. und 9. Jahrhundert*, Berliner Byzantinistische Arbeiten 53. Berlin.

Živković, T. (1999), 'The date of the creation of the theme of Peloponnese', *Byzantina Symmeikta* 13: 141–155.

Index

Note: Italicized page numbers refer to figures. Page numbers followed by "n" refer to notes.

Acharnai/Menidi: rural settlements, nucleated or dispersed 43
Acheiropoietos basilica *109*; 7th-century restoration of 108–117; cross-section of *112*; ionic impost capitals *110*; longitudinal section of *115*; south propylon *114*
Adrian Komnenos 303
Aegean, maritime routes in (7th–9th centuries) 79–97, *92*, *93*, *95*; amphorae 82–88, *84–86*; belt buckles 88–91, *88*; coins 88–91; Glazed White Ware I and II (Hayes' Saraçhane typology) 80–82, *81*, *82*; lead seals 88–91
Africa Proconsularis 79
Aghios Konstantinos 193–195, *194*
'Agioi Deka' 56
Agios Georgios stoVouno *92*
Agora of Athens 174–176, *175*; materials in 176
Aigosthena *40*
Ais Adriasstou Ai Adria to Vouno 273, *273*
Alexios I Komnenos (1081–1118) 234, 240, 285, 321
Alexios II (1180–1183) 237
Alexios III (1195–1203) 303, 308
Alexius I Comnenus 275n18
amphorae 82–88; Bojburun shipwreck *84*; Eupalinos tunnel *86*; ovoid *85*
Anastasius I 142, *143*
AngelikiMexia 237
Anna Radene 235
apothekai 315
Archbishop Paul of Hagia Sophia 227

Arethousa 13, *14*
Asia Minor: buckle types 89; economic activity 303; Glazed White Wares 82; lamp 27, *27*; military bases 184
Athanassoulis, D. 137
Athens 172; 'Dark Age' wells 173–176, *173*, *175*; map of *173*
Attic *civitates* 37–39, *40*, 44
Attic settlements, location of *39*
Avramea, A.: *Tabula Imperii Byzantini* 3; *Tabula Imperii Romani* 3

Basil I (867–886) 215
Basil II (976–1025) 308
basilikakommerkia 315
belt buckles 88–91, *88*
Bintliff, J.: *Complete Archaeology of Greece: From Hunter-Gatherers to the 20th Century A.D.* 1
Bishop Niketas of Berroia 231
Black Death 159, 212–213, *213*
Boeotia 185; countryside, defending 188–192; with inset of Antikyra Bay *186*
Boeotian Survey (Bradford and Cambridge Universities) 3, 5
Bon, A.: *Le Péloponnèse byzantinjusqu'en 1204* 2
Boura, L.: *Ê elladikê naodomia kata ton 12o aiôna* 2
Bouras, C.: *Byzantine Athens, 10th–12th Centuries* 1–2; *Ê elladikê naodomia kata ton 12o aiôna* 2
Bradford University: Boeotian Survey 3, 5
Bryennios, N. 321

Index 331

Butrint 166–177; map of *167*; Tower 1
170–172, *170*, *171*; Western
Defences 169–170, *170*, *171*
Byzantine Corinth: fortifications and
location of 147–153, *149*, *151*,
152; Late, map of *148*
Byzantine Empire 2, 253, 282, 292, 321
Byzantine Greece: pollen data for
207–211, *209–211*
Byzantine sites, map of *80*

Çaka ("Tzachas") 303
Cambridge University: Boeotian Survey
3, 5
Caraher, B. 138
Chalke 265–274; Chorio, mountainous
area of 272–273, *272*; Kellia
267–270, 275n21; map of *266*
Chalkida (Middle Byzantine) 185–188;
walls of *188*
Chalkidiki, Bhiadoudi 12, *13*, 306
charity, in Middle Byzantine Greece
281–293; episcopal responses
286–289; imperial claims 283–286;
new order 289–292
Chomatenos, D. 289
Choniates, M. 286–288, 293, 307, 317, 323
Choniates, N. 303
Chorio, mountainous area of
272–273, *272*
Chozoviotissa 275n18
Chrysostom, J.: Divine Liturgy 17
Church of Saints Sergios, Bacchos, and
Georgios *239*
city-village 38
civitas/civitates 38–40, *39*, *41*, 44, 45n19
coins 88–91; Aegean 88–91; Grande
Brèche 139–142, *139*, *146*
Constantine IX (1042–1055) 308
Corinth (Byzantine): economy of 155–159,
156; fortifications and location of
147–153, *148*, *149*, *151*, *152*
corps de metiers 322
cultural archaeology 4
Curta, F.: *Edinburgh History of the
Greeks C.500 to 1050: The Early
Middle Ages* 1

Daskaleio 190–192, *191*
dekateia 308
Deligiannakis, G.: *Dodecanese and the
Eastern Aegean Islands in Late
Antiquity, AD 300–700* 1

Divine Liturgy 17
Di Vita, A. 56
Dodecanese islands 196, *197*

Eirene Prasine 235
Eleusis: minor urban settlements
40–41, *41*
EnneaPyrgoi (Mesogeia): rural
settlements, nucleated or
dispersed 43
entrepôt 315
emporia see minor urban settlements
(*emporia*)
Episcopal Complex, Louloudies Pieria,
Western Macedonia 12, *12*
Episkope of Skyros 228, *228*
'estate holder' *(emphyteutes)* 16
EustathiosKodratos 236, 290–291

Forum of Corinth 2

Galatiani 194, *195*
GBD *see* Gortyn Byzantine
District (GBD)
Georgios Marasiatis 239
Geoponika 307
Giovanni Sercambi 141, 142
Glazed White Ware I and II (Hayes'
Saraçhane typology) 80–82, *81*,
82, 98n13
globular amphorae 85–87, *86*, 97, 99n39,
169, 175
Gortyn Byzantine District (GBD) 53–74,
62–65; collapsing roofs 69–73, *71*,
72; point of view 54–55; site
55–61, *56*, *58*, *60*; time of
66–69, *67*
Grande Brèche: bridging 137–160;
coins, cult of 139–142, *139*,
146; Corinth (Byzantine)
see Corinth (Byzantine):
earthquake 153–155; Late
Roman pottery, chronology of
142–147, *143–146*; Lechaion
153–155, *154*
Greco, El. 56
Greek Archaeological Service 3
Gregory, T. 137

Hagia Mone, Areia 236, *236*
Hagia Sophia, Thessalonike 118n47,
227, 228, 241n7; basilica's
narthex, fragments of 123,

332 *Index*

124; bell tower of *127*; classification of 122; 'Dark Age' architecture of 121–129; eastern wall of the basilica's narthex, fragments of *125*; galleries of *128*; northern column of western gallery *129*; plan of *122*; transverse section, reconstruction of 122–123, *123*; western gallery of *126*

Hagios Nikolaos touKasnitze 235

Helladic School 230

Hierissos (Middle Byzantine) 215–221; buckle with representation of Pegasus *218*; houses and tombs, ruins of *217*; *kastron* of 219, 220; Polychrome White Ware sherds *218*; Samonas of Thessaloniki, lead seal of *219*; topographic plan 215, *216*; zoomorphic padlock *218*

imperial claims 283–286

institutional Church, Early Christian Greece 11–19

Isaac I 285

Isaac II Angelos (1185–1195) 286, 308

Ittar, S. *151*

John Apokaukos of Naupaktos 281, 288–289, 291

John II 285, 308

John Tzimiskes (969–976) 308

justice, in Middle Byzantine Greece 281–293; episcopal responses 286–289; imperial claims 283–286; new order 289–292

Kalymnos Island (Middle Byzantine), defending 192–196, *196*

kanonikon 285

karpophoro 16–17

Kastelli 192, *193*

Kellia *267–270*, 275n21

keroularios 319

Kibyrrhaiotai 96–97

Kissavos: map of *23*

Kolovos, J. 215

kommerkiarioi 89, 314–316, 318

kommerkion 308, 314, 321

Konstantinos Monasteriotes 235

Kosso, C. 4–5

Kythera island *92*

Laiou, A. 4

Lambrika: rural settlements, nucleated or dispersed 43

landowners, economic strategies of 302–310

landscape archaeology 3

Late Roman pottery, chronology of 142–147, *143–146*

Lavreotic Olympus 13, *15*

lead seals 88–91

Lechaion 153–155; basilica *154*; harbour *154*

Lemerle, P. 2

Leo I (457–74) 141

Leo V (813–820) 91

longue-durée framework 1

Loukas Chrysoberges (1157–1170) 235

Malicious Man in the Guise of the Present Bishop of Thessalonike, A 291

Malta 2

Malthus, T. 155

Manuel I Komnenos (1143–1180) 235, 240, 285–286, 303

Metellus, Quintus Curtius 57

Metropolitan Philippos of Serres 231

Michael VII Ducas 320

Middle Byzantine Greece: Boeotia countryside, defending 188–192; Chalkida 185–188, *188*; charity and justice in 281–293; defences of (7th–12th centuries) 182–198; fortifications 182–183, *183*; Kalymnos island, defending 192–196, *196*; merchant in 314–323; revival 212–213; Thebes 185–188, *187*

Middle Byzantine Hierissos *see* Hierissos (Middle Byzantine)

minor urban settlements *(emporia)* 40–45

Mitropolis 56, 59

Mochlos, Loutres *95*

Mouzalon, N. 283–285

Nicephorus I (802–811) 319

Nikephoros III Botaneiates 231

NikephorosPhokas 255

Nikolaos Bishop of Lakedaimon 228

Nikolaos Droungarios 230–231

Nikolaos Kalomalos 233

Nikon Metanoeite 237, 238

Normans 303

Oikonomides, N. 314
Orlandos, A. 16
Oropos: minor urban settlements 41

Paiania (Mesogeia): rural settlements,
    nucleated or dispersed 43
Palaiopolis *92*
palynology 4, 207–208
Panagia Krena 236
Pantokrator monastery 307
Papi, E. 57
Patriarch Loukas 235
peasant farmers, economic strategies of
    302–310
Peiraeus: minor urban settlements 40
Peloponnese, church-building in
    253–260, *254, 255*; distribution
    257; geographical
    characteristics *256*
Phoinikia (southeast Attica): rural
    settlements, nucleated or
    dispersed 43
phoundakarios 320
phoundax 320
Phthiotic Thebes, *agora* of 17
Plasi (Marathon): rural settlements,
    nucleated or dispersed 43
pollen data: of Black Death 212–213; for
    Byzantine Greece 207–208, *209*,
    210; for Late Antiquity 211, *212*;
    for Messenia 259; for Middle
    Byzantine 211–212
Praktika 4
praktikon 302, 309
Procopius: *De Bellis* 158
profit maximisation approach 304
Pseira Island *93*
Pylos Regional Archaeological
    Project 259

religious foundations in Middle
    Byzantine Greece, patronage of
    (867–1204) 227–240
risk aversion 304
rural settlements, nucleated or
    dispersed 43

Saint Blasios of Amorion 319
Saint Nikon 317; *Life* of 259; *Testament*
    of 259, 261n16
Samonas of Thessaloniki, lead seal of *219*
secular Christianity 16
sgraffito 320

Skylitzes, J. 321
Southern Argolid Survey (Stanford
    University) 3
spatial asynchrony 63, 64
Stadiodromikon 96
Stanford University: Southern Argolid
    Survey 3
Steiria: minor urban settlements 41
Stephanos Pepagomenos 236
St GregoriosTheologos 229
St John Prodromos 215
Strategikon 318
Stryphnos, M. 317
Synekdemos: settlements in 38–40, 44

Tafrali, O. 2
Thebes (Middle Byzantine) 185–188;
    Walls of Kadmeia *187*
Theodore KomnenosAngelos of
    Thessalonike 281, 289
Theophylact Hephaistos 283
Thessalonike (Thessalonica) 2, 5, 26, 27,
    32, 85, 182, 184, 185, 216, 218,
    219, 220, 227, 228, 232, 241n7,
    285, 289–291, 293, 303, 306, 308,
    316–322; Acheiropoietos basilica,
    7th-century restoration of
    108–117; 'Dark Age' architecture
    of Hagia Sophia 121–129
Timarion 318
Tornikes, Demetrios 323
Type XXVIII lamps *145*
Type XXXI lamp *145*

urban fortification 5

Vardanes, G. 292
Veikou, M.: *Byzantine Epirus: A
    Topography of Transformation:
    Settlements of the Seventh-Twelfth
    Centuries in Southern Epirus and
    Aetoloakarnania, Greece* 1
Velika fortress, Kissavos coast 22–33;
    African Red Slip Ware plate with
    stamped decoration 27, *27*; Asia
    Minor lamp 27, *27*; belt buckle of
    Sucidava type 25, *26*; Central
    Greek Painted Ware 27–28, *28*;
    guard-chambers 25, *26*; lid for
    pithoi with incised decoration
    28–29, *28*; LRA amphora 29–32,
    30, 31; map of *23*; walls of 22–24,
    24, 25

334 Index

Vetranius 59
Vroulias 189–190, *190*

Willibaldi, Vita 316

xenodocheion 18

Zakythinos, D.: *Vyzantinê Ellas 392–1204* 2
Zeno (474–91) 141